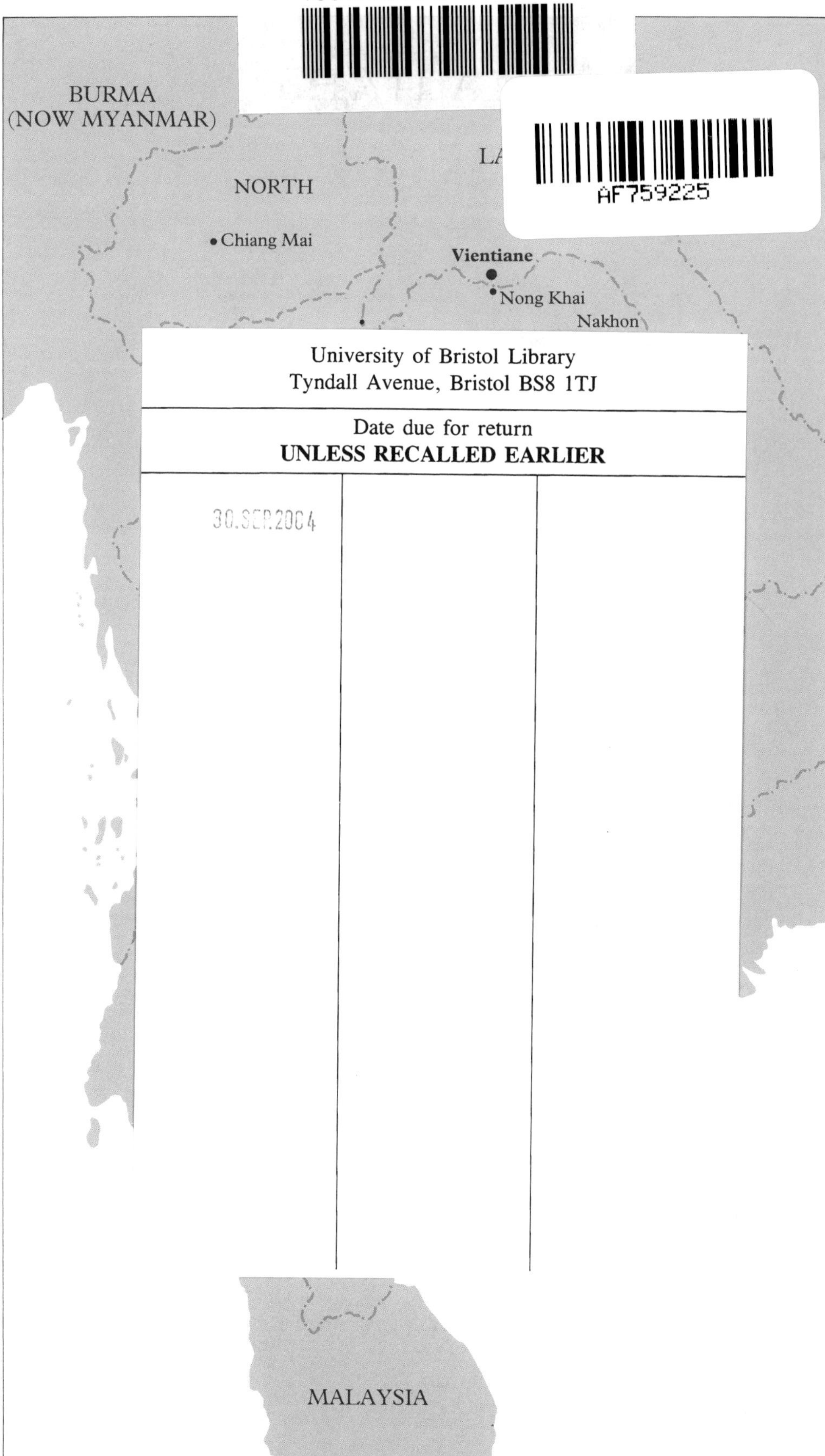
BURMA
(NOW MYANMAR)
NORTH
Chiang Mai
Vientiane
Nong Khai
Nakhon
MALAYSIA

South-East Asian Social Science Monographs

The Nation and Economic Growth

The Nation and Economic Growth

The Philippines and Thailand

Yoshihara Kunio

KUALA LUMPUR
OXFORD UNIVERSITY PRESS
OXFORD SINGAPORE NEW YORK
1994

Oxford University Press

Oxford New York Toronto
Delhi Bombay Calcutta Madras Karachi
Kuala Lumpur Singapore Hong Kong Tokyo
Nairobi Dar es Salaam Cape Town
Melbourne Auckland Madrid

and associated companies in
Berlin Ibadan

Oxford is a trade mark of Oxford University Press

Published in the United States
by Oxford University Press, New York

First published 1994

British Library Cataloguing in Publication Data
Data available

Library of Congress Cataloging-in-Publication Data
Kunio, Yoshihara, 1939–
The nation and economic growth: the Philippines and Thailand/by Yoshihara Kunio.
p. cm.
Includes bibliographical references and index.
ISBN 967 65 3054 9
1. Philippines—Economic conditions—1946– 2. Philippines—Politics and government—1946– 3. Philippines—Social conditions. 4. Thailand—Economic conditions. 5. Thailand—Politics and government. 6. Thailand—Social conditions. I. Title.
HC455.K86 1994
306'.09593—dc20
94-15914
CIP

Typeset by Indah Photosetting Centre Sdn., Bhd. Malaysia
Printed by Kim Hup Lee Printing Co. Pte. Ltd., Singapore
Published by Oxford University Press,
19–25, Jalan Kuchai Lama, 58200 Kuala Lumpur, Malaysia

To Miwa

Preface

THIS book considers the economic performance of the Philippines and Thailand, two South-East Asian countries which are similar in population size and type of economy (the market economy). In the 1970s, they also had a similar level of income, but in recent years the Thai economy has been performing much better, and in 1991, Thailand enjoyed a per capita GNP that was twice as high as in the Philippines. This is in sharp contrast to the situation in the early 1950s when it was the Philippines which enjoyed an income that was twice as high as Thailand's. At the time, the Philippines was more experienced in the practice of democracy and had a larger pool of educated manpower, and was thus considered to have the best chance for economic development in the region. But in the following years, the Philippine economy performed poorly. Why?

A typical way of explaining the turnaround is to examine such economic aggregates as investment, exports, and imports. In this book, however, non-economic differences are explored as possible reasons. The two countries differ, naturally, in fauna, flora, topography, and land area, but more relevant and significant differences lie in the areas of national tradition and organization. An examination of these differences will help to explain the disparity in economic performance. The main thesis of this book, then, is that as these fundamental differences arose and became more pronounced, affecting government attitude towards the Chinese and foreign capital, its own role in the economy, and its effectiveness in providing public goods, they changed the parameters defining the two economies in such a way as to improve the performance of the Thai economy *vis-à-vis* the Philippine economy.

My interest in the Philippine economy started in 1970 when I spent a year in the country. Since then, I have visited the Philippines numerous times, including another year's stay during 1981–2 and a seven-month stay in 1992. My interest in Thailand is of more recent origin. I visited the country for six months immediately after my year's stay in the Philippines in 1982, and since then I have made several short trips, at least for a month every year, over the past several years. Since early 1988, in preparation for this book, I have been consolidating and clarifying data collected earlier, as well as collecting more data in areas that needed more research. This book is the result, therefore, of over four years' effort to put the two countries in comparative perspective.

The data I have used come primarily from published academic works and the print media. I have supplemented the data with interviews—when information was unavailable in print or was conflicting and needed clarification—with a number of Thai and Filipino government officials and Japanese businessmen. I also depended on several Thai and Filipino scholars and intellectuals for clarification, information, and conceptualization. Their assistance is greatly appreciated, though I refrain from mentioning their names individually here.

I would, however, like to take this opportunity to thank a number of people and institutions, without whose assistance this book could not have been written. The main part of the manuscript was completed during my seven-month stay as Visiting Professor at the School of Economics, University of the Philippines. Professor Jose Encarnacion, Dean of the School, took the initiative in asking the Japan Foundation to send me there as Visiting Professor. Although this involved me in teaching (I taught one graduate course on economic development), I had adequate time to work on this manuscript. I would like to thank Professor Encarnacion and the Japan Foundation for making my stay there possible.

My Thai study was greatly facilitated by joint research with Krirkkiat Phipatseritham, Professor of Economics and former Rector of Thammasat University. This joint research, yet to be completed, provided opportunities to ask Professor Krirkkiat about various things not directly related to our project but to this book. This was especially helpful since my ability to read Thai was not sufficiently developed though I invested considerable time in it. Professor Krirkkiat also arranged appointments for me to see several high government officials in Thailand. Our joint research, which was part of the Core University Project between Kyoto and Thammasat Universities funded by the Japan Society for the Promotion of Science (JSPS), has enabled me to visit Thailand and for Professor Krirkkiat to pay reciprocal visits to Kyoto for one month in the past six years.

Because Thailand has performed better than the Philippines in terms of economic growth, in this book I tend to view Philippine institutions critically but Thai institutions positively. I hope that the reader will not think that I am pro-Thai and anti-Philippine. I do *not* wish to imply that *everything* was wrong with Philippine institutions and that all was fine with Thai institutions. But the strength of Thailand's existing institutions, which is emphasized in this book, needs to be properly acknowledged. As for the Philippines, because of its poor economic performance, its institutional weaknesses are stressed. These weaknesses are a fundamental part of national organization; they are almost certain to remain and to continue to act as constraints on economic growth. It is important for the planners of long-term economic growth to face the reality of these institutional constraints and to draw up plans to tackle them as a vital first step in promoting economic growth. The rosy economic picture painted for the Philippines numerous times in the past did not materialize largely because very little was done to rectify institutional constraints.

Economic growth is a matter of interaction among economic variables, but how these variables can be changed to promote growth cannot be adequately dealt with within the framework of neo-classical economics alone. Good economics may accelerate economic growth in the short run, but long-term economic growth is more importantly affected by the character of institutions. We have to understand a country's organization which shapes the structure and interrelationship of institutions. In this book, I stress it as a critical determinant of economic growth. However, I do not offer a complete picture of how non-economic institutions affect economic growth; I tend to concentrate on the impact of the government on the economy while not discussing other institutions (cultural and kinship institutions, in particular) at great length. Nevertheless, I hope this study will make clear a need for an in-depth study of the complete range of national institutions in relation to economic growth. The focus on institutions is not an escape hatch as it sometimes is in conventional economic analysis: their structure and interrelationship distinguishes one nation from another, and in these characteristics lies the clue to our understanding of long-term economic growth.

Any institutional discussion of two countries is difficult, for only a small number of people know both equally well. Those who are interested in how non-economic variables affect economic growth and are willing to read a two-country study (like this one) may not know much about either one of the two countries. In order that this book reach as wide a readership as possible, it is assumed that the reader does not know much about both the Philippines and Thailand.

The country or area specialists may feel that the institutional discussion is not deep enough, but they should understand that this book is not targeted at them. Although atypical in focusing on the institutional underpinning of the economy, this book is offered as an economic study. Many economists are averse to any method other than the conventional neo-classical approaches, so I have done my utmost not to lose sight of the objective, which is to offer a clear and basic explanation for the difference in economic performance between the Philippines and Thailand; at the same time I ask that they be open-minded. Institutions should not be dismissed as inconsequential factors as often happens in conventional economic analysis. I hope that this book will make that clear and stimulate further studies along this line.

Center for Southeast Asian Studies YOSHIHARA KUNIO
Kyoto University
May 1993

Contents

Tables

Figures

Appendices

Abbreviations

AFTA	ASEAN Free Trade Agreement
APT	Assets Privatization Trust
ASEAN	Association of South-East Asian Nations
BAAC	Bank of Agriculture and Agricultural Cooperatives
BOI	Board of Investment(s)
CAB	Civil Aeronautic Board
CCSF	Coconut Consumers Stabilization Fund
CIIF	Coconut Industry Investment Fund
CNL	Christians for National Liberation
Cocofed	Philippine Coconut Producers Federation, Inc.
CPP	Communist Party of the Philippines
CPT	Communist Party of Thailand
DBP	Development Bank of the Philippines
EDSA	Epifanio Delos Santos Avenue
EGAT	Electricity Generating Authority of Thailand
GNP	gross national product
IFCT	Industrial Finance Corp. of Thailand
IMF	International Monetary Fund
JPPCC	Joint Public–Private Consultative Committee
KMU	Kilusang Mayo Uno
Meralco	Manila Electric Co.
MNLF	Moro National Liberation Front
Nasutra	National Sugar Trading Corp.
NEDA	National Economic Development Authority
NEDCOL	National Economic Development Corp.
NESDB	National Economic and Social Development Board
NFA	National Food Authority
NGA	National Grains Authority
NPA	New People's Army
NPC	National Power Corp.
NRCC	National Rice and Corn Corp.
NTC	National Telecommunications Commission
PAL	Philippine Airlines
PCA	Philippine Coconut Authority

Philex	Philippine Exchange Co.
Philsucom	Philippine Sugar Commission
PKP	Partido Komunista ng Philippines
PLDT	Philippine Long Distance Telephone Co.
PNB	Philippine National Bank
PNOC	Philippine National Oil Co.
PNP	Philippine National Police
RAM	Reform the Armed Forces Movement
RCA	Rice and Corn Administration
RETELCO	Republic Telephone Co.
ROTC	Reserved Officers' Training Corps
RPB	Republic Planters Bank
SAS	Scandinavian Air System
SEC	Securities and Exchange Commission
SET	Securities Exchange of Thailand
UCPB	United Coconut Producers Bank
Unicom	United Coconut Oil Mills

1
Introduction

ECONOMISTS often make international comparisons of economic performance. This book belongs to this type of study. It focuses on two countries, the Philippines and Thailand, and attempts to explain their relative economic performance during the 1952–91 period, the most recent 40-year period for which economic data are available. This relatively long period is required to capture the dramatic change in the economic positions of these two countries. Since the Philippines is a former colony, it is appropriate to look back to the early post-war years when the colonial heritage was more strongly felt.

To focus on just two countries is to greatly limit the authenticity of the findings if the purpose is to arrive at a general understanding of economic growth. An explanation which is valid in a two-country comparison may not be valid when another pair of countries are studied, as they may face problems peculiar to themselves or to a small number of countries, or because they do not face the problems which arise in other countries. A two-country study can, however, offer insight into the problems of economic growth, and also be a building block for a general theory of growth.

In comparing the Philippines and Thailand, the most telling fact in their divergent economic performance is that during 1952–91, Thai per capita gross national product (GNP)—which in the beginning was half that of the Philippines—was more than double the latter's by the end of the period. How this reversal in fortunes came about needs explaining. Figure 1.1 gives a time profile of changes in the ratio of both per capita GNPs over the period. For the purpose of drawing up this figure, per capita GNP in national currency was converted into US dollars by use of the current exchange rate. It is assumed that the figure depicts the basic trend of the ratios of both per capita GNPs over the 40-year period. Certainly, there are some problems with the data, and short-term changes have to be interpreted with caution. The appendix at the end of this chapter lays out the statistical table on which the figure was based, and also discusses the data problems which arose in arriving at the numbers in the table.

Other data also support the more advanced position of the Philippine economy in the 1950s. In 1952, for example, the Philippines produced 660 million kilowatt hours of electrical energy, while Thailand produced

FIGURE 1.1
Philippine/Thai Per Capita GNP:
A Schematic Presentation

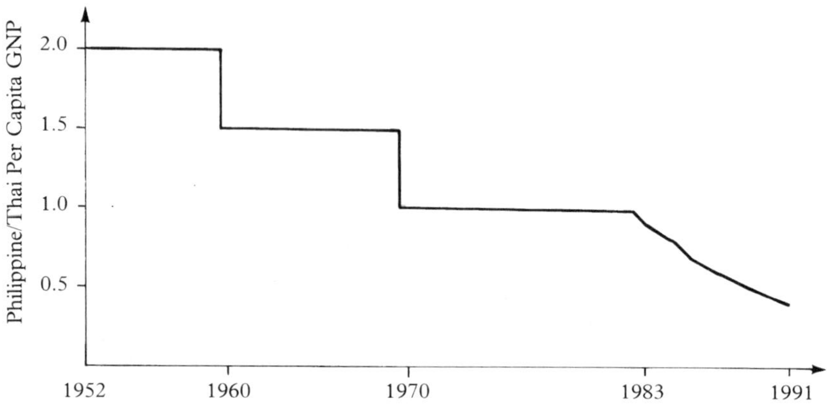

Source: Derived from Table 1.1

only 128 million kilowatt hours; the Philippines had 50,000 passenger cars and 55,300 commercial vehicles, compared with the 16,000 and 18,800 respectively in Thailand; the number of telephones installed was 34,117 in the Philippines and 7,181 in Thailand; and the Philippines' total circulation of daily newspapers was 500,000, about 18 times more than the Thai figure (75 copies per 1,000 of population in the Philippines against 4 copies in Thailand).[1] As for radio receivers, in 1954, the Philippines had about twice as many as Thailand (217,000 and 108,000 respectively).[2]

In the 1950s, the difference in per capita GNP between the Philippines and Thailand remained roughly the same.[3] In the early 1960s, however, the ratio narrowed to 1.5 and remained at this level throughout the rest of the decade. Then in 1970, Thailand caught up with the Philippines, and in the following decade or so, the two countries remained at the same level of income. During the early 1980s, Thailand started leaving the Philippines behind. The second half of the decade saw the Thai economy enjoy a boom, with the annual growth rate reaching 10.5 per cent in the years 1987–91. In 1991, Thailand's per capita GNP was about $1,600, a little over twice that of the Philippines.[4] By contrast, per capita GNP in the Philippines remained virtually at the same level over the 1980s.

The difference in income between the two countries has been affected by changes in the exchange rate, and to say, for example, that Thailand caught up with the Philippines in 1970 does not provide a true picture. It is more correct to say that Thailand caught up with the Philippines around that time. If sudden changes in the income ratio due to fluctuating exchange rates are ignored, the above time profile captures the basic trend.

How does one explain the reversal? A typical approach is to focus on the interaction among aggregate economic variables. Since such economic variables as GNP, investment, savings, and exports are interrelated, if GNP grew faster in one country than in the other, corresponding changes must have occurred in other economic variables. In trade variables, for example, Thai imports must have grown more rapidly, since a bigger increase in imports was necessary for a higher increase in output, as imports were needed for production (fertilizers and agricultural machinery for agricultural production; and various machines, raw materials, and intermediate goods for industrial production). Imports could increase as fast as exports (otherwise, there was no foreign exchange to finance the increase in imports). Exports could increase if a series of new export commodities emerged over time, for it is highly unlikely that exports could keep increasing with just one commodity. One should be able to observe a flying-geese pattern in the leading exports of Thailand up to the early 1990s.

Although such an approach may be useful, this is not the methodology pursued in this book. Instead of focusing on aggregate economic variables, the parameters defining the Philippine and Thai economies are considered, and they are assumed to have changed in such a way as to have brought about the reversal. How these parameters changed can be verified only by building an economic model for the Philippines and another for Thailand. The parameters can be estimated for every so many years (say 10), to trace the changes that have occurred. In this book, however, it is assumed that in the Philippines the parameters changed in such a way that with given changes in some economic variables, capital flight increased, foreign and domestic investment decreased, productivity declined, and so on, while in Thailand the response of those same variables changed in its favour.

The parameters defining an economy change for various reasons. Consider Figure 1.2 which depicts the 'nation' of interrelated institutions. The parameters can change if the structure of the economic institution changes. For example, if land distribution in rural areas becomes more equitable as a result of land reform, the parameters will move in new directions such that national productivity increases via higher agricultural productivity. The parameters can also change if the kinship and cultural institutions are modified. For example, if the family bond weakens and the school becomes less effective in teaching, the discipline and education of children will be affected, and with some time lag (that is, when they grow up and start to work), the parameters will be affected in such a way as to reduce national productivity.

This book focuses on the government institution because changes in its performance and relations with the economy have had the most significant impact on the parameters which brought about the reversal. More specifically, changes in government policy towards the Chinese and foreign capital, in its relations with the market economy, and in its ability to maintain peace and order are considered. It will be argued that compared with the Philippine government, the Thai government became more liberal towards the Chinese and foreign capital, thus allowing the

FIGURE 1.2
The Nation as a Set of Interrelated Institutions

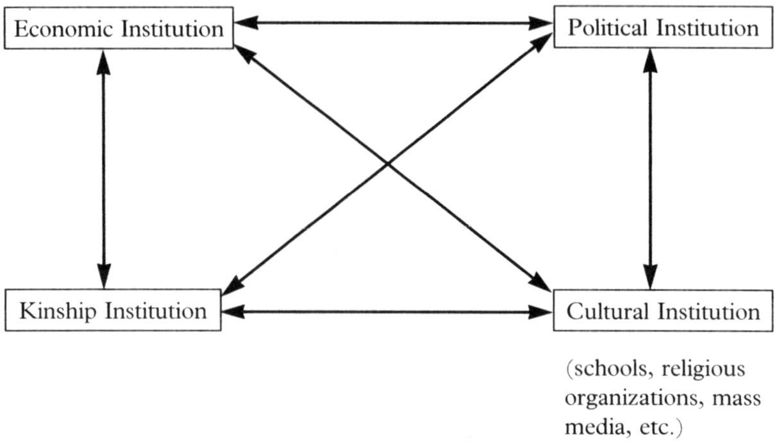

Thai economy to benefit from the business acumen of the Chinese, who accounted for over 10 per cent of the population, and to rely on foreign capital extensively in pioneering manufacturing, and more 'friendly' towards the market economy, hence permitting it to work more efficiently. The Thai government also maintained peace and order better, thus enabling foreign and domestic investors to plan with greater certainty.

Why such differences have arisen between the Philippines and Thailand is related to the manner in which they have been organized as a nation. The organization of a country is characterized by the way in which each of four main institutions is structured and how they relate to each other (Figure 1.2). Both countries' structural organization is a historical given in 1952, the beginning of the 40-year period of this study. If the organization had been stable, the parameters would not have changed; but the structural organization of both countries has changed in the course of time, and in the case of Thailand, in a favourable manner. The Philippines became particularly unstable, because its structure, inherited from the American period—without having taken deep roots in Filipino society—was somewhat artificial, being in many ways the legacy of the colonial period. The post-war change was partly a reaction to colonial order. It may appear that since independence was obtained in 1946, adjustments would have been completed by the beginning of the period under study, but since transition to independence was smooth, it took many more years for the reaction to the colonial order to surface.

In order to gauge the effect of national organization on economic performance, a study of the way the Chinese were treated is revealing. In the Philippines, during the colonial period, the Chinese were considered a genuine part of the nation and were given economic freedom (though the American administration was careful not to let too many Chinese into the country; it did not want them to use the Philippines as a stepping stone for emigration to the United States). After independence, however, the position of the Chinese changed. They were discriminated against in foreign exchange allocation and barred from many areas of economic activity (especially in retail business). The post-war structure tried to marginalize the Chinese in the Philippines.

On the other hand, in Thailand, though a number of anti-Chinese measures were taken in the early 1950s because of the rise of nationalistic feeling and to stem the spread of Communism among the Chinese in the early post-war years, the situation had settled down by the end of the 1950s. The Chinese regained the economic freedom they had enjoyed during the period of absolute monarchy (which ended in 1932). Thailand maintained *jus soli* as the principle of citizenship because Thai culture was believed to be inherently strong enough to assimilate ethnic minorities such as the Chinese, an assumption which turned out to be generally correct. This right enabled the Chinese born in Thailand to become Thai legally as well as culturally, and they played a crucial role in economic development.

Socially and economically, Thailand is a loosely structured nation.[5] Along with the dominant Thai majority, a number of other ethnic groups enjoy a great deal of freedom, especially in business. Even social control among the Thais is weak. But the country has a socially cohesive culture and a relatively strong administrative structure. In order to remain independent, Thailand developed an effective administrative structure as a matter of necessity, to defend the country against foreign aggression as well as to promote internal stability. However, administrative intervention was not extended to the economy. The country's bureaucratic capability was limited, and besides, the economy performed better that way; otherwise corruption and abuses of power were bound to become more pervasive and act as constraints on the market economy. After the 1932 Revolution which ended absolute monarchy and brought the military to power, the government handling of the economy changed because the leaders of the Revolution were ambitious though politically inexperienced, but under the threat of Communism in Indo-China and other political exigencies which required good economic performance, the relations between the two reverted (though not completely) to the situation during the period of absolute monarchy.

In the Philippines, stable workable relations between the government and the market economy have not yet been established, though the direction has been towards less intervention in the past few years. During the colonial period, the relations between the government and the economy were similar to those in Thailand, but in the post-independence period, amid the fervour of nationalism, the government adopted many interventionist measures on the assumption that these would promote economic growth. But the measures were so badly administered that government intervention became a major obstacle to economic growth. Since the mid-1980s, the pendulum has been swinging towards less intervention, but under various pretexts intervention still takes place, and the market economy is still under greater constraint in the Philippines than in Thailand.

Appendix: A Note on Data Problems

Gross National Product

GNP, the gross value added which is used to measure the economic size of a nation, is roughly the sum of the value added in the domestic economy (which consists of such sectors as agriculture, manufacturing, and services). Strictly speaking, GNP also includes the net payments of dividends, interests, and remittances, but they are usually a small portion of GNP, and are easier to estimate since the central bank keeps close track of these payments. Although GNP is often used in economic discussions, it is a rather difficult figure to arrive at. In a developing country in which statistical work receives low priority, its reliability is often questionable.

The most serious errors tend to arise in computing the value added in the service sector. Data coverage in the service sector is not as thorough and accurate as that in the agricultural and industrial sectors which have a longer history of compiling production data. The mobility and ephemeral nature of many small business establishments in the service sector make it difficult to improve data coverage. Even if data are collected by methods such as a questionnaire survey, their reliability poses a big problem. The same problem also arises in the agricultural and industrial sectors, but it is more serious in the service sector because independent checks are more difficult to carry out: there are few easily available independent data such as production capacity which in the industrial sector can be derived from the capacity of the machines installed, and in the agricultural sector, from the land acreage of a crop.

Although income data in the agricultural and industrial sectors are considered to be more reliable, there is still need for caution. A brief review of the method of collating population census figures—supposedly the easiest figures to obtain—will illustrate the problem of reliability. Every 10 years in the past few decades, a population census was taken in both the Philippines and Thailand. Given the nature of the data collected and the high priority attached to it in the government's statistical collection, it is usually thought that population census figures are the most reliable among national statistics. This may be so, but there remains the problem of reliability, at least for earlier years.

In a population census, the government divides the country into small areas, each of which can be covered by a census taker. The population of the country in the census year is the sum total of the numbers reported by census takers. In 1980, the census figure for Thailand was 44.8 million, and in 1990, 56.3 million. If these two figures are reliable, the annual growth rate of population in the 10-year period was 2.4 per cent, which is much higher than the rate which demographers think reasonable from sample data. The 1980 figure appears to be wrong. The target rate in the Fifth National Economic and Social Development Plan (1982–6) was 1.5 per cent per annum, and that in the Sixth Plan (1987–91) was 1.3 per cent per annum. These targets are believed to have been roughly

TABLE 1.1
Philippine and Thai Per Capita GNP, 1952–1991 ($)

Year	*Philippines*	*Thailand*	*Philippines/ Thailand*
1952	157	80	1.96
1953	160	88	1.82
1954	161	76	2.12
1955	166	82	2.02
1956	177	87	2.03
1957	187	85	2.20
1958	192	84	2.28
1959	203	86	2.36
1960	140	94	1.49
1961	157	100	1.57
1962	149	106	1.41
1963	169	109	1.55
1964	177	116	1.52
1965	188	126	1.49
1966	201	147	1.37
1967	216	152	1.42
1968	232	160	1.45
1969	248	170	1.46
1970	193	195	0.99
1971	203	197	1.03
1972	213	212	1.00
1973	257	273	0.94
1974	358	339	1.06
1975	375	359	1.04
1976	415	399	1.04
1977	464	453	1.02
1978	525	535	0.98
1979	628	593	1.06
1980	732	682	1.07
1981	775	719	1.08
1982	766	720	1.06
1983	655	790	0.83
1984	595	804	0.74
1985	587	709	0.83
1986	540	775	0.70
1987	598	893	0.67
1988	664	1,074	0.62
1989	732	1,230	0.60
1990	767	1,402	0.55
1991	735	1,605	0.46

Sources: Per capita GNP. The Philippines: for 1952–75, National Economic Development Authority, *The National Income Accounts, CY 1946–1975 (Link Series)*, 1978, and for 1976–91. Asian Development Bank (ADB), *Key Indicators of Developing Asian and Pacific Countries*, various years. Thailand: for 1970–86, National Economic and Social

Development Board (NESDB), *National Income of Thailand, New Series, 1970–87*, and for the earlier years, the unpublished mimeographed sheets of national income statistics of the NESDB (one set for the years up to 1969 and another for 1988–91; the latter is published, and appears also in ADB's *Key Indicators*).

Foreign Exchange Rates. The Philippines: for 1970–91, ADB, *Key Indicators*, various years, and for the earlier years, United Nations, *Statistical Yearbook*, various years. Thailand: for 1970–91, ADB, *Key Indicators*, various years, and for the earlier years, Central Statistical Office, *Statistical Yearbook of Thailand*, various years.

Notes: Per capita GNP in dollars was obtained by dividing per capita GNP in the national currency by its exchange rate for the dollar.

For 1952–5, Thailand had a multiple exchange rate system. The rates used are market rates.

For 1952–5 and 1959–61, the Philippine government sold the dollar to importers at different rates. The rates used here are the highest official dollar rates. For 1956–8, the dollar was sold at the official selling rate of 2.02, but the highest official dollar rate of 1952–5 (2.40) was used.

achieved, and Thailand is considered to be a success case in population control. During the Sixth Plan, major aid agencies which had been helping the country in spreading family planning pulled out of the country, considering that their job had been done.

The coverage and reliability of national income data today are more suspect than those of population, and they were even more so in earlier years when there was no strongly felt need for statistical data collection. Nevertheless, GNP has been estimated, and it is the best available measure of development. There are other development indicators (such as electrical energy consumed), but they show up only certain facets of the economy. For the purpose of this book, a more comprehensive indicator is needed; from this perspective, GNP is the most desirable since it is the sum total of economic activities.

Although the magnitude of the gap might be questioned, there is virtual consensus that the Thai economy was more prosperous than the Philippine economy in 1991 (even if adjusted for the population). For earlier years, in spite of the more serious questionability of GNP estimates then, the supplement of other development indicators, such as electrical energy production and number of motor vehicles, show that the Philippine economy was more advanced than the Thai in 1952. Some doubts remain as to how the subsistence sector was dealt with in calculating GNP in earlier years and whether per capita GNP was underestimated in Thailand because the economy was less monetized than the Philippine economy which has had a longer history as a money economy. This adjustment may be necessary, but it is safe to say that the Philippine monetary economy was more developed than the Thai in the early 1950s.

Exchange Rate

For international comparison, the per capita GNP of different countries is usually converted to dollars by using the foreign exchange rate. This method is, however, known to be unsatisfactory. It is more accurate to use the purchasing power parity index, which gives the conversion rate of one currency to another for buying a fixed set of goods and services needed to maintain a certain standard of living. Unfortunately, there is no purchasing power parity index for 1952, and since to construct it is a laborious process, it is not attempted here. Fortunately, the bias which arises in using exchange rates is most significant when developed and developing countries are compared. Since the Philippines and Thailand do not differ greatly in their living standards, the use of exchange rates is not inappropriate.

In 1988, for example, the US per capita GNP was $19,850. If the exchange rate is used for conversion, per capita GNP was $630 in the Philippines and $1,000 in Thailand. But if conversion is based on the purchasing power parity index, their per capita GNPs become $2,170 and $3,280 respectively. That is, if the exchange rate is used, the income gap between the United States and the Philippines is 31.50 times, and that between Thailand and the Philippines is 1.59 times. But based on the purchasing power parity index, the US–Philippine gap is reduced to about one-third (from 31 to 9 times) of the difference based on the exchange rate, while the Thai–Philippine gap remains at a level similar to that based on the exchange rate (1.51).[6]

In the 1950s, the dollar–peso exchange rate in the Philippines was more complicated than in later years when there was a unified market rate. For example, the official selling rate of ₱2 per dollar in 1952 could not have been the equilibrium rate. This is partly attested to by the fact that the peso–dollar exchange rate of the year was the same as the one in the pre-war years despite the fact that the index of the cost of living in Manila increased more than three times between 1941 and 1952, while in the United States, the consumer price index increased less than two times. Since the exchange rate tends to adjust to the different rates of increase of the cost of living index, the pre-war rate of ₱2 per dollar could not have been maintained in the free exchange market.

The overvaluation of the peso is also reflected in the big deficits in the trade account of the Philippines in the first few years after independence when there was no foreign exchange control. The deficits were, however, compensated for by the payments the US government made to the Philippines (the bulk of which was $620 million paid as war damages under the Philippine Rehabilitation Act of 1946). But in the late 1940s, American payments began to diminish, and the only way to sustain the exchange rate of ₱2 per dollar was to resort to exchange control, which started in December 1949.

Since the official rate had clearly overvalued the peso, the Philippine government soon began selling the dollar to local importers at higher rates. During 1952–5, the rates varied from ₱2.02 to ₱2.36 per dollar; in 1959, ₱2.02 to ₱2.52; in 1960, ₱2.02 to ₱3.60; and in 1961, ₱2.02 to ₱3.40. During 1956–8, selling rates were unified at ₱2.02. In January 1962, the government finally devalued the currency to about ₱4.00 per dollar.

In the 1950s, the market rate was even higher than the highest official dollar rate of the Philippine government. For example, in early 1954 when the highest official dollar rate in the Philippine was ₱2.36, the market rate was about ₱3.00 per dollar in the Hong Kong exchange market.[7] However, the market rate of the peso was probably lower than the equilibrium rate, since the demand of Philippine importers for the dollar would have declined and its supply to Philippine exporters would have increased under a cheaper peso (that is, exports would have been encouraged and imports discouraged with the lower value of the peso). The true rate was probably somewhere between the highest official dollar rate (₱2.36) and the free market rate (₱3.00).

To arrive at the exchange rate for conversion into the dollar, although there is a risk of overvaluing the peso, the highest official dollar rate each year was used for 1952–5 and 1959–61. For the three years (1956–8) when the rate was unified at ₱2.02, the highest official dollar rate of 1952–5 (₱2.36 per dollar) was taken as an approximation to what would have been the highest official selling rate if the government had decided to discriminate against importers according to the importance of the imports. In 1959 when the government began selling the dollar at multiple rates, the highest rate was ₱2.52, not significantly more than the highest figure of ₱2.36 in the earlier years. But even the highest dollar rate in 1959 seems to have underestimated the equilibrium rate, for in the following year, the highest dollar rate had to be further increased. Consequently, there was a sharp drop in per capita GNP between 1959 and 1960. This seems to indicate that the dollar value of per capita GNP in the preceding several years was overstated.

After the devaluation of January 1962, the rates used in computing the GNP are market rates. But in a number of years, they are probably not the rates which would have prevailed without government intervention in the exchange market, although the difference is most likely to have been much smaller than in the 1950s when there was exchange control. At least for a few years after the devaluation in 1962, the difference must have been very small, because the level of government intervention was low, but in the late 1960s when the government intervened in the exchange market and started to impose import controls on some commodities, the difference became bigger. Thus, when devaluation occurred again in February 1970, the peso–dollar exchange rate jumped from ₱4 to ₱6 per dollar. Reflecting this devaluation, per capita GNP declined from $248 to $193 between 1969 and 1970. Such a large drop could have taken place only if the dollar value of per capita GNP was overvalued in the preceding few years because of the overvaluation of the peso. But in most of the remaining years, such a large artificial drop was not observed. Since 1962, except around 1970, the dollar–peso rate seems to have adjusted to the market rate, without a long time lag.

The dollar–peso rate in the free exchange market can be used as an approximation of the Philippine purchasing power parity index. But the market rate is not such an ideal rate if it reflects heavy borrowings from abroad. From 1970 to 1982, the dollar value of per capita GNP grew faster in the Philippines than in Thailand, but this was possibly due to the fact that the peso was propped up by the the former's heavy borrowings from abroad. (In the 1970s, the Philippines borrowed more aggressively than Thailand.) Thus, the strength of the Philippine economy in the 1970s and the early 1980s (*vis-à-vis* the Thai economy) is partly illusory. Obviously, the short-term variations of the Philippine per capita GNP in the statistical table have to be interpreted with some caution. The best approach is to focus on the trend of per capita GNP, especially in relation to that of Thailand.

Thailand had a multiple exchange rate system in 1952. The official rate was B12.5 per dollar, whereas the free market rate was B21.4 per dollar. The official rate was used by the government primarily to pay the exporters of rice, tin, and rubber. Almost all foreign exchange receipts from the export of rice, 40 per cent of the proceeds from tin, and 20 per cent from rubber had to be surrendered to the Bank of Thailand at the official rate. Other goods could be exported at the free market rate, which was also the rate for the import of virtually all goods. It might be argued that without the official buying rate, the baht would have appreciated in the free market because exports would have increased since producers (peasants, etc.) could have received higher incomes. This might be so, but it has to be borne in mind that a considerable amount of the three commodities was being smuggled out. The extent of the response of these producers to price changes can also be questioned.

In 1955, the multiple exchange rate system was abolished, and the rate was set at B20.7 per dollar, a rate which was not much different from the free market rate in 1952. (Thailand maintained this rate for the next 25 years.) In view of this, the undervaluation of the baht in 1952 did not seem to be serious. The free market rate used to convert per capita GNP to dollar terms prior to 1955 was probably a fairly good approximation to the equilibrium exchange rate. In the early 1950s, if there was a bias in the market rate of the baht, it was in the direction of slight undervaluation. As discussed earlier, the peso in those years was probably overvalued. Hence, the two-times difference in per capita GNP between the Philippines and Thailand probably exceeded the true difference to some extent.[8]

The dollar exchange rate of the Thai baht was largely stable during the 40-year period. The rate of B20.7 per dollar set in 1955 was maintained until 1981, when the baht was devalued about 10 per cent (to B23.0 per dollar). Then in November 1984, it was devalued another 17 per cent (to B27.0 per dollar). After this, the baht appreciated slightly, and in 1991, the exchange rate was B25.5 per dollar. As in the Philippines, the dollar value of per capita GNP was affected by devaluation (especially in 1985 and 1986, as seen from the statistical table), and not too much importance should be attached to annual changes during the period around the devaluations.

1. United Nations, *Statistical Yearbook, 1953.*

2. United Nations, *Statistical Yearbook, 1956.*

3. Comparing the Philippines with Thailand in the 1950s, Harry Oshima writes: 'The Philippines led the growth of the ASEAN countries in the 1950s, when its physical infrastructure, literacy, life expectancy, and bureaucracy were among the most advanced. In contrast, Bangkok in 1961 still had all the earmarks of an ancient Oriental city, full of large buildings made of wood, hardly any concrete structures, narrow streets, and many canals running through the city' (Harry T. Oshima, *Economic Growth in Monsoon Asia: A Comparative Survey*, Tokyo: University of Tokyo Press, 1987, p. 220).

4. On the relative decline of the Philippine economy, Filipino novelist Sionil Jose said, 'After the war, we were the envy of Asia. Korea—it would never catch up! Tokyo was where you went to find a cheap lay. Now ... look at us!' (James Fallows, 'The Ilocos: A Philippine Discovery', *Atlantic*, May 1991). As reflected in this quote, many among the Filipino élite were confident right after the war that their country would have a bright future thanks to American colonial legacy.

5. An American anthropologist described Thai society as loosely structured. The phrase 'a loosely structured nation' used here is a slightly different concept. For the former concept, see John Embree, 'Thailand—A Loosely Structured Social System', *American Anthropologist*, April–June 1950.

6. United Nations Development Programme, *Human Development Report 1991*, New York: Oxford University Press, 1991, pp. 119–22.

7. *Far Eastern Economic Review*, 4 February 1954: 131.

8. See Paul Studenski, *The Income of Nations, Measurement and Analysis: Past and Present*, New York: New York University Press, 1958, pp. 229–30, which also shows a difference of about two times for 1955. For a comparison of the Philippines and Thailand in the pre-war period, see M. K. Bennett, 'International Disparities in Consumption Levels', *American Economic Review*, September 1951. This study shows that during 1934–8, the Philippines was well ahead of Thailand in terms of higher per capita income.

PART I
THE CHINESE AND FOREIGN CAPITAL

2
The Chinese and Business

Population Size

THE Chinese in South-East Asia were an easily identifiable group in the pre-war period. Most were immigrants from China, all spoke Chinese and had Chinese surnames. They did not speak Mandarin, though; instead, coming from southern China, they spoke Cantonese, Hokkien, Hakka, Teochew, or Hainanese. In the Philippines, the Hokkien accounted for about 80 per cent of the Chinese population, and the Cantonese the remaining 20 per cent. In Thailand, the Teochew were the dominant group, followed by the Hakka, Hainanese, Cantonese, and Hokkien.[1] If their mothers were local women, many Chinese children born locally lost their 'Chineseness' because they did not learn to speak Chinese, and were integrated into the local community. (In the Philippines, they were called Chinese mestizos.) Especially before the First World War, very few Chinese women migrated, thus many of the children born to Chinese fathers were 'lost' in that way. The children who were identified as Chinese spoke Chinese, retained Chinese surnames, and belonged to the Chinese community.

In the post-war period, the Chinese became a less easily identifiable group. Many were naturalized. In Thailand, locally born Chinese were entitled to citizenship. A large number of them localized their names. Because of the forced localization of Chinese schools, Chinese children could barely speak Chinese, and became socially integrated into the local community. Conceptually, it may be said that one is Chinese if he thinks that he is Chinese, but this does not serve as an objective criteria for counting the number of Chinese. In arriving at the size of the Chinese population, there was a data problem even for the pre-war period, but post-war, the conceptual problem became an additional complication.

There is, however, a consensus that there were—and still are—many more Chinese in Thailand than in the Philippines. The question is how many more. According to the Overseas Chinese Affairs Commission of the Nationalist Government in Taiwan, the Chinese population in 1950 was 3.5 million in Thailand and 180,000 in the Philippines.[2] Since the total population of Thailand was about 18 million and of the Philippines about 19 million (both countries had roughly the same population throughout the 40-year period), the Chinese proportion of the population in Thailand in that year was almost 20 per cent and that in the

Philippines a little less than 1 per cent. There is no knowing, however, how reliable these figures are.

The most often quoted figures are Victor Purcell's and G. William Skinner's. Purcell's estimates for 1947 are 2.5 million (14.4 per cent of the total population) for Thailand and 120,000 (0.6 per cent) for the Philippines.[3] Skinner's estimates for 1950 are 3 million (16.7 per cent of the total population) for Thailand and 230,000 (1.2 per cent) for the Philippines. The discrepancy was unlikely to be due to the different years of estimation. It was mostly likely due to the different data sources used.

Purcell also gives estimates for 1960. The Chinese population in Thailand increased to only 2.7 million (possibly because Chinese immigration stopped due to severe government restriction and because of fewer new marriages, there was little natural growth), while the total population grew at a little over 3 per cent per annum between 1947 and 1960. As a result, the proportion of the Chinese population fell to 10.2 per cent. In the Philippines, the Chinese population increased from 120,000 to 181,000 over the same period, and the proportion of the Chinese increased slightly to 0.67 per cent in 1960. Estimates for later years are also available, but their reliability becomes more questionable. For example, one Chinese-Filipino organization maintains that there were 800,000–900,000 ethnic Chinese in the Philippines in the late 1980s, or about 1.5 per cent of the total population.[4] However, based on the estimates of early years when the Chinese were more identifiable, this author considers the Chinese population in the Philippines to have been a little less than 1 per cent, and in Thailand to be at least 10 per cent, so that in the period under consideration, Thailand had at least 10 times more Chinese than the Philippines in percentage terms as well as in absolute numbers.

A large Chinese population was a favourable factor for economic growth. This might appear to be a simplistic proposition, but there is supporting evidence for it. This assertion, however, presupposes that the Chinese did not pose a social problem for the country concerned. In fact, they did in both Thailand and the Philippines, and how and to what extent this was overcome will be considered in the next section. This chapter is concerned with why the Chinese were a greater propelling force of economic changes than the indigenous population, and the concrete ways in which they contributed to economic growth.

Work Ethic

To make a general statement about an ethnic group is dangerous, because there are always people who do not fit into it. For example, if one says that the Chinese are diligent, one is bound to encounter a number of Chinese who are not. But a comparative statement can be made of an average Chinese with an average indigene (and this average reflects the majority of the group). It is in this sense that the statement that the Chinese have a stronger work ethic than the indigene should be understood.

The immigrants, who made up the bulk of the Chinese population in the pre-war period, are thought to have had a stronger work ethic than the indigenes because most of them had experienced poverty in southern China where the population density was high and the economic reality harsh. Although they left their homes to escape poverty, they did not lose the work ethic required for survival at home. On the other hand, historically, the population density of South-East Asia was low, and nature was bountiful, so that there was no need for the indigenes to work hard for a living. As a result, their value orientation was more towards leisure and the adaptation of man to nature.

King Chulalongkorn's statement 'I regard them [the Chinese] not as foreigners but as component parts of the kingdom' was possibly made because he needed Chinese labour.[5] Economic modernization in Thailand required a number of tasks the Thais were not able to do, or if they could, they were reluctant to perform. For instance, when the king wanted to build a railway system for reasons of national security, it was the Chinese who supplied the coolie labour for this task. In addition, they were needed as workers in new processing industries such as rice and sawmills; as stevedores in the Bangkok port; as coolies for building canals in the Bangkok area; as tin miners in southern Thailand; as artisans and mechanics; and as traders handling new exports and imports. From the king's point of view, the Chinese who were willing to offer the labour he needed were welcome.

In the Philippines also, American businessmen demanded the importation of Chinese coolies because they believed that the Chinese were more hardworking than the Filipinos. But the American administration did not allow the Chinese into the country as coolies. Those who came did so as traders, and despite their small number, they achieved control of the greater bulk of retail and wholesale trade. How can this phenomenon be explained? Victor Purcell attributed their success in business to their 'patience in adversity, adaptability, determination and good humored resilience'. The German geographer, Albert Kolb, put it down to their ingenuity and 'satisfaction with small things'.[6] The political scientist Joseph Hayden, who was Vice-Governor of the Philippines in the mid-1930s, ascribed it to 'energy, thrift, self-control, physical and spiritual endurance, cheerfulness, infinite capacity for hard work'. Hayden elaborated:

> these qualities mean that while he is struggling to establish himself the Chinese will work sixteen hours per day. So will the members of his family. He and they will live with appalling frugality in order to put every penny back into the business. No economy is too petty to be practiced; no transaction or profit too small to be sought. Small wonder that such a people have dominated the economic life of the tropical, more easy-going Philippines.[7]

It was not only foreign observers who recognized the personal qualities which made the Chinese successful in business in the Philippines.

Tomas Confesor, Filipino director of the Bureau of Commerce, told local businessmen in 1933 that if they wanted to supplant the Chinese, they must develop the economic efficiency of the Chinese and perform for the community the same services performed by the Chinese. He told Filipino businessmen that they should not use political means to supplant the Chinese, for that would not serve national interests.[8] For his pains, a storm of Filipino indignation broke over his head.

Business Networks

In the viewpoint of a Filipino businessman, the system was loaded against him. He was excluded from a Chinese network because he was not Chinese, and the reason that he could not succeed was not a matter of his personal qualities but an unfair system that shut him out. As early as 1900, the Philippine Commission set up by President McKinley in 1899 (one of its functions was to investigate conditions in the Philippines) attributed the success of the Chinese to their in-group co-operation.

> They [the Chinese] succeeded everywhere in obtaining a monopoly of wholesale and retail trade, becoming, by the unity of purpose which they possess, the proprietors of mechanical arts and trades in the country. They lend each other cooperative aid, and all work together for the same end, thus forming a vast commercial society with which it is impossible for other merchants, who work separately, to compete.[9]

It should not be assumed that the Chinese community had one integrated network. The fact is there were numerous networks, which sometimes had connections with each other, especially when one network did not serve the purpose of a group member who wanted to expand his trading; but usually the networks were independent of each other. It was essentially a co-operative business group. Those who belonged to the group could buy goods on credit, receive special price discounts from other members, and (when they got together) exchange business as well as social information. It was not a fixed group as some were brought in by the introduction of a member, and others were expelled for cheating or failing members in various ways. It was an exclusive group in that the non-Chinese, or even the Chinese who belonged to other dialect groups or had other cultural attributes, were excluded.

The network was also a performance-based group. Trustworthiness had to be maintained in order to remain in the network. Those who could not be trusted were left out, and those who were thought untrustworthy were not allowed in. It was a way to reduce risk in doing business in an uncertain world—a world where there were frequent cheatings and unkept promises arising from human frailties. A network evolved in a dynamic world. Those who could not grow with others fell behind and were marginalized, if not left out entirely. There was, therefore, pressure on members to be adaptable to new economic opportunities.

Thailand did not break up the Chinese networks, which turned out to be a blessing to the economy. The Philippines, however, did great damage to them by discriminating against the Chinese in foreign exchange allocation in the 1950s and passing the Retail Trade Nationalization Law and other measures (for example, in the nationalization of the trading and processing of rice and corn). The Philippine government used legal measures to break up the Chinese trading networks and relied on government corporations such as the Philippine National Bank to help Filipinos develop alternative networks. But this strategy did not work very well because a workable network required time, experience, and connections to build. An artificially created network was a poor substitute for one which had evolved over time, for—trust being weak among its members—it did not function well in facilitating transactions. In addition, it could not be easily connected with networks outside the country, at least not as well as a Chinese network could be with those in Hong Kong, Taiwan, or South-East Asian trading centres.

Economically, Bangkok can be regarded as a Chinese city. Half its population in 1947 was Chinese.[10] There were many Chinese traders in Thai regional cities and market towns as well (about half the Chinese population lived in the provinces).[11] They gave advances to peasants, bought their crops, and introduced them to new crops. It was through these networks that rice was brought to Bangkok for export. Later, cassava and corn were exported in the same way. As the government built more highways, Chinese trading networks expanded and, at the same time, were strengthened. Since the mid-1980s, pineapples, asparagus, bamboo shoots, mushrooms, young corn, and canned tomatoes have been exported through these networks.

Chinese networks for commercial crops were greatly helped by their connections with those in Taiwan. Many of these recent agricultural exports were what Taiwan used to export, but because the cost of production increased as the economy grew, Taiwan lost its competitiveness in agricultural products. Taiwanese exporters tied up with Thai traders in introducing the necessary capital and technology to rural areas in Thailand. Numerous Thai–Taiwanese joint ventures were set up in the North and North-east in the 1980s. In a number of other cases, however, the initiative came from the Thais, and what was obtained from Taiwan was primarily technology. A typical case was the entry of the Charoen Pokphand group (popularly known as the CP group) into shrimp culture. The group, which had grown large as a chicken processor and trader, had enough capital to diversify into new fields.

Thailand's connections with Taiwan were not restricted to agribusiness. In the 3-year period after mid-1985, the Taiwanese currency appreciated from about NT$40 to NT$26 per dollar, and many of its labour-intensive products ceased to be competitive in the export market. Consequently, some Taiwanese producers shifted their production to Thailand. In a few years, in the late 1980s, Thailand became a major producer of toys, rubber shoes and gloves, tennis rackets, and other labour-intensive products. Thai traders and manufacturers formed joint ventures with Taiwanese investors, or became their subcontractors.

During 1987–May 1990, Taiwan invested about $2 billion in Thailand, about five times more than it did in the Philippines.[12]

Thai Chinese networks were also connected to neighbouring countries. Thai Chinese traders sought out their counterparts in Laos, Cambodia, Vietnam, and Burma (now Myanmar) for business dealings. In the past, political instability in these countries caused some Chinese traders and skilled workers to move to Thailand. In particular, the coming of gem traders and manufacturers from Burma in the mid-1960s (as a result of Ne Win's anti-Chinese policy) boosted the fledgeling jewellery industry, which became a leading export industry two decades later. Another helpful factor in the growth of this industry was the availability of rubies in Thailand (which has provided about 80 per cent of the world's gem-quality rubies).[13] Many of these were apparently brought in from neighbouring countries through Chinese networks.

Many Chinese traders and producers went to some length to be independent. For example, they worked hard at absorbing technology from abroad. If necessary, they formed joint ventures with foreign companies, and then eased them out when they were no longer useful. (The textile-based conglomerate, Saha Union, absorbed technology in this manner from its Japanese partners in its early years.) Traders often tried to reduce the number of foreign intermediaries to reach final purchasers as directly as possible. In many industries, since distribution channels had been firmly established (especially in selling to the Japanese), they did not succeed, but in others (for example, textiles), they did. Foreign buyers were more willing to accept the Chinese because they could meet internationally accepted business standards as their business tradition had prepared them for internationally shared business practices. Many, of course, behaved unscrupulously, but many more imbibed the business values which brought about long-term success.

Chinese Dominance in Thailand

The Chinese population was large enough to dominate practically all business fields in Thailand. Among the large businesses, non-Chinese ones are mostly government-related, such as the government-owned public utility companies like Thai Airways International. There is also a government bank (Krung Thai Bank) and government bodies such as the Petroleum Authority of Thailand which owns petrol stations and oil refineries. There are no reasons why these had to be government-owned, but they are kept as such, possibly to keep lucrative posts for bureaucrats (military as well as civilian). In addition, there are two major companies controlled by the Crown Property Bureau: Siam Commercial Bank and Siam Cement. These were originally set up to counter the British (not the Chinese) who dominated business in the pre-war period.

Large Thai entrepreneurs are few in number. There is the Bhirombhakdi family which owns Boon Rawd, known for its Singha beer, the most popular brew in Thailand. The founder, Phya Bhirombhakdi, was a Thai of Chinese ancestry who worked as a bureaucrat for the King (rising eventually to the rank of Phya, the second highest rank conferred on bureaucrats and soldiers before the Revolution of 1932). Another Thai entrepreneur is Chaijudh Karnasuta, who controls Italian–Thai Development Corp., a major construction company set up jointly with Giorgio Berlingieri. At first, the Italian ran the company, but after his death in 1981, Chaijudh took over and managed it with the assistance of his children and sons-in-law.

Practically all other large private companies are controlled by the Chinese. The most often mentioned Chinese companies are Bangkok Bank, the largest commercial bank not only in Thailand but also in South-East Asia; the textile-based conglomerate, Saha Union; and the agri-business group, Charoen Pokphand. A recent entrant to the 'big league' is the Karnchanapas family who has moved back from Hong Kong. Mongkol Karnchanapas made money in Bangkok as the distributor of Seiko watches, and probably because in the mid-1970s Thai security was threatened by the Communist victory in Indo-China, Mongkol moved the centre of his business to Hong Kong. Having become even more successful there, the family returned to Thailand as a big real estate developer. They were the developers of two large real estate projects, Muang Thong and Thana City. They have also won a bid for an elevated mass transit system in Bangkok.

According to Board of Investment (BOI) data, Hong Kong was the largest foreign investor in Thailand in 1991. Because there has been a great deal of anxiety among Hong Kong businessmen about the status of Hong Kong after it reverts to China in 1997, there has been a large outflow of capital, and some has come to Thailand. In the late 1980s, BOI-approved investments went to such labour-intensive industries as toys, plastic products, and electronics. In addition, there must have been a large financial investment from Hong Kong. Hong Kong–Bangkok connections are close. Many Chinese companies in Thailand have offices and subsidiaries in Hong Kong, and there is a lot of travelling between the two cities. In the late 1980s, there were over a dozen flights each way daily, and the flight time was less than three hours. It was possible to go from Bangkok to Hong Kong in the morning, do business there, and come back in the evening of the same day.

A New Environment under Marcos

In the Philippines, the Chinese were less dominant. This could be seen from the existence of many big Filipino (non-Chinese) companies. Some of the best-known were the Ayala group, inclusive of the Ayala Corp. (which developed Makati), the Bank of Philippine Islands, and Insular Life Insurance; San Miguel Corp., the food conglomerate; the Lopez group, which controlled the power company Meralco and the Philippine Commercial & Industrial Bank; the Republic Flour Mills controlled by Jose Concepcion (former Secretary of Trade and Industry), and Concepcion Industries by his brother, Raul; the Cebu-based Aboitiz family engaged in shipping and trading; the engineering company A G & P headed by Roberto Villanueva; and Dante Santos's Philippine Appliance Corp. During the period of martial law, President Ferdinand Marcos's Filipino cronies wielded great power. His best-known associates were Eduardo 'Danding' Cojuangco, Roberto Benedicto, Rodolfo Cuenca, Herminio Disini, Antonio Floirendo, Ricardo Silverio, and Bienvenido Tantoco. In addition, there were a large number of sugar-based Filipino business families, such as the Cojuangcos (from which President Corazon Aquino comes), the Elizaldes, the Aranetas, the de Leons, and the Montelibanos. By the late 1970s, the Filipinos had become a more dominant group than the Chinese.

The situation, however, began to change in the 1980s. The Chinese became more visible, and the Filipinos began losing influence. The first change came about following Marcos's measures in 1975 and 1976 to make naturalization easier for the Chinese. Prior to this, naturalization was difficult, and the large majority of Chinese immigrants did not have Philippine citizenship. Since *jus soli* was not the citizenship criteria, the children also remained Chinese. These non-Filipino Chinese were discriminated against under nationalistic measures such as import control and retail trade nationalization. But thanks to Marcos's measures, a large number of them (one source cites a figure of about 160,000) obtained citizenship.[14] Marcos believed that by raising the economic position of the Chinese, he could counter the power of the old rich who were critical of him.

More immediate reasons for the rise of the Chinese in the 1980s were the collapse of sugar prices and the fall of Marcos and his cronies. Under free trade with the United States, sugar became the major export crop of the Philippines in the pre-war period, and remained so until the late 1970s. Unlike other colonies, in the Philippines, little foreign capital went into sugar production. It was Filipinos, especially mestizos, who took advantage of new economic opportunities and organized sugar production. Many of them became large sugar planters or owners of sugar mills (called centrals in the Philippines). In the post-war period, with government encouragement, some of these people diversified into banking, trading, and industry.

The sugar industry started facing problems in the 1970s. With the expiration of the Laurel–Langley Treaty in 1974, the Philippines lost its quotas in the US market which paid higher prices than the international market. But in the mid-1970s, sugar prices were good, and the loss of the American market was not felt immediately. In the second half of the 1970s, prices started to go down, but in 1980, they increased again, almost to the 1974 level of 65 cents per kilogram, the highest level recorded thus far. However, sugar prices began plummeting in 1982, and hit the bottom in 1985 when prices were down to about 9 cents per kilogram. In the late 1980s, prices recovered somewhat, but most Filipino sugar producers could not continue production with such low sugar prices, and sugar became a depressed industry in the Philippines.

The mismanagement of the National Sugar Trading Corp., which was given a monopoly on sugar trading during the martial law period, contributed to the depressed state of the sugar industry, but a more fundamental reason was change in the international market. In Europe, the supply increased as a result of government subsidies to sugar beet producers, whereas the demand declined because a cheaper corn-based sweetener became available. Moreover, public concern over the health effects of sugar reduced per capita consumption in sugar-importing countries.[15] Furthermore, the cost of sugar production in the Philippines tended to be high. In earlier years, Filipino producers had done well because they were given preferential treatment in the American market, without which many of them could not have competed.

Among Marcos's cronies were a few who 'made it big' during martial law and fell together with Marcos (or a little earlier when the economy began stagnating and Marcos was forced by international lending agencies to rationalize his economic policy). A typical example was Herminio Disini, who was little known in business before martial law. But a number of others were well known before martial law. For example, Ricardo Silverio was an assembler of Toyota cars, and Rodolfo Cuenca was the largest constructor (he owned the Construction & Development Corp. of the Philippines). These people started using their connections with Marcos for quick profits or aggressive expansion. When the economy faced a financial crisis in the early 1980s, they got into trouble too, but Marcos could not help them out because international lending agencies pressured him to impose greater rationality on government policy. Their companies were taken over by the government, or liquidated. Some left the country with Marcos because they feared that the new Aquino government would prosecute them for collaborating with Marcos in plundering the country.

Although most of Marcos's cronies were Filipinos, there were a few Chinese among them. They were Ralph Nubla, Jose Campos, and Lucio Tan. Nubla did not go into business in a big way during the martial law period. Having been Marcos's classmate at the University of the Philippines and as President of the Federation of Filipino–Chinese Chambers of Commerce and Industry, he served as a liaison between Marcos and the Chinese community. Campos (also known as Jose C. Yao) owned the largest drug company in the Philippines, United Laboratories, and used his government connections for the benefit of his business (for example, by selling his drugs to government hospitals), but the company was well managed before martial law and remained so even after it. He co-operated with the Aquino government by disclosing Marcos's assets which he had been holding, and thus survived the transition.

Lucio Tan's ties with Marcos were much closer. Before martial law, he had a small foothold in the cigarette business. It was after he went into banking in 1977 that he joined the big business league. According to a government committee, Marcos was behind his venture into banking. In that year, he took over a small bank (General Banking and Trust) and changed its name to Allied Banking Corp. In the following few years, it became a leading bank, with a large infusion of low-interest loans from the Central Bank and a rapid increase in branches. The Aquino government tried to prosecute him for his collaboration with Marcos, but he was still untouched in 1991.

The Rise of Chinese Businesses in the Philippines

With the collapse of the sugar industry and the disappearance of the cronies, the Philippine business leadership changed greatly. Chinese businessmen became more successful and visible. The most dramatic change came about in department stores. Until the early 1980s, the most prestigious department store was Rustan's, set up in the Makati Commercial Center in 1971 by Bienvenido Tantoco, who later became a close associate of Marcos. In the mid-1970s, Tantoco set up another store in Cubao. But he became more interested in making quick profits under Marcos, for example, by operating duty-free shops. While he was doing this, some Chinese ventured into the large-scale retail business. In particular, Henry Sy's Shoe Mart and John Gokongwei's Robinson's began competing with Rustan's.

Then with the fall of Marcos, Tantoco lost the monopoly on duty-free shops and sought political asylum in the Vatican where he had been serving as ambassador since 1983. He was granted asylum, but the Vatican court soon sentenced him to 3 years' imprisonment on an arms conviction. Rustan's was, however, kept open by his children, though the Makati store was burnt down and closed for renovation for over a year. In 1992, Rustan's opened a new store (Rustan's Tower) in the Shangri-la Plaza in Mandaluyong. But it was surpassed by Robinson's and Shoe Mart (SM) which had aggressively expanded while Tantoco was engaged in a 'monopoly game' or while his children were busy adjusting to the post-Marcos period. The shopping malls, Robinson's Galleria and SM Megamall, are the most recent additions to their sprawling retail empires.

The retail business is competitive. Shoe Mart is planning to set up a large shopping complex in Cebu to challenge the Gaisano family's firm foothold there. Not to be outdone by Shoe Mart's challenge, the Gaisanos built the Gaisano Country Mall, a large leisure and shopping complex. They have also diversified into Metro Manila and set up Isetan Department Stores in Quiapo and Cubao.

Henry Sy's rise was the most dramatic. He was born in Fukien around 1925. His father was probably a 'commuter' Chinese in the Philippines who had a family in China, and Henry probably came to join him when he was still a boy. It is known that his father was operating a *sari-sari* (sundry goods) store when he set up a shoe store in downtown Manila shortly after the Pacific War at the age of about 20. It is not clear how he managed to survive the Retail Trade Nationalization Law, but he probably succeeded in getting naturalized. Naturalization was a slow and expensive process, but it was not an insurmountable obstacle for those who had money and determination to go through with it. His dream was to become rich by selling a pair of shoes to all Filipinos (about 19 million of them in 1948). In the following years, he became modestly successful, but it was not until 1975 that he became prominent. In that year, he set up a large department store in the Ayala Center in Makati. However, it was only in 1985 when he set up SM City at the end of the EDSA highway that a spectacular expansion began. In 1991, his SM chain held the premier place in the Philippine retail trade, and his business empire which included banking, real estate, and aquaculture (shrimps) was probably the largest Chinese business group in the country.[16]

There are a number of other visible Chinese entrepreneurs. There is the flamboyant Tan Yu who ventured into Taiwan and came back with Taiwanese money in the early 1980s, investing it in hotels and other projects. George Ty is probably the biggest banker among the Chinese; his Metropolitan Bank challenged the Bank of Philippine Islands, the largest private bank, in the early 1990s. In terms of total assets, it became slightly larger than the Bank of Philippine Islands in the second quarter of 1992. William Gatchalian became big in the plastics industry in a relatively short time. A couple of other recent stars are William Ley in construction and the Ang brothers in the fast-food business. In addition, though in a less dramatic way, a number of other Chinese became successful by exporting labour-intensive products such as garments. When these new stars were combined with the long-established Chinese companies, such as the China Banking Corp. and the Equitable Banking Corp., the Chinese business community became a formidable force in the Philippine economy in the late 1980s.

There was some residual anti-Chinese feeling in the Philippines as late as 1990. Some so-called nationalist journalists and intellectuals were trying to foment it by essentially repeating the theme nationalist Filipinos had used in the 1950s: they asked whether or not the country was really independent with the Chinese controlling the economy, or attributed the rise of basic commodity prices to the hoarding and manipulation of Chinese merchants. But they were fighting a lost cause. In the 1950s, people had faith in the potential of Filipino entrepreneurs, and were willing to accept government intervention in promoting them. However, it turned out that many Filipino entrepreneurs were better as political entrepreneurs than as business entrepreneurs, and though not all the blame could be placed on them, they were at least partly responsible for the miserable economic condition the country was mired in in the 1980s.

Since the mid-1980s, the trend of economic thought has been in favour of competition and an open economy. People are less willing to accept the protectionist recipe of the 1950s, for the chances are that it will make the already weak economy worse. The public has become more tolerant towards the ethnic Chinese. Several of them participated in the SEA Games in 1991 and won gold medals for the Philippines; this was a big change compared with the early years when there had been a feeling against ethnic Chinese representing the Philippines in international sports events. President Aquino's pride in her Chinese lineage is also a reflection of the people's increased tolerance.

Chinese Networks: Contrasts

The resilience of Chinese businesses is a bright side of the Philippine economy today. When the economy becomes more open and peace and order prevails, these businesses can act as a catalyst for economic rejuvenation. But they cannot be so powerful a force as their counterparts in Thailand for two reasons. First, their number is limited. Even economically, Manila is not a Chinese city, unlike Bangkok. Secondly, Chinese networks in the Philippines are not as strongly established as those in Thailand. Discrimination against the Chinese in the 1950s and 1960s did great damage to these networks. In the 1970s, the monopolies set up in grain, sugar, and coconut oil trading destroyed the Chinese networks in these commodities which had survived the discrimination of the earlier decades. Government intervention, which prevailed throughout the period, affected Filipino as well as Chinese entrepreneurs. Many of the former developed political entrepreneurship to the detriment of business entrepreneurship. These legacies act as a brake on the Philippines when Hong Kong, Taiwan, and South-East Asian Chinese networks try to connect with the country.

It is true that Chinese networks in Thailand face some of the same problems of the Philippine networks. In general, however, they work better than those in the Philippines. In Thailand, the period of Chinese discrimination was short; the level of discrimination was lower; and government intervention was less. Chinese businesses and networks evolved more naturally under a freer and more competitive business environment. Unlike in the Philippines, they did not have to go through a turbulent period in which many businesses declined and some rose for non-business reasons. Thus, traditional practices could adjust to new ones more or less at their own speed to produce a workable business system.

The tragedy of the discrimination against the Chinese and of other government intervention measures in the Philippines was not only that less efficient Filipino businesses replaced more efficient Chinese ones, but also that when Chinese businesses became important in the region, Philippine Chinese networks were so weak that they could not easily connect with Chinese businesses overseas. This became a serious disadvantage to the Philippines in the 1980s when Taiwan and Hong Kong became important foreign investors.

1. The percentage distribution of the Chinese by dialect group was as follows: Teochew, 56; Hakka, 16; Hainanese, 12; Cantonese, 7; Hokkien, 7; and others, 2. Richard J. Coughlin, *Double Identity: The Chinese in Modern Thailand*, Hong Kong: University of Hong Kong Press, 1960, pp. 6–7. Quoted in Likhit Dhiravegin, *Thai Politics: Selected Aspects of Development and Change*, Bangkok: Tri-Sciences Publishing House, 1985, p. 363.

2. *Far Eastern Economic Review*, 3 July 1952: 13.

3. Victor Purcell, *The Chinese in Southeast Asia*, reprinted Kuala Lumpur: Oxford University Press, 1980, p. 3.

4. Teresita Ang See, *The Chinese in the Philippines: Problems and Perspectives*, Manila: Kaisa Para Sa Kaunlaran, 1990, p. 1.

5. D. J. M. Tate, *The Making of Modern South-East Asia*, Kuala Lumpur: Oxford University Press, 1979, Vol. 2, p. 545.

6. George Weightman, 'The Philippine Chinese: A Cultural History of a Marginal Trading Community', Ph.D. thesis, Cornell University, 1959, p. 141.

7. Joseph Ralston Hayden, *The Philippines: A Study in National Development*, New York: Macmillan Co., 1942, p. 700.

8. Ibid.

9. Quoted in Jacques Amyot, *The Manila Chinese: Familism in the Philippine Environment*, IPC Monographs No. 2, Quezon City: Ateneo de Manila University, 1973, p. 65.

10. Wendell Blanchard, *Thailand: Its People, Its Society, Its Culture*, New Haven: HRAF Press, 1958, p. 66.

11. *Far Eastern Economic Review*, 21 November 1957: 663.

12. Samart Chiasakul and Koji Taniguchi, *The Role of Foreign Capital in the Manufacturers Market Development in Thailand*, Joint Research Programme Series No. 89, Tokyo: Institute of Developing Economies, 1991, p. 32.

13. *Far Eastern Economic Review*, 9 May 1991.

14. *Far Eastern Economic Review*, 15 February 1990. This article also reports that one of the papers Marcos took to Hawaii when he fled the country shows that he received a contribution [or bribe] of $12 million from the Chinese community for these measures.

15. For changes in the international sugar market which affect the Philippines, see Joop Theunissen, 'Linkage and Alternatives: The Philippine Sugar Industry in the 1990s', Discussion paper, Tilburg University, July 1989.

16. There is not much information on Henry Sy. The most detailed and readily available write-up on him appeared in *Asiaweek*, 25 March 1988. Though less detailed, see also *Far Eastern Economic Review*, 22 December 1988 and *Asahi Shinbun* (a Japanese newspaper), 28 June 1989. This paragraph is partly based on these sources.

3
Anti-Chinese Discrimination

The Retail Trade Nationalization Law in the Philippines

In 1954, the Philippine government enacted the Retail Trade Nationalization Law, which restricted retail trade to Filipinos or 100 per cent Filipino-owned corporations after 1964. Since there was a transition period of ten years and the foreigners who were engaged in retail trade before 1954 continued to do so even after 1964 until their death or retirement, utter confusion was avoided, but it was a terrible blow to the Chinese since retail was the bastion of their economic power. Furthermore, the court interpreted retail trade fairly broadly, and some businesses not normally considered retail trade (such as wholesale activities) were eventually covered by the law.

The law was one of many nationalization laws enacted since 1903 when the Philippine Commission (which acted as an advisory body to the American Governor-General) passed the Public Land Act, which restricted the benefits of homesteading to citizens of the Philippines and the United States. Inspired by this action, the Philippine legislature passed a number of other nationalization laws after it became all-Filipino in 1916. Public utilities, banks, shipping, civil aviation, and mining were some industries nationalized before 1954.[1] The Philippine court upheld practically all these measures and sometimes extended their interpretation. For example, in 1936, agricultural land was reserved for Philippine nationals, which was understandable, but in post-war years, the court interpreted all land to be agricultural land as all land had at one time been in the public domain and initially alienated for agricultural purposes (the Krivenko decision in 1947). This decision barred foreign nationals from establishing title to land, commercial or industrial.

All these nationalization laws allow some foreign participation in 'Filipino' companies as long as the Filipinos own a majority (usually 60 per cent) of the equity. But the Retail Trade Nationalization Law allows no foreign ownership at all. This prevented the Chinese from getting around it by sharing ownership with Filipinos while retaining actual control, as happened in Thailand when it restricted a number of industries (especially those in the tertiary sector) to Thai-majority owned companies in the early 1970s. Although the Retail Trade Nationalization Law did not specifically target the Chinese (all other foreigners were covered by this law, except the Americans who were given national treatment under the Laurel–Langley Treaty until 1974), the severity of the ownership condition possibly arose from the frustration many Filipinos had experienced in trying to enter the Chinese-dominated retail trade.

The Chinese saw the handwriting on the wall when they faced discrimination in the allocation of foreign exchange for imports. In early 1949, the Philippine government reserved 20 per cent of imports for new Filipino importers. The next year, the Philippine Congress passed a law which reserved 30 per cent of import quotas for new Filipino importers and increased the percentage to 50 in the following two years.[2] It is generally believed that import control was imposed to maintain the exchange rate at ₱2 per dollar, which would have been difficult otherwise in view of large trade deficits in the second half of the 1940s. But Alfredo Montelibano, who had once served as chairman of the Import Control Commission, stated that the real intent of import control was to transfer import trade from aliens to Filipinos.[3] The aliens included non-Chinese, but the Chinese were a major target, and their share in import trade subsequently declined.

As early as 1921, the Filipinos tried to make things difficult for the Chinese by enacting the Bookkeeping Law, which required every merchant in the country to keep complete accounts of his business in English, Spanish, or a local dialect. If Chinese merchants kept records, they did so in Chinese; if the law had been implemented, it would have been a great inconvenience to them. They fought this law all the way to the United States Supreme Court, and won their case. Even after that, the Filipinos tried new bookkeeping laws, and during the Commonwealth period, they finally succeeded.[4] This was just a beginning. An inkling of what would be in store with independence came when an ordinance was enacted by the Manila Municipal Board in January 1941 to exclude all persons except citizens of the Philippines and the United States from engaging in any form of business in the public markets. However, the passage of a Retail Trade Nationalization Law was difficult at this time because Japanese merchants were venturing into retail trade; if such a law passed, Japan was likely to intervene in Philippine affairs on the ground of protecting its own nationals.[5]

The strength of anti-Chinese feeling in the Philippines is reflected also in the frequency of anti-Chinese violence. One serious anti-Chinese outbreak during the American period took place in Cabanatuan—about 120 kilometres north of Manila, and at that time a town of some 20,000 inhabitants—a centre for Chinese control over the rice-based regional economy. The Chinese were mobbed, their stores looted, and some were killed. The same scenes were re-enacted in Manila and, on a lesser scale, in other Chinese centres. Minor attacks on the Chinese and their property are said to have been a recurring feature of Philippine life: a dispute between a Chinese *sari-sari* (sundry goods) store owner and a Filipino customer may arise and attract a large Filipino crowd which turns into a mob of rioters.[6]

Given the fact of political independence and nationalistic fervour, it is surprising that it took several years for a Retail Trade Nationalization

Law to be enacted. Filipino nationalists who pushed this measure felt that the politicians had been bought by the Chinese. That may have been so, but the first few presidents of the country had some misgivings about the legality of such a law. As lawyers, Presidents Sergio Osmena, Manuel Roxas, and Elpidio Quirino are said to have been concerned with its possible violation of the due process of law, equal protection under the law, and sanctity of international obligations.[7] At the same time, like Tomas Confesor, the pre-war director of the Bureau of Commerce, they may also have been concerned with its negative economic consequences, although being politicians they could not express their concern as bluntly as Confesor had.

The Retail Trade Nationalization Law of 1954 was a severe blow to the Chinese because most of them did not have Philippine citizenship. During the American period, as in pre-war Thailand, immigrant Chinese were Chinese nationals. But unlike in Thailand, immigrant Chinese could not be easily naturalized, and their children were also Chinese nationals. (In Thailand, all children were Thai because of the use of the principle of *jus soli* in establishing citizenship.) The application of the Chinese Exclusion Act of the United States was extended to the Philippines, making it difficult for immigrant Chinese to be naturalized. The principle of *jus soli* adopted by the Philippine government during the American period did not help either because it did not apply to Chinese children born in the Philippines.[8] Then, the Commonwealth Constitution of 1935 (which remained valid until Marcos replaced it with a new one after martial law was proclaimed) rejected *jus soli* as the criterion for citizenship in favour of *jus sanguinis* [a law based on blood]. (In the Philippines, this was interpreted to mean that only children with Filipino fathers could become Filipinos; that is, children's citizenship was determined by the 'blood' (sanguinis) of their fathers.)

Naturalization as a Way around the Law

One way to get around the Retail Trade Nationalization Law was to use a Filipina common-law wife as a dummy, but this solution had two problems. One was the Anti-Dummy Law, whereby competitors might ask government officials to investigate the matter, or government officials might use the law for extortion.[9] The other problem was that it required a legal transfer of ownership to her, thus giving rise to difficulties if the common-law wife decided to have her own way. The situation could get complicated if she brought her family to her side of the dispute. But in a large number of small Chinese businesses, this arrangement was a popular solution.

For a medium-size to large business, however, the only practicable solution was naturalization. Within a family, the older members were less qualified for naturalization than the younger ones who were born in the country. The ones who were thought eligible for naturalization applied. The process was expensive, and a little humiliating. But naturalization was possible for those who could pay and were determined to go through the process. In the mid-1960s, when the exchange rate was ₱4 per dollar, middle-class Chinese needed about ₱15,000 (₱10,000 for bribes and ₱5,000 as a legal fee) to make an application. The rich Chinese paid more. For the most difficult cases (the Chinese who were not well qualified because of a criminal record or for some other reason), the maximum was around ₱100,000.[10]

Most large Chinese businesses got around the Retail Trade Naturalization Law by getting some family members naturalized. For example, Yutivo Sons Hardware, a large hardware store and a distributor (later an assembler) of GM cars, was essentially a Chinese company in the late 1940s. But by 1964, it had become 100 per cent Filipino. Principal members of the family (such as Yu Khe Tai) managed to become naturalized in the 1950s, and those who did not relinquished their shares to other members of the family who had acquired citizenship. But not all Chinese businesses were successful in this way, and some had to be dissolved in 1964. For example, there was a pre-war trading company called Uy Matio & Co. based in Dumaguete, Negros. In the early post-war years, the founder's nephew, Tirso Uytengsu, was managing the company. As in the case of Yutivo, several family members succeeded in obtaining naturalization, and the Filipino share in the company had increased to about 90 per cent by 1959. Nevertheless, the company had to be dissolved in 1963 because there were still Chinese shareholders remaining. Since a Chinese family is an extended family involving cousins, nephews, etc., adjustment of interests within a family sometimes did not go smoothly.[11]

The number of Chinese with Philippine citizenship increased as a result of naturalization, but it was a small increase. From independence to the late 1960s, there were only 300 successful applications per year; thus, the bulk of the Chinese population extant in the early 1950s remained Chinese in subsequent years. With *jus sanguinis* as the criterion for citizenship, children born to the Chinese remained Chinese. Those who were engaged in trade before 1954 continued to do so until their retirement or death if they were proprietors, but their children could not take over their business. They were unwanted people in the Philippines.

Whatever Marcos's motive was, his measures to facilitate naturalization were the most humane and possibly the most beneficial among his measures during the martial law period. Presidential Letter of Instruction No. 270 dated 22 April 1975 requested government agencies to grant qualified aliens citizenship fairly quickly after they had applied. Presidential Letter of Instruction No. 491 dated 29 December 1976 relaxed the qualification for naturalization by lowering the language and financial requirements.[12] As a result, by the late 1980s, about 38,000 Chinese heads of households (160,000 persons including dependents) had received citizenship.[13] As late as 1990, there were still a large number of Chinese who had not been naturalized for one reason or another, but undoubtedly, the situation had eased considerably. In view of the poor performance of the economy and the greater assimilation of younger Chinese into society, the Filipino attitude became more favourably inclined towards the ethnic Chinese. Some anti-Chinese feeling still remained, but the Chinese issue was dying.

'Thailand for the Thais'

In Thailand, the Revolution of 1932 changed the environment for the Chinese. The new government's policy was summed up in the slogan 'Thailand for the Thais', and the Chinese became the object of government discrimination. By putting obstacles in the path of the Chinese, the government encouraged the Thais to go into business. Starting with the measure forbidding Chinese food hawkers from selling their wares, the government had enacted laws to reserve 27 trades and professions (such as hairdressing and taxi driving) for the Thais by mid-1942. From 1936 onwards, the government increasingly entered into business on its own account.[14] For example, it set up the Thai Rice Co. in 1938 to compete with the Chinese in the trade. The government also virtually took over the salt, tobacco, petroleum, and pork businesses.[15]

One should, however, keep in mind that anti-Chinese feeling in Thailand was confined to a small group of educated Thais, especially those who had been educated in Europe and influenced by the racial bigotry of Europeans. Unlike in the Philippines, there were no anti-Chinese riots. In 1937, a Thai nationalist intellectual, Luang Vichit Vadhakarn, drew people's attention to the fact that the Chinese had been remitting large sums of money to their families in China—an amount equal to one-quarter of the total government budget that year.[16] He succeeded in stirring up anti-Chinese sentiment, but it was not translated into organized support for anti-Chinese measures. This type of activity was needed to generate general public support for the government's nationalistic policy, but its effects on the Chinese were modest at best. The move to set up the Thai Rice Co. was a more significant one because the Chinese had a strong foothold in rice distribution, but it was also influenced strongly by the need to co-operate with Japan, which had been fighting with China and thus wanted the Thai government to take measures to control the Chinese.

Unlike in the Philippines, indigenous Thai entrepreneurship was undeveloped, and government corporations became the major instrument of the government's 'Thai-ification' campaign in post-war years. According to the World Bank mission in the mid-1950s, the Thai government was 'involved directly or indirectly in a large number of commercial and other industrial enterprises'.[17] However, since government corporations were primarily found in manufacturing and public utilities, they did not pose a direct threat to the Chinese, who were weak or absent in these industries. The only major exception was the Thai Rice Co., but even in this case, the company had to depend on Chinese managerial skills because the Thais did not have expertise in rice trading. Its importance declined after 1948 when the government dropped the plan to nationalize the rice industry.

Keeping the Chinese as a Part of the Thai Nation

There were two factors which pushed the government into business. The first was, as pointed out above, the new policy of the Revolutionary government of building a country on mass nationalism; the leaders of the Revolutionary government needed to take the country in a new direction to justify their seizure of power. The second was the government's concern with the increasing number of Chinese who resisted integration into Thai society. This concern began during the reign of King Vajiravuhd (r. 1910–25) when the Republican movement of Sun Yat-sen started to stir up nationalist feelings among the Chinese in Thailand, and more and more Chinese began bringing wives from China instead of marrying Thai women. King Vajiravuhd wrote a series of press articles attacking the Chinese as the 'Jews of the East'. Later, King Prajadipok (r. 1925–35) announced measures to restrict Chinese immigration and to bring Chinese schools under government control; both measures were barely enforced. The Revolutionary government, however, took this problem more seriously. It imposed stricter control on Chinese schools, and those which tried to evade the regulations were closed. Under Phibul Songkram—he became Prime Minister in 1938—Chinese schools were closed one after another; in 1944, only two Chinese schools remained open in the whole country.[18]

After the Pacific War, during the democratic period (1945–7), many Chinese schools were reopened. The turmoil in China brought a new wave of immigrants to Thailand. To make the situation worse, a large number of Chinese, especially youths, began siding with the Communists in China and tried to take over the leadership of the Chinese community in Thailand. In 1947, violence occurred between the Communists and the Nationalists. The government acted quickly, deporting 400 Chinese and fixing the quota for immigrants at 10,000 a year (reduced to 200 in 1949).[19]

Phibul became Prime Minister again in 1948 (his first government fell in 1944 when the tide of the Pacific War began turning against Japan), and moved decisively against Chinese chauvinists and Communists. As a show of strength, the government increased the annual residence tax on aliens from B20 to B400 (about $20) in 1952. The Chinese community strongly opposed this increase, and riots broke out in Bangkok. The government responded by shooting the ringleaders and arresting and deporting many others.[20] Most of the Chinese who took part in the riots did so because they felt that the tax was heavy and unfair, but they were not Communists; however, the Communists probably acted as organizers.[21] To the Thai government, it possibly did not matter whether the participants were Communists or not; what was important was to teach a lesson to the Chinese, that the government could do whatever it wanted to do with them if they did not submit to its authority. In the same year, the government arrested and deported nine wealthy merchants. This time, the Chinese response was mute.

At the same time, the government clamped down on Chinese schools which it feared could serve overall as an institution to retard assimilation. The Phibul government did not wipe them out as completely as it had once done during the Pacific War (at which time Phibul possibly did so as part of his co-operation with Japan). But the government reduced the number of Chinese primary schools, banned all secondary schools except two foreign language schools in Bangkok, and turned the remaining Chinese primary schools into almost *de facto* Thai schools by requiring them to teach most subjects in Thai. The only feature which distinguished them from Thai schools was the teaching of four subjects (reading, writing, manners, and civics) in Chinese, but the number of hours spent on these subjects was so few that no Chinese pupil could master the Chinese language (Mandarin), let alone study Chinese history, literature, and culture.

Besides the diluted content of Chinese education, another factor which undermined the viability of Chinese schools was their dependence primarily on school fees for their finance as the government viewed school fund-raising as a political activity, which could prompt an official investigation of contributors. Since free government schools were available, Chinese schools found it increasingly difficult to operate, and many closed down voluntarily in the 1960s. In the early 1970s, the number of Chinese schools outside Bangkok was down to about 25,[22] while the number in Bangkok was not much greater than that.

From the Chinese point of view, if they did not openly resist the government policy of assimilation, the situation was more manageable in Thailand than in the Philippines. The Thai government at least let them engage in their traditional trading business. But they had to contend with harassment and extortion by government officials. If the Chinese resisted, they could be charged as Communists and arbitrarily imprisoned or, in the worst case, deported. The vulnerability of the Chinese was dramatically stated by a Thai newspaper: 'It is the easiest thing in the world to bleed [the] Chinese in our country. . . .'[23] Discrimination was not however, an insurmountable problem. The Chinese sought protection from powerful government officials, whom the Chinese had to pay regularly, but they were at least allowed to continue their business and even to prosper under their protection.

In spite of this patron–client arrangement, not everything went well for the Chinese, of course. When a patron lost power to his political rival, his major clients, especially, faced retribution. For example, Chin Sophonpanich of Bangkok Bank had to flee the country when his patron Phao Siryanon, Director-General of the Police Department, fell following his rival Sarit Thanarat's overthrow of the Phibul government in 1975. He did not come back until 1963 when Sarit died and a new government was formed. This atmosphere of uncertainty eased substantially in the following years with the establishment of the stable Thanom Kittikachorn–Prapart Charustien government. The gradual rise of democratic forces in the country made it more difficult for government officials to continue to extort or to make legal arrangements for payments (for example, by serving on the board of directors of a Chinese company), especially after the fall of the Thanom–Prapart government (1963–73). At the same time, more and more second-generation Chinese began participating in their companies, increasingly shaping them into Thai companies.

Policy Reversal under Sarit

By the time Sarit came to power, the Chinese had ceased to be a threat to national security, and it seemed that given time, they would be assimilated into Thai society. At that time, because the government was all powerful, it could do whatever it wanted with the Chinese. Of course, there was no reason to kill the goose that laid the golden eggs. The question Sarit faced was what to do with Phibul's policy of promoting government corporations as a measure to counter Chinese economic power. As pointed out above, the policy was a part of the 'Thailand for the Thais' policy of the Revolutionary leaders. But since Sarit and his supporters belonged to a new generation and were not involved in the Revolution of 1932 which overthrew absolute monarchy, they did not suffer the 'guilt feeling' of the Revolutionary leaders and had not actually rebelled against the king's social and economic order which prevailed before the Revolution.

A few other developments in the 1950s combined to move Sarit to reverse the policy of the previous government and to rely instead on private initiative for economic development. First, most government corporations were badly managed, and were losing money. This worried the Bank of Thailand as it was concerned with the resultant negative effects on the government budget and monetary policy. Secondly, though the government had largely contained the Communist penetration of the Chinese population in Thailand, the Communists were gaining influence in Indo-China; to counter them, the government needed development, especially in the rural areas of northern and north-eastern Thailand bordering Indo-Chinese states. Thirdly, the United States, which had become Thailand's major ally in the post-war period (Thailand became a member of the American-sponsored South-East Asia Treaty Organization in 1954), championed the free enterprise system, and pressured the new government through the World Bank and US missions to promote development through private initiative. The United States had considerable influence on Sarit, giving Thailand about $300 million in military aid by 1957.[24]

In 1972, the Thanom–Prapart government (which followed Sarit's growth-oriented policy), faced with the rise of economic nationalism since the late 1960s, passed two laws restricting the activities of foreigners and foreign companies. They did not specifically target the Chinese, but those who had not been naturalized were affected. For example, one of the two laws—the Alien Business Law—reserved retail trade for the Thais and Thai companies. Unlike the Retail Trade Nationalization Law of the Philippines, a Thai company which could engage in retail trade was defined as one in which the Thai owned more than half its capital. Hence, a 49 per cent foreign-owned company could engage in retail trade even after this law was enacted. First-generation Chinese who had not been naturalized could transfer majority ownership to their Thai-born children who were Thai because of the principle of *jus soli*.

Although over time the Chinese were increasingly assimilated into Thai society, they did not completely lose their Chinese identity. A minority of Thai Chinese retained their 'Chineseness', without which Chinese business networks could not easily connect with those in other countries. Chinese schools could not teach Chinese well, but pupils could at least learn basic Mandarin, and those who wanted more could hire private tutors. Many spoke Teochew and other dialects at home with their first-generation Chinese parents, and continued to use these dialects if they went into business. It was not difficult for Teochew-speaking people to learn Hokkien, the language of Taiwan, since the difference between the two is not large (smaller than between Cantonese and Teochew). A small number of Chinese who wanted more formal Chinese education went to Hong Kong and Taiwan for their secondary and tertiary education.

Anti-Chinese feeling did not disappear completely: in the late 1980s, military criticism of big businesses and money politics smacked of some anti-Chineseness. The criticism was subtle, however. The military had many third-generation Chinese among the leadership, and could not be blatantly anti-Chinese. The military were primarily worried about their loss of influence to politicians, but since the latter were supported by Chinese businessmen, the military were indirectly concerned with the rise of the Chinese as a political force. Radical military leaders were unhappy with the wealth of big Chinese businessmen which, they believed, had been accumulated at the expense of the urban and rural masses. If third-generation Chinese military leaders were critical of Chinese businessmen, it was because they felt that, in comparison with themselves who were integrated into Thai society and concerned about the national interest, second-generation Chinese in big business seemed selfish and resistant to assimilation. But overall, the level of anti-Chinese feeling was low, and it remained generally latent. It could not come alive as a force by itself. Only when combined with other factors could it become relevant.

Shutting out the Chinese in the Philippines

The Philippine Chinese fared much worse than their Thai counterparts; they were much less acceptable to the new Philippines. Although the Philippines was a colony, the Chinese situation there was somewhat different from that in Indonesia or Malaysia. Neither the Spanish nor the American administration openly welcomed Chinese immigration. The Spanish were concerned with the politically destabilizing effect of

Chinese immigration; the colony could be easily lost to rebellious Chinese because only a small number of Spaniards were living there and the bureaucracy was badly organized. The Americans applied the Chinese Exclusion Act to the Philippines and technically barred Chinese immigration. But both the Spanish and the American administrations needed the Chinese for Philippine development, and allowed a small number in—a number much less than in Indonesia or Malaysia.

The Filipinos who took over the government in 1946 resented the pre-independence system which allowed foreigners (including the Chinese) to dominate the Philippine economy. The Spaniards and Americans had done a great deal for their development, but it was not enough from the Filipino perspective. Their main grouse was the country's underdevelopment, and because they accepted the nationalistic rhetoric which had been gaining currency abroad, they attributed the cause to the colonial order, and believed that the way to improve the situation was for Filipinos to regain the economy from foreigners. Attorney Reyes, a former official of the Bureau of Commerce who worked vigorously for the Retail Trade Nationalization Law, said:

> The economic slavery of the Filipinos is now a reality. Our embarrassing and sad situation has reached the limit. It needs immediate solution. We need Economic Revolution against those who are enslaving the Filipinos economically and those who allow themselves to be their tools. We must act now to save ourselves from complete economic serfdom caused by treachery and negligence of many of us. There is need for indoctrination so that the minds, feelings and actions of those who have betrayed or are betraying our country can be adjusted. The rope that completely binds Juan de la Cruz [a hypothetical Filipino] into slavery should be untied.[25]

Senator Jose Zulueta, a political leader who sponsored the Retail Trade Nationalization Law, argued:

> At present a condition exists here which finds no parallel in other parts of the world. Ours is an independent country, and yet its independence can be illusory because aliens control the economic streams of the nation. . . . If these aliens are so minded they can paralyze our national economy and create chaos to endanger our national security and integrity.[26]

In response to the Chinese challenge to the constitutionality of the nationalization law, the Supreme Court stated in its 1957 decision (Ichong v. Hernandez and Sarmiento) supporting the law:

> If political independence is a legitimate aspiration of a people, then economic independence is nonetheless legitimate. Freedom and liberty are not real and positive if the people are subject to the economic control and domination of others, especially if not of their own race or country. The removal and eradication of the shackles of foreign economic control and domination, is one of the noblest motives that a national legislature may pursue. It is impossible to conceive that legislation that seeks to bring it about can infringe the constitutional limitation of due process. The attainment of a legitimate aspiration of a people can never be beyond the limits of legislative authority.[27]

Although some were doubtful, many Filipinos accepted the nationalistic rhetoric and supported such nationalization measures as the Retail Trade Nationalization Law as a necessary step towards economic progress. The core group was the Filipino entrepreneurs who benefited economically from such measures, and their relatively large presence distinguished Philippine from Thai economic nationalism. It was they who initiated, promoted, and benefited from nationalization measures. They grouped themselves into the Chamber of Commerce of the Philippines, the National Economic Protectionism Association, and the Association for the Nationalization of the Retail Trade. By the early 1950s, they gathered enough political support to push a retail trade nationalization bill through the Philippine Congress. In mid-1954, they finally succeeded in getting the President to sign it into law.

The strength of the Filipino entrepreneurial class can be explained by a combination of factors: the small Chinese population, government land policy, the rise of mestizo entrepreneurs, and the education and training of Filipinos during the colonial period. In contrast, a large number of Chinese came to Thailand, dominating almost every facet of the modern economic sector. It is not that there were no mestizos in Thailand. Since intermarriage was common between Chinese men and Thai women, there were many children of mixed parentage; but few distinguished themselves in business. They either merged with the Thai commoners, or entered the ranks of high government officials. During the period of absolute monarchy, there was no help for them in doing business. After the Revolution, the government tried to help them to some extent, but because the Thai business class hardly existed and to create one was too time consuming, the government decided to go into business on its own account.

In the Philippines, many mestizos (Chinese and Spanish) ventured into commercial agriculture.[28] If they could own only what they could cultivate, as in Thailand, they might not have become a conspicuous presence. In the Philippines, however, they could become large landowners by buying land from Filipino peasants, foreclosing their land against which the peasants had borrowed money at usurious rates, developing new land by hiring workers, or taking away land from their previous owners by using fake land titles or force. They sent their children to Catholic schools and later, during the American period, also to government schools of higher learning (the University of the Philippines in particular) which prepared them for the law and other professions. Some who succeeded in these professions later diversified into business.[29]

This process of advancement was not confined to Chinese or Spanish mestizos. Some indigenous community leaders (the *principalia* class) took advantage of expanding economic and educational opportunities. Later, as the economy progressed, some Filipino commoners availed themselves of the same opportunities, and became modestly successful traders or manufacturers. They developed niches in the regions where the Chinese had not gone, or in the economic fields in which the Chinese had no interest because profit margins were low. But if they wanted to expand into the more lucrative areas, they were thwarted by the Chinese. If the more successful Filipinos (including Chinese mestizos) wanted to diversify from commercial agriculture or professional fields into new areas, they tended to run into Chinese competition. The problem became more serious in the late pre-war and early post-war years when those Filipinos who were trained by American companies entered business by taking over these companies as their investors withdrew from the country.

A new concept of the nation in independent Philippines left the Chinese at the margin, if it did not leave them out completely. Philippine nationalism was expending all its energy on the creation of a new nation with Filipinos at the centre of both the political and economic stage. It was a social experiment which did not turn out well.

In Thailand, a large part of nationalistic fervour was expended on strengthening the government structure. A higher priority was attached to strengthening the military and police than to getting the economy under Thai control. Any foreign (including Chinese) attempt to challenge the government's authority or to create another nation within the nation had to be crushed. Phibul's nationalism had placed some emphasis on the economy, but it had been a small-scale experiment. One of Sarit's greatest contributions to his country was to have stopped it at an early stage. But Phibul's contribution has to be recognized at the same time. The supremacy of government he established made it possible to bring under control the agitated Chinese community in the aftermath of the Communist victory in mainland China, a success which paved the way for a more liberal Chinese policy in later years. Traditionally, the Thai government had concentrated on building the administrative structure, and relied a great deal on ethnic minorities for economic progress. With the Revolution of 1932 and the increased Chinese threat in the immediate post-war years, some adjustments became necessary, but the new equilibrium reached was similar to the old one. As in earlier years, the Chinese regained their economic freedom. It is this 'looseness' in the relationship between the government and the Chinese which has kept the Thai economy growing over the past century.

1. For a list of the nationalization laws, see Remigio E. Agpalo, *The Political Process and the Nationalization of the Retail Trade in the Philippines*, Quezon City: Office of Coordinator of Research, University of the Philippines, 1962, p. 88.

2. Caridad C. Semana, 'Some Political Aspects of Philippine Economic Development after Independence', Ph.D. thesis, Harvard University, 1965, pp. 215–16.

3. George Weightman, 'The Philippine Chinese: A Cultural History of a Marginal Trading Community', Ph.D. thesis, Cornell University, 1959, p. 185.

4. Joseph Ralston Hayden, *The Philippines: A Study in National Development*, New York: Macmillan Co., 1942, p. 707.

5. Agpalo, *The Political Process and the Nationalization of the Retail Trade*, p. 32.

6. Hayden, *The Philippines*, pp. 703–4.

7. Agpalo, *The Political Process and the Nationalization of the Retail Trade*, p. 93.

8. Author's correspondence with Alfonso Felix, Jr., 16 December 1982.

9. The Anti-Dummy Law was passed during the Commonwealth period and revised in 1947.

10. Interview with Alfonso Felix, Jr., Manila, 27 September 1982.

11. Yoshihara Kunio, *Philippine Industrialization: Foreign and Domestic Capital*, Singapore: Oxford University Press, and Quezon City: Ateneo de Manila University Press, 1985, p. 86.

12. Yuan-li Wu and Chun-hsi Wu, *Economic Development in Southeast Asia: The Chinese Dimension*, Stanford: Hoover Institution Press, 1980, p. 75.

13. *Far Eastern Economic Review*, 15 February 1990.

14. *Far Eastern Economic Review*, 21 November 1957: 663.

15. David Wyatt, *Thailand: A Short History*, New Haven: Yale University Press, 1984, p. 254.

16. Judith A. Stowe, *Siam Becomes Thailand*, London: Hurst & Co., 1991, p. 103; Vilas Manivat (comp.), *M. R. Kukrit Pramoj: His Wit and Wisdom, Writings, Speeches and Interviews*, Bangkok: Editions Duang Kamol, 1983, p. 206.

17. *A Public Development Program for Thailand*, Baltimore: Johns Hopkins Press, 1959, p. 91.

18. Keith Watson, *Educational Development in Thailand*, Hong Kong: Heinemann Asia, 1980, p. 126.

19. Wendell Blanchard, *Thailand: Its People, Its Society, Its Culture*, New Haven: HRAF Press, 1958, p. 68.

20. Watson, *Educational Development in Thailand*, p. 127.

21. *Far Eastern Economic Review*, 23 October 1952: 529.

22. Watson, *Educational Development in Thailand*, p. 128.

23. G. William Skinner, *Chinese Society in Thailand: An Analytical History*, Ithaca: Cornell University Press, 1957, p. 303.

24. Frank Darling, *Thailand and the United States*, Washington, DC: Public Affairs Press, 1965, p. 168.

25. Agpalo, *The Political Process and the Nationalization of the Retail Trade*, p. 42.

26. Ibid., p. 95.

27. Ibid., p. 247.

28. For the role of Chinese mestizos, see Edgar Wickberg, 'The Chinese Mestizo in Philippine History', *Journal of Southeast Asian History*, March 1964.

29. For diversification patterns, see Yoshihara, *Philippine Industrialization*, Chapter 6.

4
The Contribution of Foreign Investment

Japanese Investment

BOTH the Philippines and Thailand started restricting foreign investment after the Pacific War, and their first major target was foreign banks. The Philippines passed the General Banking Act in 1948, banning new foreign banks and restricting banking to companies that were at least 60 per cent Filipino-owned. The foreign banks which had been operating up to 1948 were allowed to continue, but the doors were shut to new banks. In the pre-war period, there was one Japanese bank—the Yokohama Species Bank (the predecessor of the Bank of Tokyo)—but since all Japanese companies had left the Philippines after Japan's defeat in the Pacific War, there was no Japanese bank operating in 1948. As a result, there are no branches of Japanese banks in the Philippines even today. The foreign banks which continued to function were restricted in their operation, especially in setting up new branches, and their importance declined sharply in the post-war period.

In Thailand, Japanese banks could re-enter the economy (Mitsui Bank renewed its operations in 1952 and the Bank of Tokyo in 1962). But new licences have not been issued to foreign banks for a long time. As in the Philippines, those which were allowed to function were restricted in their operation, and their importance declined dramatically after the Pacific War. In the 1980s, foreign banks accounted for only a few per cent of the total deposits in commercial banks (about 2 per cent in the late 1980s)—a big change from the pre-war period when foreign banks, especially British banks (Hong Kong and Shanghai Banking Corp. and Chartered Bank), dominated Thai banking.

In other areas, however, Thailand allowed Japanese firms to invest quite freely. In 1969, besides a large number of Japanese-affiliated companies in the manufacturing industry, there were 36 in commerce and foreign trade, 5 in building and construction, 2 in transportation, 6 in advertising and publishing, and 18 in other services. Besides these, there were 41 Japanese branches and 63 liaison offices.[1] In the early 1970s, the Board of Investment (BOI) in Thailand stated: 'Japan ... attracts special attention. The presence of Japanese in Thailand is conspicuous not only in industry but in export-import, in wholesale trade, in banking and services as well.'[2] The Philippines was, however, much more restrictive. Though it allowed Japanese investment in the manufacturing industry to some extent, it severely restricted opportunities in other areas.

Japanese Trading Companies

Attitudes towards Japanese trading companies differed widely between Thailand and the Philippines. These Japanese companies started returning to Thailand soon after Japan regained independence with the San Francisco Peace Treaty of 1951. In the Philippines, it was not until 1967 that they were allowed to set up branches to do business in the country. The legality of this re-entry was, however, challenged in the Philippine Senate, and a month later, the mayor of Manila ordered Japanese trading companies to stop business transactions until the completion of deliberations in the Senate. President Ferdinand Marcos issued a circular to override the mayor's order, but because the latter had some political backing and would not rescind his order even at the former's request, the only practical thing these Japanese companies could do was to move out of Manila to Makati, which was emerging as the business centre of the Philippines at that time.

Japanese trading companies had marketing channels in Japan and abroad, channels which Filipino trading companies could not easily establish. They also often arranged the necessary finance, which was again difficult for Filipino companies to do (Filipino nationalists thought that trading was just simple buying and selling). In Thailand, it was through the pioneering efforts of Japanese trading companies that the country became a maize exporter in the 1960s. Of course, large Japanese trading companies could not engage in low-profit operations such as dealing directly with the numerous peasants who produced maize. They tied up with Chinese middlemen, and organized export marketing with the necessary financial backing. Without these Japanese companies, the success of Thailand as an exporter of maize would have been considerably delayed. In later years, they also became involved in the export to Japan of other agricultural products such as tapioca flour, mung beans, dry mushrooms, young corn, canned tomatoes, deboned chicken, and *wasabi* (Japanese horseradish).

The promotion of Thai agricultural products was also undertaken by Western trading companies. Such commodities traders as Cargill were important promoters of tapioca flour to the European market. They not only found markets for Thai tapioca flour and made necessary arrangements for its shipment, but also contributed to the improvement of palletizing technology. But the role of Western companies was more restricted compared with that of large diversified Japanese trading companies (*sogo shosha*) because the former specialized in a relatively narrow range of products.[3]

Retail Trade

Another big difference between the Philippines and Thailand was their attitude towards foreign investment in retail trade. In the Philippines, there were no Japanese department stores and supermarkets operating in the country because of the Retail Trade Nationalization Law (see Chapter 3). But in Thailand, retail trade was open to minority foreign investment. Thus, it was possible for Japanese investors to own 49 per cent of the equity, and control the management of the company by spreading Thai ownership over many shareholders (if they did not control the company, they had at least a great deal of freedom in management). The first Japanese department store to open a branch in Bangkok was Daimaru in the mid-1960s. But Daimaru was not followed by others immediately. It was not until around 1985 that Jusco, Sogo, and Tokyu set up stores in Bangkok. They were followed by Yaohan with its first store in Thailand in 1991. In the meantime, Sogo opened its second store, and Jusco a few more in the Bangkok metropolitan area.

These Japanese stores were not outlets for goods from Japan. In the early 1980s, Daimaru was handling mostly Thai-made products. The Japanese manager of the Daimaru store stated that if the goods produced by Japanese joint venture firms (such as electrical and electronic consumer goods) were considered Thai goods, they accounted for 98 per cent of their sales.[4] Before new department stores or supermarkets or additional branches could be opened, the permission of the Ministry of Commerce had to be obtained. In the mid-1980s, one of the ministry's conditions was that they promote exports from Thailand. Around this time, the Japanese yen began appreciating, and Japanese department stores and especially supermarkets actively sought textiles, miscellaneous labour-intensive products, and frozen shrimps and other food products from Thailand. A few Japanese supermarkets, though they did not open stores for retailing in Thailand, set up purchasing offices. All these large Japanese retail outlets were involved in merchandise development since Thai goods could not be sold in Japan as they were. In the second half of the 1980s, actively seeking goods to send back to Japan, they became serious competitors of Japanese trading companies which had been traditionally involved in exporting Thai products to Japan.

Manufacturing

In Thailand

In the promotion of industrialization, Thailand depended on Japanese investment to a large extent. Industrialization was vital for Thai development because the country could not develop very far with agriculture alone. Since Thailand had no technology base for industrial development, foreign companies were welcome in practically all manufacturing fields, at least in the initial phase. In the early 1960s, the major foreign investors in the world were American companies, but they were not interested in Thailand, possibly because the market was too small. However, Japanese companies were interested, and willing to invest there. They brought capital and technology, although the amount of capital was small in each project and the level of technology introduced was low in the initial phase. But, as industrialization progressed, especially in the 1980s, many of the factories Japanese companies built were modern plants equipped with expensive machines.

In the initial phase of their investment, Japanese manufacturing companies often invested jointly with Japanese trading companies. There were exceptions, such as car and household appliance makers, but most others—for example, textile companies which were the largest investors at that time—needed internationally more experienced trading companies. Even in Japan, they depended on the trading companies of their *keiretsu* (group) for the acquisition of raw materials and the necessary machinery from abroad and the export of their products. The only overseas experience they had was their pre-war expansion to China where they had run their factories as an extension of their Japanese operation.

In the post-war period, the Japanese had difficulty adjusting to the language and customs of the country in which they invested. Japanese trading companies which had acted as a link between Japanese manufacturing companies and the world and acquired in this role a broad experience in international operation supplied the necessary information for investment purposes and often acted as the organizer for an industrial project, although they usually remained minor equity holders. For example, the Japanese trading company Marubeni tied up with the Japanese textile company Toyobo in establishing two leading textile companies in Thailand, Erawan Textile Co. and Dusit Textile Co., during import substitution industrialization in the 1960s. Later, when the conditions for textile exports improved, Marubeni spearheaded the export drive of these companies.

Japanese industrial investment in Thailand was channelled into three major areas. In the first target area, the Thai industrial base was almost absent: motor car and household electrical appliances. In the second area, production had been started by Thai companies but efficiency was low. To this sector, Japanese companies brought better machinery and raised productivity. Investment in cotton spinning and weaving falls into this second category. In the third area, Thai manufacturers lacked technical expertise even though they had been producing substitute products. Japanese investment in synthetic spinning and synthetic fibre production are good examples of this category.

In these three areas, the Japanese contributed to the diversification in Thai industrial output. Around 1970, when import substitution had made considerable progress under the growth-oriented Sarit and Thanom–Prapart regimes, Japanese-affiliated companies accounted for 40 per cent of cotton spinning, 70 per cent of synthetic spinning, 100 per cent of synthetic fibre, 100 per cent of synthetic fabric, 71 per cent of motor car, 100 per cent of motor cycle, 51 per cent of battery, 53 per cent of wire rod, 100 per cent of sheet glass, 100 per cent of printing ink, 83 per cent of refrigerator, 75 per cent of air conditioner, 47 per cent of electric fan, and 38 per cent of tyre production.[5]

The profile of manufacturing in Thailand changed as import substitution industrialization progressed. For example, Japanese companies were, in the beginning, engaged only in assembling motor car parts brought from Japan. Then, parts such as tyres and batteries began to be produced locally. At this stage, the Japanese suppliers of parts invested in Thailand to produce these parts; later, car engines were produced. Since engines were produced by assemblers in Japan—unlike their American counterparts, Japanese car companies rely on outside suppliers for most parts—these Japanese car assemblers invested in this area. Engine production was difficult earlier when the market was small, but it became viable as the Thai domestic market grew to about 300,000 vehicles per year in the late 1980s. It was also helped by the ASEAN (Association of South-East Asian Nations) complementary scheme which started in 1988. The scheme counts the parts produced in other ASEAN countries as domestic products in the domestic content requirements of an ASEAN country. (In 1991, the domestic content requirement was 55 per cent for passenger cars and 65 per cent for commercial vehicles.) For example, Siam Toyota set up an engine factory in Thailand not only for the Thai domestic market but also for its factories in other ASEAN countries, especially Malaysia.

In the household electrical appliance sector, the most dramatic change in recent years has been the establishment of Thai CRT in 1986 with a registered capital of B600 million (about $23 million at the then exchange rate), to produce colour picture tubes (cathode ray tubes) for television sets. As in the case of car engine production, an economy of scale was necessary for production to be viable. Hence, production of colour television picture tubes had to wait until the market for colour television sets became large enough to justify it. Fortunately for Thailand, the economy began growing at rates of over 10 per cent per annum in the following years. In 1990, the company even decided to expand production to 2 million units per year by investing an additional B1,200 million ($48 million).[6] The company is a joint venture between the Mitsubishi group and a Thai group centred around Siam Cement Co. The necessary technology was supplied by Mitsubishi Electric Co.

Even in the field of textiles, where it is often thought that import substitution has been completed, diversification into new fields is still going on. In the 1980s, as higher-quality garments needed to be produced for export and also to satisfy the upgraded domestic market—a result of the economic boom in the second half of the decade—the Japanese textile company Teijin decided to produce special filament yarn in 1991 instead of importing it. Teijin Polyester (Thailand), the country's largest producer of polyester yarn, decided to go into production because the demand was expected to rise further, to 1,500 tons by 1992, and part of the production could be shipped to its overseas market. Teijin has been involved in synthetic textile production in Thailand since the 1960s. In 1991, it was one of the largest textile groups in Thailand engaged in the production of polyester products (staple, ordinary filament yarn, yarn, and chips).[7]

The contribution of Japanese investment to Thai industrialization was more dramatic in the second half of the 1980s when a large number of

Japanese companies set up a production base in Thailand for their American, European, and Japanese markets. This move was a result of the sharp yen appreciation after the Plaza Accord of 1985. The currency appreciated from about ¥250 per dollar in mid-1985 to ¥165 a year later and ¥123 by the end of 1987. This sharp appreciation made production in Japan too expensive for a large number of Japanese exporters as well as those which had been producing for the domestic market. Production abroad became a matter of survival for them. Many of these companies came to Thailand because the country had been improving the environment for export-oriented foreign investors by liberalizing the regulation on foreign equity, devaluing the overvalued baht which had discouraged exports, and exempting import duties on raw materials and parts needed for export production, or if they had to be paid at the point of entry, improving the refunding procedure.

Among the various categories of Japanese industrial investment in Thailand, two received a great deal of attention. One was the motor car industry which had been an example of a badly planned import substitution programme. The domestic content programme progressed, as more and more parts were produced in the country, but car prices remained high; passenger car prices were usually about twice as high as in Japan. When Mitsubishi cars were first exported from Thailand, it was an eye-opening event for the critics of the industry. Undoubtedly, as the rate of capital utilization grew with the expansion of the car market (300,000 vehicles sold in 1990) and the rate of protection declined under the Anand Panyarachun government in 1991, prices, especially for passenger cars, came down. At the end of 1991, the prices of passenger cars were only about 60 per cent higher in Thailand than in Japan, but taxes and import duties formed a big part of this difference. Since they could be exempted from duty if exported, the marginal cost of producing passenger cars in Thailand dropped to the level that justified export production.

The production expansion of Japanese car producers in the early 1990s has, however, not been for export, but for the Thai domestic market which has been growing at a rapid rate and is expected to attain 500,000 vehicles per year in the near future. The Japanese car maker, Mitsubishi Motor Co., set up its second plant near the new port, Laem Chabang, through its joint venture, MMC–Sittipol, and has been exporting cars to Canada from Thailand, but the export volume was only around 10,000 cars per annum. The new plant was primarily for the domestic market.[8]

The use of Thailand as an export platform posed difficulties for Japanese car producers, but not through any fault of Thailand. Unlike electronic or electrical products, product specifications (for example, safety and gas remission standards) for cars differ from country to country. In one country, the driver's seat is on the right-hand side; in another on the left-hand side. But a more important reason for the difficulty is the fact that the world market is divided. Most developing countries ban car imports. The major markets already have their own car manufacturers backed by their respective governments which consider the car industry as the key industry in their economy. This importance is related to the fact that the price of a car is high, much higher than that of a household electronic or electrical product. Because of such a nationalistic policy, if Japanese car manufacturers want to penetrate a foreign market (for example, the United States), production within that market becomes a necessity.

The second category of Japanese industrial investment was in household electronic and electrical products. Japanese producers in this sector did not face trade barriers as much as car producers. They could freely use Thailand as an export platform for their global market. In the initial phase, they brought in most of the parts and components needed for assembly, but since the parts tended to be heavy and bulky, some brought with them their parts suppliers from Japan. It was their investment which dramatically changed Thailand's export structure in the late 1980s and early 1990s. In the mid-1980s, manufactured exports began surpassing agricultural exports, but at that time, major manufactured exports were labour-intensive products such as textiles. During the late 1980s, electronic products became new exports, and in 1990, they were the second largest export of Thailand, accounting for 12 per cent of total exports. (Textiles were the largest export, accounting for 14 per cent of total exports.)[9]

The first Japanese electronic company to move to Thailand in a big way in the 1980s was Minebear Co., which had originally been a producer of ball-bearings but diversified into electronic products through the production of miniature high-tech bearings. The company has invested over $500 million in its seven manufacturing plants in Thailand, and made the country its biggest production base (accounting for about 65 per cent of its world production). Its Thai factories produce not only bearings, but also such electronic products as computer peripherals (for example, floppy disk drives), magnetic recording heads, and stepping motors. In the late 1980s, it became the largest export group in Thailand. Minebear was followed by most of the large Japanese producers of electronic and electrical products, such as Toshiba, Sony, Sanyo, Mitsubishi Electric, Sharp, Daikin, Fujitsu, Murata, and NEC.

In the beginning, the markets of these producers were Europe, the United States, and a number of other countries besides Japan, but the situation began changing rapidly around 1990. Daikin and Toshiba decided to produce household air-conditioners for the Japanese market. This was their defensive reaction to Matsushita's decision to move the production centre of household air-conditioners to Malaysia. Then, Sharp decided to produce radio-cassette recorders and micro-electronic ovens in Thailand for the Japanese market. NEC followed suit with colour television sets. They had been producing these products in Japan, but, because of increasing production costs there, decided to move their lower-priced goods to Thailand, while keeping the higher-priced ones in Japan. In a way, this phenomenon was an international division of labour on a firm level.

How large the flow of Japanese investment in the second half of the 1980s was, compared with the period up to the mid-1980s, is captured in the fact that the investment figure of 1987 alone exceeded the cumulative total up to the year before. At the end of 1986, the registered capital of Japanese subsidiaries and joint ventures was B2,836 million, but by the end of 1987, the figure had risen to B6,312 million. It kept rising in the following few years, reaching B30,252 million in mid-1990 and B38,755 million at the end of 1991.

In the Philippines

Japanese industrial investment did not flow into the Philippines as it did in Thailand. Japanese companies began investing in Thailand in the 1950s, and were the main foreign investors in the 1960s. In the Philippines, it was not until early 1967 that Japanese investment was approved on a minority basis. Even this toehold was not a real beginning. In the following years, though the number of Japanese-affiliated companies increased slowly, it was still small compared with that in Thailand. According to the Bank of Japan, there were only 22 Japanese industrial projects in the Philippines at the end of 1972, compared with 131 in Thailand.[10]

After martial law was declared in September 1972, the environment for Japanese investment in the Philippines improved. In 1973, 15 Japanese companies received approval from the Bank of Japan to invest in the Philippine manufacturing sector, and in the first three months of 1974, 11 more did. As a result, the number of Japanese companies which had received approval by March 1974 was 48, and the amount of investment rose to $20.1 million. Compared with the 169 cases and $89.6 million of investment in Thailand, Japanese investment in the Philippines was still small. In Thailand, Japanese companies participated in its industrialization from the beginning, but in the Philippines, these companies, such as textile firms which were large investors at that time, were barred at that stage.[11]

Late in 1974, Kawasaki Steel decided to set up a large sintering plant in Mindanao. It was the single largest Japanese investment in the Philippines. The plant was to import iron ore from Brazil, Australia, and Canada, and produce sintered ore for export to Kawasaki's steel plants in Japan. It cost ₱1.6 billion (about $235 million at the then exchange rate). The Mindanao plant began operation in 1977. In 1980, Marubeni and a few other trading companies participated in a copper smelting plant (Philippine Associated Smelting and Refining Corp.) in Leyte. This was the second largest Japanese overseas investment in the 1970s. As the economy was performing well at that time, a number of other Japanese companies invested in the Philippines. For example, the Bataan Export Processing Zone attracted some Japanese manufacturers who were looking for an overseas base for labour-intensive production. The amount of Japanese investment which never exceeded ₱25 million per year before martial law rose to ₱67 million in 1973, and jumped to ₱693 million in 1974 because of Kawasaki's investment. In the following years, it averaged around ₱150 million per year.[12]

In the early 1980s, the economy as well as peace and order started to deteriorate in the Philippines, and a number of Japanese companies left the country. But there was no sharp decline in the inflow of Japanese investment. For example, Mitsubishi took over Chrysler's car assembly plant and invested ₱406 million in it in 1985. (It became the second largest Japanese investment in the Philippines after Kawasaki's sintering plant.) It was the beginning of the take-over of the American-dominated car industry by Japanese companies.

In 1986, when Marcos fell, the ensuing political uncertainty caused Japanese investment to decline, but in the following year, it began to rise again to new heights. Some established Japanese companies, like Matsushita, expanded their operation at this time, and new ones, such as NEC, Uniden (a producer of communications equipment), and Asahi Glass, came to the Philippines. Moreover, Japanese car assemblers prodded the parts producers in their *keiretsu* in Japan to come to the Philippines. Mitsubishi Electric set up a plant to produce motor starters, and Sumitomo Denso automotive wiring harness. Mitsubishi Motor set up Asian Transmission, and exported part of its output to its plant in Thailand.[13]

The amount of Japanese investment in the Philippines was nevertheless minuscule compared with that in Thailand. This can be seen from the investment applications approved by the BOI. In 1987, the Philippine BOI approved $29 million worth of investments from Japan, whereas the Thai BOI approved $966 million (Table 4.1). In the following years, the amount of Japanese investment approved by the Philippine BOI increased, but in 1990, it was still around $306 million, while the corresponding amount approved by the Thai BOI was $2,704 million. A year earlier, the figure in Thailand reached a peak of $3,526 million, about 22 times more than Japanese investment in the Philippines. During 1987–91, Japanese investment in Thailand was about $12,000 million, whereas that in the Philippines was only about $800 million (Table 4.2).

TABLE 4.1
Foreign Investment in the Philippines and Thailand, 1987–1991 ($ million)

	Japanese Investment		*Total Foreign Investment*	
Year	*Philippines*	*Thailand*	*Philippines*	*Thailand*
1987	29	966	167	1,948
1988	96	3,034	473	6,239
1989	158	3,526	805	7,996
1990	306	2,704	962	14,119
1991	208	1,754	787	4,972
Total	797	11,984	3,194	35,271

Sources: Philippine and Thai BOIs.
Note: The investment figures in national currencies were converted by the exchange rates of respective years.

TABLE 4.2
East Asian Investment in the Philippines and Thailand, 1987–1991 ($ million)

	Japan	*Hong Kong*	*Taiwan*	*Total*
Philippines	797	403	440	1,640
Thailand	11,984	8,655	3,343	23,982

Sources and note: As for Table 4.1.

American Investment

In the 1950s and 1960s, when Japanese investment was virtually shut out from the Philippines, the major foreign investors in the country were American companies. In the early post-war years, the Philippines decided to treat American companies as national, not foreign, companies, and this decision held until 1974. This preferential status enabled American companies to continue in the areas otherwise reserved for Filipino companies. As a result, in the 1950s, American companies were engaged not only in manufacturing, but also in sugar milling, public utilities, mining, trading, engineering and construction, and various other service industries (for example, stevedoring). As in Thailand, the Philippines had to make up for its lack of technology in manufacturing by inviting foreign companies to invest in the country. In the Philippines, American companies met this need. For example, in the car industry no Japanese companies were involved at this time, unlike in Thailand. The industry was dominated by the three American car companies, General Motors, Ford, and Chrysler.[14]

As import substitution was pushed in the 1950s and 1960s in the Philippines, American companies responded by investing more, but not up to the level expected initially. In the 1960s and early 1970s, it was American divestment (rather than investment) which attracted attention: the American companies which had been enjoying national treatment were going to lose that privilege in 1974. It was clear that those in public utilities and mining had to reduce their foreign equity to 40 per cent after 1974 as required by the Constitution. Rather than wait until the last moment, these companies began divesting in the 1960s. General Public Utilities Corp., which had been operating Manila Electric Co. since 1923, sold its holding in 1961 to Meralco Securities, a Filipino corporation headed by Eugenio Lopez. In late 1967, the General Telephone & Electronics Corp. of New York sold its controlling interests in the Philippine Long Distance Telephone Co., while the controlling American interests in Lepanto Consolidated Mining were sold the same year. Also, American ownership in Atlas Consolidated (the mining company organized by Andres Soriano, and listed in stock markets in both the Philippines and the United States) declined in the late 1960s. By the end of 1972, about $250 million had been withdrawn from the Philippines.[15]

Then in 1973 and 1974, just before the Americans lost their privilege, a further ₱539 million (about $80 million at the then exchange rate) was withdrawn from the Philippines. Part of this outflow was a continuation of the ongoing divestment. For example, it was at this time that the mining company Benguet Consolidated, in which the Americans had controlling interests, was Filipinized. But there a new development also accelerated American divestment. The Petroleum Commission, created during the oil crisis of 1973, kept oil prices unreasonably low making it difficult for foreign companies to operate profitably; hence, the American shareholders in Bataan Refining and Filoil Refining sold their holdings to the Philippine government (which created the Philippine National Oil Co.).[16]

Another problem for American companies was competition from their Japanese counterparts. In the case of the car industry, the Japanese companies (Toyota, Mitsubishi, Nissan, Honda, and Isuzu) now dominate in South-East Asia. American and European producers withdrew from Thailand because they could not compete with the Japanese there, but in the Philippines, American withdrawal was partly caused by the shrinking domestic market in the mid-1980s. In 1983, the size of the car market was around 50,000 vehicles per year, but in 1984, it fell drastically to about 12,000 and was not expected to improve soon. It was at this time that General Motors, Chrysler, and Ford withdrew from the country. The Japanese challenge in the United States and other car markets made it difficult for American producers to continue to operate at a loss. In contrast, Japanese producers felt that the market was bound to improve some day and were financially strong enough to operate in the red until then.

In both the Philippines and Thailand, though American companies are no longer as visible as they used to be, there are still a number of them left. Goodyear Tire and Rubber now supplies tyres to Japanese car makers. Most American household appliance makers have pulled out, but semiconductor producers (such as National Semiconductor) are using the region as their production base. Dole and Del Monte are still canning pineapples for export. There also remain a large number of pharmaceutical companies in both the Philippines and Thailand. In petroleum refining, Caltex have refineries in both the Philippines and Thailand, and Esso in Thailand. In tyres, semi-conductors, and food, there are Japanese companies competing with American ones. But in pharmaceuticals and petroleum refining, however, American companies are clearly dominant.

American companies had not, however, invested heavily in both countries in the 1980s. In Thailand, Prime Minister Chatichai Chunhawan said in an interview with the United Press International in 1989 that he wanted more American investment, adding: 'I don't want my children to speak Japanese. I want them to speak English. [So you must come.]'[17] This remark prompted the Japanese ambassador to send a note of protest to the Thai government. Despite the Prime Minister's plea, however, American investment lagged behind Japanese investment, and during 1987–9, it fell behind Taiwanese investment and was roughly equal to that from Hong Kong. In the early 1990s, when Japanese and Taiwanese investment declined, American investment regained its former position (becoming the largest foreign investment in 1991, surpassing even Japanese investment), but the total amount of American investment during the boom period (1987–91) was much smaller than that from Japan, or Hong Kong, and roughly equal to that of Taiwanese investment.[18] The increase in 1991 was largely due to American oil companies' expansion projects.

The Spillover from East Asian Development

Part of the Philippine problem was that East Asian investment which had made the Thai economy dynamic since 1987 did not play a corresponding role in the Philippines. American investment (such as pharmaceuticals and petroleum refining) was concentrated in the areas where it did not create many jobs, therefore East Asian investment was more desirable from the viewpoint of creating employment and earning foreign exchange. Taiwan transferred much of its labour-intensive industry to low-wage countries like Thailand. Japan acted similarly; but its level of investment was higher and products more modern. In the 1980s, the United States ceased to be a catalyst for economic change in the region. This surprised the American-oriented Filipino élite who assumed that if the Philippines needed foreign investment, it should be American investment.

During 1987–91, the Thai BOI approved about $35 billion worth of foreign investment (see Table 4.1). In the Philippines, the corresponding figure was approximately $3 billion, about one-tenth the figure of Thailand. Apart from Japanese investment ($12,000 million in Thailand compared to $800 million in the Philippines), Taiwanese ($3,343 million and $440 million) and Hong Kong ($8,655 million and $403 million) investment was also much less in the Philippines during the same period. The investment from the three countries (Japan, Hong Kong, and Taiwan) totalled about $24 billion, accounting for 68 per cent of total foreign investment in Thailand, and about 15 times the amount invested in the Philippines ($1,640 million) (see Table 4.2). This difference in the flow of foreign investment from the three countries produced a significant disparity in the growth performance of the two countries during the period.

1. Kunio Yoshihara, *Japanese Investment in Southeast Asia*, Honolulu: University Press of Hawaii, 1978, p. 79.

2. Ibid.

3. For the activities of *sogo shosha*, see Yoshihara Kunio, *Sogo Shosha: The Vanguard of the Japanese Economy*, Tokyo: Oxford University Press, 1982.

4. *Thai-Vietnam to Nihon, Tomita Takejiro Kyoju Taikan Kinen Ronbunshu* [Thailand, Vietnam, and Japan: A Collection of Essays in Commemoration of the Retirement of

Professor Tomita Takejiro], Osaka: Division of Thai and Vietnamese Languages, Osaka Foreign Language University, 1984, p. 162.

5. Yoshihara Kunio, *Philippine Industrialization: Foreign and Domestic Capital*, Singapore: Oxford University Press, and Quezon City: Ateneo de Manila University Press, 1985, pp. 77–8.

6. *Bangkok Post Weekly Review*, 21 September 1990.

7. *Bangkok Post Weekly Review*, 22 November 1991.

8. Interview with Mr Ueda Masanao, President of MMC–Sittipol, 13 January 1992.

9. For the changing export structure caused by foreign investment a few years earlier, see Suthy Prasartset, 'An Emerging Trade Pattern since the New Wave of Japanese Direct Investment in Thailand', in Kunio Yoshihara (ed.), *Japan in Thailand*, Kuala Lumpur: Falcon Press, 1990.

10. Yoshihara, *Japanese Investment in Southeast Asia*, p. 65.

11. Ibid., pp. 65–6.

12. The Philippine Board of Investments.

13. Ibid.

14. For American investment in the Philippines, see Yoshihara, *Philippine Industrialization*, Chapter 4.

15. Frank Golay, 'Taming the American Multinationals', in Norman G. Owen (ed.), *The Philippine Economy and the United States: Studies in Past and Present Interactions*, Ann Arbor: Center for South and Southeast Asian Studies, University of Michigan, 1983, p. 152.

16. In the early 1970s, there were four petroleum-refining companies. One was the Anglo-Dutch company Shell, and the other three were American: Caltex, Bataan Refining (the joint venture of Esso and Mobil), and Filoil Refining (an American-Filipino joint venture in which Gulf Oil was the majority shareholder).

17. *Bangkok Post Weekly Review*, 24 November 1989.

18. The Thai Board of Investment.

5
Attitude towards Foreign Investment

In both the Philippines and Thailand, government policy towards foreign investment changed over time. In Thailand, foreign investment really began in the early 1960s. In 1960, the Sarit government enacted the Promotion of Industrial Investment Act—replacing the Promotion of Industries Act of 1954, which had been ineffective in attracting foreign investment—revising it in 1962 to further liberalize promotion benefits and simplify legal and administrative procedures. The revised Act entitled promoted enterprises to such benefits as exemption from import duties on machinery and from income tax, complete or partial exemption from import duties on raw materials depending on the priority of the goods to be manufactured, tariff protection, and the right to remit invested capital and profits and to employ foreign nationals. The Philippines or any other South-East Asian countries did not offer such liberal benefits to foreign investors as did Thailand. The Board of Investment (BOI), set up in 1959, became the administrative agency of the Promotion of Industrial Investment Act.

Post-war Relations with Japan

Thai–Japanese relations were normalized soon after April 1952 when the San Francisco Peace Treaty went into effect and the Allied occupation of Japan ended. There were no reparations to work out as Thailand had been an ally of Japan during the Pacific War. It might be argued that Thailand was forced to become Japan's ally and that as a result property and infrastructure were damaged by Allied bombing; Japan should therefore compensate Thailand. This, however, did not become an issue in post-war years; the only thing to settle was the B1.6 billion worth of obligations the Japanese military had incurred through the issue of yen military scripts during the war: the question was how much they were worth in post-war prices. In 1955, it appeared that Thailand and Japan had reached an agreement, but it was not until late 1961 that a final settlement was reached. Japan agreed to provide Thailand with Japanese goods and services worth ¥9.6 billion ($26.7 million) over an 8-year period. The negotiations, however, did not mar relations between the two countries. Diplomatic ties were restored in the early 1950s, and both countries were on friendly terms thereafter; when Prime Minister Phibul

Songkram (who collaborated with Japan during the war) was ousted in 1957, he spent his exile in Japan and eventually died there.

In the Philippines, the reaction to Japan in the early post-war years was entirely different. The Philippine archipelago had been the scene of major battles fought between Japan and the United States. Many Filipinos fought on the American side either as regular soldiers or as guerrilla fighters (for example, by joining the Communist-controlled Hukbalahaps) and died or were executed by the Japanese military. The human toll was staggering—at least 500,000 Filipinos died during the war[1]—and property damage was extensive. According to one estimate, 50 per cent of Manila, 70 per cent of Cebu, 75 per cent of Iloilo, 90 per cent of Zamboanga, and 85 per cent of Davao suffered damage during the war.[2] In addition, the war substantially damaged the production system of cash crops (for example, sugar) which had been the foundation of economic progress in the pre-war period.

The first issue Japan had to settle with the Philippines was the question of reparations. Under pressure from the United States, the Philippines reluctantly participated in the San Francisco Peace Conference of 1951 and was one of the signatories to the Peace Treaty. However, ratification of the treaty in the Philippines pended on the settlement of reparations. Immediately after the war, the Philippines set up a commission on reparations which estimated war damage at roughly $8 billion. The Philippines presented this figure to a Japanese negotiator in 1952,[3] but negotiations dragged on for a few more years because, first, Japan felt that the Philippine claim was too large and, secondly, Japan was indecisive as to whether or not to include capital goods as part of the payments. The Philippine claim was gradually reduced, and Japan decided to supply capital goods. In 1956, Japan and the Philippines agreed that the former pay $550 million over a period of 20 years. That same year, diplomatic relations between the two countries were restored.

Japan–Philippine relations were, however, strained for another 15 years. An indication of this strain was the refusal of the Philippine Senate to ratify the Treaty of Amity, Commerce and Navigation. Philippine and Japanese government representatives signed it in 1960, and it was ratified the following year by the Japanese Diet, but the Philippine Senate did not act on it in the 1960s. There were some technical objections to the treaty, but the attitude that 'what the Japanese were unable to accomplish in war, they are trying to accomplish in peace' was the major barrier to its ratification. In 1972, the Senate finally decided not to ratify it.

In the 1960s, trade between the two countries was increasing, but the Philippines was slow in opening up the country to Japanese desiring residence there. In the early 1960s, the Department of Foreign Affairs rejected the application of a Japanese woman (Matsuko Lirag) for a permanent resident visa, despite the fact that she was married to the brother of a prominent Filipino industrialist. The negative attitude of the Philippines towards Japan's 'second coming' was not only the emotional aftermath of the unhappy wartime experience, it was also influenced by concern that Japanese entry might thwart the aspiration of Filipino industrialists.[4] At this time, some major Japanese exports were a threat to what Filipino industrialists were trying to produce; in order to protect them, the Philippine government kept the Japanese at arm's length. In the 1960s, it was hoped that this policy would pay off.

Philippine–American Relations

The attitude of the Philippine government towards the Americans was diametrically opposite to that towards the Japanese. The Pacific War was perceived as a time of horrors, and the Americans who came back to subjugate the Japanese were thought of as the angels of liberation. When the Commonwealth government was set up in 1935, the Philippines was scheduled to become independent 10 years later, and according to the Constitution of 1935, some key economic sectors (such as mining and public utilities) were to be reserved for Filipinos or majority Filipino-owned companies. But in 1946, the United States Congress passed the Bell Trade Act, which stipulated that Americans be given full parity with Filipinos until 1974 in undertaking economic activities in the Philippines. To accommodate this demand, the Philippine government amended the Constitution. While the Philippine government had to go through the complicated procedure of a constitutional amendment (including a national plebiscite) as the release of war damage payments of $600 million was conditional upon Philippine acceptance of the Bell Trade Act, nevertheless, without a deep reservoir of goodwill towards the United States, the amendment would not have been possible.

American influence was all pervasive. In the cultural area, English continued as the major language of the country. The economy was structured in such a way that it could not survive without close ties to the United States. Its major exports, such as sugar, entered the United States only under the preferential arrangement made possible by the Bell Trade Act. In the early 1950s, the Philippines still depended on the United States for about 70 per cent of its foreign trade. This is in great contrast with Thailand where, though the United States was gaining influence especially in the political and military fields, it accounted for only about 20 per cent of Thai exports. Rice, Thailand's major export at that time, was not in demand in the United States.

In 1955, to remove one-sided provisions, the Bell Trade Act was replaced by the Laurel–Langley Agreement, and one-sided provisions were removed or made reciprocal (for example, the parity rights of Americans in the Philippines were given to Filipinos in the United States). Since Americans enjoyed a special privilege until 1974, one might expect that American investment would pour into the Philippines. But, in reality, it was far from the favourite place of American investors. Besides investment regulations, the investment climate includes other factors such as the freedom to import the necessary machinery, raw materials, and parts, the freedom to remit profits, and freedom from arbitrary government regulations. On these points, the Philippines scored poorly. Until early 1962, foreign exchange control was practised, and in the late 1960s, import control began. Furthermore, remittances were controlled whenever the country suffered large deficits in the balance of payments. American investment did not come as expected under such circumstances, but the nationalistic rhetoric became increasingly shrill.

A Gradual Change in the Philippine Attitude

In the second half of the 1960s, the Philippine government began to change its policy towards Japanese and other non-American investors. In 1967, the Investment Incentives Act was enacted because it realized that foreign investment was needed for further development. But the Act was not a serious attempt to attract investment as the BOI—the administrative agency for the Investment Incentives Act—could approve foreign equity of only up to 40 per cent in preferred areas. Under the Foreign Business Regulation Act, which was enacted a year later, foreign equity in non-preferred areas was restricted to 30 per cent. In some pioneer areas, the BOI could approve 100 per cent foreign equity, but for Japanese and other East Asian investors, this was extremely difficult.

The real beginning of Japanese and other non-American investment in the Philippines took place after martial law was proclaimed in September 1972. Before that, President Ferdinand Marcos encountered opposition from various sources, including the established business élite and the national legislature, when promoting foreign investment. In his attempt to create a New Society (Bagong Lipunan) under martial law, Marcos needed new foreign investors as well as new Filipino business leaders. Old ones tended to be critical of him or supported the opposition. It was in this political setting that Marcos opened up the country to Japanese and other non-American investors soon after he declared martial law. At the same time, peace and order improved, and the number of industrial disputes declined. Moreover, Marcos made special efforts to attract Japanese investment. As a gesture of goodwill to Japan, he revived and ratified the Treaty of Amity, Commerce and Navigation which the Senate had rejected in 1972. To show that the country was forging ahead and leaving the past behind, he allowed the Japanese to build memorials for their war dead (about 0.5 million Japanese died in the Philippines and its territorial waters). Japanese visits for this purpose peaked in 1978 when the Philippine government encouraged the Japanese to visit the war battle zones as part of its campaign to attract tourists from abroad. About 150 war memorials had been built by the mid-1980s.[5]

The Thai Attitude, 1960s–1980s

At the time when the Philippines was loosening its foreign investment regulations, Thailand was reacting to the consequences of its open-door policy in the 1960s. The liberal Thai attitude towards foreign investment had resulted in the overbearing presence of the Japanese in the country. The first organized Thai reaction was the Anti-Japanese Product Week arranged by the National Students Center of Thailand in November 1972. There were frequent demonstrations in front of Japanese department store Daimaru, which had become the symbol of the Japanese presence in Thailand. Starting in the late 1960s, the feeling that Thailand needed to strengthen its control over foreign investment began to take root. One Cabinet minister (Pote Sarasin) expressed the fear that 'one day we may wake up and find the Japanese controlling this industry or that industry'.[6] In 1972, a leading intellectual magazine, *Social Science Review*, published a special issue on the Japanese presence in Thailand. One of the articles graphically described Japanese dominance:

> If all the Japanese cars in Thailand were taken away, then all the roads in the country would be empty. If all the Japanese radios, televisions and electronic and electric appliances suddenly disappeared from the Thai households, then all the households would be silent as graves. If clothing with Japanese trademarks were taken away from the Thai people, then all the Thais would be naked. How completely are the Thais under Japanese influence.[7]

Even in the 1960s, the Thai government had begun tightening control over foreign investment. The 1962 revision of the Promotion of Industrial Investment Act completely exempted machinery, raw materials, and parts from import duties, but in 1967, the maximum benefit was reduced to an exemption of one-third of the import tariff rate, and in 1969, the exemption was entirely abolished. The policy on equity also changed gradually. Until the mid-1960s, it was easy for foreign investors to obtain approval for full ownership, but thereafter the Thai government promoted joint ventures with Thai partners. Then in August 1969, the Thai government decided that except in nationally important industries, investment projects with a foreign majority would not be approved. This principle was not strictly adhered to, but the number of Japanese investments with minority ownership began increasing thereafter.

In 1972, the Thai government passed two nationalistic laws: the Alien Business Law, which reserved the retail and export trades and certain others for Thais or Thai companies; and the Alien Occupation Law reserving certain occupations for Thais. These two laws affected some foreign companies directly. For example, Japanese trading companies could no longer engage in indent business, and foreigners had to obtain work permits if they wanted to work in Thailand. Nevertheless, foreign companies were not seriously affected. The Alien Business Law defines a Thai company to be a majority Thai-owned company; hence, Japanese trading companies set up joint ventures to undertake the 'nationalized' activities, holding 49 per cent equity themselves while spreading the remaining Thai ownership over its employees and the Thai public and companies it had established relations with. This assured the Japanese of effective control over the joint venture and the freedom to run it as an essentially Japanese company. In the issuance of work permits, the Thai government was not very strict, though it undoubtedly created problems still. If the number of work permits a Japanese company could obtain from the Thai government was not enough, those who were bachelors or could come to Thailand alone were brought in on a short-term visa and left the country every few months to return soon on another short-term visa.

In the mid-1970s, the foreign investment climate in Thailand deteriorated, but this was not largely due to the two laws passed in 1972. Undoubtedly, they made the country less open to foreign investment, but it was still more open than in most other Asian countries, including the Philippines. What made the country less attractive then was the political uncertainty which accompanied the fall of the military regime (Thanom Kittikachorn–Prapart Charustien) in 1973 and that of the Saigon government in 1975. The former event led to labour unrest, frequent street demonstrations, and terrorist activities, while the latter closed Thailand's trade with South Vietnam and reduced American military spending in Thailand. Moreover, the rise of democracy in the mid-1970s led to the closure of American bases in Thailand. These developments lent credence to the 'domino theory', causing some capital to flee Thailand.

By the early 1980s, however, political stability had been restored in Thailand. The unstable democracy period was ended by the military *coup* of October 1976. The military, however, could not go back to the style of government prevailing during the 1960s. In 1978, a basically democratic Constitution was proclaimed, and the following year, the military began sharing power with the politicians elected to Parliament. This change restored political stability, but Thailand was facing difficult economic problems: import substitution industrialization which had sustained growth in the past ran out of steam around 1980, and the sharp increase in oil prices added to the difficulties of the Thai economy.

Under the first Prem Tinsulanonda government formed in 1980, Thailand began taking serious measures to promote manufactured exports. In view of the tendency of the balance of payments to run into deficit, the government decided to devalue the baht which had been maintained at the level of about B20 per dollar for the past 30 years. After the devaluations of 1981 and 1984, the exchange rate was about B27 per dollar in 1985. Furthermore, the Thai government liberalized foreign investment; foreign equity holding, which had been restricted to 50 per cent or less, was raised, for export-oriented investment, up to 100 per cent, depending on export ratios. In 1986, the government made it easier for exporters to enjoy tax exemption (duties on imported materials and business taxes on exported goods), or in case they had to pay duties and/or taxes first, improved the administrative procedure for refunding them after the products were exported. These changes benefited Thai producers of textiles and other labour-intensive products, and were the main reason why Japanese and Taiwanese investors were attracted to Thailand in the second half of the 1980s.

The Philippine Attitude, Early 1990s

From the mid-1980s, the Philippine government further liberalized foreign investment. With the deterioration of the investment climate because of the poor performance of the economy, the government wanted to make up for the decline of domestic investment with foreign investment. A number of Japanese companies which had been operating in the country with Filipino partners raised their equity by buying Filipino holdings. Then in 1991, the Philippines passed a liberal Foreign Investments Act, under which foreign investors can hold up to 100 per cent equity in a Philippine company if it exports 60 per cent or more of its output (goods and services), or if it ventures into areas which do not appear on the negative list (see below) even if it does not export its output at all.

A unique feature of the Act is that an export-oriented foreign investor can invest freely even if he does not plan to export all of the output. He can sell up to 40 per cent of the output in the domestic market. He may not be entitled to promotional privileges, but if he needs them, he can apply to the BOI. How this application will be handled is a little uncertain, but he is likely to get some incentives from the BOI—at least tax-free imports of machinery necessary for production. Even without BOI privileges, he can import raw materials and parts duty-free on a consignment basis, or if he pays duties, he can get them refunded when the goods are exported. This arrangement is possible under a customs administrative order.

In the case of investment for the domestic market (that is, less than 60 per cent of output is exported), the Foreign Investments Act is fairly specific about the negative list which is made up of three sections. The first section consists of the areas of economic activities reserved for Philippine nationals (Filipinos or Filipino-owned corporations) by mandate of the Constitution and specific laws. This includes retail trade, while banking and other financial services do not appear on the negative list of this section, though they are reserved for Philippine nationals, because they are not covered by the Act.

The second section consists of areas where foreign ownership is limited for reasons of security, defence, risk to health and morals, and protection of local small- and medium-scale enterprises. The areas which belong to this section is spelt out in the Foreign Investments Act and cannot be arbitrarily expanded. If a foreign investor wants to produce goods or services for the domestic market, he has to invest more than $500,000 in order not to be classified as a small- or medium-size enterprise. The only condition under which he can invest with less than $500,000 is if he brings in advanced technology. Whether the technology is advanced or not is determined by the Department of Science and Technology.

The third section is expandable and can be used to protect an inefficient domestic industry from foreign investors. This section contains 'the areas of investment in which existing enterprises already serve adequately the needs of the economy and the consumer and do not require further foreign investments'. As a precaution, the Act makes it clear that while the National Economic Development Authority (NEDA) determines what these areas are, its decision has to be approved by the President and promulgated in a presidential proclamation. It also lays down reasonable criteria for the NEDA in determining the areas of exclusion. The law allows three years for the NEDA to draw up the list of excluded areas; hence, it will not be until mid-1994 that it will be finalized. In the meantime, the Philippine government has published a transitory list covering only a small number of areas (such as import and wholesale activities not integrated with the production or manufacture of goods).

As a result of the new law, a large number of areas have become open to foreign investment. For example, foreign investment for the domestic market in the area of household appliances had been difficult, but under the new law—at least until the NEDA comes up with a negative list—it is open to foreign investment of more than $500,000. Even if the area is included in the NEDA's negative list in 1994, since foreign equity is allowed up to 40 per cent, the foreign investor can reduce his holding to that level while spreading Filipino ownership over a number of shareholders whom the foreign investor thinks are reliable, as was done in Thailand to get around the requirement of Thai majority ownership in such areas as retail trade. There is no doubt that under the new law the Philippines has become wide open to foreign investment. Although there are areas such as retail trade and banking which are still heavily protected, most others have become more open to foreign investors than in Thailand.

Reasons for Philippine Caution in the Early Years

It took more than 40 years for the Philippines to come around to the realization that the country needs foreign investment for development. One reason for its cautious attitude towards foreign investment was the reaction to the colonial period. Filipino nationalists argued that Philippine underdevelopment was due to the colonial policy which had relied on Chinese and foreign capital and did not nurture Filipino entrepreneurs. Although indigenous (Filipino) entrepreneurship was more developed in the Philippines than in other South-East Asian countries, the fact remains that Chinese and foreign capital occupied a dominant position in a number of industries. Filipino nationalists blamed them for the underdevelopment of the economy and argued that if the government took measures to nurture Filipino entrepreneurs, the economy would develop. They gave little thought to the possibility that this strategy might not work. But as a new nation, the Philippines was willing to undertake a new economic experiment.

The nationalistic rhetoric was backed up by the anti-Japanese feeling generated after the Pacific War. To many Filipinos, Japan was a brutal conqueror. After the Japanese surrender, the Philippines imprisoned many Japanese soldiers for their cruel acts during the war and even executed some, like General Yamashita, head of the Japanese Army in the Philippines at the time of the surrender. Although the Philippines wanted more reparations, under American pressure, it agreed to a smaller sum ($550 million) and normalized diplomatic relations with Japan. But Philippine–Japanese relations did not improve much. The ratification of the Treaty of Amity, Commerce and Navigations was for a long time not discussed in the Philippine Senate. The relations between the two countries did not improve significantly until President Marcos declared martial law.

The closing of doors to Japanese investors in the period before martial law was not entirely due to the anti-Japanese feeling created during the Japanese occupation. The feeling was exploited by Filipino entrepreneurs who wanted protection from Japanese competition. This is similar to the case of the Retail Trade Nationalization Law of 1954 which was pushed by Filipino businessmen who wanted to eliminate Chinese competition. It is not completely accurate to say that Filipino entrepreneurs controlled the government—other interests (such as landed interests) were represented in the government—but they did capture the country's trade, investment, and industrial policy. As a result, the Philippines for a long time could not change its economic policy if such changes went against their interests. It was only after the economy had performed miserably that the policy was changed. These nationalistic entrepreneurs were pursuing their vested interests while the masses were suffering from poverty. (In 1985, this included 59 per cent of Filipinos, though the ratio fell to about 50 per cent a few years later.) Marcos improved the situation to some extent, but not very much because he also needed a support base which partly consisted of protectionist entrepreneurs. President Corazon Aquino (who came to power after Marcos fled in February 1986) was blamed for many economic ills, but the Foreign Investments Act she signed in mid-1991 may turn out to be the best economic legacy she has bequeathed to her successors.

The Political Dimension in the Thai Attitude

In many ways, the Thai attitude towards Japanese investors was completely opposite to that in the Philippines. Throughout the 40-year period, the Thai attitude was warm by comparison. Even in the early 1970s, the overbearing presence of the Japanese in Thailand did not seriously damage Thai–Japanese relations. A great deal of the criticism was an indirect attack on the corrupt Thanom–Prapart government. The image of the Japanese in Thailand remained relatively good; in the 1970s and 1980s, a large number of Japanese comics were translated into Thai, and many Japanese animations were shown on television with Thai subtitles. In 1990, one television channel aired a serialized drama, *Khu Kam* [A Pair of Star-crossed Lovers], based on a popular novel written by Vimol Siripaiboon in the late 1960s. It is a love story between Lieutenant Kobori of the Japanese Army and a Thai coed during the Pacific War. It was so popular that during the drama's airtime Bangkok's notorious traffic thinned out and social engagements were often cancelled.[8]

In explaining the Thai attitude towards Japan, one academic put it this way: 'The Thais are pragmatic about Japanese investment in their country. They want Thailand to become like Japan, but they are realistic enough to know that it is difficult. So, their attitude is "grow with Japan." They don't mind that Thailand becomes the industrial backyard of Japan.'[9]

This may be so, but there is a political dimension to it, which also explains Thailand's open policy towards other foreign investors. While some Third World countries were under the strong influence of nationalistic rhetoric, Thailand was being run mostly by authoritarian regimes. The national legislature was either closed or, if it functioned, it did not have much power. As a result, party politics was undeveloped, and Thai businessmen (mostly Chinese) could not influence economic policy through politicians. The Thai bureaucracy was largely independent of influence from the business sector, though the degree of independence enjoyed should not be exaggerated. In banking, for example, although the Bank of Thailand was far from being captured by banking interests, it was partly under the pressure of these interests that the central bank restricted the operation of existing foreign banks and the entry of new ones. But in general, economic policy was not dictated by business interests, as was the case in the Philippines.

Although business interests were increasingly brought to bear on the Thai government over time, the bureaucracy had kept a great deal of its independence until recently. Especially in the 1950s and 1960s, the bureaucracy enjoyed almost complete independence. Since business was in the hands of the Chinese, Thai bureaucrats did not have to pay much attention to business interests. They could subject the Chinese to foreign competition for the sake of the national interest. Under the authoritarian setting, the Chinese could only do their best to protect their interests given the prevailing policy. Around 1970, as second-generation Chinese began taking over their fathers' businesses, a dialogue between Chinese businesses and the government bureaucracy began. However, at this stage, the bureaucrats still had the upper hand of Chinese businessmen. It was in the 1980s when Thailand began moving towards democracy that business interests began to be felt strongly by the bureaucracy through the politicians these interests backed. But by this time, since the period of nationalistic excesses was coming to an end and an open economic policy had become the established trend in the world, it was difficult to resort to such nationalistic policy as was adopted in the Philippines before martial law. Yet, a large part of the credit for the economic reform which brought about the shift to export-oriented industrialization in the early 1980s belongs to the political structure which protected the bureaucracy from political interference.

It is not always the case that economic policy is better under the democratic system. If the government is captured by vested interests, which can happen under democracy, it cannot change its policy even if it is in the national interest to do so. This has been the case in the Philippines until recently. Policy shifts came about only after economic decline forced a dramatic change in the thinking of the people. In Thailand where the political system was regarded as less developed because of its control by the military, economic policy was, ironically, more rational and flexible, adjusting to the needs of the economy in stages. Foreign investment policy was positive because the bureaucracy judged that this would promote economic progress, and could be carried out under the mandate given by the military leadership which dominated Thai politics.

1. Theodore Friend, *The Blue-eyed Enemy: Japan against the West in Java and Luzon, 1942–1945*, Princeton: Princeton University Press, 1988, p. 242.

2. These estimates are given in the 'Seventh and Final Report of the High Commissioner to the Philippines', quoted in Kunio Yoshihara, *Japanese Investment in Southeast Asia*, Honolulu: University Press of Hawaii, 1978.

3. J. Vellut, 'Japanese Reparations to the Philippines', *Asian Survey*, October 1963.

4. Diosdado Macapagal, *A Stone for the Edifice: Memoirs of a President*, Quezon City: Mac Publishing House, 1968, pp. 329–30.

5. Interview with Shimada Sakae, Manila, 22 January 1992. Mr Shimada manages war memorials for various Japanese groups.

6. *Bangkok Post*, 11 May 1968.

7. *Social Science Review*, 10 (1972): 13.

8. *International Herald Tribune*, 8 June 1990.

9. Interview with Professor Prasert Yamklinfung, Bangkok, 7 January.

PART II
GOVERNMENT INTERVENTION IN THE MARKET ECONOMY

6
Nurturing the Financial Market

THE governments of both the Philippines and Thailand have regulated their respective financial institutions, with the degree of regulation changing over time. It decreased in the 1980s, with the so-called financial deregulation (for example, lifting the ceiling on interests) of the period. The fact remains, however, that financial institutions are among the most regulated in both countries. It is imperative that newly independent countries develop their financial institutions carefully as they are the core of the money economy. If their development goes awry, the whole economy suffers. Without public confidence in financial institutions, available capital cannot be mobilized for investment, and economic growth is retarded. The time horizon for many developing countries consists of decades, not centuries as was the case of Western countries which developed their financial market without much government intervention.

Undoubtedly, not all financial institutions can be well supervised, and the government lets consumers make their own judgements on certain categories of financial institutions (for example, finance companies). In general, the government tries to supervise them so that they are worthy of public trust. The most important aim of government supervision of these institutions—besides their development, they are regulated for other purposes such as social equity—is to ensure that they are financially sound. Accordingly, the government encourages (and often legally requires) them to diversify their loan and investment portfolios so that funds are channelled to those who can use them most productively, which is, of course, what financial intermediation is supposed to do. But financial institutions often collect money from consumers and businesses and channel it to the affiliated businesses of their owners. If this works well, as it did for *zaibatsu* (family-controlled) banks in pre-war Japan, then, keeping aside the issue of equity, all is well, but in practice, it often produces bad debts and is a major cause of bankruptcy.

The government also encourages financial institutions to enlarge their equity over time, so that it can act as a shock absorber in bad times. A financial institution may be owned by a family or a small number of families. When deposits increase with an expanding economy, it is desirable for equity to increase at about the same rate, but the desired increase may be difficult to achieve if the ownership structure is to be kept constant. The government often push ownership diversification in such a case. At the same time, professionalism is also encouraged in strengthening the management.

The government can enact laws to promote some practices it thinks desirable (such as ownership diversification and imposition of a single borrower's limit), but to bring about others, it has to rely on administrative guidance. It is most effective when a financial institution gets into trouble and comes to the government for assistance. Of course, if it is really in trouble and cannot be easily rescued, the government has to let it fail as long as it does not do much damage to public confidence. In the case of a commercial bank, the government tends to help, and can attach certain conditions when it grants low-interest loans.

The government can deregulate financial institutions and still maintain public confidence in them if it can guarantee the money put into them with a deposit insurance system, but this can be very expensive if the insurance premium is high or the system runs out of money because of many bankruptcies. Even if there is a deposit insurance system, the government usually regulates the institutions and tries to make their operation profitable. For example, the government can create a large interest spread by regulating interest rates on deposits and loans, and thereby make the banking industry profitable, or the government can make public money available to banks at low interest rates, in which case the interest rate foregone is a cost to the public. Both the Philippines and Thailand have at various times resorted to rescue loans and interest regulations. In the Philippines, many banks failed and the Philippine Deposit Insurance Corp. paid their depositors what the banks owed them. In the mid-1980s, when a few commercial banks failed, the insurance system did not have enough money, and had to borrow from the Central Bank.

In both countries, the regulation and supervision of financial institutions are delegated to the Central Bank of the Philippines and the Bank of Thailand respectively. Overall, the former was less effective in developing the financial market and imposed greater costs on society than did the latter. This was primarily due to the weakness of the former in controlling financial institutions, compared with the latter. It was handicapped partly because it operated in a litigious environment which allowed financial institutions to appeal against the actions of the Central Bank in court (and they often won their cases), and partly because it was so politicized an institution that it could not develop a strong bureaucracy.

The Central Bank of the Philippines: Its Weaknesses

A Litigious Environment

The weakness of the Central Bank of the Philippines in recent years was most dramatically demonstrated when it lost a court case in December 1991. In 1985, the Central Bank closed Banco Filipino Savings & Mortgage Bank, on the ground that it was financially unsound. The

Aguirre family, who controlled the bank, was suspected of having channelled much of the money into the family's speculative businesses and to have incurred large non-performing assets. From the Bank's point of view, the savings bank could not be easily rehabilitated; it was therefore better to close it before the family could further plunder the bank and cause greater damage to the financial system. The Bank also wanted to minimize payments to the bank's depositors through the deposit insurance system. But the owner challenged the Bank's decision in court, arguing that the bank was financially solvent at the time it was closed and that the Bank's real motive behind its closure was the benefit of the commercial bank (Far East Bank and Trust Co.) the Governor of the Bank had been heading before assuming his present post.

The litigious environment in the Philippines had probably been carried over from its former colonial master, the United States. Particularly in the post-war period, the legal system in the United States made it increasingly easier for the weaker party to win a suit. The system became biased against the government or a big corporation, or it might be argued that the former bias in favour of powerful institutions was corrected. Whichever one's interpretation may be, the result was a greater chance for a consumer to win a case against a big corporation, or for a regulated company against a regulatory agency. Since many leading Filipino judges and lawyers have studied in the United States and Philippine law schools have been set up after the American model, legal developments in the United States easily influenced the Philippine system. In the Philippines, however, it was not weak consumers but big companies, like commercial banks, which benefited from the recent legal bias against the government.

The possibility of a bank winning a case against the Central Bank made it difficult for the latter to take pre-emptive action against a mismanaged bank. The Bank tended to respond belatedly to problem banks, and in the meantime, the situation aggravated. A Central Bank official has to be cautious in taking punitive action against a bank since he can be sued and may be suspended from his post, heavily fined, or end up in jail. In the mid-1980s, however, during Jose Fernandez's term, the Bank decided to close a number of other banks, besides Banco Filipino. Most were small banks (rural and thrift banks), but three commercial banks were included (Manila Banking Corp., Pacific Bank, and Veterans Bank). As expected, some, especially the commercial banks, took their cases to court, and these were still pending at the time of the Supreme Court's decision on Banco Filipino. The Central Bank also wanted to close the Producers' Bank in 1984, but it did not succeed because the court issued a restraining order against the Bank.

An issue which arose in the Banco Filipino case was the objectivity of the Central Bank's action. At the time of its closure, the Governor of the Central Bank was Jose Fernandez, a competent former commercial banker. It is alleged that he closed Banco Filipino so that Far East Bank could take it over. There is no evidence to support this allegation, but the appointment of a commercial banker—even a former one—as head of his regulatory agency shows a lack of propriety on the part of the Central Bank as a bureaucracy. This sort of arrangement is bound to create an allegation of conflict of interests. (Fernandez has been charged with violation of the anti-graft law by simulating the divestment of his shareholdings in Far East Bank.)

Fernandez was not the first commercial banker to head the Central Bank; the practice started with the appointment of the third Governor, Alfonso Calalang (formerly with the Security Bank and Trust). In the history of the Bank, governors were usually appointed from outside the Bank. The first Governor was Miguel Cuaderno, who served almost two full 6-year terms from its inception until the end of 1960. He was with the Bureau of Banking before the war, and served as Secretary of Finance under Presidents Manuel Roxas and Elpidio Quirino. At one time, he had worked for the private commercial bank, Philippine Bank of Commerce, but could be regarded essentially as a government official. Cuaderno's successor, Andres Castillo, was promoted to Governor from within the Bank, but he was the first and last one so appointed. Although his successor, Alfonso Calalang, had come from the banking sector, he was not, however, a complete stranger to the Bank. He was the Bank's first Deputy Governor, having come from the Philippine Bank of Commerce where Cuaderno had been President. After a few years, he left the Bank, and about 15 years later, in early 1968, he returned as Governor.

The fourth Governor, Gregorio Licaros, who served from 1970 to 1981 was also not a complete outsider; he had worked in the Bank in the 1950s. Later the same decade, he left for another government bank, the Development Bank of the Philippines, and in 1962, he joined a private insurance company. Licaros's successor, Jaime Laya, had been Professor of Business in the University of the Philippines, and was brought into the Cabinet as Minister of the Budget by President Ferdinand Marcos. He was not a technocrat in the real sense of the word. As a former partner of Sycip, Gorres, Velayo & Co., he remained close to this accounting firm which audited a number of commercial banks. In 1984, he was succeeded by Jose Fernandez, who after serving a full 6-year term was succeeded in early 1990 by Jose Cuisia, the head of the Social Security System. Even Cuisia had been with a commercial bank before his tenure at the Social Security System.

This history of relying on outsiders to fill the post of governor of the Central Bank is in great contrast with that of the Bank of Thailand where, except in its early years, the governors have been officials who rose from the ranks. Rather than bringing in people from outside, the Bank of Thailand served as a training ground for other government agencies and the private sector. For example, some of the governors of the Bank later moved to other government agencies and became key economic technocrats (for instance, Snoh Unakul and Nukul Prachuabmoh). Thai commercial banks have also recruited professional managers from the Bank.

Neglecting Staff Development

In 1991, several former Bank of Thailand officials were working as executives in commercial banks. This smacked a little of corruption, because to some extent they owed their positions to their connections with the Bank. But a more important reason for this development was that the Bank had a large number of competent and ambitious people who, at the upper-middle or lower executive levels, had to leave. The Bank is a strictly pyramidal organization, and new posts cannot be created even if there are competent people at lower levels. Only a small number can be promoted from the upper-middle level of the hierarchy, and after that, promotion becomes increasingly difficult. Besides, at executive levels, the Bank does not pay as well as commercial banks, so there is a strong incentive for officials to leave the Bank.[1]

A central bank can make profits easily, since—putting it simplistically—it prints money at almost zero cost and lends it with interest. Given this freedom, it can therefore pay its employees well and offer various other incentives, thus, attracting competent people. This is what the Bank of Thailand did, for it is not under the Civil Service Commission which sets the salary scales for government employees. The Bank paid its staff better than did government agencies under the Commission. For example, in 1991, the governor of the Bank was paid about ten times more than the top bureaucrats (the C-11 level) under the commission. However, commercial banks paid more than the Bank did to its executives; but for the clerical and middle-level employees, the Bank paid better than commercial banks; thus, the turnover of employees was low at these levels. The Bank has also been offering about three overseas scholarships per year since the early 1960s, hence creating a reservoir of people for the executive level.

In contrast, the Central Bank of the Philippines could not attract many good people, and if it did, it could not keep them, because commercial banks and other private companies could pay better salaries. The Bank paid, on average, 30–40 per cent more than did most other government agencies; it could not pay more than that because, as a government institution, it was difficult to justify substantially better salaries for its employees. In 1989, during President Corazon Aquino's administration, government salaries were standardized, and the Central Bank's salary scales became comparable with those of other government agencies. In 1991, the Bank lost a number of promising employees to the private sector, and a number of others took optional retirement (including compulsory retirement, a total of 246 employees left).[2]

As a weak bureaucracy, the Central Bank made a number of blunders. In December 1983, the Bank admitted that it had overstated its international reserve by about $600 million; this error greatly tarnished its international reputation. It intervened in the foreign exchange market to defend the peso when economic fundamentals could not support it. It suffered large losses because too much of the international reserve was held in weak dollars and too little in strong yen, resulting in cross-currency losses. It also made procedural mistakes in taking disciplinary actions against commercial banks, and consequently lost some of the suits the banks had brought against it. Its legal department could not attract competent lawyers, nor was it free to hire outside lawyers for its defence. However, private banks could hire good law firms, and in court, they often had the upper hand of the overworked and underpaid lawyers of the Central Bank. Even with competent legal staff, the defence would be difficult if there was a corruption charge involved. It was alleged that Bank officials sometimes took actions against banks to enrich themselves, for example, by collaborating with those who wanted to take over the banks. Not all complaints of the commercial banks suing the Central Bank were unjustified; the former owners of Interbank and Allied Bank who are suing the Central Bank may have genuine complaints.

Under Heavy Political Pressure

The Central Bank was under heavy political pressure from the beginning. The most serious problem it first faced was that of financing government deficits. Like a typical developing country, the Philippine government tended to increase spending, but lacked the determination to tax the people, as a result of which the budget tended to run into deficits. In the 1950s, Cuaderno was a strong Governor, standing up against this pressure.[3] But his successors gradually succumbed, and the rate of inflation accelerated during their terms of office. The consumer price index which increased only 0.7 per cent per annum in the 1950s rose 5.6 per cent in the 1960s, 13.9 per cent in the 1970s, and 15.1 per cent in the 1980s. As a result, the external value of the peso depreciated dramatically in the 40-year period (1952–91) under study in this book, from ₱2 per dollar in the early 1950s to about ₱26 per dollar in the early 1990s.

In contrast, there was greater monetary stability in Thailand. The rate of price increase was higher in the 1950s (2.1 per cent per annum) in Thailand than in the Philippines, but in subsequent decades, it was lower (2.0 per cent in the 1960s, 9.7 per cent in the 1970s, and 4.6 per cent in the 1980s). The external value of the baht was therefore more stable. In the 40-year period, the baht depreciated only about 25 per cent, from about B20 to about B25 per dollar.

The Central Bank of the Philippines also came under the influence of politicians who wanted to use it to their own advantage. In late 1961, after Cuaderno had retired, in order to keep a foothold in the incoming administration, outgoing President Carlos Garcia appointed his Secretary of Finance, Castillo, as Governor, an action which incoming President Diosdado Macapagal branded as a 'midnight appointment'. However, the appointment was upheld by the Supreme Court. (Castillo had been serving as Acting Governor after Cuaderno's retirement.)

It was, however, Marcos who most abused his presidential power to appoint a governor. His first appointee was Calalang. During his term when Marcos was running for re-election in 1969, the Central Bank is said to have made money available for his campaign.[4] In that year, the consumer price index, which had increased only 1 per cent in the previous year, rose almost 15 per cent. Licaros was Marcos's second appointee. Marcos probably first met Licaros in the 1950s when the latter was in charge of foreign exchange allocation in the Central Bank. Marcos is said to have made his political influence available to businessmen to get foreign exchange from the Central Bank, thus making a lot of money for himself.[5] Soon after Marcos became President, while Licaros was with a private insurance company, Marcos, apparently liking his subservient attitude, put him back into the Development Bank of the Philippines (he had been the head of the DBP during the Garcia administration) and later made him Calalang's replacement at the Central Bank. During his 12-year tenure at the Bank, it is said that he made the Bank's facilities available for not only Marcos but also for a number of his own clients in the private sector. Many allegations of corruption have been hurled against him; he is said to have been the most corrupt Governor in the Bank's history.[6]

Financial Mismanagement

The 43-year history of the Central Bank of the Philippines is a story of decline. As it evolved into a politicized, weak bureaucracy, it also became too diversified an institution for a central bank. This was partly its own fault. In the 1950s, it was engaged in foreign exchange allocation. Thailand also practised exchange control, but the Bank of Thailand delegated the authority to approve most transactions to commercial banks.[7] But in the Philippines, the Central Bank was directly involved in approving transactions. Although exchange control was lifted in early 1962, later in the decade when the country began experiencing large deficits in the balance of payments, the Bank began imposing import control and was directly involved in selecting the goods to be controlled and in issuing import licences. Through such involvement, the Bank became a hotbed of corruption. The fact that Imelda Marcos's sister, Alita Martel (married to a businessman whose family owned the Marsteel Group), was heading the import control department during martial law provided plenty of grist for the mills of the Bank's critics. Alita fled the country with the Marcoses during the EDSA Revolution of February 1986. Under pressure from the International Monetary Fund, the Aquino administration later reduced the number of goods under import control.

In 1991, the Central Bank's losses amounted to about ₱21 billion ($776 million), with its accumulated losses amounting to a little over ₱300 billion.[8] The losses were partly the result of rescue operations undertaken by the Bank in the mid-1980s when a large number of financial institutions faced problems, but it is alleged that a big portion of it had arisen from the undertakings that should not have been embarked on. During the height of crony capitalism, it was said that the Bank had guaranteed loans from foreign financial institutions to private companies and was also engaged in currency swaps (borrowing money from abroad and lending it in the peso). As the economy deteriorated in the following years, many private borrowers could not return foreign loans, and the

Bank had to shoulder their responsibility if it had acted as their guarantor. As the peso devalued, currency swaps must have caused large losses to the Bank. The Central Bank, however, denied these charges, saying that the losses were mainly due to the costs of operations by the Bank to avert the collapse of the financial system in 1983–4, as well as the costs related to foreign debt restructuring.[9] Even if that is true, the losses still reflect the costs of mismanaging the country's financial market.

With the Central Bank weak as it was, the financial system became a little chaotic. This was well manifested in the financial crisis triggered by the case of Dewey Dee, a Filipino-Chinese businessman who fled the country in early 1981, leaving behind an unsecured debt of about $100 million. His family owned a textile factory, which he headed after his father retired, but not content with small profits in textile manufacturing, he went into gambling and speculation for quick profits. It is said that he not only frequented casinos in Manila but also those abroad. He also speculated on commodities and stock, and lost especially heavily on sugar and gold futures. He took advantage of financial institutions' confidence in his family to keep borrowing in the hope of recouping his previous losses.[10]

The financial institutions directly hit by the Dewey Dee affair were non-banking institutions. They guaranteed higher returns to investors, and with their money bought debt instruments from businessmen who could not borrow from the banking sector, because either their credit was not good or their borrowings had already reached the limits. Naturally, they were more risky borrowers, but non-banks had to take risk in order to earn more interest. Dewey Dee and other speculative businessmen who should have been stopped earlier from issuing commercial papers kept doing so, and non-banks were willing to accept them since the economy was doing well. But the bubble burst when the news broke that he had fled the country. Then, public investors suddenly wanted their money back, and many major non-banks (such as Bancom Development Corp., Philippine Underwriters Finance Corp., and Atrium Capital Corp.) went bankrupt, unable to collect money from their borrowers.

A similar incident took place in Thailand in January 1979 when Raja Finance, a medium-size company, went bankrupt, causing a crisis which was felt more on the stock market than by the banking system (as will be explained in the next section, only finance companies were affected). The affair wreaked havoc on the stock market, and it was not until 1987 that its turnover returned to the level before the Raja Finance debacle. In the Philippines, the Dewey Dee affair triggered off a major banking crisis because some banks (Associated Citizens Bank, Philipinas Bank, Producers' Banks, Commercial Bank of Manila, and Interbank) had lent heavily to non-banks.

The Philippine banking sector is too fragmented: at the end of 1991, there were 31 commercial banks (including 4 foreign banks), 102 thrift banks (7 savings and mortgage banks, 39 private development banks, and 56 stock savings and loan associations), 796 rural banks, and 3 specialized government banks, making altogether 932 banks. Many banks were not well managed, and the Central Bank closed 277 (6 commercial banks, 3 savings and mortgage banks, 6 private development banks, 28 stock savings and loan associations, and 234 rural banks) during 1970–91. Most of these were closed in the 1980s (only 26 in the 1970s).[11]

There is some instability in commercial banking, which accounted for the bulk of deposits in the banking sector (about 87 per cent in 1990). In the 1960s, a number of weak commercial banks were born as about 20 commercial banks were created. From time to time, weak banks were absorbed by stronger ones, and some were closed by the Central Bank. As a result, the number of commercial banks declined slightly in the 1970s and 1980s. In 1974, there were 33 domestic commercial banks, but the number was reduced to 27 in 1991. The decline in number was not a steady one despite closures and mergers in the 1970s and 1980s, because some thrift banks increased their amount of equity and were upgraded to commercial banks. The instability of commercial banks was made up to some extent by the deposit insurance system—it covered the non-commercial banks as well—that became operational soon after a banking crisis in 1968. But the maximum coverage was small: it was originally ₱10,000; in 1978, it was raised to ₱15,000; and in 1984, to ₱40,000. Consequently, during the banking crisis of the 1980s, many large depositors took their money to the 4 foreign banks operating here; those who had the means to do so took money out of the country.

The Bank of Thailand: Building a Sound Financial System

In contrast, the Bank of Thailand did a much better job in creating a modern banking system. In the 1950s, most domestic commercial banks were run by Chinese merchants in a traditional way, and public confidence in the banking system was low. (The Philippine banking system was more modern at that time.) The Bank of Thailand could not overhaul the financial system, and its task was to do its best with what prevailed. It set down rules and regulations to shape commercial banks into professionally run public institutions. But this could only be done in phases over time. The first systematic set of banking rules was embodied in the Commercial Banking Act of 1962. Stricter rules were legislated in the Commercial Banking Act of 1979.

The Bank of Thailand became a strong bureaucracy especially after Puey Ungphakorn became Governor (June 1959–August 1971). Unlike the Central Bank of the Philippines, there were practically no charges of corruption hurled against the Bank of Thailand.[12] Under Puey, it became the best-run civil bureaucracy. It used the large degree of discretionary power it enjoyed to intervene in the operations of commercial banks, and imposed appropriate reforms so that they could meet the needs of an expanding economy. The Bank's task was to make them worthy of public confidence in the beginning, and later, when this had been accomplished, to ensure that they maintained it. Substantial progress had been made in the first task by the mid-1960s; depositors had begun to feel safe about putting their money in commercial banks.[13] In the following years, bank deposits increased rapidly. The ratio of bank deposits to gross national product (GNP)—which can be taken as an indicator of banking development—increased from about 25 to about 80 per cent between the early 1960s and early 1990s. In the Philippines, however, because of one banking crisis after another, the ratio hovered around 20 per cent until the late 1980s, when it exceeded 25 per cent for the first time.[14]

The Bank of Thailand's policy was not to fragment the banking sector, which consisted of only commercial banks, and the number was restricted to slightly over a dozen. Many of them were set up during the Pacific War when Western banks were closed. A few more were set up in the immediate post-war years. After 1950, only two more banks were approved: the Thai Military Bank, founded during the Sarit Thanarat period, and the now-defunct Asia Trust Bank, a few years later.[15] If there was any trend in the number of commercial banks, it was one of decline.

The Bank of Thailand did not just take over a bank whenever it got into trouble. Usually, it offered help with some strings attached (such as requiring the bank to recruit more professionals from outside and to raise equity by inviting new investors). But in 1966, it took over two badly run banks (Provincial Bank and Agricultural Bank) and merged them to become a government-owned bank (Khrung Thai Bank). Then in the mid-1980s, the Bank of Thailand had to intervene in a few more banks (for example, Asia Trust Bank and First Bangkok City Bank, formerly Thai Development Bank) which suffered foreign exchange losses and problem loans. In the case of Asia Trust, it was renamed Sayam Bank and later absorbed by Khrung Thai Bank.

The Bank of Thailand required the other problem banks to change their management and ownership structure, reducing the existing equity capital to absorb losses and issuing new shares to new investors. In return, the Bank gave rescue loans at low interest rates. The owners of Asia Trust and First Bangkok City Bank, instead of suing the Bank of Thailand as their counterparts did in the Philippines, fled the country. The Bank of Thailand enjoyed greater freedom in taking pre-emptive actions before the situation worsened, when some problems were detected through regular inspections or through other indications. This freedom was judiciously exercised by the Bank; it became a big contributing factor in boosting public confidence in the banking sector.

The Bank of Thailand encountered more problems in regulating finance companies. Since the licensing authority of finance companies was under the Minister of Finance, when this post was assumed by politicians, businessmen could obtain licences more easily in return for their past or new contributions. At one time, there were over 100 finance companies, many of which acted as securities firms, and became involved in speculative activities. The failure of Raja Finance was the most famous debacle in the local history of finance and securities firms. After manipulating its own shares, Raja Finance went bankrupt in early 1979. At this time, facing runs on deposits, a number of other finance companies also faced difficulties. A few months later, the government enacted the Finance, Securities and Credit Foncier Act, which strengthened the power of the Bank of Thailand; its supervisory powers were broadened and it became easier to take punitive actions against mismanaged finance companies. But there were too many of them to supervise (and a large number of them were managed in a traditional way), and in the mid-1980s, with the economy in recession, many finance companies got into difficulties again. The Bank of Thailand did not, however, rescue all of them. Its attitude was that although it would do its best to prevent the failure of finance companies, the possibility of their collapse was the risk depositors had to take in trying to earn more interest than commercial banks could offer.

Developing a Stock Market

Another important concern of the Bank of Thailand was the development of a stock market. There is great advantage in having an active stock market; companies can raise equity capital there, and become strong in recession times by reducing the debt–equity ratio. In 1962, a private group organized a stock market, but it did not become an active market. Determined to create a better-organized market, the Bank formed a working group in 1969, and 5 years later, succeeded in getting the Securities Exchange of Thailand Act passed. On 30 April 1975, the Securities Exchange of Thailand (SET) started its first trading day. Established companies were reluctant to get listed on the SET, because this required disclosure of certain information on their operations; hence, the government gave a 5 per cent tax reduction on corporate profits as an incentive. For the first few years, the SET expanded smoothly, but following the Raja Finance debacle, public confidence was shattered, and the stock market entered a period of low trading. It was not until 1987 that, helped by the booming economy and some reforms in the stock market, public confidence returned. In the following years, the volume of trading expanded rapidly, and the SET became a bigger market than the Manila and Makati Stock Exchanges combined, though the latter two have a longer history than the SET. (The Manila Stock Exchange was set up in 1927.) In 1991, the market capitalization of listed companies was bigger in Thailand than in the Philippines; its ratio to GNP was roughly 30 per cent in Thailand and a little over 10 per cent in the Philippines.[16]

The Manila and Makati Stock Exchanges are under the purview of the Securities and Exchange Commission (SEC), but each has its own board consisting exclusively of people from the private sector, mostly the heads of securities firms which trade in the market, and which runs the market without direct government supervision, though certain disciplinary actions (for example, suspending the trading right of a securities firm) have to be taken by the SEC at the board's request.

In contrast, the Thai government was more involved in the activities of the SET. Its board consisted of 9 directors; at least 4 of whom were government representatives. In the beginning, the Bank of Thailand had better control of the SET's board. For example, the first few presidents of the SET came from the Bank of Thailand. But over time, the Bank of Thailand began losing influence on the board. What concerned the Bank most in the late 1980s was the aggressiveness of securities firms which could lead to the ruin of public confidence in the stock market. As securities firms gained more influence on the board, it became easier for companies to be listed on the stock exchange, which was to the advantage of their business but also attracted speculative companies which wanted to manipulate the stock market to their advantage. In 1991 alone, 61 companies were newly listed with the SET (the total number of listed companies was about 290 in mid-1992). Unless the SET was properly regulated, things could go wrong at any time since most investors were buying and selling short-term.[17] From the viewpoint of the Bank of Thailand, because the stock market was underdeveloped compared with the banking sector which had experienced the Raja Finance debacle, another fiasco had to be avoided.

Under the Anand Panyarachun government, the Bank of Thailand initiated the creation of the Securities and Exchange Commission (SEC), which is controlled by a 9-member committee consisting of the Minister of Finance, Under-Secretary of Finance, Under-Secretary of Commerce, Governor of the Bank of Thailand, and five representatives form the private sector (mostly professionals), but none from the securities industry.[18] The deputy governor of the Bank of Thailand (Ekamol Kiriwat) became chairman of the SEC. The SEC sets down regulations on the operations of securities firms, requirements for the listing of a company on the stock exchange, and rules on information disclosure for a listed company. A bill to create the SEC was passed in March 1992. The Bank of Thailand felt that a government-supervised agency independent of securities brokers could better control the market. Any stock market has many crooks (some of them are the chief executive officers of listed companies) trying to cheat public investors, so there is a need for supervision in order to minimize the damage they can do to the market.

The Bank of Thailand also wants the SET to let listed companies use it to issue debt instruments, such as bonds and commercial papers. Since there is no market for private debt instruments, the only source of borrowing for companies is financial institutions, especially the banks. But if creditworthy companies can borrow through the SET, they can reduce their dependence on commercial banks. This can have a large impact on the financial market, since large companies might be able to raise as much money in the SET as they can borrow from banks, thus posing a serious challenge to the banking sector. Banks then have to compete not only among themselves but also with the SET, and the cost of financial intermediation is therefore expected to decline.

Summary

In sum, the modernization of the financial system was bureaucratically guided in Thailand. Commercial banks in the early 1950s were mostly run by Chinese merchants in a non-professional manner, and the task of the Bank of Thailand was to guide them to become modern institutions which could meet the needs of an expanding economy for financial intermediation. Later, the Bank became involved in creating a stock exchange and making it a viable financial institution which could channel savings to long-term investment. The Bank of Thailand was rather effective in these tasks because it was a strong bureaucracy. In contrast, the Central Bank of the Philippines was a weak bureaucracy, not being able to attract, and if it did, to keep, good staff. It came under the influence of politicians, and has been charged with corruption and mismanagement. The litigious environment that prevailed in the country did not help either. As a result, the Central Bank's regulatory power was eroded, and public confidence in banks tended to suffer. In the case of the Manila and Makati Stock Exchanges, the SEC is their regulatory agency, but it is an even weaker bureaucracy than the Central Bank, leaving their operations largely to self-regulation. There have been no major scandals, but no strong public confidence in them could be built because of suspicion of malpractices among securities firms, especially some of those dealing in the Manila Stock Exchange, which had been traditionally a bigger market than the Makati Stock Exchange (which, many people felt, was better run). The lack of effective supervision by the SEC was one major reason for the inability of the stock market to develop further in the Philippines despite its long history.

1. Information on the Bank of Thailand in this and the next paragraph is based on an interview with Vijit Supinit, Governor of the Bank of Thailand, Bangkok, 14 January 1992.

2. *Central Banker* (the Bank's in-house magazine), January–March 1992.

3. Miguel Cuaderno, *Problems of Economic Development*, Manila, privately published, 1964, various pages.

4. Michael Onorato (interviewer and ed.), 'Salvador Araneta: Reflections of a Filipino Exile', Oral History Program, California State University, Fullerton, 1979, p. 16.

5. Primitivo Mijares, *The Conjugal Dictatorship of Ferdinand and Imelda Marcos I*, San Francisco: Union Square Publications, 1986, p. 262.

6. One allegation is that Licaros helped Lucio Tan and Willy Co to take over a medium-size bank, General Banking and Trust, for much less than its current value and making it (renamed Allied Banking) the third largest commercial bank in a few years. It is said that Licaros liberally approved their requests for the opening of new branches and special loans.

7. In May 1990, the Thai government liberalized foreign exchange transactions with regard to trade in goods and services by accepting article 8 of the International Monetary Fund Agreement.

8. The Central Bank has not published the amount of its accumulated losses, but Governor Cuisia testified in a hearing in the House of Representatives that they amounted to ₱308 billion (*Philippine Daily Globe*, 11 November 1992).

9. Jose Cuisia, 'Clarification on Various Newspaper Reports and Commentaries Regarding the Central Bank's Income Position', *Central Banker*, January–March 1992.

10. This paragraph is largely based on the so-called financial white paper which circulated privately in 1981. Reputedly, it was written by the Bank of Philippine Islands. The paper is entitled 'Recent Developments in the Chinese Community'. The amount of debts he left behind, $100 million, comes from the 1990 annual report of the Philippine Deposit Insurance Corp.

11. Philippine Deposit Insurance Corp.

12. There was a minor scandal related to a contract regarding the printing of Thai currency notes in the 1950s, but that is the only corruption which surfaced in the Bank of Thailand's history. The scandal is mentioned in *A Siamese for All Seasons: Collected Articles by and about Puey Ungphakorn*, Bangkok: Kamol Keemthong Foundation, 1981, p. 308.

13. Piti Sithi-Amnuai, *Finance and Banking in Thailand*, Bangkok, privately published, 1964, pp. 163–4.

14. International Monetary Fund, *International Financial Statistics Yearbook 1992*. The ratio of bank deposits to GNP is affected by many other factors besides confidence in banking institutions. For example, people may have confidence in the banks but their rates of interest for deposits may not be attractive. But the ratio indicates the degree of banking development, of which the people's confidence in the banks, at least in the initial stage, is an important determinant.

15. The military wanted its own bank to handle its defence budget and US military assistance. In the case of this licence, the Bank of Thailand seems to have yielded to pressure from the military. For a military-owned bank, it has been managed fairly well. But in the mid-1980s, it seems to have accumulated a large amount of bad loans. Bank of Thailand officials were sent in, and since then, two of them have become its managing director. Military officials still sit on the board, but they do not seem to interfere in its management extensively.

16. The year 1991 is not a particularly good year to compare because share prices were low in the Philippines and high in Thailand. In November 1989, when Philippine share prices were the highest, the ratio of market capitalization to GNP was roughly 30 per cent. But the amount of market capitalization then was about $13 billion, a much lower figure than that of about $40 billion in Thailand at the end of 1991.

17. Most are individual investors; there are few institutional investors in Thailand today. Their time horizon is short. A medium term can be three days. Interview with Pakhawat Kovithvathanaphong, president of Securities One Limited, Bangkok, 16 January 1992.

18. Finance Minister Suthee Singhasaneh appointed two economists as representatives of the private sector: Virabongsa Ramangkura and Narongchai Akrasanee. But Narongchai was chairman of GF Finance and Securities, and Virabongsa was adviser to the chairman of the Bangkok Bank of Commerce whose share issue became controversial in November 1992 (many people felt that there was some share price manipulation). They were charged with conflict of interest, and later resigned from the SEC committee.

7
Government Corporations

Thailand in the Mid-1950s

In the mid-1950s, Thailand had numerous government corporations in various sectors. The World Bank mission which visited the country at that time reported the situation as follows:

> [T]he Government is ... involved directly or indirectly in a large number of commercial and other industrial enterprises. In manufacturing it monopolizes tobacco, potable and industrial spirits and playing cards; it dominates timber, sugar, paper, gunny bags and minerals other than tin; it has large interests in cement, glass, pharmaceuticals, batteries, tin, tanneries and textiles, sometimes in direct competition with established producers; and finally, it operates a number of small plants making such diverse products as shoe polish, alum, rubber footwear, metal cabinets, paper clips, ceramics, and many others. In all, it controls some 60 establishments (including 15 distilleries), of which perhaps 40 can be classed as large in the sense of employing more than 50 workers.[1]

During the period of absolute monarchy, the Thai government was hardly involved in business ventures. The only exceptions were the two companies the king participated in: Siam Commercial Bank and Siam Cement. Under the guidance of conservative British Financial Advisers, the Thai government largely restricted its role to providing general government services (maintenance of peace and order, defence, education, etc.); building infrastructure (primarily railways); and collecting taxes to pay for these. Since it was afraid of getting into financial trouble—which could be an excuse for foreign intervention—the government did little in the way of developmental functions. The economy was left primarily to Chinese merchants and Thai peasants.

The situation changed with the Revolution of 1932. The Revolutionary Party, whose leadership consisted of Western-educated civil and military bureaucrats, stripped the king of absolute power, but retained him as a constitutional monarch. To justify such a drastic action (drastic at that time in the Thai context), they had to explain the benefits that would be brought about under their new government. They promised, among other things, to bring the economy under Thai control. In their view, the Chinese—at least those not integrated into Thai society (the first-generation Chinese and those of the second generation who resisted integration)—were not Thai, and the economy was underdeveloped because foreigners were controlling it. They reasoned that if the economy was brought under Thai control, it would improve. They therefore encouraged Thais to go into trade and industry, but because the Thai entrepreneurial class was virtually non-existent, this strategy did not work well. As an alternative, they soon created a large number of government corporations.

By the mid-1950s, this economic experiment was developing problems. Most government and government-backed corporations were losing money, and thus draining the Treasury. Unlike some other South-East Asian countries, the government did not have the natural resources to indefinitely finance these money-losing ventures. The most notorious case was that of National Economic Development Corp. (NEDCOL), a private company set up in 1954 by a number of prominent people connected with the War Veterans Organization. Its authorized capital was B50 million, but only B3 million was paid up by private shareholders. Most of its capital came from loans, especially foreign loans, guaranteed by the government. By the end of 1957, when the first loan repayment was due, NEDCOL had become bankrupt with a total debt of about B700 million (of which $30 million was foreign loans).[2]

Policy Reversal under Sarit

The conservative economic bureaucrats centred around the Bank of Thailand who wanted the government to leave entrepreneurial activities to private initiative engineered a World Bank mission. After studying the situation in the country, the mission recommended that the government rely on private enterprise for economic development (industrial development in particular). This recommendation was adopted by the newly established Sarit Thanarat government, which in the late 1950s began disengaging itself from the financial, commercial, and industrial sectors of the economy. Thereafter, the government restricted direct involvement largely to the public utilities sector (railways, air transportation, telecommunication, electric power generation and distribution, etc.)

Events did not proceed exactly as the conservative economic bureaucrats wanted. In the late 1980s, there were two government corporations losing money heavily: the State Railway of Thailand and the Bangkok Mass Transit Authority. These two bodies provide transportation for the masses, thus raising fares to cover expenses was politically difficult. Their losses were at least partly the result of the populist demand initiated by student and union leaders and supported by publicity-seeking politicians, often the case in a developing country.

Fortunately for Thailand, the situation did not get out of control. Most other state enterprises were earning profits, and as a whole, they were not a direct drain on the Treasury. In contrast, a number of government corporations in the Philippines were a big drain on the Treasury. The government had to heavily subsidize, for example, the National Power Corp., National Electrification Administration, Metropolitan Waterworks and Sewerage, and National Food Authority.

In Thailand, although Sarit decided in the late 1950s when he became Prime Minister that the government should withdraw from the economy, some government corporations remained in manufacturing and finance. One such example is the Petroleum Authority of Thailand, which is engaged in oil and gas exploration, refining, petrochemical manufacturing, and distribution. But in manufacturing, Thai government involvement was less than that of its counterpart in the Philippines. At the beginning of martial law, the Philippine National Oil Company was set up to play a role similar to that of the Petroleum Authority of Thailand. However, compared with the former, the latter is better run; normally, the Petroleum Authority of Thailand sets up joint ventures with private companies, and there is greater economic rationality in these operations.[3] Also unlike in the Philippines where the government-owned National Steel Corp. has a monopoly over major steel products, all steel companies in Thailand are privately owned. However, there are still several small government corporations undertaking industrial production in Thailand, but their negative effects on the economy are not large. The biggest of them is Thailand Tobacco Monopoly. The Philippine government, through the National Development Company, is a co-investor in fertilizer production (Philippine Phosphate Fertilizer Corp.) and copper smelting (Philippine Associated Smelting and Refining Corp.).

The Financial Sector: Contrasts

In Thailand

The biggest difference between the Thai and the Philippine attitude with regard to government intervention can be seen in the financial sector. In the late 1980s, four Thai institutions were considered government specialized banks: the Government Savings Bank, Government Housing Bank, Bank of Agriculture and Agricultural Cooperatives (BAAC), and Industrial Finance Corp. of Thailand (IFCT). They were small banks, accounting for about 11 per cent of the total assets of financial institutions. Of these four, the Government Savings Bank is the largest, having half of their total assets. Its deposits were invested largely in government bonds and promissory notes. The Government Housing Bank channelled its funds into government housing schemes for low-income people and government employees, while the BAAC lent money to the agricultural sector. The IFCT was the smallest of the four, and could not be really considered a government bank as in the late 1980s about 85 per cent of its equity was owned by the private sector. It was being run essentially as a private bank engaged in long-term lending. For these reasons, there was little room for cronies or government-connected entrepreneurs to obtain large loans from these banks. The only exception may be the BAAC which lent money to large agri-businesses, but no major problems have surfaced even here.

Khrung Thai Bank, the government-owned commercial bank which was created in 1966 by merging two badly run commercial banks

(Provincial Bank and Agricultural Bank), remains a government bank, although it is not clear why the government keeps it so. As it did with the First Bangkok City Bank in the mid-1980s, the Bank of Thailand could have restructured its ownership by inviting new private investors, but it gave control of the bank to the Ministry of Finance. In the late 1980s, Khrung Thai Bank took over the trouble-ridden Sayam Bank and became the second largest commercial bank (surpassing Thai Farmers Bank), accounting for about 15 per cent of the total assets of commercial banks and about 10 per cent of the total assets of all financial institutions. Thus, if Khrung Thai Bank was added to the four specialized government banks, the share of government financial institutions was about 21 per cent.

Khrung Thai Bank had some similarities to government banks in the Philippines. In the mid-1980s, it had a large portfolio of non-performing assets. Large borrowers which could not pay back their loans at that time were Cha-am Pineapple Cannery Co., the Metro Group (a diversified commodities-trading conglomerate), and Siam Vidhya (a real estate company). Their indebtedness was reportedly as much as B10 billion ($340 million at the then exchange rates). These companies were headed by politically connected entrepreneurs. Cha-am Pineapple Cannery's chairman, Colonel Phol Rerngprasertvit, was a Member of Parliament at that time and a leader of the small opposition party, United Democratic Party. The bank was being run bureaucratically, and could not have been as large as it was without large deposits from government corporations (which accounted for about half its deposits). The loss it suffered from bad loans to the three companies was contained as they made up less than 10 per cent of its assets. It even had enough discipline left to file criminal charges against Tamchai Kambhato, who had approved loans beyond the limits of his authority during his five-year term which ended in January 1986.[4] In July 1992, after he was sentenced to 20 years in prison, he immediately petitioned the Court of Appeals, and of this writing, the case is still pending.

In the Philippines

Philippine government financial institutions played a much more important role in the sector. In the early 1980s, a Filipino economist described their position in the financial sector as follows:

> Another important feature of the [financial] system is the presence of a large public sector—the Philippine National Bank (PNB), a commercial bank, the Development Bank of the Philippines (DBP), an investment bank, and the semi-public rural and development banks. The last two are saving banks with a development-oriented lending objective. The PNB has been the largest commercial bank whose assets comprise from 20 to 30 percent of the total commercial banking sector. The DBP assets have been about 15 percent of total banking assets. Counting [semi-public] rural and development banks, the share in assets of the public and semi-public banks amount to more than half of the total.[5]

In the last five years of President Ferdinand Marcos's rule, the operations of both the PNB and the DBP expanded rapidly. Between 1980 and 1985, PNB's assets doubled from ₱38 billion to ₱76 billion, while DBP's assets increased more, from ₱27 billion to ₱72 billion. Then, after Marcos fled the country, under the new Corazon Aquino administration, these government banks went through massive rehabilitation. The new management team which took over the DBP reported the situation as follows:

> During the first semester of 1986, we found that the DBP was in a dismal state, financially and otherwise, resulting from mistakes of the past. Foremost among its problems was the massive amount of Non-Performing Assets still carried in its books which accounted for more than 90 per cent of its portfolio. Another was the large and unwieldy organizational structure which at the very least needed to be trimmed down and streamlined.[6]

The state of affairs in the PNB was not much better than in the DBP. The government took over the non-performing assets of both banks to put them on a financially sound basis. Non-performing assets of ₱110 billion in book value were transferred to the government, which also took over ₱117 billion worth of their liabilities.[7] As a result, both became smaller banks. PNB's assets were halved in 1986, and its share of total assets in the banking sector declined from 26 to 12 per cent between 1985 and 1987, though it still maintained the leading position in the commercial banking sector. DBP's assets were drastically reduced, from ₱72 billion to about ₱10 billion between 1985 and 1986. In size, the DBP became comparable to the larger private commercial banks. Privatization of the PNB began in 1987, and in 1991, 30 per cent of its equity was held by the private sector.

Both the PNB and the DBP had faced some problems before martial law, but they were not serious ones. After martial law was declared, they began losing economic rationality almost completely. Marcos needed to dispense favours to a large number of his supporters throughout the country, not just his cronies; he used the two institutions to meet their financial needs. Some of them, of course, gave him a certain percentage of the loans they received from the banks or a share in their projects. Money came easy for them. A large number of new projects were 'cooked up' just to obtain money from the two banks; often, it did not matter whether or not the projects were economically viable. By launching projects, they made money, and if the projects floundered later on, they could be given to the banks. For example, in the mid-1970s, although the sugar market did not look good, a number of sugar mills were built by Marcos's supporters with money from the two banks (primarily the PNB). These projects, of course, turned out to be non-viable.

If the banks had been using the private sector's money, they would have been more careful. But a large part of their funds came from the government, the Central Bank, or foreign financial institutions (with the government's guarantee). If the money from these sources was not enough, the banks guaranteed foreign loans to the private sector. Since the PNB was a commercial bank, its lending operations were not as liberal as those of the DBP, but as a government bank too, it was also expected to play the part of an investment banker, like the DBP. Already in the pre-war period, the PNB was performing such a role in the sugar sector (by financing construction of sugar mills), but its developmental function broadened during the Marcos period. Besides diversifying its lending activities (so that Marcos's associates such as Ricardo Silverio, the assembler of Toyota cars, could borrow from it), it also bought equity through its subsidiary, the National Investment Development Corp. The DBP was in worse shape than the PNB because it gave large 'behest loans'—given at the behest of Marcos—to his cronies and continued to do so even after they began experiencing difficulties in the early 1980s. Its funds came almost exclusively from the government, the Central Bank, and foreign borrowing.[8] Even if it had gone bankrupt, the public would not have been seriously affected as they were not its major depositors. It was easier for economic rationality to break down in such a bank.

Not all the non-performing assets taken over by the government were useless. The Assets Privatization Trust (APT), which took over these assets, sold a large number of them and remitted about ₱18 billion to the Treasury. The APT had also taken over some assets from the Philippine Export and Foreign Loan Guarantee Corp. (a government corporation set up by Marcos, essentially for guaranteeing foreign borrowings) and the National Development Co., thus not all assets sold came from the DBP and the PNB, but their assets constituted the bulk of APT's assets. The APT recovered about 15 per cent of the non-performing assets of the two government financial institutions, with some assets yet to be privatized. These are the more difficult assets to dispose of, but the APT may be able to sell some of them eventually and remit more to the Treasury. But the fact remains that a large sum, probably about ₱95 billion, was lost by the PNB and the DBP.[9]

Undoubtedly, Marcos was the most culpable in causing such huge losses. But those bank executives who often executed the so-called 'behest loans' were accessories to his criminal acts, and the new Aquino government should have filed charges against them. But it was more concerned with the 'big fish', and had enough problems dealing with them. The wheel of justice turns slowly in the Philippines, and no 'big fish' have been convicted yet. Compared with them, the bank executives were 'small fish', and the government has not filed any charges against them. None took proprietary interests in the PNB or the DBP nor did they protect their integrity. Everything is blamed on Marcos, but he needed collaborators to wreak such serious damage on the country. After he was overthrown, the collaborators, big or small, should have been tried in court, as a warning to others. PNB's ₱2-billion loan to the Construction & Development Corp. of the Philippines—owned by Marcos's crony Rodolfo Cuenca and in which Marcos had a stake—was a clear violation of the rules by PNB executives since it exceeded a single borrower's limit, which was 15 per cent of its net worth.[10]

The Thai government filed criminal charges against the head of Khrung Thai Bank for the losses incurred by the bank in the first half of the 1980s. In the late 1910s, during the colonial period in the Philippines, the American administration convicted and jailed Venacio Concepcion, the first Filipino head of the PNB, for the large losses of the bank ($30 million, a very large sum at that time); he had granted fat loans to many of his friends with little collateral in return. Much of the discipline of the Philippine bureaucracy in the early post-war years was created during the American period, but this started crumbling as a new generation of Filipino politicians took over the country. The degeneration reached an acme during Marcos's martial law period. The PNB and DBP debacle in the mid-1980s was a part of this decline of discipline in the government bureaucracy.

Electric Power Generation: EGAT and the NPC

In the Philippines, the problems of government corporations were not confined to the financial sector. The differences in approach between Philippine and Thai government corporations were most clearly demonstrated in electric power generation and air transportation. The government corporation Electricity Generating Authority of Thailand (EGAT) has a monopoly on electric power generation. There have been no serious complaints about EGAT; rather it is known for its record of efficiency and profitability. In the Philippines, however, the National Power Corp. (NPC), which has a monopoly on power generation, has often been criticized, its reputation reaching a nadir in 1992. A power shortage began developing towards the end of 1989, and worsened in mid-1992 when the country began experiencing daily brownouts lasting four or more hours. It is estimated that in the two and a half years since 1990 the damage to the national economy caused by brownouts has amounted to over ₱100 billion. In November 1992, President Fidel Ramos said, '[E]lectric brownouts . . . have cut down the productivity of manufacturing enterprises by nearly a third.'[11] In the first 9 months of 1992, exports declined by 2.45 per cent and gross domestic product by 0.41 per cent (however, the gross national product increased by 0.91 per cent largely due to the remittances of Filipino contract workers overseas).

The power shortage became critical only recently, therefore it is not a major factor for the poor performance of the Philippine economy in the 40-year period ending in 1991. However, the NPC's problems are indicative of the problems of other government corporations. But a couple of them are unique to the NPC.

One is the question of environmental protection. Given a liberal intellectual atmosphere and broad exposure to English writings which have increasingly become environmentally conscious in recent years, it is not surprising that the country has produced strong environmentalist groups. Since thermal power plants tend to cause air and water pollution, hydroelectric plants environmental disruption, and nuclear power plants safety problems, it has become difficult in the past several years for a power project to get clearance from the Department of Environment and Natural Resources, which is under the strong influence of environmentalist groups. New power projects were opposed for one environmental reason or another, and no new major power plants has been built since the end of the Marcos administration. The 630 megawatt nuclear power plant in Bataan, which was to increase the country's total generation capacity by over 10 per cent, was almost completed in 1986 when new President Corazon Aquino stopped it partly because of environmental and safety concerns. Anti-nuclear groups have been adamantly opposed to its reopening. If the government tried to push through a power plant project over the objection of environmentalists, the latter got in touch with their counterparts in developed countries which were financing it (the Philippines was too short of foreign exchanges to carry it out alone) to put pressure on their governments.

The second problem, while not entirely unique to the NPC, cannot be too generalized either. Prior to the 1970s, the NPC was in charge of hydroelectric power generation, primarily for the provinces. But after martial law was declared, it took over the thermal power plants of the Manila Electric Co. (Meralco), and electric power generation became its monopoly. If Meralco had kept their thermal plants and kept expanding as it did in the 1960s, the situation might have been better today, but the political power balance in the early 1970s did not allow it. Meralco was controlled by Eugenio Lopez, Marcos's political enemy at that time. The Lopezes (Eugenio and his brother Fernando, Vice-President under Marcos) belonged to the old oligarchs whom Marcos wanted to purge from his New Society; hence, Meralco had to be taken away from them. Power generation and distribution were separated; Meralco retained the latter function and the company was given to Imelda Marcos's family while the NPC took over the former.[12]

Not so unique to the NPC is the charge that the Bataan nuclear power plant was a project tainted with corruption. Its major contractor was Westinghouse Electric Corp. When the Philippine government was leaning towards another contractor (General Electric), Westinghouse approached Marcos through its Filipino agent Herminio Disini, a crony whose wife is a cousin of Imelda as well as her personal physician. Westinghouse paid Disini $17 million as a sales fee, and part of it (probably, a large part of it) went to Marcos as a bribe. Marcos seems to have taken a certain percentage from all major government-related projects, including this nuclear power plant. This factor plus the tendency of bribers to overcharge their clients inflated the costs of government projects. For the nuclear plant, it is said that the government paid twice as much as other governments did for a similar plant.[13] Soon after Aquino became President, she stopped the project, and sued Westinghouse for bribery. In this project, which did not produce any power, the NPC incurred a foreign debt of $2 billion to be paid over the 10-year period ending in 1995.[14] Under martial law, like many other government corporations, the NPC did not have clear control over its operations.

A more common problem the NPC faced as a government corporation was the lack of revenues for the maintenance and expansion of its plants. It could set rates on its own (they were not set by the Energy Regulatory Board which regulated energy prices), but any attempt to increase rates was opposed by politicians who were backed by populist groups such as trade unions. Their thinking was that electric power (or any public utility service) should be made available cheaply with government subsidies. But with the budget in deficit, that was not possible. During the Marcos period, his solution was to borrow from abroad, but this could not go on indefinitely. When foreign creditors found out that the country was heavily indebted and that there was a risk of default, foreign loans were no longer easily available, and government projects, such as power plants, had difficulties in raising finance. The only way to keep expanding the power supply to meet increasing demand is to make consumers (household, industrial, and commercial users) pay for the costs. If this principle is not clearly established, privatization of power plants, which is gaining popularity now, will be futile.[15]

Aquino appointed Ernesto Aboitiz as head of the NPC in 1987. Many people say that he was an incompetent administrator. He was not, however, inexperienced in running a power company. Before coming to the NPC, he had managed one such company in Davao City in southern Mindanao. It is said that during Aquino's presidential campaign in 1986, Aboitiz was her active supporter and that his NPC appointment was her reward for his support (in the election, Davao City voted overwhelmingly for Aquino). But his critics contended that operating a large organization like the NPC required more capability than running a small power company and they charged that he did not know what to do with it. They say that if he had wanted to expand the power supply, the government was willing to finance it, but he did not do anything to prevent the shortage which was forecasted. Some even charge that he deliberately caused the power shortage because it was good for his family's business which included selling generators. But probably from his point of view, the NPC was too politicized and undisciplined (with so many employees and so many entitlements) an organization for an outsider like him to put right in a short time. In the past, the head of the NPC had changed frequently, being a political appointee.

The NPC's malaise was a result of its failure to develop a strong bureaucracy, a common fate of government corporations and administrative agencies in the Philippines, with the NPC being one of the worst. One journalist, fed up with the frequent brownouts in 1992, wrote that 'besides being callous and shameless, it [NPC] is also grossly negligent, extravagant and incompetent'.[16]

Contrasting Philippine Airlines and Thai International

Phillipine Airlines (PAL) was another badly run government corporation. Many people used to say jokingly that PAL stood for 'Planes Always Late'. International travellers tended not to take PAL if there was an alternative airline flying the same route. During the Marcos period, PAL passengers were left stranded abroad, sometimes for days, while their aircraft were diverted to fly Imelda and her entourage. Sometimes an extra jumbo jet was sent along for the luggage. During the Aquino administration, PAL's performance improved, but in the year ending March 1991, only about two-thirds of its international flights could leave within 15 minutes of schedule.[17] The Aquino administration took over its losses amounting to $520 million to make it saleable to private investors.

In contrast, Thai Airways International, owned by the Thai government, is a model airline of a developing country. It was one of the 24 top airlines which received super excellent classification in 1991 from the International Travel Research Institute.[18] It has earned profits during most of its 32-year history; 1990/1 was its twenty-seventh consecutive year of profit, contrasting sharply with PAL's dismal financial record in the past 20 years. Thai International expanded its fleet by buying new aircraft according to plan, and by the end of 1991, had reduced the average age of its aircraft to 5.6 years (one of the youngest fleets in the industry). It has become a full partner in AMADEUS, the computerized global travel distribution system which feeds information on the airline's schedule, tariff, and reservations to 30,000 travel trade terminals, worldwide. In 1992, having met the listing requirements of the Securities Exchange of Thailand (SET) (which include profit records in the recent past), its shares were listed on the SET.

One of PAL's problems was that it had to serve many domestic destinations because the Philippines is an island nation. Thailand built a good road system so that land transportation was a good substitute for air conveyance within the radius of a few hundred kilometres from Bangkok. For outlying areas also, there was no strong need to create many destinations, since it was enough to link Bangkok to a small number of regional cities, to which nearby small towns were connected by good roads. In 1991, PAL was serving about 43 domestic destinations, twice Thai International's domestic destinations. The domestic tariffs were controlled by the Civil Aeronautic Board (CAB), which tended to set tariffs so low that PAL could not make profits on most routes even with full capacity. The problem was similar to the one the NPC faced with its regulatory agency.

PAL's problem, however, was more deep-seated than that. PAL has a history that is 20 years longer than Thai International, but it is more unstable as an organization because ownership changed a few times and new management did a poor job of running the company. Originally, it was privately organized and managed by Andres Soriano, head of Soriano y Cia, under a contract. (Soriano's style was for Soriano y Cia to become a minority shareholder of a company and obtain the contract for its management. In this way, Soriano successfully built a few major companies, such as San Miguel Corp.) In the 1950s, the Philippine government became PAL's majority stockholder. At first, because of Soriano's good relations with the country's presidents, the airline's operation continued smoothly but in early 1961, he resigned from his position as president. The immediate reason was two airplane accidents at the end of 1960, but he also seemed to have become fed up with increasing attacks by nationalists on him. Though he was born in the Philippines and had served as a captain in its Army and as Secretary of Finance in President Manuel Quezon's government-in-exile in Washington, he became an American citizen soon after the Pacific War. Together with his American friends, he managed PAL, an arrangement which was, however, disagreeable to Filipino nationalists.[19]

After Soriano resigned, the government took over the management of PAL, and soon after Diosdado Macapagal became President, he gave control of it to Benigno Toda, one of the major financiers of his presidential campaign. Toda eventually bought the government's equity and became PAL's controlling shareholder. PAL was once again a privately owned and managed company, but this did not do much good for PAL. Toda was not interested in building up the airline as a business organization. Instead, he was milking it for his family businesses. For example, his flagship company, Rubicon, had a management contract with PAL, receiving 5 per cent of its profits before taxes.[20] In 1970, he had a conflict with the pilots, who eventually staged a mass resignation, thus making it necessary to reduce domestic and international flights.

Imelda Marcos often utilized PAL's planes when she went abroad. It is said that soon after Marcos asked Toda to send him a bill for her use of the aircraft—Toda sent a bill but not for the full amount (reported to have been around $6 million)—an angry Imelda made sure that he lost the company. But a more plausible reason was probably that the company was not under good management and had to be restructured to meet the increasing demand for international travel in the mid-1970s. In 1977, the government took over the company and made Roman Cruz, head of the Government Service Insurance System as well as one of Imelda's lackeys, its executive officer.

During Cruz's term, PAL incurred large losses which are often attributed to his incompetency.[21] When he took over the company, PAL needed a large infusion of capital for building up its fleet, for this he borrowed from abroad.[22] In 1979, the second oil crisis sent the Philippine economy (affected further by political instability) into a tailspin. Domestic operations were affected by this economic downturn, as well as by the inability to obtain fare increases from the regulatory agency (CAB) despite the increase in aviation fuel prices. The peso devaluation at this time was another source of difficulty since PAL had borrowed heavily in foreign currencies and planned to use its peso revenues for partial debt servicing. Imelda's indiscriminate use of PAL's aircraft continued to be a problem.[23]

A large part of the losses was probably due to circumstances beyond Cruz's control. His culpability was a little different from that of the executives of the PNB and the DBP, who often knowingly created nonperforming assets. Cruz nevertheless seems to have been a corrupt official. In June 1985, the *San Jose Mercury News* (which exposed

Marcos's wealth in the United States) reported that he is one of several government officials who had 'huge' hidden wealth there. (Another is Geronimo Velasco, Minister of Energy, who had supervised the NPC.)

Ironically, the better-run Thai International was always headed by the Air Force Chief. Many government corporations were headed by former military officers, but Thai International was one of the few headed by an active-duty military officer. Many retired officers went to Thai International from the Air Force (in the early 1990s, at least half of its top 24 managers were said to have come from the armed forces, mostly from the Air Force). One might suppose therefore that it was one of the badly run, military-controlled companies observed in developing countries. But the Thai military were careful about management. In its first decade, the flights were only within Asia. Furthermore, it invited the Scandinavian Air System (SAS) to be a shareholder, and was run under SAS tutelage. In the early 1970s, after gaining experience in regional flights, it started intercontinental flights. A few years later, it bought out the SAS holding, but maintained a co-operation agreement with it, under which some SAS personnel continued to work for Thai International.

The advantage of Thai International was in its organizational stability. But as a military-controlled company, it had problems of its own. Factionalism within the Air Force was sometimes reflected in the power struggle among the top management. The professional managers who rose from the ranks were not happy with military officers occupying high positions as a sinecure. Furthermore, corruption was a recurrent problem. For example, the management under Air Force Chief Kaset Rojananil (who had been serving as chairman since 1989) was accused in early 1992 of malpractices ranging from costly land acquisition to questionable selection of aircraft engines. But the Thai Air Force gave stability and protection to Thai International, and by relying a great deal on professional expertise, it has built a fairly well-run airline.

1. *A Public Development Program for Thailand*, Baltimore: Johns Hopkins Press, 1959, p. 91.

2. Frank H. Golay et al., *Underdevelopment and Economic Nationalism in Southeast Asia*, Ithaca: Cornell University Press, 1969, p. 308.

3. A typical ownership structure is 49 per cent for the Petroleum Authority of Thailand, 2 per cent for a quasi-government organization (such as Crown Property Bureau), and 49 per cent for private investors.

4. *Asian Wall Street Journal*, 4 and 5 December 1987.

5. Edita Tan, *The Structure and Growth of the Philippine Financial Market and the Behavior of Its Major Components*, Working Paper No. 81–94, Makati: Philippine Institute for Development Studies, June 1981, p. 2.

6. Development Bank of the Philippines, 1986–7 Report, p. 22.

7. According to the annual reports of the PNB and the DBP for the 1986 financial year, the government took over ₱47 billion worth of non-performing assets and ₱55 billion worth of liabilities from the PNB, and ₱61 billion worth of non-performing assets and ₱62 billion worth of liabilities from the DBP.

8. Mario Lamberte, *The Development Bank of the Philippines (DBP) and the Financial Crisis: A Descriptive Analysis*, Staff Paper Series No. 84–07, Makati: Philippine Institute for Development Studies, November 1984, p. 10.

9. '5-Year Performance Report', Asset Privatization Trust, Makati [1992].

10. This was one of Jaime Ongpin's 'eleven major infuriating problems' when he was attacking Marcos in the mid-1980s. Ongpin became Secretary of Finance after Aquino became President (Nick Joaquin, *Jaime Ongpin: The Enigma*, Makati: Jaime V. Ongpin Institute of Business and Government, 1990, p. 211). Belatedly, in mid-1992, the Philippine government filed graft charges against Panfilo Domingo, then president of the PNB, and Marcos's former crony, Rodolfo Cuenca, for having defrauded the government of some $29 million (roughly ₱727 million) in behest loans.

11. Edward R. Kiunisala, 'Hang Napocor', *Philippines Free Press*, Part II, 14 November 1992. National Power Corp. is often abbreviated as Napocor in the Philippines.

12. For Meralco's history, see *66 Years of Service*, Manila: Manila Electric Co., 1969 and *A Brief History*, Manila: Manila Electric Co., 1976.

13. Ricardo Manapat, *Some Are Smarter Than Others: The History of Marcos' Crony Capitalism*, New York: Aletheia Publications, 1991, p. 325.

14. *A Short Story of the National Power Corporation, 1936–1986*, Quezon City: National Power Corp., 1986, p. 59. This debt incurred in connection with the nuclear power plant was later taken over by the government.

15. Another way to ensure enough revenues is to bribe the regulators. It is said that this can be more easily done if the NPC is privatized.

16. Edward R. Kiunisala, 'Hang Napocor', *Philippines Free Press*, Part I, 31 October 1992: 4.

17. *Asian Wall Street Journal*, 30 January 1992.

18. 'Thai Airways International: 32nd Anniversary', *Sawasdee* [Thai International's flight magazine], May 1992. After the political unrest of May 1992, Thai International faced some difficulties in going ahead with its plan to list its stocks on the SET because of chairman Kaset's close link to the disgraced army strongman, Suchinda Kraprayoon, who pro-democracy groups hold responsible for the shooting of demonstrators by the military that month. By scaring away foreign tourists, the unrest caused a decline in the airline's passenger load to about 50 per cent (from a little over 60 per cent before the unrest).

19. This and the next paragraph are partly based on 'A History of Philippine Airlines' [1989].

20. Bernard Wideman, 'Philippine Airlines: A Presidential Landing', *Insight*, July 1978: 52.

21. Manapat, *Some Are Smarter Than Others*, pp. 368–71.

22. Soon after the government take-over, PAL's capital was increased 10 times, from ₱25 million to ₱250 million.

23. 'Philippine Airlines: 50 Years . . . and Counting' [1991].

8
Government Monopolies of Agricultural Products

The Rationale for Government Monopolies

DURING the martial law period in the Philippines, President Ferdinand Marcos created several monopolies, of which the two most disreputable were the National Sugar Trading Corp. (Nasutra) and United Coconut Oil Mills (Unicom). Since their products were mostly exported, the rationale behind these monopolies was the strengthening of the country's bargaining position in the world market, thus bringing greater benefits to domestic producers. Sugar-cane producers and millers and coconut farmers were supposed to benefit from these monopolies, but the results were otherwise.

Marcos was not a poorly educated military dictator in a developing country, but he may not have had a good understanding of how the economy works. In particular, he may not have understood that it is competition which drives the economy. Competition does not have to be atomistic. Even in an oligopolistic industry, if competition prevails between large firms, the results can be beneficial to the economy. Since these large firms emerge through competition over time, they usually have an internal mechanism to keep themselves efficient. But an artificially created monopoly is prone to fail due to mismanagement, or if it continues to exist, it becomes a burden on the economy. Nasutra and Unicom were such examples.

If Marcos understood the merit of competition, he probably did not see much importance in the role of middlemen. There is no doubt that Unicom in particular greatly simplified the trading channels for coconut. Since the industry was dominated by the Chinese, although he was probably not anti-Chinese, it was politically easier to get rid of the middlemen. Undoubtedly, there is little merit in a fragmented distribution channel. If it can be simplified by the emergence of large traders, distribution may become more efficient, but competition between them must remain. Otherwise, a large trader becomes a monopolist (or monopsonist), and then even if distribution becomes better organized, producers get lower prices and/or consumers have to pay higher prices.

Unicom could not determine the price of its product (coconut oil) in the international market because of the availability of substitutes (such as palm oil and soybean oil), although that was its original purpose. As the dominant buyer in most areas in the Philippines, it became a monopsonist and depressed its purchasing prices. After Unicom was formed, the spread between domestic and export prices of copra became larger. In 1979, when Unicom started operation, the spread was about 10 per cent, but in the next year it rose to 26 per cent, and remained at this level in the following two years.[1] Since the spread was about 10 per cent originally, the spread beyond that could be considered as the loss to coconut farmers due to the formation of Unicom.[2]

Nasutra

There was a political purpose to the creation of Nasutra as well. Martial law was declared in order to create a New Society, which meant that the Old Society, which had opposed Marcos, had to be destroyed. Sugar was the financial basis of many politicians in the Old Society because as a major export commodity, wealth was created in the industry and used to fund political activities. More specifically, because the allocation of American quotas, which gave preferential treatment to Philippine sugar until 1974, was often a political decision and because the Philippine National Bank (PNB), a government financial institution, was heavily involved in the financing of the industry, sugar became a politicized industry, prompting sugar barons to get into politics. Many of the politicians who represented the sugar industry were Marcos's political enemies: the Lopez brothers (Eugenio and Fernando) were prime examples.

The sugar monopoly was probably a means to bring the industry under government control. The best way of doing this was to give a trading monopoly to its major financier, the PNB. This is what the government did initially. For sugar trading, the PNB set up a subsidiary called Philippine Exchange Co. (Philex). Philex mismanaged trading and incurred large losses, and was thus dissolved. Sugar trading was then put under the newly created Philippine Sugar Commission (Philsucom), of which Nasutra was a trading arm. Marcos put Roberto Benedicto, one of his closest cronies, in charge of Philsucom. Benedicto, who had headed the PNB from 1966 to 1970, also kept a careful watch on the PNB, because its loans were an important means by which Philsucom kept the industry under control. Benedicto also went into banking on his own. He bought a controlling interest in the Republic Bank and renamed it Republic Planters Bank (RPB). Given low-interest loans from the Central Bank and designated as the depository of the sugar industry by a presidential decree, the RPB quickly became one of the largest commercial banks (the fifth largest in 1980 in terms of assets).

The shortage of sugar in the domestic market gave the government an excuse to take over sugar trading in 1974—the same year that saw the end of the American quota system which paid higher prices to Philippine sugar than did the international market (about 38 per cent higher in the 1960s).[3] Fortunately, it was the year when the international sugar market was recording the highest prices in its history (about

65 cents per kilogram). Sugar producers had been required to meet the domestic demand at the prices set by the government, but with the surge of prices in the international market, they did not want to sell their sugar in the country. As a result, the domestic market suffered a shortage, prompting the government to step in.[4]

Philex had made money at first. Since sugar prices were going up in the international market, the sugar it bought in the country could be sold abroad at higher prices. At that time, the question was to whom the profits belonged. Many sugar producers thought that Philex was their trading agency, and thus, profits should be handed over to them. But this was probably not what Marcos had intended. In the following years, however, Philex incurred huge losses, and there was no more money to distribute. Sugar prices came down to 45 cents per kilogram in 1975, 25 cents in 1976, and 18 cents in 1977. Philex probably did not understand the volatility of the international market at that time. Since sugar prices fell in the mid-1970s, it ended up with sugar for which it had paid higher prices, and it kept the sugar, hoping that prices would go up. But prices did not rebound, and when it began unloading the large stock it had accumulated (probably over 1 million tons), it had to take substantial losses (moreover, some stock had deteriorated due to poor storage facilities).[5]

Nasutra, which took over sugar distribution from Philex in 1977, strengthened its role by setting up offices in London and New York (the two world centres of sugar trading), getting directly into the transport, bulk storage, and handling of sugar, and even expanding into sugar milling and refining.[6] Complaints about Nasutra were not about its losses, as in the case of Philex, though sugar prices were volatile around 1980. Probably, having learnt some lessons from the earlier Philex debacle, Nasutra was more cautious about speculation. Instead, the complaints were that it underpaid sugar producers. It was said that 'while ... Nasutra sold at $63.70 per picul in the 1979–80 period, it bought at $18.16; when it sold at $40.05, it paid $14.20'.[7] There may have been some such profitable operations for Nasutra, but the average spread between its purchase and sales prices was probably much smaller. Undoubtedly, however, Nasutra was a milking operation for Marcos and his cronies (especially, Benedicto). One study estimates that during 1972–82, the net income loss for sugar producers was about 30 per cent.[8]

Unicom

The coconut industry was organized differently from the sugar industry. Unlike Nasutra, Unicom was heavily involved in production (coconut oil); in the case of sugar, processing was done primarily by private sugar mills. Furthermore, Unicom did not have complete control over distribution as Nasutra did with sugar. Unicom did not have much control over the direct export of desiccated coconut or copra. It was the dominant manufacturer of coconut oil, controlling 80–90 per cent of the country's milling capacity, making it a dominant player in the coconut industry, which, like the sugar industry, was very much export-oriented. In the 1970s, coconut oil was the dominant coconut export; in 1980, it comprised 85 per cent of total coconut exports.[9] In the earlier decades, coconut oil was less important, but as the Board of Investments (BOI) gave incentives to coconut oil mills to add more value to their exports, a number of new mills were created in the 1970s, and coconut oil became the dominant coconut export.

The ease with which Unicom could establish such a dominant position in a short time was due to the rapid expansion of milling capacity which took place under BOI incentives. Furthermore, in 1979, a number of newly established mills were facing difficulties because coconut oil prices did not increase much despite a large increase in copra prices. They were glad to be bought out. In addition, the presidential letter of instruction which led to the formation of Unicom stipulated that it control at least 55 per cent of the country's oil milling capacity. This made large foreign-affiliated oil producers (such as Legaspi Oil and Granexport) vulnerable to take-over. The provision of the letter of instruction that 'the government shall give its total support for [Unicom] which includes financial and other assistance' also made it difficult for private mills to operate independently of Unicom. For example, the domestic price of coconut oil was set by the government, and if subsidies were required, they were restricted to firms which co-operated with Unicom. Three private mills (Interco Group, Southern Island Oil Mills, and Lu Do & Lu Ym) became participating mills under the co-ordination scheme of Unicom.

Criticisms of government intervention in the coconut industry during the martial law period were not confined to Unicom. Another major issue was the levy on copra and its use. This started, however, before martial law, with the so-called Cocofund levy. In 1971, a law was passed to collect a fixed levy (55 centavo per 100 kilograms of copra) for a period of 10 years starting in 1972. The levy was to be used to set up the Coconut Investment Co. to be owned by the coconut farmers of the Philippine Coconut Producers Federation, Inc. (Cocofed), which would invest the levy in the processing and trading of copra. It was reasoned that coconut farmers would gain under this scheme since they would share in the profits of the processing and trading operations (which otherwise would go to middlemen).

The Cocofund levy was modest, but in August 1973 during martial law, a much larger tax (the Coconut Consumers Stabilization Fund (CCSF) levy) at the rate of ₱60 per kilogram was imposed on copra. Initially, it was intended as a temporary levy to stabilize the domestic prices of coconut-based products through subsidies when the world price of copra rose abruptly during 1973–4. Even after copra prices had stabilized, the levy remained, and became a sort of a development tax on the industry (administered by the government agency Philippine Coconut Authority, PCA). Part of the CCSF levy (₱20 per 100 kilograms of copra) was earmarked for the industry's development programmes, including the nation-wide coconut hybrid replanting programme and the acquisition of a bank for coconut farmers.

In 1975, the PCA was authorized to buy a small bank, the First United Bank, by using the CCSF levy. The PCA paid about ₱29 million for 72 per cent of its equity, and renamed it United Coconut Producers Bank (UCPB). Eduardo 'Danding' Cojuangco, another of Marcos's close cronies, negotiated the acquisition and was made president of the bank. Later, in order to meet the Central Bank's ₱100 million minimum paid-up capital requirement for a universal bank (a commercial bank allowed to undertake diversified functions, such as selling securities and undertaking equity investment in industrial firms), the PCA poured an additional ₱80 million of the CCSF levy into the bank. With this increase in capital and as the depository of all coconut levies, the UCPB quickly became one of the largest commercial banks (the seventh largest in terms of assets in 1980). With the existence of the UCPB and a large CCSF levy, what was envisioned when the Cocofund levy was imposed became a reality. In 1978, the Coconut Industry Investment Fund (CIIF) was created with part of the CCSF levy, and it was put under the control of the UCPB. The next year, the UCPB and the CIIF bought almost two-thirds of the country's total milling capacity, and put the acquired mills under the newly created organization, Unicom.[10]

In principle, there is nothing particularly wrong with a development programme funded by a tax on the industry. However, for most coconut farmers, benefits from the CCSF levy were few compared to the amount they paid. From 1972 to 1982 when the levy was lifted, coconut farmers paid about ₱9.7 billion. The levy fluctuated during the period; starting at 4 per cent of export prices in 1973, it went up to 21 per cent in 1974, stayed roughly at this level until 1980, though it fell to 13 per cent in 1979, and rose to 31 per cent in 1981.[11] At first, coconut farmers did not understand what was going on; they did not pay the levy directly but received the balance due to them from traders. It was traders and processors who paid the levy, and knowing in advance how much they had to pay, they deducted it from their offer prices to coconut farmers. Thus, it was coconut farmers who bore the burden of the levy. However, they gradually caught up with what was going on, and began complaining bitterly. The levy was finally lifted in 1982.

The levies and monopolies were supposed to benefit Filipino producers (sugar producers and coconut farmers), and they might have done so if they had been well managed. Instead, they were used to benefit a small group of privileged people. In the case of sugar, the key beneficiary was Roberto Benedicto, and in the case of coconuts, they were Eduardo Cojuangco and Juan Ponce Enrile, a lawyer by profession and a Minister of Defense, who also served as chairman of the PCA. How the levies were used and the monopolies were run are not well documented, though there is a general consensus of opinion that Benedicto, Cojuangco, Enrile, and their 'sub-cronies' (the landlords who dominated Cocofed and some large sugar planters and millers who collaborated with Benedicto) benefited enormously. They received high salaries, lucrative commissions, preferential treatment from the monopolies, and used the monopolies to generate profits for their own businesses. The Marcoses also had a share: Imelda used the levies for her extravagant projects (such as the Miss Universe Pageant), while Marcos received $8.3 million in contributions from the coconut levies for his 1986 presidential campaign.[12]

The Decline of the Sugar and Coconut Industries

The sugar and coconut industries became depressed in the 1980s, but the levies and monopolies were not the major cause, though they were undoubtedly a contributing factor. The two industries, which had developed as export industries, faced weakening prices during the decade. This was not obvious of the sugar industry until the early 1980s, though there were signs of weakening prices in the mid-1970s. The international sugar price, which, in 1980, rebounded almost to the level of 1974 (65 cents per kilogram, the highest price in its history), started to plummet in the following years, hitting the bottom in 1985 (about 9 cents per kilogram). In the second half of the 1980s, the price recovered somewhat, rising to about 28 cents per kilogram in 1990, but by then, the Philippine sugar industry had become a much smaller one (as evidenced by the dramatic decline in exports to about 10 per cent of the mid-1970s level). Copra prices took a sharp decline during the same period. The decline in purchasing power was worse. In 1982, when 1 ton of copra sold for $314, the sum purchased less than half of what it did in the first half of the 1950s.[13] The 1990 price of $230 per ton was even below the 1982 price.

The basic problem for sugar and coconut oil (the dominant coconut product exported) was that their demand in the international market declined and/or their supply increased. The demand for coconut oil declined because of the increasing availability of soybean oil and palm oil as its substitutes in the United States (the major market of Philippine coconut oil). Furthermore, the campaign against coconut and palm oil launched by the American Soybean Association was fairly successful in planting an image in the minds of American consumers that coconut and palm oils are bad for the health. Affected by this, rightly or wrongly, consumers in other developed countries generally began to form a similarly negative view of coconut and palm oils.

Increasing concern about the unhealthy effects of sugar consumption also had a dampening effect on demand; between 1973 and 1984, per capita consumption of sugar declined in developed countries.[14] But a decline in the demand of sugar from the food industry (soft drink makers in particular) was more sharply felt by the sugar industry. In the 1960s, there was a technological breakthrough in the production of corn-based sweeteners (the most popular was High-Fructose Corn Syrup, known as HFCS), and over time, they became a serious competitor of sugar. On the supply side, an increase in sugar beet production in Europe reduced its dependence on cane sugar from the tropical region.

Beet sugar is not competitive with cane sugar, but under the protection and subsidies given for the self-sufficiency programme in food production, beet production in Europe increased rapidly, even to the extent of exporting the excess.

The Philippine sugar industry was known to be a high-cost industry. The cost of sugar production in the Philippines was already high in the pre-war period. In the mid-1930s, it was about twice as high as in the other two major centres of production, Cuba and Java.[15] Despite this, the Philippine sugar industry prospered because of the free trade arrangement with the United States. In the post-war period, the cost situation did not improve much in the Philippines as it continued to enjoy privileged access to the US market under a quota system. In the meantime, new low-cost sugar producers were emerging. In the late 1970s, the heavily mechanized Australian sugar industry could produce sugar at less than half the cost in Negros, the major sugar-producing area in the Philippines.[16]

The Rise of Thailand as a Sugar Exporter

The rapid rise of Thailand as a major sugar exporter is another indicator of the strength of Thai agriculture. In the post-war period, protected by an import ban, the sugar industry expanded rapidly, and by 1960, the country had become self-sufficient in sugar. Exports began slowly in the 1960s, increasing dramatically in the following decade. Sugar exports rose from 150,000 to 1.16 million tons between 1971 and 1981.[17] In the 1980s, Philippine sugar exports declined (from 1.5 million tons in 1980 to about 0.15 million tons in 1990), while Thai sugar exports increased and reached the level of 3.0 million tons in 1991, making Thailand the third largest exporter in the world.

This increase in Thai sugar exports was not, however, solely the result of a production increase guided by market forces. Faced with the sharp decline in prices in the mid-1980s, the Thai sugar industry pressured the government to give it assistance in the form of reduced business taxes, low-interest loans, and subsidies. The subsidies came from consumers, who paid the higher domestic prices set by the government. The Thai sugar industry is unique in that it was the only agricultural sector sustained by government assistance. All others were either taxed or left to market forces. According to one estimate made in the late 1980s, the Thai sugar industry would have shrunk to one-quarter of its size at that time if government assistance was withdrawn.[18]

Distribution of Grains by the Government: Contrasts

The Thai government started taxing rice soon after the Pacific War. In the early 1950s when there were multiple exchange rates, the government paid rice exporters B35 per pound sterling and sold the pound sterling at B55–60 to importers. The difference was revenue to the government. When a direct tax on rice exports was added, the combined tax burden on rice was about 58 per cent of the domestic wholesale price or 33 per cent of the free on board price. In 1955, the exchange rates were unified, and the implicit export tax was replaced by a rice tax (called rice premium in Thailand), which imposed a similar level of burden on rice in the following years.[19]

This burden, similar to that borne by Filipino sugar and copra farmers, did not retard the rice industry in Thailand. On the contrary, both production and exports rose in the following decades. Over time, however, rice exports became less important as new exports emerged. Rice production became particularly difficult in the late 1980s because the cost of production increased as a result of sustained economic growth in the country, while rice prices tended to stagnate as the United States and Vietnam entered the export market. Since the rice tax was lifted in 1986, it did not have anything to do with the difficulties of the rice industry in the early 1990s. There was, however, one fundamental difference about this tax from the Philippine situation. The rice tax collected over the three decades was government revenue, and therefore used to finance government expenditure.

Immediately after the Pacific War, the Thai government agreed to deliver 1.5 million tons of rice to the Allies, free of charge, as a sort of war indemnity, and could have used this as an excuse to set up a monopoly over rice exports. However, it did not do so, though its rice policy was not *laissez faire* as in the pre-war period. The government ensured that rice was available in the domestic market at reasonable prices and let only surplus rice be exported. Since domestic prices were set below export prices, the government took a large part of the difference from rice exporters through the rice tax, not through a monopoly as the Philippine government did in the 1970s. The Thai method of ensuring the availability of rice in the domestic market was somewhat cumbersome, but worked better than the monopoly system of the Philippines. In Thailand, rice exporters had to obtain licences to sell rice abroad. The government allocated the difference between production and domestic consumption of rice to exporters on the basis of their past export performance.[20]

The Philippine government's intervention in agriculture had a clear anti-middlemen bias. In Thailand, rice trading was under the jurisdiction of the Ministry of Commerce, which did not get involved in distribution directly. In the Philippines, however, a government agency undertook commercial operations. This started with a government corporation, the National Rice and Corn Corp. (NRCC), set up in 1936. It had a monopoly on rice and corn imports which it distributed through government-sponsored agencies such as agricultural co-operatives. (This monopoly was politically important for the party in power because it could be used to lower food prices in the years of national elections and as a source of patronage for party supporters in the provinces.) The NRCC's role was taken over by the Rice and Corn Administration (RCA) in the early 1960s. In the same decade, the RCA went into rice milling and warehousing because it was felt that distribution could not be left to unscrupulous merchants. In addition, the RCA ensured the implementation of the Rice and Corn Trade Nationalization Law (passed in 1960) which Filipinized the rice and corn industry in 1964 (akin to what the Retail Trade Nationalization Law did for retail trade). In 1972, at the start of martial law, the RCA became the National Grains Authority (NGA) to strengthen the government's power to 'stabilize the supply and prices of grains and benefit farmers and consumers'. In 1981, it was renamed the National Food Authority (NFA) and put under Imelda Marcos, Minister of Human Settlements. Under the new head, the NFA became more broadly involved in distribution (for example, by setting up direct distribution outlets called Kadiwa stores), diversifying its functions to all basic foods.

In the distribution of domestic grains, however, the NFA relied a great deal on private distributors. For example, in the case of the most important commodity, rice, although the NGA or the NFA increased the number of its warehouses, the private sector bought more rice from farmers (90 per cent sold in the country in the early 1990s). But in the areas where warehouses were not adequate (in the second half of the 1970s, rice production rapidly increased, and a few hundred thousand tons were exported), the government agency became the major procurer of rice. For the country as a whole, despite the government's efforts (to increase warehousing facilities in particular), post-harvest losses were becoming a serious problem. The private sector was not responding to meet this problem, despite there being a large number of merchants involved in the distribution, because profit incentives tended to be weak; the government set support prices for farmers and price ceilings for consumers. It was within this range that private distributors and processors could operate—they could operate only by the grace of the government. The NFA, for example, was given the power to register, license, and supervise merchants (including processors) in the distribution of rice.

This situation may seem good to those who view middlemen as hoarders, black marketeers, manipulators of prices, or exploiters of the masses, but it was very damaging to the rice industry and the rural economy as a whole. Because of corruption, inertia, lack of incentives, and bureaucratic red tape, a government agency was a poor substitute for merchants, despite the rhetoric to the contrary. Being government-directed, if not -dominated, the rural distribution channel in the Philippines became inefficient.

Economic Consequences

In Thailand, agriculture was the leading sector of the economy in the 1950s and 1960s, and provided the basis for industry-led growth in the following decades. This was made possible partly by owner (mainly) cultivation and infrastructural development, but an important contribution arose from the way distribution was structured. Rice was exported largely through Chinese networks, but new agricultural exports (for example, maize and tapioca) were initially handled by foreign trading companies with the assistance of Chinese domestic distributors. It was through this Chinese network that foreign price signals were transmitted to the rural sector, finances were arranged, and processing was undertaken. For example, to increase maize production to satisfy the large market in Japan in the 1960s, Thai peasants needed small tractors (two-wheel and light four-wheel) which could till land when the soil was still too hard (before the beginning of the rains) for draught animals to plough. These were imported by Japanese trading companies from Japan, and distributed by Chinese middlemen with their finances. The Chinese distribution network also made possible further mechanization (for example, in the introduction of threshing machines), rural motorization, increased storage facilities, and better processing technologies, which conjoined to reduce post-harvest losses and improve product quality.

In the Philippines, the distribution network connecting the rural sector and the international market was weak. A reason for this weakness was government restriction of the entry and operations of foreign trading companies (see Chapter 5). Another reason was the weakening of domestic distribution by government discrimination and intervention. In this, the first blow came with the Retail Trade Nationalization Law. The Chinese who survived it by becoming naturalized then faced government intervention. In the 1970s, their predicament was compounded when rice, sugar, and coconut oil exports became government monopolies. Some distributors and processors were bought out by the government; others who remained as private entities became sub-agents, distributing and processing under the guidance of their supervising agencies. Evolving into a bureaucratic system, in efficiency and dynamism, the rural distribution channel in the Philippines was a far cry from its Thai counterpart. This factor is a major reason why Philippine agriculture never became the leading sector of the economy in post-war years.

1. *Philippine Daily Inquirer*, 28 April 1992.

2. According to one estimate, Unicom paid between 9 and 15 per cent below the price it would have paid under competitive conditions (Robert Dohner and Ponciano Intal, 'The Marcos Legacy: Economic Policy and Foreign Debt in the Philippines', in Jeffrey Sachs and Susan Collins (ed.), *Developing Country Debt and Economic Performance*, Chicago: University of Chicago Press, 1989, Vol. 3, p. 468).

3. A University of the Philippines study estimated that in the period 1960–71, if the International Sugar Agreement price was taken as the relevant border price for the Philippines, there was a net income transfer to Philippine sugar farmers averaging 38 per cent of the value of the output (Dohner and Intal, 'The Marcos Legacy', p. 462).

4. Ricardo Manapat, *Some Are Smarter Than Others: The History of Marcos' Crony Capitalism*, New York: Aletheia Publications, 1991, p. 103.

5. Dohner and Intal, 'The Marcos Legacy', pp. 462–3.

6. Ibid., p. 464.

7. Manapat, *Some Are Smarter Than Others*, p. 107.

8. From a University of the Philippines study quoted in Dohner and Intal, 'The Marcos Legacy', p. 463.

9. Ramon Clarete and James Roumasset, *An Analysis of the Economic Policies Affecting the Philippine Coconut Industry*, Working Paper No. 83–08, Makati: Philippine Institute for Development Studies, 1983, p. 6.

10. This and preceding paragraphs are based on 'IBON Primer on the Philippine Coconut Industry', Manila, IBON Databank Phils., Inc. [1979]; Clarete and Roumasset, *Economic Policies Affecting the Philippine Coconut Industry*, pp. 1–21; and 'How the Coco Levy Worked', *Philippine Daily Inquirer*, 26, 27, and 28 April 1992.

11. Clarete and Roumasset, *Economic Policies Affecting the Philippine Coconut Industry*, p. 15.

12. Manapat, *Some Are Smarter Than Others*, p. 184. The Philippines' former ambassador to the United States, Emmanuel Pelaez, is quoted to have said that the coconut levy resulted in 'the biggest robbery in Philippine history' (Teodoro Benigno's column, *Philippine Star*, 26 August 1992).

13. *1950–1983 Commodity Trade and Price Trends*, Baltimore: Johns Hopkins University Press, n.d. [1985], the statistical table on copra prices.

14. Joop Theunissen, 'Linkage and Alternatives: The Philippine Sugar Industry in the 1990s', Discussion paper, Tilburg University, July 1989, p. 9.

15. *Report of the Joint Preparatory Committee on Philippine Affairs*, Washington, DC: US Government Printing Office, 20 May 1938, p. 1072.

16. Alfred W. McCoy, 'The Restoration of Planter Power in La Carlota City', in Benedict J. Kerkvliet and Resil B. Mojares (eds.), *From Marcos to Aquino: Local Perspectives on Political Transition in the Philippines*, Quezon City: Ateneo de Manila University Press, 1991, p. 116.

17. Theunissen, 'Linkage and Alternatives', p. 18.

18. Ammar Siamwalla and Suthad Setboonsarng, *Trade, Exchange Rate, and Agricultural Pricing Policies in Thailand*, World Bank Comparative Studies, Washington, DC: World Bank, 1989, p. iii.

19. Ibid., pp. 29–31; James Ingram, *Economic Change in Thailand, 1850–1970*, Stanford: Stanford University Press, 1971, p. 246.

20. Ammar and Suthad, *Trade, Exchange Rate, and Agricultural Pricing Policies in Thailand*, p. 31.

9
Trade Barriers

Import Substitution Industrialization

In post-war years, both the Philippines and Thailand attributed their underdevelopment to the virtual absence of a manufacturing industry. Both were importing manufactured goods for consumption, and exporting primary products (the former exported sugar, copra, and abaca, while the latter rice, tin, rubber, and teak). Undoubtedly, if they aspired to become developed countries, they had to move on to produce higher value-added exports, which tended to be manufactured goods. However, industrialization could not be accomplished under free trade because new, inexperienced manufacturing firms could not compete with imports. Thus, the Philippine and Thai governments erected tariff and non-tariff barriers to the importation of the manufactured goods whose production they wanted to promote in their respective countries.

Industrialization started with consumer goods whose demand was relatively large and production relatively simple, for example, textiles. Later, industrialization progressed to the production of more sophisticated consumer goods, industrial raw materials, machinery, and machinery parts. Today, both countries produce a wide variety of manufactured goods. Actually, the major purpose of industrialization was not to meet domestic demand with domestic production, but to transform the economic structure such that the terms of trade would improve with the export of more value-added manufactured goods. (Otherwise, the living standard of the people could not be uplifted.) The structure of exports had to change; the emphasis shifted from agricultural products to light manufactured goods and then to more sophisticated manufactured products, which would fetch better prices. In reality, this progression did not take place smoothly. Industrialization tended to end with import substitution, producing inferior goods at higher prices, and was protected by trade barriers. It did not become the propelling force of economic development as initially planned.

Tariff Protection

Thailand, however, handled the matter of industrialization better than the Philippines did, succeeding in making manufactured goods the major exports in the 1980s. It did not make the mistake of protecting its industry too much. However, there did not seem to have been a big difference between the two countries in tariff protection. In fact, it is not clear which country imposed the higher tariffs. According to the Customs Tariff Code of Thailand, in 1960, the average tariff rate for non-durable consumer goods was 34.3 per cent; durable consumer goods, 42.0 per cent; intermediate goods, 32.6 per cent; capital goods, 19.3 per cent. In the 1960s, tariff changes tended to increase, rather than reduce, rates.[1] In the Philippines, the respective 1961 and 1965 average tariff rates for consumer goods were 64.1 and 70.1 per cent; intermediate goods, 24.6 and 27.4 per cent; and capital goods, 16.2 per cent in both years.[2] Though the classifications are not the same, it seems that the Philippines imposed higher tariffs on consumer goods, but lower tariffs on intermediate and capital goods in the 1960s than did Thailand. In 1980, the average tariff rate of the Philippines was 43 per cent, higher than Thailand's 31 per cent, but it went down to 29 per cent in 1986, which was probably lower than the Thai average since it remained at a little higher than 30 per cent in the first half of the 1980s (34 per cent in 1985).[3]

Exchange and Import Control

The two countries took vastly different approaches in the area of exchange and import control. In December 1949, the Philippine government began exchange control. The problem began when the pre-war exchange rate of ₱2 per dollar was re-established right after the Pacific War. The war had considerably weakened the Philippine economy (for example, destroying its export industries, such as sugar), and caused a large increase in prices, but after the war, the Philippines and the United States agreed to restore the pre-war rate. This produced massive deficits in the Philippine balance of trade, but the receipts of dollar exchange in the form of war damage payments, veterans pensions, and other American expenditures in the Philippines made up for the deficits for a while. These American expenditures began dwindling in 1949, and as a result, the Philippines experienced a large drop in international reserves.[4] At this time, the Philippines could not unilaterally devalue the peso since it needed the consent of the American government (as stipulated in the Bell Trade Act of 1946). Instead of seeking American approval for devaluation of the peso, the Philippine government decided to undertake foreign exchange budgeting.

Until lifted by President Diosdado Macapagal in early 1962, foreign exchange budgeting caused all sorts of problems. It was a very effective means for promoting industrialization, because it reduced import competition and encouraged production of goods, especially consumer goods, which received a low priority in dollar allocation, but it created great uncertainty among businessmen and also produced unscrupulous rent-seekers. An industrial entrepreneur who depended on imported raw materials for his production worried whether or not he could get enough foreign exchange. He might need foreign exchange to replace machines with new ones, or to buy spare parts; if he did not get foreign exchange, machines would stop working. Chinese and foreign businessmen were more concerned about these problems because they were the target of discrimination. The Americans enjoyed parity rights, but they also faced uncertainty because the rights assured them only of the same treatment as Filipinos, not the allocation of foreign exchange.[5]

Foreign exchange allocation was a bureaucratic as well as a political decision. Entrepreneurs who wanted to ensure the availability of foreign exchange for their businesses cultivated good connections with high government officials or powerful politicians. This was not, however, cost-free as they had to entertain these officials and politicians and pay bribes or contributions. Otherwise, they could buy foreign exchange from brokers, but the peso rates were higher than those offered by the government. As a last resort, they could approach the government for allocation on the basis of business merit, but chances were that they would not get it. At the overvalued exchange rate of the peso, the demand for the dollar was much greater than its availability. In 1950, the first year of exchange control, imports (which reflect the demand for dollar exchange) had to be reduced to three-fifths of their volume a year earlier.

Ferdinand Marcos was a rising star in Philippine politics in the 1950s, but he was not among the most powerful politicians at that time. Yet, he amassed a large fortune as a patron of businessmen who needed foreign exchange. Primitivo Mijares, Marcos's top confidential pressman in the early martial law years who defected to the United States in 1975 (he later disappeared; many people believe that he was executed by Marcos's agents), wrote of his role:

> It was definitely the import-control law which Marcos authored, pushed in Congress and conned his fellow Ilocano, President Elpidio Quirino, into signing into law that must have skyrocketed the Marcos accumulation of cash. . . . Marcos was the lord tong [grease money] collector of every sizable import license approved by the Central Bank. He had full time staffs both at his office in Congress and at his residence at San Juan, Rizal to process, follow up and receive 'cumshaw' from grateful businessmen. According to Heherson Alvarez, delegate from Isabela province who is now in exile in America, the minimum fee demanded by Marcos for every import license release was ₱10,000 [₱2 per dollar at this time].[6]

Exchange control not only became a hotbed of corruption but also a source of distortion of market forces in the Philippines. Thailand never went into exchange budgeting, though there was an Exchange Control Act (enacted in 1942) which was primarily applied to the foreign exchange earned. For most transactions, dollar exchange was available at the rate set by the government (roughly B20 per dollar until the early 1980s when the baht was slightly devalued). Moreover, the Bank of Thailand delegated authority for the approval of transactions to commercial banks (foreign as well as domestic). Then in May 1990, the

Thai government accepted Article VIII of the International Monetary Fund (IMF) Agreement, liberalizing foreign exchange transactions with regard to trade in goods and services.

One of the first acts of President Macapagal was to devalue the peso from ₱2 to ₱4 per dollar; he also lifted exchange control. The 1960s was a decade of decontrol, but at the end of the decade, the Philippine government, through the Central Bank, began selective import control, and the list of goods under control expanded in the following decade. In 1977, 62 per cent of all consumer goods, 24 per cent of mineral fuels and lubricants, 23 per cent of intermediate goods, and 17 per cent of capital goods were subject to control.[7] In 1980, 37 per cent of imported goods in the Philippines were restricted items. Thailand also restricted imports for the protection of domestic industries; for example, imports of new and used cars were banned to protect the car assembly industry. Similarly, imports of construction materials (steel bars and cement), sugar, silverware for hotels, sanitary ware, animal feeds, and a number of agricultural and food products were restricted. But the extent of restriction was much smaller than in the Philippines. In 1980, the percentage of imported goods restricted was probably just a few per cent.[8]

Trade Liberalization in the Philippines from the 1980s

Under pressure from the World Bank and the IMF, the Philippine government began reducing tariff and non-tariff barriers in the 1980s, but it was under the Aquino administration that significant progress was made on this front. The percentage of goods under import restriction fell from around 34 per cent in 1985 to 17 per cent in 1986, and further to 8 per cent at the end of 1989.[9] In 1991, the government began taking steps towards full deregulation of foreign exchange, but as late as mid-1992, the Filipino business tycoon Enrique Zobel, head of the Ayala Group until 1983, lamented that 'importing a tractor can easily dishearten any ordinary mortal—with all the red tape involved from the many government agencies one would have to go through to get the all-important permit to import'.[10] He made this point to pressure the government to take measures to improve productivity in agriculture—the sector he has had a long-standing interest in.

In the meantime, tariff rates were reduced, though not as dramatically as initially planned. In a turnaround in early 1991, the government imposed a surcharge of 9 per cent on imports in order to increase tax revenues. Although this was reduced to 5 per cent in August, it offset the tariff reduction of the past few years to some extent. In Thailand, trade liberalization was pushed also, and its tariff rates in 1991 might have been lower than in the Philippines. For example, the Philippine tariff on general machinery was 35 per cent, and if a surcharge of 5 per cent was added, importers had to pay 40 per cent of the value of imported machines as a tax to the government, a figure which was much higher than the tariff rate of 5 per cent in Thailand. However, both countries faced difficulties in reducing tariffs because of opposition from domestic industries. For example, in Thailand, tariff rates on plastics and textile fabrics remained at 35–60 per cent.

Reasons for Lower Non-tariff Barriers in Thailand

The major reason why Thailand did not depend a lot on non-tariff barriers was that the exchange rate of about B20 per dollar could be maintained without them. This was possible partly because the Bank of Thailand managed the money supply better than did the Central Bank in the Philippines. In the Philippines, with government expenditure tending to exceed its tax revenues, the end result was chronic budget deficits, which were financed by the issue of new money by the Central Bank. In the 1960s, the rate of increase of consumer prices in the Philippines was 5.6 per cent; in the 1970s, 13.9 per cent; and in the 1980s, 15.1 per cent. They were respectively 2.8, 1.4, and 3.3 times the rates of consumer price increase in Thailand.[11] As a result, there was constant pressure on the peso to devalue because the rate of consumer price increase there tended to be higher than in the United States, thus overvaluing the existing rate. The Philippine government resorted to import control in the 1970s in order to defend the peso. It was a way to hide (or at least minimize the effect of) its monetary mismanagement, as devaluation would have aggravated the inflationary trend by raising the prices of imported goods.[12] The Thai government's firmer commitment to monetary stability reduced the temptation to print money, a temptation to which the Philippine government succumbed.

A more important factor for greater exchange stability in Thailand was its better performance in exports. In the early 1950s, its traditional exports of rice, tin, rubber, and teak accounted for over 80 per cent of Thai exports, but the rise of new exports, such as maize, cassava, and kenaf, reduced their importance to 70 per cent in 1960, and 50 per cent in 1969. The combined exports of maize, cassava, and kenaf (including jute) in 1966 were B3.7 billion, more than the combined exports of tin, rubber, and teak, and only a little less than the exports of rice (B4.0 billion).[13] In the second half of the 1960s, these agricultural exports did not expand much because of weak prices, but there was a rise in tourist income and American military spending related to the stepped-up activities of the Vietnam War. (Thailand served as a major base for American operations in Vietnam.)

Yet in the early 1970s, Thai exports were still less than Philippine exports. As shown in Table 9.1, it was in the 1980s, especially the second half of the decade, that a big gap in export performance emerged between the two countries. Although the difference in exports was still small in 1980, Thailand exported three times more than the Philippines ten years later. Thailand accomplished this feat because it successfully transformed its composition of exports in favour of manufactured exports. Table 9.1 shows a large increase in the percentage export share of two SITC categories (machines and miscellaneous manufactured goods) in the 1980s. Even in the case of basic manufactures, in 1970 a

TABLE 9.1
Percentage Share of Exports by Commodity Group in the Philippines and Thailand, 1970–1991

Exports	*1970*	*1975*	*1980*	*1985*	*1990*	*1991*
By SITC classification						
Food						
Philippines	23.9	36.1	24.3	17.8	13.1	13.9
Thailand	47.1	59.0	44.6	44.7	28.2	26.5
Beverage and tobacco						
Philippines	1.3	1.6	0.6	0.7	0.7	1.0
Thailand	1.4	1.2	1.0	0.8	0.4	0.5
Crude materials						
Philippines	51.4	28.4	24.9	10.4	6.7	5.4
Thailand	28.9	15.1	14.3	10.2	5.7	5.2
Mineral fuels						
Philippines	1.8	1.6	0.9	0.9	2.2	2.4
Thailand	0.3	0.6	0.1	1.3	0.8	0.9
Animal, vegetable oil, and fats						
Philippines	8.6	10.2	9.9	8.0	4.6	3.5
Thailand	0.1	0.1	0.2	0.3	–	–
Chemicals						
Philippines	0.4	1.0	1.5	3.3	3.2	3.4
Thailand	0.2	0.6	0.7	1.3	1.4	1.9
Basic manufactures						
Philippines	7.8	10.4	9.2	10.1	9.3	8.0
Thailand	14.8	14.3	22.1	18.5	18.3	16.7
Machines, transport equipment						
Philippines	0.1	0.4	2.3	6.9	12.5	13.9
Thailand	0.1	1.3	5.7	8.8	22.2	24.4
Miscellaneous manufactured goods						
Philippines	0.8	4.4	10.5	11.6	16.4	16.3
Thailand	0.4	3.5	6.4	12.4	21.4	22.7
Unclassified goods						
Philippines	3.9	5.9	15.9	30.3	31.3	32.2
Thailand	6.7	4.3	4.9	1.7	1.5	1.2
Total exports ($ million)						
Philippines	1,142	2,294	5,788	4,629	8,186	8,839
Thailand	710	2,208	6,505	7,119	23,053	28,351

Sources: Asian Development Bank, *Key Indicators of Developing Asian and Pacific Countries*, various years.

Notes: Export figures for Thailand were given in baht. They were converted into dollars by using the year's average exchange rate. SITC = Standard International Trade Classification.

large part of it was tin (considered a manufactured good under SITC classification), but by the end of the 1980s, its share had become negligible, and the largest component of basic manufactures became textiles (yarn, fabrics, and other textile goods, excluding garments, which are classified under miscellaneous manufactured goods).

Table 9.2 shows the decline of the importance of traditional exports. In Thailand, the most dramatic decline was in two major primary exports, rice and rubber. In 1960, the two accounted for 60 per cent of total exports, but the percentage was down to 9 in 1990. A similar decline is also observed in three other primary commodities (tapioca products, maize, and tin), and during the 30-year period, the percentage share of the five primary products in total exports declined from 75 to 14 per cent. One should note, however, that the Philippines experienced an even bigger decline in traditional exports. The four major products (sugar, copra and coconut oil, copper concentrates, and logs and lumber) accounted for 76 per cent of total exports in 1960, but only 41 per cent in 1980 and 10 per cent in 1990. This big drop in the 1980s was primarily because their exports declined in absolute terms. In Thailand, although primary goods increased in absolute terms, manufactured exports rose much more rapidly.

TABLE 9.2
Decline of Primary Exports in the Philippines and Thailand, 1960–1990 (percentage share of total exports)

Export	*1960*	*1970*	*1980*	*1990*
Philippines				
Sugar	24	17	11	1
Copra and coconut oil	32	20	14	5
Copper concentrates	5	17	9	2
Logs and lumber	15	24	7	2
Total	76	78	41	10
Thailand				
Rice	30	17	15	5
Rubber	30	15	9	4
Tapioca products	3	8	11	4
Maize	6	13	5	1
Tin	6	11	9	–
Total	75	64	49	14

Sources: Asian Development Bank, *Key Indicators of Developing Asian and Pacific Countries*, various years.

Manufactured Exports Become Significant in Thailand

A large increase in manufactured exports took place in the 1980s, but changes in that direction had started in the early 1970s when, despite a relatively smooth increase in agricultural exports, total export increase tended to lag behind import increase because the progress of import substitution industrialization required increasing imports of machines, raw materials, and parts. There was a clear need for new exports, especially manufactured goods, as the prices of agricultural exports tended to be weak. But to export manufactured goods was difficult because Thailand had built a high tariff barrier which increased the cost of production and made its products uncompetitive in the export market. For example, the prices of Thai textile goods were about 30 per cent higher than their international prices. Yet it was around this time that textile exports began. In 1976, textile exports exceeded imports for the first time in Thai history.[14]

In the early 1970s, the textile industry was depressed by a glut created by the rapid expansion of production capacity in the late 1960s. The traditional way for textile firms to survive was by reducing prices, but this time, the textile association decided to impose a B5 levy on each spindle (there were over a million spindles at that time) and to use it as a subsidy for exporters (as a 'reward' for not dumping their products in the domestic market). This reduced the differential between domestic and international prices to 20 per cent. Then, the association obtained concessions from the Bank of Thailand in the form of lower interest discounts on the trade bills of textile exporters. At a time when the commercial rate of discount was 12 per cent, thanks to the Bank of Thailand's discount facilities, textile producers could get their trade bills discounted at 7 per cent.

Furthermore, since business taxes and import duties were additional barriers to international competitiveness, the association succeeded in persuading the government to refund them after the products were exported. After this, exports were possible, although at the beginning, as a measure for dumping abroad, they were not very profitable. But once the export channel was established, being a low-wage country, Thailand had a definite advantage in textile exports. An uncertainty was whether the government would refund taxes without much delay; this type of scheme is often thwarted by a poorly functioning bureaucracy. The Thai bureaucracy worked well enough to keep the scheme going, though there were a lot of complaints of long delays in the refunds.

The rise of gem and jewellery exports came in the mid-1970s, a little later than that of textiles. Thailand was among the top five gem-bearing areas of the world, and its domestic supply was supplemented by the gemstones (particularly rubies) smuggled in from Burma and Cambodia. In the late 1950s, the industry was still small, with exports of less than B20 million. In the early 1960's, it was strengthened by the relocation of Chinese gem traders and manufacturers from Burma because of the anti-capitalist (and anti-Chinese) policy of the newly formed Ne Win government there.[15] The purchases made by American soldiers who were stationed in or who came to the country on rest and recreation leave during the Vietnam War also gave a boost to the industry.

In order for gems and jewellery to be major exports, government-created barriers, especially the high import duty on rough stones and the business tax on finished gems and jewellery, had to be removed. Gem traders and jewellery manufacturers organized the Thai Gems and Jewelry Traders Association and started lobbying for the removal of these trade barriers. The government lifted the import duty on rough stones in 1977 and the business tax on finished jewellery in 1981. The association also obtained government support for the trade fairs and exhibitions it held to attract foreign buyers.[16] Under these favourable circumstances, exports began to grow.

In the 1980s, gemstones of various types (emeralds, sapphires, topazes, etc.) were brought from Africa, Latin America, and Asia (India and Sri Lanka in particular) for cutting and polishing. In addition, European firms began sending small-size diamonds to Thailand, and as this expanded, the country became one of the major diamond-cutting centres of the world. In 1990, gem and jewellery recorded B34.5 billion ($1.36 billion) in exports, making the industry the country's third largest exporter (after textiles and electronic products).

It was government–private co-operation which brought about this dramatic transformation, a co-operation formalized under the Prem Tinsulanonda government in 1982 when the Joint Public–Private Consultative Committee (JPPCC) was set up. One of its important functions was to feed the government information on the problems Thai firms (including foreign-owned companies operating in the country) faced in exporting their products. There were many complaints from the private sector about long delays in tax refunds, excessive customs formalities, cumbersome procedures for getting export clearance (especially for food products), limited government office hours for customs processing and export clearance, etc. The period when the JPPCC was active was short, but government–private consultations, especially at industry level, continued, and the government accommodated many of the demands of the private sector. But trade barriers (especially tariffs) had been created to protect or benefit certain groups, and there were conflicting views on what needed to be done, depending on their interests. The government listened to the views of the private sector, and made decisions on a number of problems with the better overall performance of the national economy in mind, often overriding objections from certain groups. Without this objectivity, the government could have become immobilized by conflicting views.

Attracting Export-oriented Foreign Investment

At the same time, the Thai government took measures to promote export-oriented investment. If a newly established firm was to export all its output (later this figure was reduced to 50 per cent), it could apply to the Board of Investment for exemption of import duties on raw materials and parts and of business taxes on output. (Under the system of exemption, unlike the one of refund, an exporting firm did not have to pay duties and taxes. However, they had to be paid for the portion sold in the domestic market. Many foreign firms preferred to ship their goods abroad, and then import them if they were needed in the domestic market, since selling directly to the domestic market entailed negotiations with the government on the amount of taxes they had to pay.) Even if the application was not approved (or partially approved), the firm could get the duties and taxes refunded when the products were exported, but approval could greatly simplify the problem and become an attractive feature for an investor. In 1983, the government liberalized foreign equity, letting it go up to 100 per cent in the case of export-oriented investment. Furthermore, the government began promoting industrial estates to help foreign investors in finding industrial sites (11 of the 13 industrial estates extant in 1990 were built in the 1980s).

These measures, when matched with the devaluation of the baht in the first half of the 1980s, made Thailand an attractive site for foreign investors. As discussed in Chapter 4, a couple of years after the Plaza Accord of 1985—which sharply appreciated the yen—there was a surge of Japanese export-oriented investment into Thailand. There was also a large inflow of investment from Taiwan, whose currency also appreciated in the second half of the 1980s. The uncertainty caused by the British decision to return Hong Kong to China in 1997 also brought investment from that island. These foreign investments created new exports or expanded the exports of labour-intensive goods which had started in the 1970s, and contributed greatly to export expansion in Thailand after the mid-1980s.

Reasons for Non-tariff Barriers in the Philippines

In the Philippines, non-tariff barriers were substantial during most of the 40-year period (1952–91) under study in this book. Because of the tendency for the government to overspend, there was constant pressure on the external value of the peso. The peso was devalued from ₱2 to about ₱26 per dollar between the beginning and the end of the 40-year period (recording about ₱28 per dollar in late 1990 and early 1991), but the government often put off devaluation when it was necessary. The only alternative was to increase exports rapidly, but its performance in exports tended to be poor. Under this situation, a non-tariff barrier (exchange or import control) was a convenient measure by which the government hid from the people the weak economic fundamentals it had caused. Clearly, import control was retained not just because it was a convenient measure for delaying devaluation. But it would not have been needed if responsible monetary management or a better export performance had eased the pressure to devalue the peso.

Given the pressure on the peso, exchange or import control could be justified on the ground that it could stabilize consumer prices. However, the businesses protected from foreign competition were the more important beneficiaries of control. Like exchange control, it also gave opportunities for corrupt gain to politicians and government officials. Also, the industries whose products were subject to import control worked hard to keep their products on the control list. High tariffs could be a substitute, but they were too obvious; import control could disguise the degree of protection better. In the early Aquino years, these industries fought against import liberalization.

The Thai government did its best to avoid devaluation by controlling the increase of money supply and taking measures to expand exports. Even with these efforts, if the balance of payments did not improve and the choice was between devaluation and exchange or import control, the Thai government took the former path, as it did in 1981 and 1984. It never resorted to exchange or import control to ease the pressure on the baht. The Thai government should be commended for its discipline. In contrast, the Philippine government tended to use exchange or import control to camouflage its mismanagement of the economy, make the cost of protection of domestic industries ambiguous, and secure opportunities for corruption for politicians and government officials in the process. The tragedy is that, although exchange or import control was becoming a cancer of the economy, the Philippine government did not act to stem it until the late 1980s.

1. James Ingram, *Economic Change in Thailand, 1850–1970*, Stanford: Stanford University Press, 1971, p. 283.

2. John Power and Gerardo Sicat, 'The Philippines: Industrialization and Trade Policies', in John Power and Gerardo Sicat (eds.), *The Philippines and Taiwan*, London: Oxford University Press, 1971, p. 93.

3. A 1987 World Bank study quoted in Robert Dohner and Ponciano Intal, 'The Marcos Legacy: Economic Policy and Foreign Debt in the Philippines', in Jeffrey Sachs and Susan Collins (eds.), *Developing Country Debt and Economic Performance*, Chicago: University of Chicago Press, 1989, Vol. 3, p. 574. Another study, however, shows that in 1978, for each of the SITC Codes 0–9, the Philippine tariff rates were higher than the Thai rates (Romeo Bautista, 'The 1981–85 Tariff Changes and Effective Protection of Manufacturing Industries', *Journal of Philippine Development*, 8, 1–2, 1981).

4. Miguel Cuaderno, *Guideposts to Economic Stability*, Manila: Central Bank of the Philippines, 1955, p. 220.

5. *American Chamber of Commerce Journal*, March 1960: 128.

6. Primitivo Mijares, *The Conjugal Dictatorship of Ferdinand and Imelda Marcos I*, San Francisco: Union Square Publications, 1986, p. 262.

7. Dohner and Intal, 'The Marcos Legacy', pp. 442–3.

8. Less than 5 per cent according to the 1987 World Bank study quoted in ibid., p. 574. In 1989, there were only 75 items subject to import restriction, out of 4,000 import items. The percentage was less than 2 that year (Narongchai Akrasanee et al., *Thailand's Export-led Growth: Retrospect and Prospects*, Policy Study No. 3, Bangkok: Thailand Development Research Institute, 1991, p. 15).

9. Filologo Pante and Erlinda Medalla, *The Philippine Industrial Sector: Policies, Programs and Performance*, Working Paper Series No. 90–18, Makati: Philippine Institute for Development Studies, July 1990, p. 27.

10. Enrique Zobel, 'Philippine Agriculture in the Year 2020: An Endangered Sector', *Manila Bulletin*, 6 July 1992.

11. In the 1950s, the Philippines controlled price increases better than Thailand (0.7 per cent per year vs. 2.1 per cent). A large part of the credit goes to Central Bank Governor Miguel Cuaderno, who fought the pressure from politicians on the Central Bank to finance government deficits (Miguel Cuaderno, *Problems of Economic Development*, Manila, privately published, 1964). Also, see Caridad C. Semana, 'Some Political Aspects of Philippine Economic Development after Independence', Ph.D. thesis, Harvard University, 1965, pp. 335–43.

12. In 1969, to forestall another devaluation, there was a move in Congress to restore exchange control (Alejandro Lichauco, *Nationalist Economics*, Quezon City: Institute for Rural Industrialization, 1988, p. 183).

13. Ingram, *Economic Change in Thailand*, p. 312.

14. This and the next two paragraphs are based on Fujinaga Takahiro, *Thai wa Ima: Kyu Seicho o Togeru Ajia Power* [Thailand Today: A Rapidly Growing New Asian Power], Tokyo: Diamond-sha, 1989, pp. 80–2 and an interview with him in Bangkok, 22 January 1987. Mr Fujinaga was in charge of the textile department in the Japanese trading company, Marubeni, at that time.

15. *Far Eastern Economic Review*, 9 May 1991.

16. Anek Laothamatas, *Business Associations and the New Political Economy of Thailand: From Bureaucratic Polity to Liberal Corporatism*, Boulder: Westview Press, and Singapore: Institute of Southeast Asian Studies, 1992, pp. 97–8.

10
Government Intervention in the Price Mechanism

Appeasing the Masses

THE ideal way to re-distribute economic equity is through direct taxes such as progressive personal income, inheritance, and property taxes, but both the Philippines and Thailand depended heavily on indirect taxes, which tend to have retrogressive effects on income distribution. (In the second half of the 1980s, 70 per cent of tax revenues in the Philippines and 77 per cent in Thailand came from indirect taxes.) In Thailand, there was neither inheritance nor property tax. To compensate for the lack of a re-distributive mechanism through taxation, both governments used price support and control to appease the masses. In Thailand, it was in more recent years that the government began this practice, and hence, the damage inflicted on the economy was more contained. In contrast, the history of price support and control in the Philippines is longer, and its effects on the economy were more harmful because the government was more populist and/or because economic circumstances made it difficult for the government to later reverse the trend.

The rural masses enjoyed some benefits from price support and control in both the Philippines and Thailand. The government made some low-interest loans available to peasants, supplied them fertilizers at subsidized prices, gave price support for some agricultural products, kept transportation cost low (especially railway fares), and provided electricity at low rates. In Thailand where the rural sector had been historically taxed heavily, the government has become more supportive of peasants since the mid-1970s.[1] For example, the Bank of Thailand required commercial banks to lend a certain portion of their deposits to the rural sector (the target was 7 per cent for 1976). In the 1980s, the government became more involved in procuring rice from peasants at support prices. When sugar prices plummeted in the early 1980s, the government raised its domestic price to help sugar producers. But still the extent of government involvement was small. Although there was a measure to ease the tight credit situation in rural areas, the large part of the lending of commercial banks went to agri-business, not directly to peasants. The government's procurement of rice tended to be less than 10 per cent of the total rice marketed. It was probably only the well-organized sugar producers who could claim substantial benefits from the government's price support scheme.

The Thai government had to pay more attention to the urban masses who were prone to publicly protest government actions directly affecting their daily lives, and to the newspapers which tended to take a populist stand (the television and radio stations were controlled by either the government or the military). In early 1980, the Kriangsak Chomanan government resigned because of its unpopular decision to raise domestic oil prices during the second oil crisis: the middle class depended on cars for transportation, and the Bangkok poor feared the price increase of goods and services related to oil (electricity in particular).

The Thai government also let the Bangkok Mass Transit Authority (the capital's bus monopoly formed in 1976 by merging several private bus firms) keep losing money. It was the biggest money loser in the 1980s among government corporations. The government wanted to increase bus fares, but hesitated to do so. In the late 1960s when bus services were then offered by private companies, student leaders used the fare issue to mobilize students and workers, triggering the movement which led to the fall of the Thanom Kittikachorn–Prapart Charustien government in 1973. Also in 1982, when the Prem Tinsulanonda government decided to increase bus fares from B1 to B2, students marched to Government House and, together with workers, threatened strong action unless the increase was reduced. The government consequently rolled back the increase.[2] In a way, low bus fares were a penalty the government had to pay for the neglect of past administrations in developing an effective mass transit system. (Bangkok is notorious for its traffic problem.)

In general, whether in Thailand or in the Philippines, the government trod carefully when it had to raise the prices of basic goods and services. Oil prices, passenger fares for various modes of transportation (railway in particular), electricity charges, and telephone charges were controlled, with the government reluctantly approving their increase. In addition, the prices of food and industrial products might be regulated. In terms of the number of goods and services under government price control, Thailand probably fared worse than the Philippines. It is reported that there were 110 products on the price control list as late as mid-1991.[3] The list included such goods as motor cars, motor cycles, cement, detergents, margarine, fish meal, roasted coffee beans, sanitary napkins, and cooking oil. But the Thai government approved price increases rather promptly if they were justified; in the case of public utilities, the government was more willing to grant it. This is a major reason why public utilities are in better shape in Thailand than in the Philippines.

Rate Regulation in the Philippines and Its Consequences

When the Philippine Long Distance Telephone Co. (PLDT) and Manila Electric Co. (Meralco) were owned by Americans, the Public Service Commission dragged its feet over applications for rate increase.[4]

It sat on, and frequently rejected, applications for a rate increase.[5] During the first oil crisis of 1973, the government created the Petroleum Commission to regulate oil prices. At that time, there were four foreign-owned refineries, and none Filipino-owned, though Filipino investors had a minority interest in one of the four refineries (Filoil Refinery). The commission made it difficult to operate profitably by keeping domestic prices low; as a result, two American-owned refineries were closed. It was at this time that the government created the Philippine National Oil Co. and let it take over the other two refineries: the one in Bataan which was formerly owned jointly by Mobil and Esso was kept open, while Filoil was closed.

The American investors who pulled out of the Philippines may have thought that rate or price regulation was a weapon to be used specifically against them, but it continued to be a problem for Filipino-owned public utility companies. Because government regulatory agencies did not approve fare increases—or when they did, it was after a considerable delay—the services of public utility companies deteriorated over time or did not expand much. Inadequate revenues made it difficult for them to invest in the improvement of existing services or in expansion. In the late 1980s, even to maintain some existing services became difficult.

As explained in Chapter 7, the Philippines began suffering from long brownouts in late 1989, and the Philippine Airlines is the worst in the South-East Asian region. The telephone system is also in bad shape; one Filipino newspaper columnist wrote that 'it is known as the "most religious network on earth" because you pick up the receiver and pray for a dial tone'.[6] In 1990, there were 688,000 lines in the Philippines, a substantial increase from 420,000 a decade earlier, but there were almost twice as many telephone lines in Thailand that year. The telephones in the Philippines are heavily concentrated in Metro Manila. In the mid-1980s, 81 per cent of municipalities did not have telephones. (A province is divided into municipalities, and there were 1,595 municipalities at that time.) In Thailand also, there was a concentration in the Bangkok Metropolitan area, but it was not as high as in the Philippines. In the mid-1980s, 30 per cent of telephone lines were in the provinces, and there were no districts without a telephone. (A Thai province is divided into districts, which is a geographically larger unit than a municipality in the Philippines.)

In the Philippines, the government does not allow telephone companies to earn more than a 12 per cent rate of return on their invested capital. This ceiling was set in 1935 when the rate of interest was around 4 per cent. This is a disincentive for telephone companies to invest in expansion as the rate of interest has increased in more recent years. For example, in the early 1980s, when the rate of interest for 12-month time deposits was around 14 per cent, the PLDT was earning less than 10 per cent on its invested capital. A major reason for its poor rate of return was the depreciation of the peso. To finance its imports of equipment, it had borrowed heavily from abroad since the rate of interest overseas was cheaper. But the peso depreciated rapidly in the 1980s and since its repayments were based mainly on its peso revenue, the depreciation reduced the company's earning capacity.

In 1983, the PLDT asked for a 60–70 per cent increase on domestic tariffs (so that it could earn the maximum 12 per cent rate of return in spite of the rising rate of interest), but the National Telecommunications Commission (NTC, which replaced the Public Service Commission as the regulatory agency of the telecommunications industry) approved only a 35 per cent increase. In recent years, the PLDT has been asking the NTC to increase the maximum ceiling on the rate of return to 15 per cent and to let it use the additional 3 per cent for investment in expansion. The NTC has not approved the request as yet, despite a strong need for the expansion of the telephone service. From the PLDT's point of view, the tariff for the local service is so low that there is no economic incentive to invest in its expansion. The PLDT says that it is the international telephone service which enables it to earn profits, thus the areas where not many international calls are made (such as rural areas) become low-priority areas, which may be a disadvantage from the perspective of the country's development.

In general, the attitude of government regulatory agencies was not forward-looking; they were more interested in containing the rate increase, even if this meant a deterioration in the quality of the service. For example, the number of buses running on the streets decreased 20 per cent (from 18,016 to 14,667) between 1980 and 1990.[7] Many of those in Metro Manila are museum pieces. On the antiquated bus service, one Filipino columnist wrote:

> Metro Manila ... is a twisting spool of commuters, waiting, almost endlessly for that ride back home. The wait takes one, two, three hours, even more at times, an almost unbearable agony for those who reside in Cavite or Bulacan, or any of the near-by provinces.
>
> There are tens of thousands of such commuters, and I do not know where they get their grit, their forbearance and their patience. In many places, such as the entrances to residential villages and subdivisions, they stand in line, staring ahead and speechless, living in a world I never lived in.
>
> When I was such a commuter for many years, we went home within the half hour, certainly within the hour. It was a breeze going home to Quezon City or Pasay or Baclaran. . . .[8]

The same columnist contrasted the water situation between earlier and recent years:

> [In earlier years,] the faucets always gushed water. Taking a shower then was like standing in a driving rain. Today, the water often trickles and there is a dry gurgling in the pipes. Times there are when you have soap all over and the water suddenly stops . . .[9]

Interisland shipping also deteriorated. In the pre-war period, the Philippines enjoyed an advantage over Thailand since its sea transportation was more developed and less expensive than land transportation, but in the post-war period, with the progress of motorization and an extended network of highways, Thailand began enjoying an advantage in this sector. By the end of the 1960s, all but 6 of the 71 provincial capitals in the country became accessible by paved roads.[10] The highway connecting Bangkok to Nong Khai on the Mekong River opposite Vientiane was completed in the mid-1960s, and along this road many agricultural products (rice, maize, cassava, vegetables, pineapples, canned tomatoes, etc.) were sent to Bangkok (often for export), and imported and domestically produced goods were brought back (detergents, kitchen utensils, motor cycles, washing machines, television sets, etc.). This highway also facilitated the movement of people, especially between their home towns and Bangkok where they migrated as temporary or semi-permanent workers. Today, even from Nakhon Phanom, a remote north-eastern city facing the Mekong River, there are several air-conditioned and non-air-conditioned buses leaving for Bangkok daily.

In contrast, slow-moving antiquated ships are the mode of transportation for ordinary people and cargoes between the Philippine islands. Multinational companies like Dole and Del Monte, which operate plantations in Mindanao, charter ships to export their products directly, but small producers in Mindanao have to contend with the poor links to Metro Manila and abroad. When Negros tried to diversify from sugar into other goods (such as shrimp) in the 1980s, it was foiled by poor shipping connections. It was more expensive to ship a container from Manila to Negros than from Manila to Taiwan, a route over which the Philippine government did not have sole jurisdiction.

The investment climate for foreign oil companies was not conducive during the Aquino period. In 1987, when the country faced a balance of payments crisis, the government asked oil companies to postpone payments to their suppliers. They agreed because the government promised to pay the cost of borrowing the necessary money from abroad—this relieved the government of the burden of using foreign exchange to pay for oil imports—but this promise was challenged in court, and the Supreme Court finally ruled against it.[11] The government was reluctant to approve an oil price increase and preferred to give subsidies to oil companies when international oil prices went up. But the government was short of money and saddled with large foreign debts; when international prices increased sharply after Iraq's invasion of Kuwait in mid-1990, the government ran out of money to pay subsidies to oil companies. A price increase was the only way out, a step which the government eventually took. However, fearful of providing a rallying point for anti-government groups, the government did not make the increase large enough to eliminate subsidies. Moreover, the government had difficulties in funding the subsidies, and usually delayed payments. This entangled relationship between the government and oil companies was hardly conducive to investment for expansion. It was reported that Caltex (Philippines) could not ask its parent company for money for expansion (while its other subsidiaries in the region were getting

$2 billion in the early 1990s), and that its geothermal project for the Philippines was also put off. (The prices of oil and energy were under the jurisdiction of the Energy Regulatory Board.)[12]

The trouble with the Philippine government was that it did not want to make unpopular decisions. When the economy got worse, as it did during the Aquino period, such decisions became more difficult, but even before that, the government preferred to keep the rates for public utilities low, and if their increase had to be approved, they tended to delay it. Politicians who opposed (even) economically justifiable increases were heroes: they were applauded by students, workers, and the public. To approve rate increases promptly would antagonize the people, particularly the urban masses, and might expose the government for the bad job it was doing in macroeconomic management. The expedient way was to please the people, even if it meant grave economic harm over the long run.

Minimum Wage Legislation

This characteristic of expediency is best demonstrated in minimum wage legislation. In 1991, the minimum daily wage in Metro Manila was about ₱127 ($4.70), in contrast with about B97 ($4.10) in Bangkok; and Thailand's per capita gross national product was about $1,600, a little over twice that of the Philippines. Minimum wages were introduced in the Philippines in 1951, but in Thailand it was not until 1972. At this time, though per capita income was roughly the same for both countries, minimum wages in the Philippines were twice as high as those in Thailand. There were certain groups of workers who benefited from artificially high minimum wages, but a large number of workers, especially in traditional and small-scale sectors, could not enjoy them. Employers used various means to pay less, not so much out of greed as the inability to pay. Foreign investors had to think twice before they decided to invest in the Philippines, not just because the wage tended to be high but also because it reflected the incapacity of the government to impose discipline on labour.

In the Philippines, trade unions were strong. In the 1980s, the leftist national federation, Kilusang Mayo Uno, became a powerful political force. During the Aquino administration, it used *welgang bayan* (people's strikes) to press its demands on the government, such as an increase in the minimum wage. But even during martial law when trade unions were better controlled, the government kept increasing minimum wages. Whenever prices increased because the government had overspent, inflation resulted, and minimum wages had to be adjusted upwards. To please workers—not necessarily militant ones—politicians often resorted to minimum wage increases.

In 1972, when a minimum wage was introduced in Thailand, the government set it at B12 (60 cents) per day. In subsequent years, it was raised, but the increases were modest. This restraint might be explained by the fact that the government was run mostly by the military so that politicians had little opportunity to make the minimum wage a big issue. But in the 1980s when politicians increased their power, they did not make it a big issue either. A more important reason for moderation was the fact that workers were not well organized. Trade unions were banned by the government between 1958 and 1971 and again between 1976 and 1980.[13] Even when they were legal, they had to register with the Department of Labour in the Ministry of the Interior (to which the Police Department also belongs), and receive a licence. Before issuing a licence, the Department of Labour made sure that the applicants were not a threat to national security. After the licence was issued, their internal operation was under the close supervision of the department. For example, no general meeting was lawful without the presence of public officials. Union leaders were sometimes dismissed by the government. This high-handed attitude towards workers did not change much even during the period of full democracy from mid-1988 to early 1991.

In the 1980s, however, the unions of government corporations became strong, and troublesome for the government (for example, they stopped international telephone calls for quite some time in 1982 and in the late 1980s, and opposed the privatization of the Klong Toey port and the newly created Laem Chabang port in the Eastern Seaboard industrial complex). The military clique which took over the government in February 1991 disbanded them as one of its first measures. They protested vehemently against the decision with the help of their overseas affiliates, but there was no strong public support for them—the people were probably fed up with the frequent use of their stranglehold on vital services for their selfish purposes—and the government stood firm on its decision. (For some unknown reason, a prominent labour leader of their national federation has been missing since then.)

'Market-friendly' Regulation in Thailand

The Thai government, as explained earlier, could seldom raise bus fares in Bangkok. Nor could it increase railway fares either, although there was a need to improve railway services. But then buses and trucks had become much more important modes of transportation for the outer provinces. The government also had to be careful of increasing oil prices because it might incur the wrath of the urban middle class who depend on cars for transportation as well as of the urban poor who depend on cooking gas for household fuel. But the government did not freeze oil prices for long, and let them go up when international prices went up, although providing some cushion by delaying the increase for a while. At least the business environment was not so bad as in the Philippines as to discourage foreign oil companies from expanding their refining capacity. In the early 1990s, Esso was planning to invest $950 million in refinery expansion, and Caltex had similar plans ($1 billion plus).

There were a lot of complaints about the inadequacies of public utilities, but clearly the situation was not as bad as in the Philippines. The inadequacies of Thai public utilities were not because they, suffering from losses and not receiving enough subsidies, could not afford to improve and expand the facilities. Except for the State Railway of Thailand and the Bangkok Mass Transit Authority, all other major government corporations earned profits in the late 1980s. For them, the rates were high enough to cover the operating costs and the amortization of the loans they had incurred for expansion of facilities. In the early 1980s, the Metropolitan Waterworks Authority was one of the three big losers (together with the railway and bus companies). But, in a few years, after a new head was appointed, it started earning profits. It had been badly run as a government corporation, and this had to be rectified, but the rate increase was an important part of its transformation into a profitable enterprise.[14]

Since the mid-1970s, politicians have become more influential, with some taking a populist stand, opposing rate increases and arguing for greater government subsidies. Around 1980, one of them even argued for free bus services and hospital care.[15] But these politicians did not become a significant force. Most government corporations were expected to cover costs with revenues. For this purpose, though the government did not freely grant rate increases, they were usually granted if they were justified by increasing costs.

Where the telephone service was concerned, government policy was not such as to deter private companies from entering the field; in the early 1990s, the government decided to rely on private companies to expand the telephone system on a revenue-sharing basis from 1.5 million to 4.5 million lines. In 1991, the government gave a subsidiary of the Charoen Pokphand group a licence to install an additional 2 million lines in the Bangkok Metropolitan area. In July 1992, the government approved the plan of Thai Telephone and Telecommunications (a consortium led by Loxley of Bangkok) to install 1 million lines in the provinces.

In short, the Thai government was less populist than the Philippine government; it was more determined to make users pay for the services they were receiving. However, it should be added that since the late 1980s the government has been greatly helped by a healthy economy which reduced public resistance to rate increases. In contrast, the situation in the Philippines was a vicious cycle. The economy was so bad that public resistance to rate increases was strong (and fuelled by irresponsible politicians), and if they were not granted, the consequent lack of revenue for expansion or even for maintenance caused services to deteriorate.

Poor Government Planning in the Philippines

Undoutedly, the major reason for the poor conditions of public utilities in the Philippines was the government's slow response to applications for rate increases, but it was not the only reason. In the case of telephones, another major factor was poor planning on the part of the government. Besides the PLDT, there are about 40 other private telephone companies today. In addition, there are a few government operators, one of which is the telecommunications office in the Department of Transportation and Communications which operates the local telephone service in some rural areas as well as the long-distance domestic toll service; the other government operators are local governments.

Although the PLDT dominates the telephone industry, accounting for over 90 per cent of telephone lines in the country, with most major cities serviced by it, it does not have a franchise over the whole country. The 40 or so small companies have their own franchise areas. They cannot raise capital as well as the PLDT can, and cannot invest much in expansion. There are also problems in interconnections with the PLDT; the exchanges of some telephone companies are obsolete or technically incompatible with the PLDT's system. The PLDT is not enthusiastic about (or sometimes refuse) interconnections (for an economic reason). It does not want to improve the facilities needed for interconnection, either because not much revenue is expected as a result, or because it feels that small companies are not paying their due share in the revenue which arises from interconnections. Also in some cases, the facilities of small telephone companies are so limited that they cannot take too many incoming calls.

Then, there is the telecommunications office (in the Department of Transportation and Communications) which has been competing in some areas with the PLDT since the mid-1950s (in earlier years, the government telephone service was under the Bureau of Telecommunications), taking advantage of access to reparations and Official Development Assistance (from which, the PLDT was excluded until a few years ago). For example, in the Cagayan Valley, the PLDT and the telecommunications office operate separate telephone exchanges, and both have transmission facilities from Metro Manila. The government should not have gone into the telephone service in the first place. Its involvement started in early post-war years when a large need for telephone service could not be met by the PLDT and other private companies, especially in the provinces. The government could have given subsidies to encourage private companies to expand their services to needed areas, or even if it went into the service directly, it could have privatized it when a private company was ready to undertake it, thus avoiding a duplicate system. Instead, the government stayed on to take care of the needs of bureaucrats and politicians.

There has not been a concerted effort to rationalize and integrate the country's telephone system. There has been some progress, however, since the mid-1970s; for example, the PLDT absorbed the Republic Telephone Co. (RETELCO) in the early 1980s, and has been serving all of Metro Manila since then. Formerly, to call a RETELCO number from Makati or any PLDT area in Metro Manila was extremely difficult. There is still no single government agency in charge of all telephone systems in the country. The NTC supervises all private companies, but does not have jurisdiction over the telecommunications office's telephone operation. Government policy has been *ad hoc* at best, and often immobilized by vested interests in the industry and the government. People often blame the PLDT for the poor telephone system, which may be justifiable to some extent, but the real problem is poor government planning and regulation. The sorry state of the telephone service in the Philippines is part of the overall picture of the incompetent bureaucracy messing up the economy.

1. For the role of workers in getting the government to pay more attention to rural development in the mid-1970s, see David Morell and Chai-Anan Samudavanija, *Thailand: Reaction and Revolution*, Cambridge: Oelgeschlager, Gunn & Hain, 1981, p. 193.

2. Ross Prizzia, *Thailand in Transition: The Role of Oppositional Forces*, Honolulu: University Press of Hawaii, 1985, pp. 81–4.

3. *Bangkok Post*, 21 June 1991. At this time, 46 products were dropped from the price control list.

4. Meralco was sold to Filipino investors in 1961, and the PLDT in 1967.

5. Frank Golay, 'Taming the American Multinationals', in Norman G. Owen (ed.), *The Philippine Economy and the United States: Studies in Past and Present Interactions*, Ann Arbor: Center for South and Southeast Asian Studies, University of Michigan, 1983, pp. 142–3.

6. Max Soliven's column in the *Asian Wall Street Journal*, 28 January 1992.

7. Pete Nicomedes Prado, 'Transportation and Communication', in *The Aquino Administration: Record and Legacy (1986–1992)*, Quezon City: University of the Philippines Press, 1992, p. 267.

8. Teodoro Benigno, *Here Is the Score*, Manila: Philippines Today Inc., 1990, p. 62.

9. Ibid., p. 397.

10. James Ingram, *Economic Change in Thailand, 1850–1970*, Stanford: Stanford University Press, 1971, p. 277.

11. *Far Eastern Economic Review*, 18 June 1992.

12. *Manila Chronicle*, 16 June 1992.

13. Anek Laothamatas, *Business Associations and the New Political Economy of Thailand: From Bureaucratic Polity to Liberal Corporatism*, Boulder: Westview Press, and Singapore: Institute of Southeast Asian Studies, 1992, p. 46.

14. Pisit Leeahtam, *Thailand's Economic Adjustment in the 1980s: From Crisis to Double Digit Growth*, Bangkok: Dokya Publishing House (1988) Co., 1991, p. 59.

15. The economic platform of Kukrit Pramoj (he served as Prime Minister for about a year from March 1975) included free bus transportation for low-income people and a national minimum wage of $50 per month (at this time, the government's daily minimum wage was $1.25 in Bangkok and $0.80–0.90 in the provinces). He also advocated nationalization of rice mills and the rice market. Kukrit blamed the military for his 1976 election defeat (Vilas Manivat (comp.), *M. R. Kukrit Pramoj: His Wit and Wisdom, Writings, Speeches and Interviews*, Bangkok: Editions Duang Kamol, 1983, p. 129).

11
The Fundamentals That Led to Intervention

WHY was the Bank of Thailand a more effective institution than the Central Bank of the Philippines? Why did the Philippine government get extensively involved in the capital market and record such a dismal performance (as reflected in the huge losses of the Philippine National Bank and the Development Bank of the Philippines)? Why were Philippine government corporations badly managed compared with their Thai counterparts (for example, Philippine Airlines cf. Thai Airways International, and the National Power Corp. cf. the Electricity Generation Authority of Thailand)? Why did the Philippine government create monopolies (for example, Unicom and Nasutra) and weaken distribution channels? Why did the Philippine government erect higher trade barriers and intervene in the price mechanism more extensively than did the Thai government?

There are specific answers to these questions, but the common factor underlying them all concerns the nature of government. Sustainable economic growth is a vital national interest, since it is the means to liberate people from poverty, thus giving them greater freedom to consume goods and services. Free market advocates tend to give the impression that government everywhere functions in the same way. But the fact is otherwise. At worst it is tantamount to a crime syndicate controlling people with armed forces and extorting money from them. This is not an exceptional case, certainly not in history when such was the character of many governments.[1] A government may be run, more ideally, with the welfare of the nation as its prime objective, but it is a mistake to think that such is the norm. Leaders often govern for private gain, at the expense of the well-being of the national economy. When developing countries such as the Philippines and Thailand are discussed, how well national interests are taken care of by government leaders is an important question for investigation.

The ills of government intervention were more pronounced in the Philippines than in Thailand because the Philippine government became a vehicle for private gain and the good of the nation was neglected. There were Filipino politicians and private citizens who worked for the national welfare, but they were usually overwhelmed by politicians and their supporters who put their private interests above national interests.

In Thailand also, there were a large number of such government leaders. There has been a great deal of corruption in the Thai government,[2] but not enough to overwhelm its administration of the country; many Thai government leaders paid a lot of attention to national interests.

Corrupt leaders do not always pursue private gain only. Some are literally corrupt because they take bribes, but they may still push measures to promote the national welfare at the same time. Their corruption is limited so that no great harm is done to the overall working of government for the national good. There were no Thai leaders like Marcos, who borrowed from abroad almost irrationally, leaving a legacy of debt to the country. The Thai military leaders who ran the country in the 1960s—Sarit Thanarat, Thanom Kittikachorn, Prapart Charustien, and Narong Kittikachorn—are said to have been corrupt. Sarit amassed about $150 million, and the last three (sometimes called the three tyrants) $70 million.[3] These sums are 'peanuts' compared with the $5–10 billion Marcos is alleged to have stolen from the country. Besides, the economy of Thailand kept growing several per cent per annum during their regimes, unlike that of the Philippines which was badly scarred by Marcos.

When Democracy Does Not Work

The government exists to tackle problems which cannot be solved privately, and people are supposed to elect government leaders for this purpose. Campaign issues are supposed to be public issues, and people should be able to understand them and elect the candidates who they think can best contribute to their solution. But even in countries with higher incomes and better education, democracy has often failed, what more in developing countries with a great deal of poverty and a low level of education. Many people sell their votes or vote for people who pander to their selfish needs. Public issues are incomprehensible to them, or do not solve their immediate needs.

After independence, Philippine democracy decayed, culminating in Ferdinand Marcos's assumption of the presidency in 1966. His successful political career is an indication of the inherent faults of Philippine democracy. Marcos was arrested in 1938 for the murder of his father's political rival in Ilocos Norte, his home province. He had a motive (revenge for having defeated his father in the congressional elections) and the ability to commit the crime (he was a crack shot and a member of the ROTC pistol and rifle team at the University of the Philippines). He was found guilty by the Court of First Instance, but appealed to the Supreme Court, and in 1940, was acquitted by Chief Justice Jose P. Laurel (who had earlier faced a similar problem as Marcos and who later became President of the Second Republic during the Japanese occupation).

In spite of his record, Marcos was elected to Congress in 1949. He was intelligent and ambitious, but coming from a modest middle-class family, he did not have the wealth to support his political ambition, unlike those who belonged to 'the oligarchy'. To make up for this lack, he used whatever powers he had as a Congressman for wealth accumulation and became one of the most corrupt politicians in the country. In 1959, after having served as an 'outstanding' Congressman, he successfully ran for the Senate. A few years later, he became Senate President, and finally in 1966, President of the country.

Several years later in 1972, he declared martial law supposedly to improve the political and economic situation; the move proved disastrous for the country. In the mid-1980s, opposition to the government became strong, and in February 1986, he was chased out of the country. One relatively conservative American diplomat-turned-scholar (his liberal foes call him an ultra conservative) wrote that '[Marcos] fled like a thief in the night and like a thief, arrived in Honolulu loaded with plunder stolen from the country he had promised to make great again'.[4] The Aquino government filed a lawsuit against him (he was living in Hawaii at this time) in the US District Court in California, characterizing his government as a 'RICO [Racketeer Influenced and Corrupt Organization] enterprise' as defined in the US criminal code.

President Aquino must have thought that there was a consensus in the country that Marcos and his cronies are to blame for the miserable state of the country. Yet in the 1992 presidential election, 10.3 per cent of the voters chose Imelda Marcos, and another 18.2 per cent voted for Marcos's former top associate, Eduardo Cojuangco. Apparently, many people still respect them. Marcos once said that his wife was an important asset in his campaigns—good for a million votes, because she sang and danced and turned election rallies into big budget entertainment.[5] However, in the 1992 election, she collected not just a million, but a little over two million votes. In early 1991, a prominent Filipino newspaper columnist expressed amazement at Imelda's popularity among a certain group of people:

> Each time I walk through Hong Kong's Statue Square and the Star Ferry landing area, where our 63,000 Filipina domestic helpers or housemaids now staffing HK households congregate on weekends, I am reminded of how we 'deserve' what we've got. Here we have thousands of Filipino women, some of them with college degrees, forced by economic adversity to become *achays* in a foreign city, but do they blame Marcos and Imelda for their plight? On the contrary, if you stood in the middle of the throng and shouted, '[Imelda] is a no-good!' (as one German executive, married to a Filipina warned me) you would be in great danger of being lynched.[6]

Francis Sayre, Professor of Law at Harvard University, served for a few years as Adviser in Foreign Affairs to King Rama VI (r. 1910–25) of Thailand. When the King asked him whether or not the country should go for democracy, he argued against it:

> A workable Parliament is absolutely dependent upon an intelligent electorate. Without intelligent control by the people such a body would be sure to degenerate into a corrupt and tyrannical body. Until the rank and file of people in Siam have generally received a higher degree of education than at present it would seem therefore to be exceedingly dangerous to try to set up a popularly controlled

Parliamentary body. It therefore seems inescapable that at least for the present absolute power must continue to rest in the King.[7]

Sayre did not argue against democracy to please the King, who also had a negative view of it, but he sincerely questioned the advisability of democracy in a country where the masses were illiterate. He later served as High Commissioner in the Philippines where he harboured the same doubt when President Manuel Quezon amended the Constitution so that he could seek re-election.[8] However, since the Philippines had been preparing itself for full democracy under Amcrican tutelage, he could not argue against democracy.

Many post-war Thai leaders also cautioned against democracy. Thanat Khoman, Minister of Foreign Affairs in the Sarit and Thanom–Prapart governments and widely regarded as their leading spokesman, argued eloquently against democracy in 1959:

We now find ourselves at the crossroads, we must look hard into ourselves, we must know where we are, what we want and what we can do … it is of no avail to try to ape those who, after all, are different from us in many respects. The fundamental cause [of unstable governments in the past], for many of us, lies in the sudden transplantation of alien institutions on to our soil without careful preparation and more particularly without proper regard to the circumstances which prevail in our homeland, the nature and characteristics of our own people, in a word the genius of our race, with the result that their functioning has been haphazard and even chaotic.

How can representative government function if those who are elected to represent the people in the National Assembly forget the interest of the country as a whole and pursue only their selfish gains. More particularly, how can the electorate hope to choose representatives worthy of their trust if it is hardly able to distinguish between promises of an election campaign and the genuine determination to carry out a national program and to uphold political ideals. . . .[9]

Kukrit Pramoj said in an interview in mid-1976 that most Thai politicians were after personal gain and thought more about the next election than the welfare of the country.[10] Even Prime Minister Anand Panyarachun, who is sympathetic to the cause of democracy, questioned the wisdom of moving to full democracy right away:

The Western concept of democracy remains, to an extent, an alien import to Asia. Human rights is also a foreign concept. While it is true Thailand is moving towards the Western model, the time-frame by which this is achieved cannot be dictated from without, but only from within.[11]

In the mid-1970s, amid euphoria among pro-democracy people after the fall of the Thanom–Prapart regime in October 1973, students in the nation's top university, Chulalongkorn University, gave a cool assessment of democracy. When asked whether or not they considered democracy suitable for Thailand, only 33 per cent thought it was, while 29 per cent said it was unsuitable; the rest were uncertain. As to whether or not they would want a dictatorial government like Sarit's from the late 1950s to the early 1960s, 17 per cent said they would want it because it would give them peace and economic growth, and another 46 per cent said they would want it if there was no corruption. Only 29 per cent rejected it offhand.[12]

In the Philippines also, there were people who questioned the merits of democracy. These were mostly the people who sided with Japan before and during the Pacific War, and their views were completely ignored after the defeat of Japan. For example, Jose Laurel (father of Vice-President Salvador Laurel, who served in the Aquino administration) argued for authoritarian government:

> The whole history of government shows that public affairs would be better administered and the welfare of the people better served in the hands of a moral and intellectual aristocracy.... A good and efficient government, a benevolent government, may exist and continue indefinitely functioning with admirable harmony, when men of superior moral and intellectual endowments are in control of the state. And this benevolent government is the result ... of a traditional practice of allowing the best-endowed men in the service of the state ample scope and latitude in the exercise of governmental powers.[13]

Laurel was President of the Second Republic during the war, and in the immediate post-war years, he was detained in Sugamo prison in Tokyo on the charge of collaboration with the Japanese military. At this time, he faced the prospect of the end of his political career, but he was cleared of any wrongdoings, and made a political comeback in the post-war period. In the process, however, he conveniently set aside his earlier conviction on authoritarian government.

Democracy in the Philippines, however, became the nightmare come true of people like Sayre. Public office became the means to gain fame and/or accumulate wealth. For the purpose of wealth accumulation, the more the government intervened, the better. Some economists and good-intentioned people argued against intervention, and exceptional politicians (such as President Diosdado Macapagal who decontrolled foreign exchange) had reduced the scope of government intervention, but over time, the Philippine government was captured by irresponsible politicians and private individuals who wanted to use it for private gain. A young college graduate, when asked (probably in the 1950s or early 1960s) why he wanted to be in politics, said, 'Politics is the only short-cut to popularity and wealth in the Philippines. Unless you become a big politico here, you will never be rich in a few years.'[14]

In the late 1940s, when the Philippine government was still functioning quite well, there was a case of corruption into which President Elpidio Quirino ordered an investigation. The Senate President, who was one of the accused, questioned the wisdom of the President's order:

> If you [the President] cannot permit abuses, you must at least tolerate them. What are we in power for? We are not hypocrites. Why should we pretend to be saints when in reality we are not? ... When Jesus Christ died on the Cross, He made a distinction between a good crook and the bad crooks. We can prepare to be good crooks.[15]

During the 1953 presidential campaign, a Liberal Party candidate, instead of avoiding the charge of corruption, met it head on, appealing to the electorate:

> [D]on't vote for the Nacionalistas because they are hungary for jobs, hungry for power, hungry for everything. They are like mosquitoes famished for human blood. Since they have not enjoyed power for almost eight years, they'll swoop down on you, bite you and suck your lifeblood and kill this nation, I tell you.
>
> On the other hand, we, the Liberals, have been in power since 1946. We have had enough of privileges, everything. We won't suck you any more because we have already sucked you. So, between the Nacionalistas, who are out to suck you, and the Liberals, who are now satisfied and contended, whom would you prefer to run our government? Of course, you can't make a mistake. Think it over carefully my friends.[16]

Campaigns became more expensive as time went by. People wanted to be paid, entertained, showered with gifts, and feasted. For senatorial and presidential candidates, the nation was their constituency. In order to win, they needed a national organization, which they could finance only with money amassed through corruption or from their supporters' contributions—supporters who expected to be repaid after they had won. Probably, despite the rhetoric to the contrary, the level of corruption was not higher in the Philippines than in Thailand in the 1950s, but the situation got worse in the 1960s. This is what comes of democracy when the masses are poor and badly educated.

Because corruption became rampant in the Philippines, even those who had supported democracy earlier lost faith in it. When Marcos declared martial law in September 1972, the masses were not perturbed. A large number of businessmen and professionals supported martial law, hoping that the situation would improve. There were oppositions, but they were quickly suppressed. What was a little surprising was the ease with which Marcos could institute a martial law regime. The military forces or the Supreme Court could have joined the oppositions, but they supported Marcos. At that time, there was no mass movement like the People's Revolution of February 1986, for the people had little at stake in the poorly functioning democracy.

One cannot argue for the Philippines that an authoritarian regime worked better than democracy did. Marcos's dictatorial rule from September 1972 to February 1986 probably did greater harm to the economy than democracy would have done. In democracy, if the government is really hopeless, an opposition presidential candidate will at least make an issue of it, and can win, although there is no guarantee that the new administration will be any better. Democracy gives people a chance to replace the existing corrupt government with a new one. Under dictatorial rule, this is difficult, and while a badly run dictatorial government lingers on, the economy suffers.

Marcos's martial law regime is characterized as a kleptocracy (a rule of theft). Although he may not have intended it to be so at the very beginning, the government became an institution which enabled him, his wife Imelda, and his cronies to accumulate wealth through kickbacks, extortion, and deception. Marcos himself had simple taste (though he was also probably busy accumulating money abroad), but his wife enjoyed an expensive lifestyle. She often went together with her coterie to European and American cities for shopping sprees, commandeering one or two jet airplanes from Philippine Airlines for the trip. (It is said that the second airplane was on standby or for carrying their luggage.) Even Marcos's loyal military aide was dismayed at the extent of her shopping: Imelda 'bought irrationally—expensive jewelry, clothes, bags, shoes, till one wondered how much she needed to buy to be happy'.[17] Furthermore, she spent hundreds of millions of dollars on such building projects as the Cultural Center, International Film Center, and Heart Center. These were not a waste of money like her shopping sprees, but they were low-priority projects which were carried out only at her fancy.[18]

For some reason, Marcos could barely control Imelda. It is said that he agreed to let her do as she pleased in exchange for her co-operation with him after his love affair with an American actress came into the open, embarrassing her deeply. As his health deteriorated, his control of Imelda became increasingly difficult. The same lack of control was true of his cronies. Initially, they acted on his approval, but as he weakened bodily, he paid less and less attention to their activities, often losing control of them altogether. But it was Marcos himself who was responsible for the unparalleled extent of corruption in Philippine political history. He would do anything, it seems, to remain in power. After the assassination of Senator Benigno Aquino in August 1983, the economy went into a tailspin, and a large majority of people lost faith in his government, but he clung on. The Aquino government was partly responsible for the economic ills of the second half of the 1980s and the early 1990s, but basically the problems were of Marcos's creation. The economy was heavily indebted to foreign countries (to an amount of about $28 billion) because of his government's corruption, and the country became divided because of his misrule.

Democracy was restored amid great expectations in February 1986 when Marcos fled the country and Aquino became President. In February 1987, a new Constitution was ratified, and national elections for the Senate and the House of Representatives were held a few months later. Almost 15 years after Marcos dissolved Congress, it was reopened as an independent branch of government. But as the economy stagnated, people began blaming the politicians. A prominent Filipino newspaper columnist, after pointing out that democracy rarely works in Third World countries, made a scathing remark on the Philippine Congress:

> In the Philippines, Congress is Vaudeville Inc., its denizens more attuned to the television camera and the photographer's flash bulb than they are to the needs of the nation. None among them has been able to raise above the herd to catch, inspire and illumine the people's imagination. What is worse is that many of them are crooks, and thus the infinite pleasure one derives in calling them *trapos* [traditional politicians, or rugs in Tagalog].[19]

The Military and Thai Government

The Thai government during the 40-year period (1952–1991) under study in this book was dominated by the military, although the latter have begun sharing power with politicians since the early 1980s. In the 1950s, the Phibul Songkram government kept Parliament open. Belonging to the Revolutionary Group of 1932, one of whose promises was to install democracy in the country, Phibul may have found it psychologically difficult to abolish Parliament (he did not give it much power either), but the real reason may have been that since he did not enjoy strong support in the military, he wanted to manipulate Parliament to his advantage. Sarit got rid of it after the 1957 *coup d'état*. Coming from a new generation of leaders, he was not bound by the promises of the Revolutionary group; and since he controlled the military, he did not need Parliament in the way Phibul had. It remained closed for a little over a decade. In early 1969, the Thanom Kittikachorn–Prapart Charustien government reopened it, but during this brief period, it did not have much power. After about two and a half years, it was abolished again.

The student-led revolt in 1973 ushered Thailand into full democracy in the mid-1970s, but Parliament was closed again in October 1976. A national election was held in April 1979 under a new Constitution, and Parliament was reopened. This time, it remained open almost 12 years until February 1991 when another military *coup* abolished it. In the 1980s, however, politicians gained influence, and for about two and a half years from mid-1988, the government was led by an elected prime minister (Chatichai Chunhawan). During the 40-year period, twice, for a total of about 4 years, the government was administered by elected prime ministers, but the time span was too short for democratic forces to substantially change the authoritarian structure of Thai government.

The military ran the government without a Parliament for almost 15 years, without giving much power to Parliament for another 8 years, by delegating considerable authority to a civilian prime minister they appointed for about 1 year (the Anand Panyarachun government in 1991), and shared power with politicians for about 9 years, keeping the position of prime minister for their leaders (Kriangsak Chomanan and Prem Tinsulanonda). Even during the period of elected prime ministers, the military kept the portfolios of defence and the interior (which supervise provincial governors and the Police Department). Despite the dominant position of the military, the Thai government was more effective than Philippine democracy—in promoting economic growth. It therefore cannot be argued that because authoritarian government does not work in one country (for example, the Philippines), it is bound to fail elsewhere.

Thai authoritarian government worked better than Philippine democracy, because Thailand had certain groups of people who had proprietary interests in making the government work. The Philippine tragedy was that there were no such groups. A political party can be such an institution vested with these interests, but in the Philippines, it was a collection of people primarily interested in private gain (reflected in their deeds). The Catholic Church is not a political institution, and became involved in Philippine politics only in critical times. The Philippines was like a large public corporation whose ownership was widely spread and which did not have major stockholders watching over its management to safeguard stockholders' interests.

In Thailand, a kind of ruling class tradition prevailed. During the period of absolute monarchy, government officials (*kha ratchakan*) were, as the servants of the king, feared and respected by the people. Many bright people, if they chose not to join the military, became *kha ratchakan*. They probably often used their positions for private gain, but many of those who did well in the bureaucracy were conferred such titles as *Chao Phya* and *Phya* and rewarded financially as well, and developed pride in government service. To them, it was a noble career above peasants and traders, and this view was also accepted by society.[20] Many of their children became *kha ratchakan*, and the tradition of government service continued among these upper and upper-middle class families. Thailand was not, of course, an ascribed society, but these families could give better education to their children, and could provide them with the necessary connections and material support if they decided to enter government service. As they wanted to hand down this tradition of government service to posterity, they could not unscrupulously use their positions for private gain, and since the families gave them some support, they did not have to do so. This factor helped to reduce the level of corruption, and they focused their attention on the good of the nation. In the Anand government of 1991, Anand Panyarachun (Prime Minister), Nukul Prachuabmoh (Minister of Transport and Communications), and Suthee Singhasaneh (Minister of Finance), three highly respected former government officials (Anand from the Ministry of Foreign Affairs and the other two from the Ministry of Finance), came from families which had distinguished themselves in government service over the past century.[21]

Contrary to what their critics say, the military conscientiously acted in the national interest, especially in the task of sustaining growth over time. However, they also used their power for their personal interests. It was alleged that they were involved in drug trafficking, received kickbacks from the private contractors of arms, received high salaries and stipends by serving as corporate directors while on active service or after retirement, used the government budget for private gain, and used the government corporations they controlled for the profit of their (or their families') businesses. (For example, it is said that Class 5—the fifth batch to graduate from Chulachomklao to which General Suchinda Kraprayoon belongs, had a construction company which undertook military contracts.)[22] One foreign military analyst said, 'The Thai armed forces at the top are not here to defend the country, they are here to do business, to make money.'[23] Numerous other charges have also been hurled against them.

Nevertheless, the military has also produced such political leaders as Sarit and Prem. Sarit is widely credited as the initiator of the country's sustained economic growth.[24] It was during his administration that the government decided to withdraw from the industrial sector by reversing the previous government's policy; the central bank was strengthened to nurture the development of modern commercial banking; the Board of Investment was created to promote investment (particularly foreign investment) in new industries; and the National Economic Development Board was created and the first Development Plan (1961–6) implemented. As for General Prem, he filled key economic ministries and government agencies with technocrats and relied on them in overcoming the second oil crisis in the early 1980s, and in carrying out the economic restructuring which led to export-led growth in the second half of the decade. Even pro-democracy people would probably admit that Prem was a respectable Prime Minister.

One feature which differentiated the military domination of government in Thailand from that in Indonesia is the fact that it was the military institution as a whole, not a single person, which dominated the government. Furthermore, the Thai military has a better tradition than their counterparts in most developing countries where the history of the military is short. The history of the Thai military may be traced back to 1892 when the Ministry of War was created. Military men themselves regard as their predecessors such warrior kings as Borommaracha II, who captured the Khmer capital in the mid-fifteenth century, or King Naresuan, who defended the kingdom from the Burmese in the mid-sixteenth century. After the end of absolute monarchy, they regarded themselves as guardians of the country, executing that responsibility for their predecessors who had sacrificed themselves for their country as well as for posterity. This is what they were taught, and it was this ideal of the military (that their loyalty was to the country) which exerted moral pressure on military leaders to perform, whether in government or in the military.

It is said that there is nepotism in the application of criteria in entrance to the Chulachomklao Military Academy; for instance, the sons of generals are said to be admitted on a preferential basis. But most students have entered the academy on the basis of merit, with the academy attracting the best and the brightest of the country. After graduation, those who pass out in the same year form a clique and help each other up the military hierarchy. They are competent, ambitious, and disciplined. They can easily stand up to their superiors for not sticking to the norm of the military; the Young Turks are an example. Unlike the Philippine military during the Marcos period, there are only a few generals who have stayed beyond their retirement age (and that only for a year) in Thailand's post-war history. (In the Philippines, there were over 20 generals who overstayed at one time during martial law, blocking the promotion of younger officers and thus demoralizing them.)[25] Practically all Thai generals retire at the age of 60, and some even before that to pave the way for the earlier promotion of their juniors. The Thai military is an autonomous body which politicians cannot touch, and all its generals are Chulachomklao graduates who move up the seniority-based hierarchy step by step, unlike the Philippines where Marcos could promote his soldier-chauffeur, who was not even a graduate of the Philippine Military Academy, to Chief of Staff.

The monarchy was another constraint on the Thai military. The job of the military is soldiering; in theory, the military should not run the country. During his government, Phibul had the military-supported parties invite him to become Prime Minister. But after the *coup d'état* in 1957, which abolished Parliament, the military needed a new form of legitimacy. They sought this in the king. (At that time, King Bhumibol was about 30 years old. Although he had returned from his studies in Switzerland several years earlier, he was left on the sidelines by Phibul.) The military (specifically, Sarit) brought the king back to the centre stage of Thai politics. They made it appear that they had obtained the mandate to run the government from the king. Under this political scheme, sovereignty was returned to the king (or if sovereignty was still with the people, the king represented the people's will), but not power. Young and inexperienced, King Bhumibol did not have a say about the matter at this time. Sarit ran the government for the next several years in the way he wanted.

Over time, King Bhumibol has become an increasingly important constraint on the military, primarily because he is intelligent, morally righteous, and dedicated to the good of the nation. Anti-monarchists claim that this is the image created by government propaganda, but it is the perception of a large majority of people who respect the king, and not just because he is king. People can be critical about the royal family, as judged from criticisms privately expressed not only in Bangkok but also in the provinces about some members of the family. (If a person expresses such criticisms publicly, he will be charged with lese-majesty). Furthermore, over time, the King became experienced in politics. In this, he was assisted by the Privy Council which consists of respected former government officials. Increasing numbers of people began looking up to him as the symbol of national conscience and unity. As a result, he became a moral force the military could not ignore.

From the King's perspective, Thailand is the country rebuilt by his great-great-great-grandfather (Rama I) after the destruction of Ayutthaya by the Burmese; it was his great-grandfather who opened up the country to foreign trade and put the country on the course of modernization; it was his grandfather who reformed the government and saved the country from Western colonization; and his father, although he never became king, went abroad to study medicine so that he could serve the people. During the period of absolute monarchy, the country was the king's country. Although the present King does not enjoy the same right, he nevertheless contributes to the good of the nation so that the dynasty will be perpetuated. This is his obligation to his predecessors; therefore, he cannot let the military mismanage the country.

Under these constraints, the military shared power with civilian bureaucrats when they had absolute control, and protected them when they shared power with politicians during the period of 'half-way democracy' in the 1980s. Prime Minister Anand called this an 'unholy alliance'.[26] From the late 1950s to the early 1970s when the military had absolute control, most Cabinets had only a few military men. The Sarit Cabinet had only 4 against 10 civilian bureaucrats. The first Thanom Cabinet (December 1963–March 1968) had 5 military men and 13 civilian bureaucrats. It was only in the last Thanom Cabinet (December 1972–October 1973) that military men outnumbered civilian bureaucrats,[27] and only a few ministers came from the private sector in that period. In the brief full democracy period in the mid-1970s, the situation was reversed: civilians outnumbered bureaucrats in the Cabinets. In the period of half-way democracy, this new trend continued, but Prime Minister Prem kept such key economic portfolios as finance for civilian bureaucrats until towards the end of the period.

The Military and Thai Technocrats

Since the mid-1970s, as the military lost absolute power with the advent of democratic forces, economic technocrats have been facing problems in maintaining conservative monetary and fiscal policy. Politicians such as Kukrit Pramoj wanted to make bus fares free for low-income people, increase the minimum wage by more than 50 per cent, and give away money to the rural sector. Another politician wanted to expand the service of the public utilities sector by keeping prices low while borrowing money from abroad for expansion. Many politicians wanted to increase government spending, especially on infrastructure, so that they could claim credit for it in their constituencies and get some kickbacks from their contractors, which was needed for their next campaign. Not all these demands could be fended off. The government borrowed from abroad to finance infrastructural development, but around 1982, under Prime Minister Prem, as the government's foreign debt became alarming (it increased from $623 million to $6,865 million between 1975 and 1983), economic technocrats argued strongly for a return to conservative monetary and fiscal policy, and succeeded in curbing the debt increase.[28]

Puey Ungphakorn, who served as Governor of the Bank of Thailand from June 1959 to August 1971 and is widely regarded as the father of modern banking, was brought into the government by Sarit and given the power and his support to make the Bank of Thailand a strong institution. Puey needed Sarit's support for a commercial banking law which would empower the central bank to take measures against traditional commercial banks. A few months after Sarit passed away, Puey told Thai bankers: 'His Excellency [Sarit] had nursed and led our present Commercial Banking Law [of 1962] successfully through its various stages. The merits of the present law are due in no small measure to his sympathy and efforts.'[29] After Sarit's death, Puey depended on his successor, Field Marshal Thanom, for support:

> The Prime Minister who had given me the most kindness during my work had been Field Marshal Thanom Kittikachorn. In addition to being in the same class

as leader [*sic*] in the National Defense College he also gave [me] much trust. While he was Deputy Prime Minister he often spoke up for me and if there was an important piece of work from the Cabinet he usually proposed my name.

Personal relations between him and myself were very close.[30]

Puey later became Rector of Thammasat University, which was founded by the liberal political leader Pridi Banomyong in 1933, and which since the early 1970s has become known for pro-democracy movements. Partly because of his new position, Puey became a severe critic of the military, and fled the country shortly after the military *coup* of 1976. Because of his support for the students, many of whom were leftists and later joined the Communist Party, he was accused of being a Communist. In the 1960s, however, he was a key technocrat who collaborated with the military in putting the economy on a growth trajectory. Soon after Thanom became Prime Minister, Puey said, 'Field Marshal Thanom Kittikachorn, our present Prime Minister ... is famous for his honesty and integrity.'[31] This is the Prime Minister the students accused of rampant corruption (a charge they also hurled against Prapart and Narong) and dragged down from power in October 1973.

Puey became a liberal after he left the government, but he was a conservative economic technocrat during his term in government. Other key economic technocrats who worked with the military were also generally conservative. The government agencies which kept spending in check, limited borrowing from abroad, and argued for the market economy were the Ministry of Finance, the Bank of Thailand, the National Economic and Social Development Board (NESDB), and the Budget Bureau. The heads of these agencies thought alike partly because there was some exchange of top personnel between them (for example, Puey at one time headed the Budget Bureau; Snoh Unakul was brought by Puey from the NESDB to the Bank of Thailand, became its Governor, and later returned to the NESDB). They were also insulated from political pressure. The Bank of Thailand is an independent agency, but the Ministry of Finance has some jurisdiction over it. The NESDB and the Budget Bureau are directly under the control of the Prime Minister. Conservative monetary and fiscal policy could be maintained (or at least could not be torpedoed) as long as politicians were barred from the positions of prime minister and finance minister. In the 40-year period (1952–1991) under study in this book, it was only for about one and a half years in the mid-1970s and two and a half years from the late 1980s to early 1990s that politicians took over both positions. Given the bureaucratic tradition, these were too short for politicians to subjugate the bureaucratic structure which maintained conservative monetary and fiscal policy.

The question that remains is why the economic technocrats who gained the support of the military were conservative. Practically all of them had studied abroad, and were exposed to socialistic ideas, Keynesian economics (which encouraged government spending for growth), and the concept of big push industrialization under government sponsorship. The 1950s were the decade when governments were encouraged to play an active role in the economy. This trend of economic thought afflicted the Philippines, but not Thailand because some of these ideas (for example, government-sponsored industrialization) were tried unsuccessfully by the Phibul government in the 1950s; they were a drain on the Treasury. Economic technocrats like Puey argued for government withdrawal from the economy partly because of this failure. But a more important reason lay with the Ministry of Finance: its conservative tradition and its strength among economic ministries.

In retrospect, it can be said that Thai kings knew how to run a government, whose three most important tasks were to defend the country, control the people, and tax them to finance these tasks. The Ministry of War (later changed to Defense) was in charge of the first task; the Ministry of the Interior, the second; and the Ministry of Finance, the third. These three key ministries attracted the best Thais (who could not venture into the economy because it was controlled by the Chinese). Many of the best Thai graduates of the Faculties of Economics and Commerce in Thammasat and Chulalongkorn Universities proceeded to the Ministry of Finance. Then, a number of them were sent abroad by the government for further studies. On their return, they did not dare to try the newfangled ideas which were gaining currency in the West at that time. Socialistic ideas were out of the question if they wanted to be promoted in the ministry, for, if they tried advocating these ideas, they could be easily accused of being Socialists or Communists.

In 1933, the prominent lawyer-turned-politician Pridi Banomyong was accused of being a Communist after he published a plan calling for extensive socio-economic reform. He had to leave the country until the situation cooled down. When he returned, he regained power, but in the early post-war years, he was accused of regicide—Rama VIII, the present king's elder brother, was found dead under mysterious circumstances when Pridi was Prime Minister—and eventually left for the People's Republic of China. He later moved to France and died there, but his first country of exile gave his critics further 'evidence' to argue that he was really a Communist.

Even moderate new ideas were resisted by the Ministry of Finance which had been under the strong influence of British Financial Advisers until the early post-war years. In the pre-war period, the paramount task of the ministry was to raise enough tax revenue so that the government did not have to borrow from abroad, as this might give lending countries the pretext to intervene in Thailand's internal affairs, and in the worst-case scenario, bring it under their control, especially if the money borrowed could not be returned. A budget surplus was an ideal, but if this was not possible, at least the budget should balance—what British Financial Advisers taught the Thais—and this became an established tradition of the Ministry of Finance. This policy changed somewhat in the post-war period (for example, borrowing sometimes for infrastructural development), but remained relatively conservative. Young officials who returned to the ministry after several years of study abroad fitted themselves to this tradition, and made themselves acceptable to their senior officials who determined their promotion.

Given a corruption-prone government and a shortage of educated manpower, conservative economic policy turned out to be a blessing to Thailand.[32] In the Philippines also, there was such a tradition, but it was maintained by the colonial administration. Given the nationalistic rhetoric during the independence movement, politicians could not but argue that the government, not the market, was a solution to under-development. For example, President Manuel Quezon said,

> We look upon our government as the fountain source of living to which we are reluctant to give anything, but from which we expect every bounty and help.[33]
>
> We don't believe in the economic philosophy of 'laissez faire.' We favor government leadership in production activities. We believe in planning the national economy. The world has learned at a cost of untold economic waste and human suffering ... that governments cannot allow unlimited free enterprise without jeopardizing the public welfare in the interest of human greed.[34]

In the Philippines, post-war politicians, supported by this sort of rhetoric, gradually undermined the pre-war traditions of sound macro-economic management. The situation was not too bad until the mid-1960s: for example, corrupt presidents were voted out when they ran for re-election; in fact, there were no presidents who served two full four-year terms. The moral standards of politicians were, however, definitely on the decline. The decay of democracy culminated in Marcos's assumption of the presidency in 1966 and his declaration of martial law in 1972. Under martial law, the state was treated like his personal property. But unlike Chakri kings who 'owned' Thailand, Marcos was a parvenu and did not have legitimacy for his dictatorship. To make up for this lack, he created a loyalist group consisting of military officers, government officials, crony capitalists, and local leaders; there were hundreds of them, if not thousands. In exchange for their support, he let them loose on the spoils of his office. Many politicians have harmed the economy by using the government to advance their own or their allies' interests, but none comes close to Marcos, who, while 'serving' as President for almost 20 years, plundered the country. Contrary to what Quezon said, it was government leaders who 'jeopardized the public welfare', not the 'human greed' manifested in the market economy. It is only in recent times that more and more people have begun realizing how costly a mistake the country had made.

1. Charles Tilly, 'War Making and State Making as Organized Crime', in Peter Evans et al. (eds.), *Bringing the State Back In*, Cambridge: Cambridge University Press, 1985.

2. There are numerous writings on the corruption of Thai governments. See, for example, Clark D. Neher, 'Political Corruption in a Thai Province', *Journal of Developing Areas*, July 1977.

3. Sarit's total assets are often quoted to have been around $130 million to $150 million. For example, see Fred W. Riggs, *Thailand: The Modernization of a Bureaucratic*

Polity, Honolulu: East–West Center Press, 1966, p. 245. The amount for the 'three tyrants' is from Neher, 'Political Corruption in a Thai Province'.

4. Lewis E. Gleeck, *President Marcos and the Philippine Political Culture*, Manila: Author, 1987, p. 273.

5. *International Herald Tribune*, 18 and 19 January 1992.

6. Max Soliven's column in the *Philippine Star*, 22 February 1991.

7. Quoted in Benjamin A. Batson (comp. and ed.), *Siam's Political Future: Documents from the End of the Absolute Monarchy*, Data Paper No. 96, Southeast Asian Program, Ithaca: Cornell University, July 1974, p. 27. Of course, Sayre was not the first to argue that it requires an intelligent electorate for democracy to work; this has been argued since the time of Plato.

8. Francis B. Sayre, *Glad Adventure*, New York: Macmillan Co., 1957, p. 198.

9. *Bangkok Post*, 10 March 1959. Quoted in Frank Darling, 'Marshal Sarit and Absolutist Rule in Thailand', *Pacific Affairs*, December 1960: 356–7.

10. Vilas Manivat (comp.), *M. R. Kukrit Pramoj: His Wit and Wisdom, Writings, Speeches and Interviews*, Bangkok: Editions Duang Kamol, 1983, pp. 131–2.

11. *Bangkok Post Weekly Review*, 6 March 1992.

12. Somsakdi Xuto (ed.), *Government and Politics of Thailand*, Singapore: Oxford University Press, 1987, p. 135.

13. Jose P. Laurel, *Forces That Make a Nation Great*, Manila: Bureau of Printing, 1944, p. 103.

14. Quoted in Caridad C. Semana, 'Some Political Aspects of Philippine Economic Development after Independence', Ph.D. thesis, Harvard University, 1965, p. 185.

15. Quoted in David Joel Steinberg, *The Philippines: A Singular and a Plural Place*, Boulder: Westview Press, 1990, p. 3.

16. Quoted in Semana, 'Some Political Aspects of Philippine Economic Development', pp. 179–80.

17. Arturo Aruiza, *Ferdinand E. Marcos: Malacanang to Makiki*, Quezon City: ACAruiza Enterprises, 1991, p. 281.

18. For more details, see Primitivo Mijares, *The Conjugal Dictatorship of Ferdinand and Imelda Marcos I*, San Francisco: Union Square Publications, 1986; and Ricardo Manapat, *Some Are Smarter Than Others: The History of Marcos' Crony Capitalism*, New York: Aletheia Publications, 1991.

19. Teodoro Benigno, *Here Is the Score*, Manila: Philippines Today Inc., 1990, p. 446.

20. Until relatively recently, businessmen were complaining that government officials looked down on them as 'aliens' (*khon taeng daw*).

21. *Far Eastern Economic Review*, 19 December 1991.

22. Elliott Kulick and Dick Wilson, *Thailand's Turn: Profile of a New Dragon*, London: Macmillan, 1992, p. 24.

23. *Far Eastern Economic Review*, 19 December 1991.

24. From 1951 to 1958 (during the Phibul period), the GNP grew at 4.7 per cent per year, but the growth rate accelerated to 8.6 per cent from 1959 to 1968 (James Ingram, *Economic Change in Thailand, 1850–1970*, Stanford: Stanford University Press, 1971, p. 223).

25. Aruiza, *Ferdinand E. Marcos*, pp. 41–2.

26. *Far Eastern Economic Review*, 19 December 1991.

27. Likhit Dhiravegin, *Thai Politics: Selected Aspects of Development and Change*, Bangkok: Tri-Sciences Publishing House, 1985, p. 238.

28. The figures for the government's external debt are taken from Supote Chunanuntathum et al., 'Trade and Financing Strategies for Thailand in the 1980s', Paper presented at the Seminar on New International Economic Order, Faculty of Economics, Thammasat University, 1986. The main borrowers were the Electricity Generating Authority of Thailand (the largest borrower), the Telephone Organization of Thailand, the Provincial Electricity Authority, the Metropolitan Waterworks Authority, and the State Railway of Thailand.

29. Puey's speech at the Annual Dinner of the Thai Bankers Association on 20 February 1964. *Sunthonraphot, Bothbaht, la Lhamkhwahn doi Dr Puey Ungphakorn*

[Speeches, Articles, and Congratulatory Messages by Dr Puey Ungphakorn], Bangkok: Bank of Thailand, 1964, p. 77.

30. *A Siamese for All Seasons: Collected Articles by and about Puey Ungphakorn*, Bangkok: Kamol Keemthong Foundation, 1981, p. 316.

31. *Sunthonraphot, Bothbaht, la Lhamkhwahn*, p. 77.

32. One might think that an authoritarian government is a strong government, but it is not necessarily so. One Thai scholar argues that strong government (in the sense of a government which seriously attacks accumulated national problems) has been rare in Thailand. Somsakdi, *Government and Politics of Thailand*, p. 204.

33. Quoted in Semana, 'Some Political Aspects of Philippine Economic Development', p. 337.

34. Quoted in Onofre D. Corpuz, *The Bureaucracy in the Philippines*, Quezon City: Institute of Public Administration, University of the Philippines, 1957, p. 219.

PART III
PEACE AND ORDER

12
Winning the War against the Communists in Thailand

THE Communist Party of Thailand (CPT) was probably at its peak strength in the late 1970s when, according to government sources, its military arm, the People's Liberation Army of Thailand (established in early 1969), was 13,000 strong. At that time also,[1] 36 provinces (out of 72) were declared infiltrated provinces including almost the whole North-east, South, and West, and all those bordering Laos. Altogether, 4,000–5,000 villages were said to be controlled by Communist insurgents.[2] If these claims were true, they then controlled 8–10 per cent of total villages in Thailand, and its armed strength was about half the size of the New People's Army (NPA) in the Philippines at its peak. In the late 1970s, many leftists undoubtedly believed that the 1980s would be a truly revolutionary decade.[3]

The Decline of the Communist Insurgency

In the early 1980s, however, the strength of the CPT fizzled out. It is said that one reason for this development was the amnesty policy of the Prem Tinsulanonda government. A little earlier, the Kriangsak Chomanan government had made an offer of amnesty to students, intellectuals, and others who had joined the insurgents, either in protest against or to flee persecution under the new government installed after the October 1976 *coup*. In the early 1980s, the Prem government offered an amnesty to all insurgents who were willing to lay down arms and renounce Communism. Of those who joined the insurgents in 1976, only a few hundred had accepted Kriangsak's amnesty offer, but a greater number (probably a few thousand) took up Prem's offer. In addition, numerous insurgents who had joined the CPT for different reasons surrendered. For example, in December 1982, more than 3,000 CPT members and sympathizers in Tak Province surrendered *en masse*.[4]

Another reason for the decline is said to have been the spillover effect on the CPT from the newly arisen Sino-Vietnamese conflict. In the late 1970s, the Pathet Lao was under the influence of Vietnam, whereas the Khmer Rouge was allied with China. In December 1978, Vietnam invaded Cambodia and threw out the Khmer Rouge. In retaliation, China invaded Vietnam in 1979. This series of events posed a dilemma to the CPT; it had depended heavily on China, Vietnam, and the Pathet Lao for financial, material, and moral support. Most CPT leaders were of Chinese ancestry, many of them were trained in China, and were pro-China. Even after China's invasion of Vietnam, they did not change their pro-China stance. Consequently, the Pathet Lao told the CPT to close its sanctuaries in Laos, thus necessitating the relocation of training schools, hospitals, supply stockpiles, and personnel from there. The supply line from China running through Laos was also cut.[5]

These two factors must have undoubtedly contributed to the decline of the CPT, which is today a very weak force with some remnants still fighting in remote areas. In retrospect, one wonders how real the strength of the CPT in the late 1970s was. In the 1960s and early 1970s, at least, the Thai government used the insurgency as a pretext for increased aid from the United States. It was also a useful pretext for repressive policies. For all the threats which were said to exist, the damage done to the economy as a result was small. The Communist threat was also inflated by the anxiety generated by a combination of the withdrawal of American troops and the Communist victory in Indo-China in 1975. Thailand had been serving as a major base for American air operations over Vietnam, and the closing of American bases in 1976, which the military opposed, caused a sense of crisis. Thailand feared that the Vietnamese Communists might, after toppling the governments of South Vietnam, Laos, and Cambodia, retaliate against it, the collaborator of American 'imperialists'.

The fall of Saigon and the closing of American bases affected the confidence of the business community in Bangkok. The black market exchange rate became B30 per dollar at a time when the official rate was B20 per dollar. There were a number of businessmen buying $100 notes and airplane tickets, with passports ready, so that they could leave the country at a moment's notice. People jokingly said, though with some sense of realism, that with a good highway from the border with Cambodia, it would not take long for the Vietnamese to reach Bangkok. Some Thai businessmen were also taking money out of the country (by manipulating trade invoices or other means). But the sense of crisis in the business community soon subsided, and the spread between the official and black market rates became small again.

The CPT itself, however, did not affect the business environment or the rural economy much. Unlike in the Philippines, there were no Communist-infiltrated radical trade unions calling for national strikes or making strong demands on management, causing businesses to close (except for a few years in the mid-1970s when some radical unions emerged in the aftermath of the collapse of the Thanom–Prapart government). Nor were there urban guerrillas exploding bombs in major establishments or kidnapping businessmen for ransom. Even in the rural sector where the CPT concentrated its activities after the mid-1960s, no major infrastructural projects were stalled by Communist insurgents, no power lines to mines or factories cut, and no crops and machinery destroyed because of refusal to pay their 'taxes'. Agricultural diversification into maize, cassava, pineapples, sugar, etc. went on without disruption from the insurgents. At least there are practically no reports of such incidents. In the villages under the control of insurgents, their production was obviously affected, but they were located in remote areas, and primarily engaged in subsistence agriculture.

Why did Thailand not become another domino which toppled like its Indo-Chinese neighbours before the Communist onslaught? It had also withstood the attempts of France to colonize it or a large part of its territory (especially the North-east) and those of other powers, bespeaking its ability to withstand the spread of Communism in the region in the modern era. In its endeavour to maintain independence, it strengthened the structure of the state, especially the military and police forces.

Thai Strength in Meeting the Communist Challenge

In the post-war period, the first threat of Communism came from Chinese youths who, influenced by events in mainland China, tried to infiltrate various Chinese organizations in the hope of using them to further their cause. But the Thai government acted swiftly and decisively against them. In 1949, the government restricted Chinese immigration to less than 200 per year. Then in 1952, the government outlawed Communism. (In 1946, to please the Soviet Union and thus gain admission to the United Nations, the Thai government repealed the Anti-Communist Act of 1933.) In the same year, the government increased the alien residence tax from B20 to B400 per year, an action which aroused a great deal of resentment among the Chinese. The Communists tried to take advantage of the situation by organizing a demonstration against the government.[6] The Police Chief, General Phao Siryanon, who commanded 50,000 militarized policemen, did not allow it to go on.

Around the same time, Phao also ordered the arrest and deportation of seven prominent Chinese merchants for opium smuggling and Communist racketeering. There was no avenue of appeal open to them, though they may not have had anything to do with Communism. To extort money from the Chinese, the police often threatened to charge them with being Communist or having such tendencies. But in demonstrating its power to arrest and deport even influential merchants, the government showed clearly to the Communists who was in command of the country. Hundreds of Chinese were arrested as 'Communists' (many were merely Chinese 'chauvinists'). Faced with the tough anti-Chinese chauvinist and anti-Communist stand of the government, many Chinese youths (most were possibly Communist-leaning) left for China.

The Communists needed sympathizers for their cause, but in this the government also made it difficult for them. No courses on Communism were taught in universities, nor were books on Communism available in bookstores, before October 1973. Until around this time, there were no student organizations which arranged activities under the command of the CPT or which acted as its recruiting agents, and trade unions were banned in most years. Leftist writers were imprisoned, and their books banned. For example, the socialist author Kularb Saipradit was arrested by the Phibul Songkram government around early 1953, and never allowed to write again in Thailand. During the Sarit Thanarat period, he requested and was granted political asylum in Peking. The Phibul government was harsh towards Communists, but in keeping Parliament open, it gave some breathing space to socialist politicians. Those from the North-east tended to be left-leaning and anti-government, because of separatist tendencies and possibly because of the influence of the Pathet Lao. After the *coup* in 1957 which abolished Parliament, Sarit arrested a number of them, and even executed some (for example, Krong Chantawong).

In the 1970s, especially after October 1973, the military and police did not enjoy 'absolute' power, but the operational space of leftist scholars and intellectuals was much more limited in Thailand than in the Philippines. To advance the cause of Communism, they had to attack Thai institutions and values, but this was effectively difficult because many of them were directly or indirectly tied to the royal institution; they were thus constrained by lese-majesty, a charge which the military, police, or Village Scouts (a civilian organization created under royal patronage to combat the Communists) often brought against them. Apart from lese-majesty, leftist intellectuals had to be careful in their utterances; Marxist scholars can now engage in scholarly analysis (though the collapse of Communist governments in Eastern Europe has caused them a great deal of embarrassment), but to incite the people to direct action can get them into trouble with the police.

After the mid-1960s when the CPT, following the Maoist strategy, moved the centre of its activity to the rural areas, and organized armed rebellion against the government, it was the military which fought the Communist insurgents. A factor in favour of the Thai military was its large force. (In the Philippines, people criticized Marcos for increasing the size of the military; in 1985, the Philippine military (including the Constabulary) had 158,000 men, which was certainly a big increase from 57,100 in 1971, a year before martial law was declared, but still smaller than that of the Thai military.) Around 1990, the Thai military commanded over 280,000 troops.[7] Out of this total, about 190,000 were in the Army, which was directly responsible for fighting Communist (and Muslim) insurgents. (In contrast, the Philippine Army numbered about 67,000 in 1990, with little change in size during the Aquino administration.)[8] Probably because of the Communist threat from Indo-China and the dominance of the military in Thai politics, the Thai Army could get a budget allocation sufficient to maintain such a large force. It was a waste of money if it was not needed, but undoubtedly, in counter-insurgency operations, it was a helpful factor.

The Thai military also had a reputation for better discipline than the Philippine military. There were no reports on the defection of military officers to the side of insurgents, or the sale of arms to insurgents by soldiers—problems which plagued the Philippine military. The Thai military may have killed villagers or burnt their houses and crops in mistaking them to be Communists or their supporters; in counter-insurgency operations, such incidents are bound to take place. In January 1974, the Thai military moved into a village called Ban Na Sai in Nong Khai Province in the North-east, burnt down the village, and killed a number of villagers. It was reported that the military took this action because the village had been Communist-infested. A student leader, Thirayut Boonmi, investigated the incident and claimed that the military had made a mistake. The military then conducted their own investigation but found that no mistakes had been made.[9] It is not clear which side is right.

It is a little amazing, however, that few military abuses have been reported. There are no reports of soldiers raping village girls, extorting money and food from villagers, or getting drunk and killing villagers—incidents often reported in the Philippines, prompting many villagers to join the insurgents. The mass media were better controlled in Thailand. All radio and television stations were under the control of the government or the military, but the print media were not. One might counter that since their licences could be arbitrarily revoked, the print media had to be careful about what they print. But military operations were reported, and if there were frequent abuses of military power, they would have leaked out. Thailand was not such a heavily censored country; there were enough leftist journalists, intellectuals, and scholars venturing into the provinces who would have written on such matters if they had heard them. The fact is there are few reports or writings touching on this issue. Military abuse is unlikely to have been a factor which strengthened the cause of insurgents in Thailand, as it did in the Philippines.

Rural Development

The Thai civil bureaucracy also had a role to play in reducing the Communist threat. The living conditions of the rural areas had to be improved in order to prevent people from joining the insurgents out of poverty. In the North-east where Communist insurgents were the most serious problem, the first major task the government undertook was road building, which began with US assistance in the 1950s. The United States—which eventually built four airbases in the North-east: Udon Thani, Nakhon Phanom, Korat (Nakhon Ratchasima), and Ubon Ratchathani—assisted Thailand in building highways connecting Bangkok and the North-east. The highway between Korat and Nong Khai, called Friendship Highway, was the major one built with US assistance. With its completion in the mid-1960s, Bangkok was connected to Nong Khai on the Mekong River opposite Vientiane by all-weather roads. In the early 1960s, the initiative for road building was taken over by the Thai government, and the road network in the region continued to improve. After the Friendship Highway was completed, the highways between Ubon Ratchathani and Khon Kaen (on the Friendship

Highway) via Roi Et, between Khon Kaen and Nakhon Phanom through Kalasin, between Udon Thani (on the Friendship Highway) and Nakhon Phanom, and between Nakhon Phanom and Ubon Ratchathani were built by the early 1970s, and the highway between Korat and Ubon Ratchathani was almost complete. This road network in the region was further developed in the following two decades with more highways and feeder roads.

This road network made villages in the North-east less isolated, and made it easier for the military to move into areas where Communist insurgents were active. Besides, with the progress in land transportation, it became easier for young people to move to Bangkok (and regional cities). Many were absorbed into factories, households (as maids and drivers), commercial establishments, and various informal sectors. The economy, which had been growing at a healthy rate, provided employment opportunities for the people who moved to Bangkok, and they sent part of their earnings to their parents. From the late 1950s, peasants in the region diversified into new crops, which were transported on the highways to Bangkok and other consuming and processing centres. Remittances and new sources of agricultural income changed the economic life of the North-east significantly. In the early 1970s, the people began owning motor cycles (or commercial vehicles if they were better off), television sets (radios for sure), and household electrical appliances (for example, electric fans and refrigerators). Buses plied more routes, and people became more mobile. Despite these advances, because other regions changed faster, the North-east remained the poorest in the country, but material life improved, and the grip of poverty loosened.

The development in the North-east started with Field Marshal Sarit Thanarat. His parents met during the latter years of the reign of King Rama V when his father was stationed in Nong Khai and his mother came to visit her relative there from her village near Mukdahan (an independent province today, but a district of Nakhon Phanom at that time). They married and moved to Bangkok where Sarit was born. But something must have gone wrong between the parents: Mother returned with Sarit to her village where he grew up until he was ready for schooling. After he became Prime Minister, the North-east might have occupied a special place in his mind, and probably, he wanted to do something for the region. In addition, the problem of security—the region was vulnerable to Communist propaganda from adjacent Indo-China—required the government to improve the economy there. In 1961, Sarit headed a special commission for developing the region, and a North-east Development Plan was subsequently drafted.[10]

Rural development was a slow process, and since Sarit died a few years later, he could not do much during his lifetime. But the government continued to make efforts to improve the economy of the North-east. Besides roads, the government brought electricity to the villages, which led to the introduction to radio, television, and household electrical appliances. Rural development projects were not badly administered as the Ministry of the Interior made efforts to post some of its best people there as district officers and governors. The situation was somewhat different from the provincial administration of the Philippines which was often controlled by the landed élite, who themselves were the reason for the Communist insurgency. The authoritarian nature of the Thai government made it easier to allocate public funds to a priority area such as the North-east where the Communist insurgency was growing with the support of the Pathet Lao who were criss-crossing the Mekong River dividing Thailand and Laos.

A Lower Level of Rural Discontent

An important factor which worked against the Communists was the strength of Thai traditional values and institutions. A typical village has several hundred people, an elementary school, and a Buddhist temple. It is led by a *puh yai baan* selected by the villagers; he acts as a liaison between the village and the sub-district office under a *kam naan* (who is selected by village heads in the sub-district) or the district office (the lowest line office of the Ministry of the Interior) headed by the *nai ampher*, a ministry official. The general level of education of villagers is low and they are not interested in politics, but through the school and temple, they develop a sense of pride in being Thai. This is re-enforced by the pep talks of visiting government officials and through television and radio whose stations are under the control of the military and government. (In earlier years, if the village was prosperous, movies were screened for some festive occasions.) The Communists who came to the village spoke of a social order which was quite alien to what the people had been steeped in. They also disparaged the institutions (such as the monarchy and Buddhism) the villagers hold to be good and are proud of; the people found it difficult to swallow what the Communists were telling them. The resistance to the insurgency was stronger in a village which was better exposed to the outside world.

A more fundamental reason for the resistance to Communism was the general contentment of villagers with the economic situation. In the thirteenth century, King Ramkhamheng said, 'In the water there is fish, in the fields there is rice.' This statement is often referred to as a manifestation of the country's fertility and freedom from hunger. There is a danger of this saying giving a false picture of total contentment in conflict-free rural life in Thailand, but the peasants did freely expand and exploit the land for cultivation for a long time. Based on the impression he gained during his stay in the 1920s, Francis Sayre wrote:

> Among the Siamese peasantry I found very little discontent. They tended their paddy fields and grew their rice as their fathers and grandfathers had done before them. Fundamentally they were a happy people. They accepted without question their King and his beneficent rule. Theirs not to meddle in the public affairs of their country. What took place in the government offices in Bangkok or among the princes and royal family was out of their world.[11]

The peasants were generally contented because they owned the land they cultivated. This landownership pattern was born partly because there was plenty of land. There was a vast tract of fertile land in the Chao Phraya basin, and another of flat land in the North-east belonging to the Mekong basin, with the latter being less fertile. Moreover, the population did not expand to make the man–land ratio comparable to that in other regions like Java. One reason for this may be related to the fact that not being a colony, the country was slow to introduce public health measures which would have reduced the death-rate (and thus increased the population).[12]

The main reason for the more equitable landownership is institutional. During the period of absolute monarchy, the king was referred to as *Phra Chao Paen Din* (Lord of the Land) because he, at least in theory, owned all land in the kingdom. The people could cultivate a plot of land in return for taxes paid and/or personal service rendered to the king. In this system, there was no place for the landlord class. The intermediaries between the king and peasants were the king's servants (*kha ratchakan*), whose important function was to collect taxes from the peasants. From the viewpoint of the king and his servants, it could not be tolerated if a plot of land was claimed but not cultivated, because then it did not yield taxes. It had to be cultivated by the claimant for him to enjoy the right of its use; otherwise, the right of use of the land reverted to the king.[13]

The claimant to a large tract of land could hire people to cultivate it, but Thai peasants were not familiar with the capitalist world which promotes such a scheme. The Thais who were not peasants were the king's servants, who derived their incomes solely from the government (possibly supplemented by bribes). The only people who thought about and carried out such a scheme were Chinese merchants or foreign investors. The king thought of the welfare of his peasants and ruled against the introduction of capitalistic undertakings.[14] This does not mean that the king did not grant land to those who would then rent it out. He sometimes gave land to the servants who served him well. He also granted large plots of land to the companies which dug canals in the Bangkok area, but the amount of land given out was a small portion of the total.

The king's land system was helped by the fact that the money economy had not penetrated deeply into the rural sector, which seems odd in view of the rise of export crops, especially rice, after the mid-nineteenth century when the Bowring Treaty was signed and the Thai economy was opened to foreign trade. There is no question, however, that peasants became more involved in commercial production after the mid-nineteenth century, but compared with other countries in the region which had been colonized and into which foreign capital had flowed on a large scale, the extent of Thailand's development of a money economy was more limited. In the mid-1930s, for example, Thai exports amounted to only about half those of the Philippines. A Thai economic historian argues that the economy was basically a subsistence economy:

> Thailand, before 1950, was still in the first phase of market production which may be considered as growing simply by bringing in an increasing number of peasant family [*sic*] into export production, each family producing the export crop while continuing to produce all its subsistence requirements. In con-

sequence, the Great Depression in 1931 did not have such serious effects on Thai farmers as indicated by J. M. Andrews, a Harvard professor, who conducted the rural survey in 1934. He pointed out that 'the survey found none of the general suffering and misery which have become commonplace in most other countries the world over' as the farmers 'grew [*sic*] their own food, make [the] little clothing they require, and construct their own houses with materials which can be obtained at little if any cost'.[15]

The king's land system, of course, was not ideal. Already in the pre-war period, there were tenants. According to one estimate, the tenancy rate in 1937 was 25.6 per cent in the Central region, 18.6 per cent in the North, 1.8 per cent in the North-east, 2.4 per cent in the South, and 15.7 per cent in the country as a whole.[16] In the post-war period, although the population increased at a much higher rate, the tenancy rate did not rise significantly. The Agricultural Census of 1963 showed that only 18 per cent of the peasants did not own land. Another estimate put the tenancy rate for 1976 at 20.84 per cent.[17] In spite of the problems in estimation and definition and considerable regional variation, it appears that the bulk of the peasants (over 80 per cent) had their own land to cultivate, at least until the mid-1970s. This high rate of peasant landownership was a direct consequence of the king's land system which prevented the exploitation of land with hired workers.

In Thailand, the Communists did not have the issue of land reform which the Hukbalahap and the NPA could play upon in the Philippines. In the mid-1970s, the peasants formed an association (Peasants Federation of Thailand) and took a militant stand against the landlords. But the association's focus was on land rent control, not ownership change, and its activities were centred around some areas in the North where both the tenancy rate and rent were high. The immediate reason for its decline may have been the assassination of its leaders (possibly by the people backed up, directly or indirectly, by the landlord class) and its suppression by the military-backed regime installed after the *coup* of October 1976. But if peasants' grievances had been serious, their movement could have gone underground and prospered; instead, it fizzled out. Rent given to the landlord in some areas in the North was as high as around 50 per cent of the crop, but this was probably because of high land productivity due to irrigation; peasants there were not necessarily worse off than those in other areas who paid lower rent. A general picture of the rural situation for the country as a whole showed low tenancy and moderate rent. This reduced the level of rural discontent, and thus, the appeal of Communism.

1. Ross Prizzia, *Thailand in Transition: The Role of Oppositional Forces*, Honolulu: University Press of Hawaii, 1985, p. 23.
2. Andrew Turton et al. (eds.), *Thailand: Roots of Conflict*, Nottingham: Spokesman, 1987, p. 133.
3. See ibid., p. 2, for example.
4. Prizzia, *Thailand in Transition*, pp. 23–4.

5. Kanok Wongtrangan, 'The Revolutionary Strategy of the Communist Party of Thailand: Change and Persistence', in Lim Joo-Jock (ed.), *Armed Communist Movements in Southeast Asia*, Aldershot: Gower Publishing Co., 1984, p. 136.

6. *Far Eastern Economic Review*, 23 October 1952: 529.

7. International Institute for Strategic Studies, *The Military Balance 1992–1993*, London: Brassey's, 1992, p. 162.

8. The Philippine figures come from *The Final Report of the Fact-finding Commission*, Manila: Bookmark, 1990, p. 52.

9. David Morell and Chai-Anan Samudavanija, *Thailand: Reaction and Revolution*, Cambridge: Oelgeschlager, Gunn & Hain, 1981, p. 171.

10. Thak Chaloemtiarana, *Thailand: The Politics of Despotic Paternalism*, Bangkok: Thai Khadi Institute, Thammasat University, 1979, p. 256.

11. Francis B. Sayre, *Glad Adventure*, New York: Macmillan Co., 1957, p. 89.

12. Erich Jacoby, *Agrarian Unrest in Southeast Asia*, 2nd edn., Bombay: Asia Publishing House, 1961, p. 239.

13. Vilas Manivat (comp.), *M. R. Kukrit Pramoj: His Wit and Wisdom, Writings, Speeches and Interviews*, Bangkok: Editions Duang Kamol, 1983, p. 196.

14. Benjamin A. Batson, *The End of the Absolute Monarchy in Siam*, Singapore: Oxford University Press, 1984, pp. 97–8.

15. Sompop Manarungsan, *Economic Development of Thailand, 1850–1950*, Bangkok: Institute of Asian Studies, Chulalongkorn University, 1989, p. 82.

16. James Ingram, *Economic Change in Thailand, 1850–1970*, Stanford: Stanford University Press, 1971, p. 268.

17. Andrew Turton, 'Thailand: Agrarian Bases of State Power', in Gillian Hart et al. (eds.), *Agrarian Transformation: Local Processes and the State in Southeast Asia*, Berkeley: University of California Press, 1989, p. 60.

13
Floundering in the Face of the Communists in the Philippines

AT the end of the first quarter of 1992, according to the Secretary of Defense, Renato de Villa, the New People's Army (NPA) had 13,480 armed regulars and 9,910 firearms, and had infiltrated 3,416 *barangay* (villages). The situation then was a considerable improvement over that of a few years earlier. The NPA reached its peak strength of some 25,800 regulars in 1988; had some 15,500 firearms in 1987; and had infiltrated 8,496 *barangay* (about 19 per cent of the total *barangay* in the country) by 1986.[1] The military was optimistic that it would soon win a strategic victory, but fighting was still going on in early 1992. Clashes between the two sides were often reported from the Cagayan Valley and the rugged Cordillera Mountains of northern Luzon, the Bicol region of southern Luzon (around Naga and Legaspi), the central islands of Samar and Negros, and northern and eastern Mindanao.

The Huk Insurgency

The history of Communist insurgency in the Philippines goes back to early 1942 when the Hukbalahap (Hukbong Bayan Laban sa Hapon, or People's Anti-Japanese Army) was set up. The Huks (members of the Hukbalahap) fought guerrilla wars against the Japanese Army which occupied the Philippines during the Pacific War, but they were not ordinary guerrillas. The Hukbalahap was organized as the military arm of the Communist Party (set up in 1930), which was originally urban-oriented, but in the course of its evolution, it became more involved in peasant organizations in central Luzon. In this region, the rate of land tenancy was the highest in the country, and there were numerous agricultural workers as well. Such peasant organizations as the Katipunang Pambansa ng mga Magbubukid sa Pilipinas and the Aguman Ding Maldang Talapagobra were set up to advance their cause, and their organizers later became members of the Communist Party. The ordinary peasants who joined or supported the Hukbalahap did not gain anything in particular by fighting the Japanese Army, but the Japanese invasion gave Communist leaders the legitimacy to organize a military force.

During the war, the Japanese Army and the Philippine government could not maintain peace and order in central Luzon well. The Huks sometimes killed landlords to settle old scores; thus, many fearful landlords left for Manila or nearby cities. Away from their lands, they lost bargaining power *vis-à-vis* tenants and agreed to let peasants retain a greater share of the crop. Those who remained co-operated with the Japanese garrison, but for fear of becoming the target of 'Huk justice', they could not be as harsh to peasants as before the war. The Huk insurgency in central Luzon improved the conditions of landless peasants.[2]

When the war ended, there was no more legitimacy for the Hukbalahap, and they were told to disband. But peace and order was not restored in central Luzon. Landlords wanted to re-establish the rights they possessed before the war (of which the most important was higher rent), whereas the tenants who had enjoyed better terms (of tenancy) during the war wanted to keep them. This time, landlords could count on the newly independent Philippine government and the US Army. In August 1946, Luis Taruc, the Huk leader during the war, organized the peasants who were determined to fight the landlords into the Hukbong Mapagpalaya ng Bayan (People's Army of Liberation).

Encounters between Huk and government forces intensified in the late 1940s, and wreaked havoc on various parts of central Luzon. Later, former Central Bank Governor, Miguel Cuaderno, recalled that the Huk insurgency had been a major reason for the economic deterioration of many rural areas from the late 1940s to the early 1950s.[3] At one stage, the Huks even threatened Manila. As their attacks drew closer to the capital, highway approaches were sandbagged. As a precaution, President Elpidio Quirino kept a motor launch moored at Malacanang to evacuate him and his family should the guerrillas enter Manila.[4] In view of the Communist take-over of China and a few other Asian countries at that time, the possibility of the Huks coming to power could not be entirely ruled out.

Around 1950 when insurgency was at its most virulent, there were probably about 12,000 armed Huks. Then their strength began declining, and after their commander Taruc surrendered in May 1954, Huk forces were demoralized and became seriously fragmented. A number of reasons have been offered for their decline, but the mistake in military strategy on the part of the Communists was the overestimation of the capability of their forces. In the early 1950s, the leadership of the Communist Party, over-confident and a little impatient with the prolonged struggle, went all out for a quick, decisive military victory by mobilizing large combat units for positional warfare.[5] But Huk forces were no match for the military revitalized under Ramon Magsaysay (who became Secretary of Defense in September 1950). The military mounted counter-attacks and devastated large Huk troop concentrations.

Huk forces were not, however, completely destroyed. In the late 1960s, armed Huk forces, probably numbering a few hundred, were fragmented into a few factions. They stole or extorted food and money from rich landlords and shared them with poor peasants in Robin Hood fashion; they ensured peace and order for peasants, and thus received their support in the areas of central Luzon which were neglected by the government; they ran protection rackets which thrived on gambling and prostitution in Angeles City (where the American Clark Air Force Base was located); or they simply robbed anyone who had money.

In the meantime, the Communist Party was undergoing change. In the mid-1960s, young, better-educated, and Maoist-oriented members tried to take control of its leadership, but failed and were expelled. In December 1968, one of them, Jose Maria Sison, a former student of English at the University of the Philippines, organized a new Communist Party of the Philippines (CPP). (In order to distinguish the two, the older one is often referred to by its Tagalog name, Partido Komunista ng Philippines, or PKP.) A year later, the new party attracted one of the Huk faction leaders, Bernabe Buscayno (popularly known as Kumander Dante), who founded the NPA.

Renewed Communist Insurgency

The new CPP was supported by radical, but legal, organizations (infiltrated or directed by Communists) which existed in the 1960s. They included the Kabataang Makabayan set up by Sison in late 1964 when he was with the PKP (he recruited radical student leaders at major universities in Manila as its core group); the Malayang Samahan ng Magsasaka (Democratic Union of Peasants), a militant peasant organization; the National Association of Trade Unions, a militant trade union linked to the Moscow-oriented World Federation of Trade Unions; and the Movement for the Advancement of Nationalism, formed by a group of intellectuals, politicians, and businessmen (Sison was their leader). These organizations spread Communist ideology, destabilized the political situation by mass demonstrations, and recruited new members. But the spectacular growth of the CPP and the NPA came after Marcos declared martial law in September 1972.

Like the Japanese invasion, martial law gave people the legitimacy to take up arms and fight the government. The declaration of martial law was unconstitutional in the eyes of many moderate critics. Some took the issue to the Supreme Court, but possibly influenced by the new perquisites and privileges Marcos promised, the court supported Marcos. To others (especially radicalized students), it appeared that dictatorship was declared to defend and strengthen the social structure (based on feudalism) which created massive poverty in 'cahoots' with American imperialism. They thought that the only way to fight Marcos was to join the NPA, the only organization which resorted to force to fight the Marcos government then. The NPA's strength grew from a few hundred in 1972 to several thousands by the end of the decade, and possibly exceeded 20,000 in the mid-1980s.[6] This time, the Communist insurgency spread to various parts of the country, and was not just confined to central Luzon as in the case of the Huk insurgency.

The benefits of martial law for the NPA were not, however, immediate. In fact, in the mid-1970s, it appeared that the Communist movement had been effectively contained by the government. At least in the first few years, by tightening the repression apparatus, martial law did great damage to the movement. While avoiding military operations, the CPP was quietly recruiting new members and extending its influence to new areas, such as the non-Muslim areas of Mindanao and the islands in the Visayas.[7] Then under the leadership of Rudolfo Salas, who became its head in early 1978, the CPP heightened its military activity around 1980, transferring most of its members from political to military operations. It was the first half of the 1980s which witnessed a spectacular increase in encounters with the military.[8] It coincided with the period when the Marcos regime was being weakened by economic decline and the growth of opposition among the middle class who had remained largely apolitical in the 1970s.

The NPA concentrated its forces on rural areas—true to the Maoist strategy of capturing the rural areas before strangling the cities. But it did not ignore the cities altogether; in 1982, as a trial run for its urban revolutionary tactics, the NPA began infiltrating Davao City, the country's third largest city, in southern Mindanao. From the slum area (Agdao) it had taken control of, the NPA spread its influence to other parts of the city, and around 1985, it appeared on the verge of bringing the entire city under its control. But in 1986, its influence declined rapidly.

While its operations in Davao City were going well, the NPA made Metro Manila another target of its urban revolutionary tactics. Its guerrilla units in Manila were responsible for the killing of policemen, soldiers, and government officials, the bombing of major establishments, the robbery of banks and stores, and the kidnapping of foreign businessmen. The NPA has openly admitted killing some policemen, soldiers, and government officials (saying that they have meted out 'revolutionary justice'); one famous 'execution' was the murder of General Tomas Kringal at a Quezon City beer hall in May 1984 by a Sparrows unit of the Alex Boncayao Brigade (ABB).

The NPA has not, however, taken responsibility for the other crimes attributed to them. Alfred de Leon, who was head of the Red Scorpion Group undertaking kidnappings and bank robberies, used to head the ABB, and had created the group out of the brigade. The NPA said, however, that de Leon had been expelled and that he was working for police and military generals who were the real masterminds of the criminal activities attributed to Communist urban guerrillas. The Philippine government (especially the Department of Defense), however, thought that the group was still part of the NPA, and was raising money for it in unconventional ways. Even if de Leon was not working for the NPA then, in the beginning of his kidnapping and robbery activities, he was certainly working for the NPA. Since 'revolutionary taxes' did not flow in smoothly from time to time, the NPA needed other sources of income.

In November 1986, Wakaoji Nobuyuki, general manager of the Manila branch of Mitsui & Co., a large Japanese trading company, was kidnapped. After five months of captivity, he was released on payment of a ransom reported to be $2 million. In view of the professional manner of the kidnapping and the way the payment of the ransom was handled (through a Catholic priest), it is suspected that the Red Scorpion Group was behind this kidnapping. After this incident, Japanese business executives tightened up their security arrangements. They stopped telling their Filipino employees of their schedules in advance and began changing the routes their cars would take between office and home. One Japanese trading company (not Mitsui) which rents 2 floors of office space in a building facing Ayala Avenue in Makati hired about 12 security guards in late 1991. The 2 floors were guarded 24 hours, with 2 guards per floor, and 1 at the entrance of the building. In addition, 1 was assigned to the head of the company.

Partly because they became more cautious, Japanese executives ceased to be the target of kidnapping. Another major reason was because, under diplomatic pressure, the Philippine government made more effort to solve these cases. Kidnappers then turned their attention on American executives (about 10 were kidnapped in the early 1990s). The kidnapping of Michael Barnes in January 1992 at a car park in Makati took place in broad daylight and right in the heart of the Makati financial district. He was the general manager of Philippine Geothermal, Inc. (a subsidiary of the American oil company Unocal), which operates the National Power Corp.'s geothermal plants in Laguna and Albay. Philippine Geothermal had been receiving demands from the insurgents in Laguna to pay 'revolutionary taxes', and it is believed that Barnes was kidnapped because he had refused the demand. A few months later, Philippine police rescued Barnes from the Red Scorpion Group.[9]

The Impact on the Business Environment

The Philippines is a strike-prone country because of radical trade unionism. The origin of its trade unionism can be found at the beginning of the American period. In 1930, the organizers of the Communist Party who represented the urban sector were trade union leaders. In the mid-1950s, during the Phibul Songkram period when Thailand was losing several hundred workdays due to industrial disputes (even this annoyed Sarit Thanarat, who abolished unions when he came to power a few years later), the Philippines was losing several hundred thousand workdays. Many unions were Communist-infiltrated. Those affiliated with the National Federation of Labor Unions became the core of the radical trade union formed in mid-1980, the Kilusang Mayo Uno (KMU). In a few years, the KMU became the second largest labour federation, claiming several hundred thousands in membership. The number may be an exaggeration, but it was a highly visible labour federation, organizing various demonstrations and national strikes (*welgang bayan*) in the cause of the poor (peasants, workers, and slum dwellers).

The decline of Bataan Export Processing Zone—the country's first—is partly attributed to the militancy of the KMU. The federation also made it difficult for the government when it needed to increase oil prices, by organizing a transport strike (for example, in August 1987), or its actions led moderate unions to become more militant and to put pressure on the government to keep increasing the minimum daily wage. In the mid-1980s, the Philippines was losing a few million workdays to strikes.[10] Furthermore, the KMU succeeded in bringing workers in a number of foreign multinational companies under its umbrella. As a result, industrial discipline tended to become weak in many of these companies. Those export-oriented ones suffered in particular because, as industrial discipline eroded with rising labour militancy, the production cost tended to increase or the product quality to suffer.

The situation in Metro Manila around 1990 resembles the one in Davao City in 1984. In the mid-1980s, as the NPA's influence increased in Davao with its success in bringing slum areas under its control, law and order broke down. Kidnappings of rich businessmen for ransom, armed robberies, murders, and other violent crimes became almost daily occurrences. Several years later, Metro Manila began facing a similar situation. Banks were protected by security guards with shotguns, yet they were still robbed by those armed with superior weapons. If banks could be robbed, jewellery and other shops which carried valuables were even more helpless before such robbers. Filipino-Chinese businessmen in the Binondo area reached a frenzied state when many of them were kidnapped for ransom. Kidnappings of Chinese businessmen started first in Cotabato City and General Santos City in Mindanao and Iloilo City in the Visayas, and then spread to Metro Manila.

Many of these crimes were probably not committed by the NPA, but, through its breakaway factions, it was most likely to be involved in some.[11] In Davao, soon after the government sent a crack regiment there, peace and order was restored. But in Metro Manila, though the situation did not become as bad as in Davao, peace and order remained a serious problem. In the May 1992 general election, former police general Alfredo Lim was elected Mayor of Manila on the issue of crime. Other newly elected mayors in Metro Manila (for example, Mel Mathay of Quezon City) are also serious about reducing crime in their cities.

The case of the Philippine–Taiwanese joint venture Luzon Petrochemical Corp. was also blamed on the NPA. In January 1988, the Taiwanese company USI Far East obtained from the Board of Investments (BOI) a permit to set up a naphtha cracking plant in Bataan. Shortly after this, USI Far East announced that it would move the site of the plant to Batangas Province. A survey revealed that Bataan was a stronghold of NPA guerrillas and KMU leaders. The BOI approved the relocation, but the Congressman from Bataan, Enrique Garcia, and the Philippine National Oil Co. (PNOC), which was to become a minority shareholder of the petrochemical venture, strongly objected. The PNOC has an oil refinery in Bataan which it had taken over from two American oil companies in the early 1970s. If the planned site was to be moved to Batangas where the Shell refinery could feed naphtha to the plant, there was no reason for the PNOC to participate in the venture. The Congressman took the case to court, and the

Supreme Court decided against the BOI in 1990. The case involved nationalism to some extent, but this large investment project would have been carried out smoothly if there had been no insurgency problem, which the Taiwanese company, inexperienced as it was in the Philippines, had probably not dreamed of. As a large foreign-owned installation, it could have been an ideal target for NPA extortion.

It is easier for the NPA to commit acts of sabotage or extort money in rural areas. In 1987, its guerrillas blew up a railway bridge and a few road bridges in the Bicol region in southern Luzon, causing severe delays in transport between the region and the other parts of the island.[12] They cut a power line to a mining company in southern Negros as a 'taste' of NPA justice; residents near the mining site had complained that it was polluting the environment.[13] The NPA imposed 'revolutionary taxes' on rice producers, coconut planters, and companies (mining, logging, plantation, etc.) operating in rural areas. If they refused, the guerrillas burnt their crops and destroyed their machinery, or kidnapped their owners.

The 'revolutionary taxes' were not cheap. The NPA did not receive much support from abroad, and had to raise money internally, especially for buying weapons. Although the NPA could not let companies get off too cheaply, it had to consider their ability to pay: it demanded more from multinational companies. In the case of Philippine Geothermal, it had received a demand of $5 million before the kidnapping of its general manager.[14] A logger in Quirino Province in northern central Luzon had his sawmill destroyed because he did not pay ₱1 million ($50,000); he promptly paid after he saw what the NPA could do.[15] In 1987, the government estimated that the NPA had raised about ₱300 million ($14.6 million) outside Metro Manila.[16]

A response of the landlords and companies operating in rural areas was to arm themselves as they could not always depend on government forces (which could be expensive too, since they had to pay for this service). Eduardo Cojuangco, a close crony of Marcos who had a number of plantations and businesses in Luzon, the Visayas, Mindanao, and Palawan, had a private army estimated at more than 5,000 men at its peak. After he fled the country with the Marcoses in February 1986 (he later returned and ran in the 1992 presidential election), government troops raided his cement factory in Pangasinan, and found a cache of firearms, explosives, and ammunition:

1 Chinese submachine-gun
1 .30 calibre machine-gun
2 Thompson sub-machine-guns
1 M-60 machine-gun (used in helicopter gunships)
2 AK-47 rifles
1 armalite rifle
1 model 77 Ruger rifle
1 Mark IV .380 calibre rifle
1 M-1 pistolized carbine
1 double-barrel rifle

1 .32 calibre survival rifle
1 .22 calibre Winchester rifle
1 .44 calibre magnum revolver
2 .45 calibre automatic pistols
1 .45 calibre Colt Commander automatic pistol
1 Walther PPK .22 calibre pistol
1 Browning .22 calibre target pistol
1 flare gun, 200 flare cartridges
200 smoke grenades
50,000 rounds of M-16 bullets
1,000 rounds of 7.62 mm bullets (for M-60 machine-guns)
500 blasting caps.

This cache was only a part of Cojuangco's collection.[17]

The size of Cojuangco's army and arsenal may have been exceptional, but, as pointed out above, to have a private army was not. Many big landlords had private armies of their own. In Philippine politics, it is often said that if a person wants to be elected to office, he needs the three Gs: Guns, Goons, and Gold. In rural areas, powerful politicians were often big landlords who simply used the existing first two Gs and added 'gold' at election time. They needed the first two to protect their property from the NPA, or in earlier years from Huk guerrillas.

A Higher Level of Rural Discontent

Communist insurgency, which prompted rich landlords and rural businessmen to arm themselves, began earlier and became more serious in the Philippines than in Thailand, basically because a large number of people were landless (tenants and agricultural workers). In the late 1930s, only 3 out of 10 peasants in Pampanga Province in central Luzon had land of their own.[18] Landlessness made the province the hotbed for radical peasant organizations, and later Huk guerrillas. As President Diosdado Macapagal wrote, '[T]he genesis of [Communism] . . . was the hunger of the peasants for land.'[19]

The 1930s was a decade of rural unrest. In early 1931, there was a spontaneous peasant uprising at Tayug in Pangasinan. Landlessness in the province was not as bad as in Pampanga (only 3 out of 10 peasants were tenants in Pangasinan as a whole), but in certain municipalities, the problem was serious. Four hundred men armed with knives and shotguns entered the town of Tayug, killed two government officials and several Constabulary men (the Constabulary was a sort of national police to maintain peace and order in the country), and set fire to many houses.[20] Later, Joseph Hayden wrote on the cause of the Tayug uprising:

> The reasons why the Filipino leaders did not want the Tayug incident to be investigated by a body containing the appropriate members of the Governor-General's staff of advisers are obvious. Such an inquiry would inevitably be pushed into the whole realm of the oppression of the poor peasant by the local boss, the usurer, the Constabulary, and the local official. The fact that the machinery for the registration of land titles is years behind in its work and that

the rich and influential 'land grabber' is taking advantage of this situation to despoil the homesteader and small farmer would come up for consideration. The bitter and dangerous discontent of large number[s] of peasants in many parts of the central plain of Luzon would be revealed. Here is a situation that many people believe would be extremely perilous should the support of American authority be withdrawn from the Government of the Philippines. Indeed, one of the highest officials in that Government, a Filipino, declared to the writer that the Tayug incident should not be called an agrarian uprising because the term might very well give rise to similar outbreaks elsewhere in the Islands.[21]

A few years after the Tayug uprising, another rebellion called the Sakdal uprising occurred in the provinces around Manila. The Sakdal was a political party for landless peasants, founded by Benigno Ramos. It had a large number of followers, and in the 1934 election, had elected three members of the House of Representatives, one provincial governor, and many local officials. In mid-1935, believing that the Commonwealth would strengthen the hand of the already repressive Nacionalista regime, a few days before the plebiscite on the Constitution (which would establish the Commonwealth), several thousand peasants (Sakdalistas) rose in insurrection and were brutally suppressed. A. V. H. Hartendorp, American editor of *Philippine Magazine*, wrote on the cause of this uprising:

Granted that Benigno Ramos is a 'racketeer' and his lieutenants are scoundrels, the Sakdal party remains a party of protest, and that is where its strength lies. Its members are not sycophants feeding at the political trough, but belong to the common people. Granted that the principles the Sakdalistas have espoused are vague, foolish, and uncoordinated, they show, nevertheless, a groping for remedies that have not been brought them by the politicians.

We cannot brush the matter aside by stating that the Sakdal movement is instigated by racketeers or that it is due to temporary depression. Its roots go much deeper than that—go down into a substratum of class conflict that is present here as elsewhere in the world. It is a movement of the dispossessed, of the exploited, of those who are given no chance. . . .

The only answer is to give these people a chance. The political party that can arrange that will be the political party of the future.[22]

Francis Sayre, who returned to the United States after serving as Adviser to Rama VI in Thailand in the 1920s, came to the Philippines as the last High Commissioner before the Pacific War. In the last report he sent to Washington, he gave the following assessment of the rural situation in the Philippines:

The agrarian socialist element, particularly that led by Pedro Abad Santos in Pampanga province was exceptionally active. . . . The viewpoint of . . . dissident groups was expressed not only in speeches, parades, demonstrations, and passive resistance, but also, in several instances by violence. Several persons were killed or wounded in a number of tenant uprisings. As a result, Pampanga . . . was placed under Constabulary control. By June 1941, the Constabulary had taken over all municipal police forces in the provinces of Central Luzon: Pangasinan, Pampanga, Tarlac, Bulacan, Nueva Ecija, Bataan, Zambales, Cavite, Rizal, Batangas, and Laguna. Tenant troubles at Candaba, Pampanga province resulted in the murder of six persons. On June 18, the Secretary of the Interior announced that the Constabulary had been strengthened and was prepared to strike quickly against radical elements at any time.[23]

After the war, Sayre recalled, in his autobiography, the plight of landless workers in Philippine sugar plantations:

An all-important item in the Philippine economy was sugar; and the problems connected with sugar production gave me considerable concern. In Pampanga, where great quantities of sugar cane were produced, thousands of Filipinos worked under disgraceful conditions and often for less than a living wage. They had to fight poverty all their lives, whereas the owners of the estates, living in Manila, grew inordinately rich and profited heavily from the free entry of their sugar into the United States. Here was a pernicious social problem—the indefensible and shocking contrast between the rich, lordly landowners living in Manila and the impoverished workers in Pampanga. The Huk troubles which arose after the war were part of the price which had to be paid for intolerable exploitation.[24]

Clearly, landlessness was a more serious problem in the Philippines than in Thailand. Land was more scarce in the former; the latter had about 60 per cent more territory, and its population was slightly smaller. As a result, the population density in the Philippines was 70 per cent higher. If the population density of cultivated areas was computed, the Philippine situation was probably much worse, since its territory contains many mountainous areas, whereas Thailand is essentially a large flat country except in the North. But all these data merely say that the average landholding of a peasant in the Philippines had to be smaller than in Thailand. The basic reason for the large number of landless peasants in the Philippines must lie somewhere else.

Landlessness in the Philippines must have been due to the fact that landownership was unequal. The inequitable distribution of land was partly because, in the Philippines, there was none (like the king in Thailand) who looked out for the interest of the peasant, that each peasant should be entitled to the land he tilled. During the Spanish period, the Spanish king could have fufilled this role, but he lived far away from the Philippines and it was of minor concern to him. He often alienated large tracts of land to the Catholic Church and Spaniards (he did this much more than the Thai king did for private investors). He left the governance of the Indios to colonial administrators, many of whom were corrupt. The Catholic Church did not ignore the welfare of the Indios but did not pay attention to their material base either. (Ironically, in the 1970s, liberation theology made this the Church's central concern.) No one cared much.

Then during the American period, seeing that rural unrest was one basic reason for rebellions (for example, the Philippine Revolution) against the Spanish regime, the Americans tried to rectify the situation by, for example, buying the large holdings of the Catholic Church for redistribution to peasants and passing the Land Act of 1902 to encourage homesteads. But the Americans did not do a good job of implementing their land policy. Especially after the mid-1910s, the Americans began transferring power to the Filipinos and became less involved in actual administration. As peasant leaders argued in the 1930s, the result was that the Philippine government (especially local government) came under the control of the landlord class.

Another obstacle to equitable landownership was the progress in commercialization, which started in the nineteenth century, picked up some speed late in that century, and accelerated during the American period. The Philippine rural sector was increasingly brought into the orbit of international trade. During the Spanish period, copra, sugar, and abaca (the raw material for rope) became major exports. Contrary to the negative views on the Philippine economy during the Spanish period, there was progress in commercialization at that time. On the life of the upper class in a coffee-producing region in Batangas, an American historian wrote:

> In Lipa, Batangas, which produced 4.4 million kilograms of coffee in 1887, the upper society splurged money on clothes, interior decoration, pictures; on rare crystals and china ordered from Europe; on curtains of the finest silk, on stuffed chairs from Vienna, on exquisite table wines and foods. They sought to equal the halls and banquets of Spain herself, the metropolis, the Guiding Star, the Ideal.[25]

The Americans, however, did a better job of promoting commercialization. In particular, they developed the infrastructure to promote entrepreneurial activities in rural areas, and opened up the Philippines more widely to foreign trade. In 1909, the US Congress enacted the Payne–Aldrich Tariff Act as the first step towards free trade between the United States and the Philippines. Under this Act, however, certain Philippine agricultural products were still subject to quotas, but in 1913, the US Congress passed the Simmons–Underwood Tariff Act removing these quotas and authorizing unlimited free trade.

None Cared about the Rural Masses

As the Philippines became the important supplier of agricultural products such as sugar and copra, land increased in importance. This development exacerbated the problem of the unequal distribution of land because a small minority enjoyed an undue advantage in claiming land as their private property. The system which emerged was, to put it strongly, a feudal one in which a (land) lord owned a large expanse of land worked by his peasants. In fact, the Communists claimed that feudalism was one of the three ills which plagued the country (the other two being bureaucratic capitalism and American imperialism).

Who became the 'lord' and how did he become one? Landlords were of two groups of different origins. One group hailed from the *principalia* class of the indigenous population who had collaborated with the Spaniards in running the country, and were therefore given certain privileges and had more resources under their command. In the second half of the nineteenth century, as the Spanish administration made higher education available to the indigenous people, many of their children became better educated. Being richer, better connected, and better educated (often as lawyers), the *principalia* class could appropriate public land as their property. The other group comprised immigrants (especially Chinese and Spaniards) and their descendants, many of whom married indigenous women. The women they married may have come from the *principalia* class; if not, many of their sons' wives did. Being immigrants or their immediate descendants, they had fairly strong commercial values and went into commercial agriculture after the Philippines was opened up to international trade. While undertaking commercial agriculture, they also became moneylenders and enlarged their landholdings by acquiring the land their peasant borrowers defaulted, or by using peasants for clearing public land to enlarge their holdings.[26]

The concept of private property was nebulous during the Spanish period, but the American administration in its very beginning introduced the Torrens system, which granted land titles after applicants had complied with appropriate requirements in surveys and proofs of ownership. The American administration also introduced homesteading which let peasants claim 16 hectares from public land for cultivation. (In 1924, this figure was raised to 146 hectares.) Many peasants benefited from the homesteading Act, but there were also many who were cheated. They cultivated and improved lands, believing that they would become their owners, but later found that the lands belonged to someone else.

The land registration system also victimized ignorant peasants in other ways. The lands which they thought belonged to them, because they had been cultivating them since the days of their fathers, were sometimes taken away because they were not properly registered as the owners. There are numerous reports on land grabbing by powerful landlords; this obviously intensified the sense of injustice in rural areas. A peasant who participated in the Tayug uprising of 1931 stated:

> Many of us, including myself, were formerly owners of big pieces of land in Tayug and Santa Maria. We have been driven from our lands by the hacenderos, from the lands which our fathers and grandfathers cleared or have occupied since time immemorial. Because of this grievance we have long planned ... to drive away the hacenderos and get [our] lands back.[27]

The Effect on Agricultural Productivity

Rural unrest led to the Communist insurgency, which affected the economy negatively in various ways: in urban areas, the NPA-directed kidnappings and other crimes created unstable conditions, leaving a bad image in the minds of investors (especially foreign ones); in rural areas, there was destruction of the infrastructure, crops, and machinery, 'revolutionary taxes', and increased security costs for those who decided to defend themselves. But more important were the psychological effects on landlords who made decisions on investment and farm management.

A major problem restraining Philippine economic growth was the lack of dynamism in the agricultural sector. During the American period, copra and sugar became major exports, which continued to be major exchange earners in the post-war period. In the case of sugar, it was fortunate in not only enjoying a large quota which was allowed duty-free access to the American market until the early 1970s, but also having it increased (especially in getting part of the Cuban quota). But the sugar industry is in bad shape today—worse than the Thai sugar industry. In 1991, the cost of sugar production was around 14 cents per pound, compared with 7 cents in Thailand. In the case of coconuts, there have been no major efforts in replanting, and 50 per cent of the trees are said to be senile.[28] There has been no diversification into palm oil either (as carried out in Malaysia).

Not only did the sugar and coconut industries become 'sick' industries in the 1980s, there was hardly any major agricultural diversification in the post-war period. Unlike Thailand, the Philippines did not produce new agricultural exports, nor did export-oriented agri-business spring up. In Thailand, the agricultural sector supported the industrial sector until it could start earning foreign exchange on its own. Without dynamic agriculture, industrialization is difficult.

A reason for the 'failure' of Philippine agriculture was high tenancy. Tenancy may not necessarily be bad for productivity growth, but it is if landlords are absentee ones or do not undertake an entrepreneurial role even if they live in the same area as tenants. Such landlords are simply parasites on the rural sector. In the Philippines, the most negative development was the rise of absentee landlords. One writer gives the following account of the development:

> As early as the revolutionary period [around 1900], wealthy provincial landlords began to leave the countryside. This migration, however, took on the character of a gathering exodus during the American regime. The landlords moved away physically, socially, and psychologically from the tenants and barrios [villages] toward new economic opportunities, socio-political involvement, and intellectual advancement in the towns, in Manila, and beyond. With their new world, they began to leave behind the world of the tenants to the management and care of farm managers or *katiwala*. With absentee landlordism, the personal and paternalistic social institution which supported the tenancy structure was reduced to an impersonal economic setup between a landlord and his tenants through the intermediary of his katiwala. The katiwala, who did not have the paternal solicitude of the landlord, often considered the tenant as a mere factor of production in an economy that was capital- and profit-oriented. His principal interest in tenants was not their welfare but the economic efficiency and productivity of their labor. With the migration of the landlords to the towns and cities went their obligations to give rations, loans, and other guarantees of survival.[29]

Many landlords also left their villages involuntarily. When high tenancy led to rural unrest and eventually the Communist insurgency, their personal safety was threatened. For example, soon after the Japanese invasion, many landlords in central Luzon left for Manila to escape the Huk insurgents. Since the Huk insurgency continued for several years after the war, many landlords lost interest in making their true homes in the rural areas. Even if they kept a rural residence, they tended to spend more time in nearby cities or Manila, leaving the farms to their tenants or their managers. Under this condition, investment for agricultural improvement was often kept to the minimum.

Many landlords who stayed on to manage their farms broke off relations with their tenants because peasants became troublesome as Communist influence spread. To compensate for the loss of their labour, landlords introduced mechanization, but to a level far ahead of that required by resource endowments. This made the cost of production higher, but when the transaction costs (the cost of implementing a lease contract) were taken account of, or when there was a possibility that leasing land could lead to its loss (through a land reform programme, for example), it was wiser not to have tenants. Even if it meant that the land taken back was not going to be cultivated right away, it was better that way since there would be no constraint when a new plan was made. Long-term investment was also difficult in a number of areas because crops, machinery, and the irrigation structure, etc. could be destroyed by insurgents or their peasant allies who resorted to violence during disputes. The only way out was to provide their own security by creating a private army, but this was expensive, especially if it was to be effective. For many landlords, it made sense to take money out of agriculture and invest it elsewhere (perhaps abroad). For example, coconut landowners found it difficult to replant trees or to replace them with oil palm, for coconut lands were a breeding ground for insurgency.

Other Contributing Factors

Intellectual Freedom

Landlessness was the basic cause of the Communist insurgency, but there were other contributing factors. One was the intellectual freedom prevailing in the Philippines. The Communist Party (PKP) itself was outlawed in 1957, and to proclaim one's membership in the party would have led to imprisonment, but anyone arrested for being a party member was entitled to the due process of law; without sufficient evidence it was difficult to convict him. (Until the early 1970s, anyone charged as a Communist in Thailand could be imprisoned right away.) To study Marxism or teach it was not illegal. Before martial law, there were a large number of leftist intellectuals, some of whom were teaching in universities. It was thus easier for the Communists to organize groups for indoctrination, mass mobilization, and recruitment of new members. The Kabataang Makabayan, which recruited students mostly, was one such organization. The University of the Philippines in Diliman, Quezon City, where it was active, was the breeding ground for future Communist leaders: Jose Maria Sison, the founder of the new Communist Party (CPP), was a student of English literature and later a lecturer; Rodolfo Salas, who took over the party after Sison's arrest, was an engineering student; Benito Tiamzon, who assumed the top position after Salas's arrest, was also an engineering student; and Jose Luneta, another CPP leader who was still active in 1991, was a political science major.

Weak Institutional Moorings

Another contributing factor to the insurgency was the weakness of institutional moorings which could have stabilized the social order in the Philippines, especially in remote rural areas. In Thailand, Buddhism is a counter-force against the spread of Communism in rural areas. A typical Thai village has a temple, and its priest teaches moderation and socially acceptable behaviour. In the Philippines, however, as will be explained shortly, the Catholic Church helped the Communists, to some extent, to increase their influence, especially after martial law. In Thailand, the priest's teaching goes hand in hand with moral education in a school. Religion is one of the compulsory subjects in school, and it is taught essentially as Buddhist moral education.

A Thai school also plays an important role in exposing children to the outside world and implanting a sense of identity with the established order. The teaching may have been inadequate in many ways, but children learn about national institutions and culture and also the national language, which later enable them to understand news programmes (as well as entertainment) on television. In the Philippines, the teaching is ineffective partly because there is no national language, but a more important reason is that with the government letting teachers' salaries decline in real terms, schools cannot keep or attract good teachers. Many village children leave school (if they ever attend it) without a sense of identification with their country and the language skill which would have enabled them to understand through the mass media the goings-on in the country. As Mao Zedong said, it is easier to paint on a blank wall. When this lack of national consciousness is combined with grinding poverty, it is not difficult for Communist insurgents to recruit young villagers.

The Radicalization of the Catholic Church

The Catholic Church and the CPP are poles apart in dogma under normal circumstances, but in the Philippines, liberal segments of the Church began helping the Communists in the early 1970s. The Church was traditionally concerned with spiritual, not temporal, matters, but after the Second Vatican Council concluded in the mid-1960s, the Church began paying more attention to the social and economic order because it came to believe that religious life could grow and be strengthened only in a sound economic and social milieu. This belief was first pursued in Latin America, and a result was the birth of liberation theology. The priests and nuns who espoused this theology argued that unless the existing economic order of capitalism which, according to them, had been creating massive poverty was replaced by socialism, poor people could not pursue a truly religious life. In the early 1970s, this theology began to find a following among a number of Filipino priests and nuns.[30]

From their perspective, a 'pie' is large enough for everyone to share, but if someone (a capitalist or landlord) takes an unduly large share, there is not enough for others. The capitalist or landlord has to reduce his share so that others can justly have more. If he will not, they will have to organize themselves to confront him. In order to protect his interest, the latter might use force to eliminate 'radical' leaders. Faced with this situation, liberation theologians would approve the use of force by the poor. If necessary, they would accept Communist help, or work with the Communists to achieve their objectives. After all, the Communists were also fighting the capitalist and big landlord.[31]

The majority of Catholic priests and nuns in the Philippines probably did not have anything to do with the Communists, though some may have been sympathetic to their cause. Those who collaborated with or joined the Communist rebels were a small minority. Possibly, about a dozen priests joined the NPA as rebel commanders.[32] In addition, there was a much larger group of priests and nuns who belonged to Christians for National Liberation (CNL), a radical Catholic organization (created in 1972) which collaborated with the Communists in the establishment of a new social order (socialism).[33] Remaining within the Catholic Church, they helped peasants, workers, and slum dwellers organize themselves in their quest for social justice. Some foreign missionaries were particularly active in the Philippines.

In Mindanao where there was a high percentage of foreign missionaries, the Marcos government ran into conflict with the Catholic Church. One government official charged in 1983 that the 'entire Catholic clergy of Mindanao are helping the rebels'.[34] In Negros also, the government had its hands full with Bishop Antonio Fortich, who was supporting priests and lay workers involved in Basic Christian Communities in his diocese. (This is a small religious community organized under a lay leader where there is no resident priest, and it is engaged also in educating people about their rights.) In 1984, the government arrested three priests (two were foreign missionaries) and six lay workers for having allegedly murdered a local government official and for involvement in the CNL.[35] The government also raided 22 church establishments between 1973 and 1984.[36] One of these was the August 1974 raid on the Jesuit Sacred Heart Novitiate near Manila in search of Jose Maria Sison, the head of the CPP; 2 Jesuit priests and some 20 students were arrested.

Liberation theology was an experiment which did not work. It is easy to preach social justice, but to bring it about by force is a different matter altogether. After all, the Church is not a revolutionary political or military organization. By the end of the 1980s, especially after the fall of socialist states in Eastern Europe, the theology was losing its appeal to the liberal segment of the Church, except those who had been attracted to it and had joined forces with the Communists, helping them gain legitimacy in the eyes of common people. This sort of experiment can be tried more easily in the Philippines where the Church is independent of the state. Besides, as an international organization centred in the West, the Church cannot insulate itself from newfangled liberal ideas that arise there. The separation of Church and state has advantages (for example, in bringing down an unpopular dictator, as happened in

February 1986), but Church support of Communist rebels was clearly a negative side of it.

Weak Military Discipline

The military is also to be blamed for the spread of the Communist insurgency. After martial law was declared, the military forces expanded, spectacularly in fact in the first several years. Between 1972 and 1976, regular forces grew from 62,000 to 142,000 men, and appropriations from ₱900 million ($134 million) to ₱6.9 billion ($927 million) (the ratio of military appropriations to gross national product grew from 1.7 to 5.2 per cent).[37] Despite the increase in resources, the military were not effective in combating the NPA. Troops in the field were often poorly trained, badly led, and suffered from a poor line of communications. NPA guerrillas often succeeded in ambushing platoons, and sometimes companies, killing scores of soldiers in the process. Of course, the Philippine military scored numerous victories over the guerrillas, but given the few resources it commanded, the NPA's various tactical successes were impressive. In the mid-1980s, according to an American military observer, not more than one in eight combat units was properly prepared to take the field against the guerrillas.[38]

Government soldiers sometimes abused their power and antagonized the people. In the areas where the NPA was strong, they did a poor job of identifying NPA members and sympathizers. Since it was difficult to make an arrest based on evidence, they tended to depend on informants, and thus made a number of mistakes. They were also charged with torturing suspects, killing them (called 'salvaging'), and even raping women.[39] In a number of areas where the Philippine military did not have enough forces stationed, it depended on the vigilantes of the Barrio Self-Defense Units (later renamed the Civilian Home Defense Force). As the vigilantes had hardly any training, their co-operation with the military magnified the issue of human rights violations. They fired at protesting peasants and workers, and resorted to 'salvaging' peasant and union leaders.

Military abuses drove many people into the ranks of the NPA or to sympathize with them. Francisco Claver, Bishop of Malaybalay in Bukidnon, Mindanao, from 1969 to 1984, recalled that military abuses had been the primary issue exploited by the NPA in his diocese. Foreign priests in Region 11 (southern Mindanao around Davao) said that military abuses were the main cause of anti-government, pro-NPA sentiment in the area. Bishop Fortich of Negros maintains that most NPA recruits in Negros were so not because they believed in the Communist ideology but because they had grievances against the military.[40]

The Philippine military was a badly organized institution. Discipline was lax, soldiers were badly trained, morale was low, and corruption pervaded the whole institution from top to bottom. For example, Fabian C. Ver, who became Marcos's security officer (cum chauffeur) when he became President, was promoted to General in 1971, and to Chief of

Staff 10 years later, because of his loyalty to Marcos, despite the fact that he was not even a graduate of the Philippine Military Academy. Ver reached mandatory retirement age in 1974, but Marcos would not let him go; nor did he release about 20 other loyal generals. The result was the decline of morale of younger officers, whose promotion was blocked by overstaying generals and who saw the spread of corruption at the top with their own eyes. Ver was among the most corrupt. Even Marcos's military aide states that Ver 'grew rich, very rich' as the godfather of smuggling and gambling syndicates.[41] Ver became a role model for other military officers, and institutional discipline broke down. One American political scientist wrote:

> The military learned that it was 'permissible to use official positions for personal gain.' They became involved in almost every type of business activity—legal and criminal. Officers controlled or extorted payments from the black market for dollars; they controlled car-theft rings, marijuana syndicates, illegal logging, gambling, prostitution, fishing, mining, gunrunning, and robbery. Smaller rackets were principally the province of junior-ranking officers and enlisted men whose basic pay and living conditions had not significantly improved; field grade officers and their superiors controlled larger enterprises such as illegal logging and drug smuggling. Military units even began to attack each other in struggles over the control of rackets.[42]

Summary

The Communist insurgency was helped by intellectual freedom, the weakness of traditional institutional moorings, radicalization of the Catholic Church, and the ineffectiveness of the military, but the root cause was the severe inequity in rural landownership (which caused massive poverty). As it led to rural unrest and eventually the Communist insurgency, peace and order deteriorated, making it difficult to undertake long-term plans for agricultural development. As a result, agriculture lost its potential to become a leading sector of the economy, and the performance of the whole economy became lacklustre. In the meantime, the population increased, and partly as the result of inmigration from rural areas, poverty also became serious in urban areas (especially Metro Manila), creating a ripe condition for the spread of Communism and radical unionism there. Radical unionism (especially by the KMU), bombings, kidnappings, and killings by NPA urban guerrillas in the 1980s scared off foreign as well as Filipino investors. At the same time, the sugar and coconut industries which had been major foreign exchange earners became 'sick' industries as their costs exceeded their prices (and also partly because they had not invested in productivity improvement); the rural sector as a whole stagnated with no new major export crops—a result of no major investments in diversification in the past. The deterioration in the investment climate was possibly the most serious effect of the Communist insurgency. It affected the rural economy first, and eventually, the whole economy.

1. Renato S. de Villa, 'National Defense and Security', in *The Aquino Administration: Record and Legacy (1986–1992)*, Quezon City: University of the Philippines Press, 1992, p. 93.

2. Teodoro A. Agoncillo and Milagros C. Guerrero, *History of the Filipino People*, 5th edn., Quezon City: R. P. Garcia Publishing Co., 1977, p. 524, and Onofre D. Corpuz, *The Philippines*, Englewood Cliffs, New Jersey: Prentice-Hall, 1965, p. 110.

3. Miguel Cuaderno, *Problems of Economic Development*, Manila: Author, 1964, p. 40.

4. Amando Doronila, *The State, Economic Transformation, and Political Change in the Philippines, 1946–1972*, Singapore: Oxford University Press, 1992, p. 53.

5. Gareth Porter, *The Politics of Counterinsurgency in the Philippines: Military and Political Options*, Philippine Studies Occasional Paper No. 9, Honolulu: Center for Philippine Studies, University of Hawaii, 1987, p. 131.

6. The estimates for 1972 range from 35 (the NPA's figure) to 1,030 (the government's number). Raymond Bonner, *Waltzing with a Dictator: The Marcoses and the Making of American Policy*, New York: Times Books, 1987, p. 359.

7. The Visayas cover central islands such as Samar, Leyte, Bohol, Masbate, Cebu, Negros, and Panay.

8. David Timberman, *A Changeless Land: Continuity and Change in Philippine Politics*, Singapore: Institute of Southeast Asian Studies, and Metro Manila: Bookmark, 1991, pp. 114–16.

9. *Far Eastern Economic Review*, 2 April 1992. All suspects were killed in the rescue operation. It is sometimes said that it is not clear whether they really belonged to the Red Scorpion Group. Some suspect that the real culprits were scallywags in uniform.

10. Elias T. Ramos, *Dualistic Unionism and Industrial Relations*, Quezon City: New Day Publishers, 1990, p. 200.

11. The Philippine National Police announced in March 1992 that the RSG planned to abduct 14 prominent businessmen, including presidential aspirant Eduardo Cojuangco (*Tulay*, the monthly newspaper of KAISA, an organization of Chinese Filipinos, 12 April 1992).

12. James B. Goodno, *The Philippines: Land of Broken Promises*, London: Zed Books, 1991, p. 14.

13. Yamamoto Munesuke, *Negurosu: Nageki no Shima* [Negros: An Island of Grief], Tokyo: Dai-san Shobo, 1991, p. 157.

14. *International Herald Tribune*, 3 March 1991.

15. Gregg R. Jones, *Red Revolution: Inside the Philippine Guerrilla Movement*, Boulder: Westview Press, 1989, p. 239.

16. Richard J. Kessler, *Rebellion and Repression in the Philippines*, New Haven: Yale University Press, 1989, p. 75.

17. Ricardo Manapat, *Some Are Smarter Than Others: The History of Marcos' Crony Capitalism*, New York: Aletheia Publications, 1991, p. 219.

18. Benedict J. Kerkvliet, *The Huk Rebellion: A Study of Peasant Revolt in the Philippines*, Quezon City: New Day Publishers, 1979, p. 24.

19. Diosdado Macapagal, *A Stone for the Edifice: Memoirs of a President*, Quezon City: Mac Publishing House, 1968, p. 165.

20. Martin Noone, *The Life and Times of Michael O'Doherty*, Manila: Historical Conservation Society, 1989, p. 249.

21. Joseph Ralston Hayden, *The Philippines: A Study in National Development*, New York: Macmillan Co., 1942, p. 381.

22. Quoted in David R. Sturtevant, *Popular Uprisings in the Philippines, 1840–1940*, Ithaca: Cornell University Press, 1976, p. 247.

23. Ibid., p. 254.

24. Francis B. Sayre, *Glad Adventure*, New York: Macmillan Co., 1957, p. 195.

25. Glenn Anthony May, *Battle for Batangas: A Philippine Province at War*, New Haven: Yale University Press, 1991, p. 10.

26. For further discussion on the *principalia* class and their involvement in commercial agriculture, see Dante Simbulan, 'A Study of the Socio-economic Elite in Philippine

Politics and Government, 1946–1963', Ph.D. thesis, Australian National University, 1965. For the role of the mestizos in commercial agriculture, see Edgar Wickberg, 'The Chinese Mestizo in Philippine History', *Journal of Southeast Asian History*, March 1964; and John A. Larkin, *The Pampangans: Colonial Society in a Philippine Province*, Berkeley: University of California Press, 1972.

27. Quoted in Sturtevant, *Popular Uprisings in the Philippines*, p. 189.

28. *Manila Bulletin*, 14 January 1992.

29. Wilfredo Fabros, *The Church and Its Social Involvement in the Philippines, 1930–1972*, Quezon City: Ateneo de Manila University Press, 1988, pp. 5–6.

30. For further details on the Church's involvement in socio-economic issues in the Philippines, see Fabros, *The Church and Its Social Involvement in the Philippines*, and James H. Kroeger, 'Human Promotion as an Integral Dimension of the Church's Mission of Evangelization: A Philippine Experience and Perspective since Vatican II—1965–1984', Ph.D. thesis, Pontificia Universitas Gregoriana, Vatican, 1985.

31. For more on liberation theology, see Alberto Rossa (comp.), *The Theology of Liberation*, Manila: Historical Conservation Society, 1986.

32. Kessler, *Rebellion and Repression in the Philippines*, p. 48. The figure is based on reports in the *Washington Post*.

33. The membership of the CNL (including seminarians and lay workers) in the second half of the 1980s was possibly a few thousand. See Kessler, *Rebellion and Repression in the Philippines*, p. 88 and Jones, *Red Revolution*, p. 212. The number of priests and nuns in the organization may have been around 1,200 in the mid-1980s. Ross Munro, 'The New Khmer Rouge', *Commentary*, December 1985, p. 26. Quoted in Timberman, *A Changeless Land*, p. 137.

34. Quoted in Kroeger, 'Human Promotion as an Integral Dimension', p. 246. The remark of the Minister of State for Political Affairs, L. Perex.

35. For an account of their trial, see Alfred W. McCoy, *Priests on Trial*, Ringwood, Victoria: Penguin Books Australia, 1984.

36. Robert L. Youngblood, *Marcos against the Church*, Ithaca: Cornell University Press, 1990, p. 115.

37. Felipe Miranda and Ruben Ciron, 'The Philippines: Defence Expenditures, Threat Perception and the Role of the United States', in Chin Kin Wah (ed.), *Defence Spending in Southeast Asia*, Singapore: Institute of Southeast Asian Studies, 1987, p. 136. Quoted in Timberman, *A Changeless Land*, p. 84.

38. Carl H. Lande, 'Introduction: Retrospect and Prospect', in Carl H. Lande (ed.), *Rebuilding a Nation: Philippine Challenges and American Policy*, Washington, DC: Washington Institute Press, 1987, p. 15.

39. Porter, *Politics of Counterinsurgency in the Philippines*, p. 89.

40. Ibid., p. 22.

41. Arturo Aruiza, *Ferdinand E. Marcos: Malacanang to Makiki*, Quezon City: ACAruiza Enterprises, 1991, p. 85.

42. Kessler, *Rebellion and Repression in the Philippines*, p. 125.

14
Muslim Separatism in the South

A Higher Level of Violence in the Philippines

MINDANAO, which accounts for about one-third of Philippine territory, is an ideal site for plantation agriculture. It is a large empty land of fertile soil; no typhoon afflicts it (unlike the Visayas and Luzon). In 1920, California Packing set up a pineapple plantation and a packing plant, and it was followed in the early 1960s by Castle & Cooke of Hawaii (known for the Dole brand). But the plantation industry has not flourished in Mindanao, a Moro land where there are frequent clashes between Moros and Christian Filipinos.

In the early 1970s, the violence escalated into a civil war. The Moro National Liberation Front (MNLF), the largest of the Moro rebel groups, with 50,000–60,000 guerrillas at its peak, mounted major offensives in Sulu, Cotabato, and Zamboanga in 1973 and 1974. It was as if the Moros had declared a war of independence on the Manila government. The Philippine military responded by sending battalions and putting jet bombers, tanks, and heavy artillery into action.[1] In the mid-1970s, the level of violence declined, but the MNLF and its splinter groups (the Moro Islamic Liberation Front and the MNLF Reformist), with reduced forces (about 10,000 regulars in the early 1980s), kept fighting, and peace and order remained a serious problem.[2]

In the meantime, the centre of pineapple production shifted from Hawaii and Taiwan to Thailand, bypassing the Philippines. Dole, for example, invested in Thailand, instead of expanding in the Philippines, when the cost of production in Hawaii made it imperative to expand production abroad. In 1984, Thailand overtook the Philippines in pineapple exports, and eventually became the world's largest exporter.[3]

A Lower Level of Insurgency in Thailand

Thailand too faced the problem of Muslim separatism, but the level of violence in this conflict was much lower and restricted to smaller, economically less significant areas.[4] In the late 1970s, there were about one million Muslims in southern Thailand, accounting for about 2.8 per cent of the total population (Muslims comprised 5.2 per cent of the total population in the Philippines), and they were concentrated in the four border provinces of Pattani, Narathiwat, Yala, and Satun, which together make up about 2.6 per cent of Thai territory.[5] In these areas, the roots of Islam had taken hold too deeply for Buddhism to penetrate, and religiously and culturally, they were closer to the Malay states than Buddhist Thailand. However, they became a part of Thailand because their sultans were vassals of the Thai king.

Four states in northern Peninsular Malaysia (Kedah, Perlis, Trengganu, and Kelantan, comprising about 39 000 square kilometres) used to be part of the kingdom also, but in 1909, Thailand was pressured to cede them to the British, who administered them as part of British Malaya in the following three decades. After Japan brought Malaya under its control during the Pacific War, Thailand, as an ally of Japan, got them back; but they were returned to the British after the war. They became part of the Federation of Malaya (and eventually Malaysia) set up in 1957. Thailand has never claimed them as part of its territory since then, but it regards the four provinces in the South as a genuine part of its territory. But from the viewpoint of many Muslims in these provinces, the boundary had been drawn arbitrarily, and they feel that they should be together with the Muslim Malays in Malaysia. This feeling is the basis for the Muslim separatist movement in southern Thailand.

The separatist tendency was exacerbated when the government tried to bring religious schools (*pondok*) under its control and to spread Thai education in the four provinces. In the late 1960s and the 1970s, disillusioned Muslim intellectuals formed organizations to fight for greater autonomy or secession. These rebel groups depended on foreign Islamic countries for financial assistance, especially the Arab countries which had oil money, but they also had to raise money from within the country. For this purpose, they extorted from Thai and Chinese merchants and small (rubber) plantation owners. It was reported that between August 1978 and July 1979, there were over 100 cases of extortion in Pattani, Narathiwat, and Yala (through kidnapping, for example), and each case involved a sum of money between B50,000 ($2,500) and B150,000 ($7,500).[6] However, the problem of extortion declined in the following years.

Muslim rebels also resorted to terrorism and sabotage; they burnt government buildings (schools and police stations), destroyed bridges, and killed Thai teachers who they thought were agents of destruction of the Islamic way of life. Between January 1979 and March 1980, 26 such cases were documented.[7] The incidents which attracted the attention of the international media were the bombing of Bangkok's Don Muang International Airport in 1977; the bomb attack during the royal visit to Yala in 1977; and the bombing of the Hat Yai Railway Station in 1980. They appeared to be also behind the mass mobilizations of the 1970s. In 1975, the killing of Muslim residents in Pattani by the Thai military triggered a large protest meeting. The situation was aggravated when a bomb exploded at the meeting. About 70,000 Muslims from the border provinces gathered in Pattani to protest the repressive measures of the Thai government.[8]

In Thailand, however, the violence did not escalate as it did in the Philippines; on the contrary, it declined in the 1980s. Thai Muslim grievances were primarily about the preservation of the Islamic way of life, they were not material in nature as in the case of Mindanao. A number of Muslims felt that the Thai ethnic majority was trying to assimilate them into Buddhist Thai culture. But unlike the Philippines, there were no serious grievances about land grabbing. It has been reported that some 100,000 Thais from the North-east were relocated to Pattani, Yala, and Narathiwat between 1960 and (possibly) the end of the 1970s, and that the government was planning to relocate at least another 650,000.[9] The veracity of any charge that the relocation was for the purpose of taking land from the Muslims is questionable. Overall, the inflow of Thais (including Thai-Chinese merchants) was largely restricted to the towns and unoccupied rural areas (where small rubber plantations were set up). From the viewpoint of Muslims, these unoccupied lands may have been theirs, but the inflow was much more limited than in Mindanao (the rural population in these four provinces are still predominantly Muslims), and the conflict which could arise from it was therefore much better contained.

The Thai government could not let the religious schools in the four Malay provinces become the centres of separatism (which aspired to take the form of independence or merger with Malaysia). Its unequivocal policy was to do the utmost to keep them as part of Thai territory; for this, Thai culture had to penetrate these provinces more deeply. The obvious target in this strategy was the schools, and this development, coinciding with the Islamic resurgence in the world, caused a great deal of tension and violence, but the Thai government stood firm, though it later adjusted its policy to allow teaching in Malay in the lower grades of primary school and Muslim religious instruction in schools under government supervision. From the Thai point of view, the result was far from satisfactory, but the policy has paid off. More and more Muslim youths began speaking Thai, especially those who received education beyond primary school. Their number has been increasing with the rise of the educational level in the Muslim provinces.

The Thai government was also experienced in dealing with Muslims—more so than the Christian Filipinos who were ignorant of the Muslim way of life when they took over the government. A major task of the Chulalongkorn government (1868–1910) was to centralize the government; thus, various local power centres in the country were brought under the direct control of the Bangkok government. But for the Muslim provinces in the South, exceptions were made—hereditary rulers were allowed to hold office until death. In Pattani and Narathiwat, it was not until 1940 that they were replaced by governors appointed from Bangkok.[10] Where Muslim customs were concerned, the Thai government was flexible; for example, it appointed Muslim judges to settle civil disputes among Muslims. The conflicts between Muslims and Buddhist Thais had to be brought to Thai courts presided over by Thai judges, but because Thai courts were relatively free from corruption, no blatant cases of Thais favoured over Muslims have been reported.

Since the early 1960s, and especially since the early 1970s when violence erupted in the Muslim areas, the Thai government has made efforts to specially train officials before sending them there, by teaching them the Malay language, Islam, and Malay culture. At the same time, the government has hired Malay university graduates (special quotas were allotted for Malay students in state universities) and tried to wipe out the image that the Thai bureaucracy is the preserve of Buddhist Thais. These efforts, especially the one to prepare officials for the Muslim areas, have had some effects on reducing tension between Muslims and Thais. After all, the Ministry of the Interior, which control all local administration including that of Muslim areas, has recruited competent university graduates and assigned them to the South to improve the administration there. Once assigned, they had to perform well to obtain a favourable evaluation from their superiors—an important condition for promotion. The experience and tradition of local administration was one definite advantage Thailand had over the Philippines.

The problem of Muslim insurgency in Thailand is, however, not over, and though the level of violence has come down, it can flare up again. A basic grievance of the Muslims is the low level of development in the four provinces. The rate of land utilization is low, and rice lands are flooded almost annually. The level of education, which is correlated to the level of income, is also low. The Thais might say that Muslim resistance to Thai education is the basic cause of the lower level of education, but if Thai administration is to be accepted, the government has to put more resources into education. The economic underdevelopment of the Muslim areas should not be overly stressed since their income level is not very low (less than 30 per cent lower than the national average in 1980).[11] Small-scale rubber production has provided them with cash income, and there is no deepening sense of material deprivation as experienced by the Moros in Mindanao. Nevertheless, there is a strong feeling that they are being discriminated against under the Thais and that their Muslim brothers in Malaysia (a higher-income country) have been faring better. Among the various minorities, the Muslims have been the most resistant to assimilation, and have been testing the capability of the Thai administration.

The International Dimension

Thailand has also handled the international connections of Muslim rebels much better than has the Philippines. The increased violence in Mindanao attracted more international attention and thus more aid from Islamic countries, but it all started with the mishandling of the Malaysian connection. In contrast, the Thai administration handled its problem with considerable tact, though there was a greater danger of Malaysian involvement in southern Thailand. In particular, it did not antagonize the Malaysian government by raising the issue of the four states which had been incorporated into Malaysia, and co-operated with it in fighting Malaysian Communist insurgents—also a means by which to discourage the Malaysians from getting involved in the Muslim issue in southern

Thailand. Islamic fundamentalists, especially Parti Islam leaders in Kelantan, have helped Thai Muslim insurgents by giving some material aid, but the Malaysian government, although a Muslim-dominated coalition, has never openly supported Thai Muslim rebels.

The Philippine government blundered in claiming Sabah (rich in timber and other resources) as part of its territory in 1968. Though Sabah (and Sarawak) is separated physically from Peninsular Malaysia, the Malaysian government has no intention of handing it over to the Philippines. The Philippines asked the Malaysian government to let the World Court arbitrate, but the latter objected, asserting that it was a non-issue since the people had voted in the plebiscite of 1963 under the auspices of the United Nations to join the Federation of Malaysia. The tactic of the Malaysian government later became that of aiding Moro rebels in order to put pressure on the Philippine government to drop its claim on Sabah. Such organizations as the MNLF probably obtained substantial material aid from Malaysia. Moreover, the former Malaysian Prime Minister, Tunku Abdul Rahman, as Secretary-General of the Organization of the Islamic Conference, promoted international support for the Moro cause.[12]

At state level, Tun Datu Mustapha Harun, Chief Minister of Sabah (1968–76), actively supported Moro rebels, allowing Sabah to be used as a training camp, supply depot, communications centre, and sanctuary. It is said that he was particularly interested in aiding the Moros because he wanted to take Sabah out of Malaysia to form a new state of his own consisting of Sabah, Mindanao, Palawan, and Sulu.[13] Besides such a political scheme (if true), being a native of Sulu who had migrated to Sabah, Tun Mustapha was sympathetic towards the plight of his brethren in Mindanao and particularly incensed with the Philippine claim to Sabah. In 1977, President Ferdinand Marcos promised to take steps to annul the Philippine claim, and Malaysian assistance to the Moro rebels dwindled. The Philippine claim had brought no benefits to the country; it had only exacerbated the Moro insurgency by prompting Malaysia's involvement.

Mindanao: Frontier Land for Christian Filipinos

The Muslim problem in the Philippines was serious, but the Christian Filipinos who came to control the government failed to realize it.[14] The Moros constituted a nation within the nation. They never submitted to Christian Filipinos in the pre-war period. They became part of the Philippines because they had submitted to the Americans in exchange for religious freedom, but the entire territory under American rule was handed to Christian Filipino leaders at independence. From the viewpoint of many Moros, this was an act of grievous irresponsibility. They had a number of times expressed to the Americans their wish not to be subjugated by Christian Filipinos, and that if the Americans withdrew, they wanted a separate state.[15] Some Americans were sympathetic towards the Moro cause and argued that the region under the Department of Mindanao and Sulu (which was later incorporated into the Bureau of Non-Christian Tribes) should be separated and granted independence or kept under American rule. But Christian Filipino nationalists objected, and in a hurry to get out of the Philippines, the United States acceded to their demand.[16] Some Americans predicted that to do so would cause the Moros to take up arms.[17]

Mindanao was a frontier land, rich in resources (forests, mines, fertile agricultural and grazing lands), and thus naturally attractive to Christian Filipinos, especially landless Filipinos. During Spanish times, the latter could not go there in large numbers because a large part of the island was Moroland, under Muslims who were not subjugated by the Spaniards; only some coastal areas of the island came under Spanish control. But the new conquerors, the Americans, were mightier and more considerate (at least not interested in converting them to Christianity), and the Moros submitted to their rule. Unfortunately, the peace and order under the Americans opened their land wide to Christian Filipino migration. The American government also needed better-educated and better-motivated Christian Filipinos in the administration of the land. As a result, the Christian Filipino population rose to 66 per cent by the end of the 1930s.[18] By 1960, it had risen further to about 80 per cent, and stabilized at this level. As the Christian population increased, the Moros were pushed back further into the hinterland, and today they remain a majority only in the provinces of Lanao del Sur, Maguindanao, Tawi-Tawi, and Sulu. In North Cotabato and Lanao del Norte—two provinces often regarded as Moro—in the mid-1970s, Moros made up only 37 and 23 per cent of the population respectively.[19]

From the viewpoint of the Moros, Christian Filipinos had taken away their ancestral lands (forest and agricultural) unjustly, but they could not appeal to the government or the courts, since the Christian Filipino officials or judges did not recognize Islamic law or local customary law (*adat*) concerning their land. To the officials, all lands not registered with the government were public lands which could be claimed by anyone as homesteads or leased to corporations (if they were forest lands or there were mines). There occurred a repetition of land grabbing, as had happened in Luzon and the Visayas (see Chapter 13). As Christian Filipinos became a majority, they began to control the politics of the area, and got away with many blatant acts of injustice. Most of the traditional Moro leaders, who were co-opted by the Manila government into the local and central administration, did not defend the interests of the community vigorously enough. The rising population of Christian Filipinos and their increasing control of land resources fuelled a deep anger among Moros.[20] As early as the mid-1950s, a number of them felt that justice could best be served by fighting the Christian Filipino 'invaders', and the violence thus assumed menacing proportions.[21]

The Rise of the MNLF

The turning point in the violence came in 1968 when the Muslim Independence Movement was formed by Governor Datu Udtog Matalam of Cotabato Province. Its formation is said to have been triggered by the execution of Moro recruits a few months earlier in Corregidor (an island in Manila Bay), by the Philippine military. (Moro recruits were apparently undergoing training for the infiltration of Sabah to ferment a pro-Philippine uprising.) The independence movement itself did not have its own army (at least not openly), but the bands of armed Moros who appeared thereafter ('blackshirts', 'barracudas', etc.) were not entirely unrelated to the movement. They attacked and pillaged Filipino settlements and towns. But the Filipinos had the upper hand in the fighting. They formed vigilante groups (the best and strongest was the Ilagas) and fought with the help of the Philippine military. In June 1971, some 70 Moro men, women, and children were massacred by the Ilagas at a mosque in North Cotabato; in July 1971, a grenade exploded inside a mosque, and over 60 Moro homes were burnt by the Ilagas in Lanao del Norte; in October 1971, the Philippine military slaughtered 66 Moros in the town of Magsaysay in Lanao del Norte in retaliation for their killing of a 22-man Constabulary patrol; and in November 1971, in Barrio Tacub in Lanao del Norte, the Philippine military massacred at least 40 unarmed Moros who were returning after dark in several trucks from the voting station in Magsaysay (Tacub Massacre).[22]

The MNLF was formed around 1971 by such people as Nur Misuari of Sulu and Abul Khayr Alonto of Lanao del Sur in preparation for secessionist guerrilla warfare (some were being trained abroad). However, the MNLF did not surface until after martial law was declared. The situation was bad enough before martial law; President Marcos said that the conflict between Moros and Christians had resulted 'in the killing of over 1,000 civilians and about 2,000 armed Muslims and Christians, not to mention the more than five hundred thousand of injured, displaced, and homeless persons as well as the great number of casualties among our government troops, and the paralyzation of the economy of Mindanao and Sulu'.[23] The Moro problem was one of the reasons for Marcos's declaration of martial law, but it worsened the crisis by broadening Moro support for their radical leaders. For example, Marcos's demand that civilians surrender their arms to the government forced the Moros with arms to make an immediate choice between surrendering arms and joining the rebels—many took the latter option. In Mindanao where peace and order had frequently broken down after independence, for many men (not only Moros but also Christians), it was a part of their manhood to bear arms.

From late 1972 to early 1973, the Moros attacked and took Marawi, overran much of Cotabato Province, and occupied most of Basilan and Sulu Islands. After martial law, the MNLF emerged as the strongest and best disciplined of the rebel groups. They went into a frenzy of activity in 1973 and in the first quarter of 1974.[24] The government fought back by deploying 70 per cent of its military manpower there, backed by tanks, heavy firearms, and airplanes. As a result of the escalated fighting between government forces and rebels, some towns were reduced to ashes (for example, Jolo in Sulu in 1974); as many as 1.5 million people, Muslim and Christian, were displaced;[25] and a large number of people were killed. (According to one estimate, the number of deaths was about 20,000 per year during the few years following the declaration of martial law.)[26] The fighting engulfed 13 provinces in Mindanao and Sulu.

Casualties came down to about 4,000 in 1977, as a result of the Ceasefire Agreement—the immediate result of the Tripoli Agreement concluded in Libya—signed between the government and the MNLF earlier that year. It was hoped that fighting would stop after the Ceasefire Agreement, but it was honoured more in the breach than in the observance. The agreement did not make clear the extent to which the Philippine government would yield to MNLF demands (how much autonomy, on what matters, and in which provinces). The Ceasefire Agreement broke down after October 1977 when an MNLF force killed Brigadier-General Teodulfo Bautista and 34 other Army officers at Jolo. (The details of this incident are unclear, but the government, which controlled the mass media, used it to arouse the indignation of Filipinos.) To further complicate the matter, the MNLF was split into a few factions, and some former MNLF forces became so-called 'lost commands'. Becoming essentially bandit groups, they resorted to kidnapping for ransom and extortion, giving rise to different dimensions of the problem of peace and order in Mindanao.

Marcos committed greater financial resources to Moroland and met the various demands of moderate Muslim leaders. By keeping them on his side, he succeeded in weakening support for the MNLF, whose forces numbered about 10,000 in the early 1980s, a significant drop from the 50,000 to 60,000 in the mid-1970s. Thus, although the ceasefire broke down, the level of fighting never returned to the level of the mid-1970s, and in many parts of Moroland, law and order improved. But when Marcos fell in early 1986, his Moro supporters lost the backing of the Manila government, and became vulnerable to the attack of their political enemies in some areas (for example, Marawi) where the situation worsened as a result. It then spilt over to nearby predominantly Christian Filipino areas (for example, the burning of Iligan City's commercial centre).[27]

The war waged by the MNLF and other radical Moro groups forced the Philippine government to realize that some autonomy had to be given to the Moros. They were distinct from other ethnic groups who would eventually succumb to the 'juggernaut of Filipinization'. They were too cohesive religiously, and could appeal to the Islamic World for help if their way of life was greatly threatened. (For example, they accused the Philippine government of 'genocide' in 1971 when a number of Muslims were 'massacred'.) In 1989, in 13 provinces in Mindanao, the government held a referendum on whether or not the people wanted to join the proposed Autonomous Region of Muslim Mindanao. As a result, the four provinces where the Moros are a majority (Lanao del

Sur, Maguindanao, Sulu, and Tawi-Tawi) were incorporated into the newly created region. This, however, did not stop the rebels from fighting. Many of their leaders decided that instead of pursuing secession they would settle for autonomy because the former course did not receive international backing (they depended on Islamic countries for financial assistance, and so could not ignore their views), but they still called for a boycott of the referendum of 1989. As they feared, the results did not enhance the rights of Moros in the provinces where they are a minority. Though the level of fighting declined in the late 1980s, rebel forces still numbered around 20,000, affecting about 1,200 places in mid-1992.[28] Badly split, however, they are not in a position to resume large-scale hostilities.[29]

In the 1950s and 1960s, despite incidents of violence, Mindanao was possibly a positive factor in the national economy. It was rich in forest resources and agricultural lands; a large number of homesteads as well as new plantations were set up. It was also a suitable place for industrial plants; for example, Iligan became the site for large industrial establishments. But the escalation of violence since the early 1970s has reduced its contribution to the national economy. Mindanao covers about one-third of the country's land surface. Although not the whole of Mindanao was affected by rebel forces, fighting took place in most provinces (Zamboanga del Norte, Zamboanga del Sur, Lanao del Norte, Lanao del Sur, North Cotabato, South Cotabato, Sultan Kudarat, Maguindanao, Davao del Sur, and Davao del Norte, and the three island provinces, Palawan, Tawi-Tawi, and Basilan). The MNLF and other radical Moro groups shook the very foundation of the Mindanao economy by threatening personal safety and private property. One might blame the Philippine government for not containing Filipino migration, but it was too attractive a frontier for Christian Filipinos in Luzon and the Visayas to leave to the Moros. The unassimilable Moros occupying a rich land was what the Philippines inherited at the time of independence: it was a time bomb which was bound to explode in due time.

1. T. J. S. George, *Revolt in Mindanao: The Rise of Islam in Philippine Politics*, Kuala Lumpur: Oxford University Press, 1980, p. 202.

2. The three groups are split along regional lines. The MNLF under Nur Misuari consists mostly of Tausogs and operates mainly in western Mindanao; the MILF under Hashim Salamat consists mostly of Maguindanaos (headed by Salamat himself) and operates in southern and central Mindanao; and the MNLF Reformist Group under Dimasangkay Pundato consists mostly of Maranaos concentrated in the Lanao provinces (Cesar Tapia, 'The Moro National Liberation Front', *Solidarity*, 110 (January–February 1987): 138).

3. The spread of the NPA in Mindanao was another reason why foreign pineapple producers avoided investing there. The Del Monte and Dole plantations and processing centres are located in Christian areas and were not threatened by Muslim rebels. Their problems were more with the KMU. But the MNLF, coupled with the NPA, made Mindanao generally unsuitable for the plantation industry.

4. W. K. Che Man, *Muslim Separatism: The Moros of Southern Philippines and the*

Malays of Southern Thailand, Singapore: Oxford University Press, and Quezon City: Ateneo de Manila University Press, 1990, p. 114.

5. Surin Pitsuwan, *Islam and Malay Nationalism: A Case of the Malay-Muslims of Southern Thailand*, Bangkok: Thai Khadi Research Institute, Thammasat University, 1985, p. 16.

6. Ibid., p. 241.

7. Ibid., p. 243.

8. Hashimoto Takashi, 'Thai Nanbu Kokkyo Ken Mondai to Malay Muslim Togo Seisaku' [Problems in Southern Border Provinces and Malay-Muslim Integration Policy], *Tonan Ajia Kenkyu,* September 1987: 247.

9. Reported in Surin, *Islam and Malay Nationalism*, p. 229.

10. Michael Vickery, 'Thai Regional Elites and the Reforms of King Chulalongkorn', *Journal of Asian Studies*, August 1970: 877.

11. Che Man, *Muslim Separatism*, p. 36. In the Philippines in 1970, Region XII, where there was a concentration of Moros, had a per capital income about half the national average. The Moros' average income must have been even lower, since Christian Filipinos slightly outnumbered Moros in the region and probably enjoyed a higher level of income. For the income level in Region XII in 1970, see National Economic and Development Authority, *Regional Development Information: Region XII*, Metro Manila, 1978, p. 19.

12. Ibid., p. 139.

13. This is the charge of Tun Mohammad Fuad, founder of the Berjaya Party (Sabah). Reported in George, *Revolt in Mindanao*, p. 237.

14. Moro–Christian conflicts are here considered to have arisen primarily from land disputes and the ignorance or insensitivity of Christian Filipino officials. But the negative stereotypes of Muslims created during the colonial period were probably an underlying factor. The massacres of Muslims described below briefly were probably related to this. For a concise discussion of the negative stereotypes, see Mark Turner, '"One Whole Sorry Mess": The Zamboanga Hostage-taking Incident', in Mark Turner et al. (eds.), *Mindanao: Land of Unfulfilled Promise*, Quezon City: New Day Publishers, 1992, p. 190.

15. W. Cameron Forbes, *The Philippine Islands*, Cambridge: Harvard University Press, 1945, pp. 289–92.

16. Joseph Ralston Hayden, *The Philippines: A Study in National Development*, New York: Macmillan Co., 1942, pp. 13–15.

17. For example, Clarence Miller who travelled in Mindanao in the mid-1910s (Forbes, *The Philippine Islands*, p. 293).

18. Che Man, *Muslim Separatism*, p. 25.

19. George, *Revolt in Mindanao*, p. 218.

20. Peter Gowing, *Muslim Filipinos: Heritage and Horizons*, Quezon City: New Day Publishers, 1979, p. 190.

21. *Far Eastern Economic Review*, 24 March 1955: 355. The novelist Sionil Jose also recalls the situation in 1949 when he was with the *Manila Times*:

'[F]or a month I covered the Kamlon campaign together with a veteran army reporter, Jose Vera. Colonel Lao was the commanding officer of Sulu then. We were briefed on the military movements—the Navy boats and the Air Force were to strafe this area, blocking battalions would be set up, and so on—to trap the old man Kamlon and his 30 men. Yet the very next day, Kamlon and his men disappeared from the place where they were supposed to be surrounded by the military. We spent millions of pesos in that campaign. Aside from the terrible expense, there was the waste of human lives' (*Solidarity*, 110 (January–February 1987): 81).

22. Gowing, *Muslim Filipinos*, pp. 193–4.

23. Ibid., p. 196, quote.

24. George, *Revolt in Mindanao*, p. 202.

25. Simeon A. Datumanong's figures in *Papers on the Tripoli Agreement: Problems and Prospects*, Manila: International Studies Institute of the Philippines (Faculty of Law), University of the Philippines, 1986, pp. 6–7.

26. An Associated Press dispatch in August 1975, quoted in Gowing, *Muslim Filipinos*, p. 235.

27. For the situation in Marawi after the fall of Marcos, see G. Carter Bentley, 'People Power and After in the Islamic City of Marawi', in Benedict J. Kerkvliet and Resil B. Mojares, *From Marcos to Aquino: Local Perspectives on Political Transition in the Philippines*, Quezon City: Ateneo de Manila University Press, 1991.

28. *Manila Bulletin*, 11 July 1992.

29. *Philippine Star*, 6 June 1992.

15
Crime

THE impression that Thailand is a peaceful country is generally correct. Muslim violence was restricted to the four small provinces in the South, and Communist insurgency to the remote provinces in the North-east and the North. Furthermore, the duration of the violence was relatively short, and its intensity low. Violent crimes were also contained. On the occasion of the fifth anniversary (1963) of his administration, Prime Minister Sarit Thanarat told the people with great pride that the country had won foreigners' praise for being a peaceful country and that the Thais could thus devote themselves entirely to national development.[1] He was not flattering his people: a number of foreign observers were reporting that Thailand was a peaceful country. One American scholar wrote in the early 1960s that 'Thailand remains calm. Indeed, it is safer to travel from the northermost [*sic*] to the southernmost borders of Thailand than to walk through the city streets of Chicago. This domestic calm has been extremely useful in terms of developing communications and in spreading the central authority throughout the land.'[2] In the early 1970s, another foreign observer wrote that 'general conditions of public order and safety are normally good'.[3]

In the Philippines, land disputes gave rise to Communist insurgency, and many big landlords, as a defence, set up private armies. Government forces were often not strong enough to maintain peace and order in the countryside. The situation was very different from Thailand where government forces were generally effective in controlling the country. In the process of centralization of power during the reign of King Chulalongkorn, practically all local lords were replaced by governors appointed from Bangkok (except those in the Muslim provinces in the South). The government also suppressed large Chinese secret societies before they became too powerful. In fact, the military build-up in the pre-war period was partly to maintain law and order in the country, not only to defend the country from foreign aggression. In some cases, the two were interrelated. For example, in the North-east, which the French wanted to bring under their sphere of influence, rebellions could easily give them an excuse to intervene in Thai affairs. They sometimes even tried to abet a rebellion in order to create a pretext for intervention.

The government crushed all armed resistance and maintained peace and order in the country in the pre-war period, and quickly brought guns under control after the war (there were some armed resistance groups); hence, in post-war years, it was only Communist insurgents and Muslim separatists who had the arms to carry out large-scale violence. But they were restricted to remote areas; even in the 1970s when fighting was at the peak, most of Thailand was peaceful. One felt safe travelling in the country, unless one ventured into remote fighting zones. But even during Sarit's time, numerous petty crimes (thefts) and some violent crimes (murders) were being committed in Bangkok, while small groups of bandits were roaming some parts of the country. The Thai government was fairly adept at handling large-scale organized violence, but was not so effective in controlling crime and lesser violence.

The Thai Police: Corrupt at the Fringes

The task of combating crime and violence was left to the police. Since the 1950s, the police have been known to be corrupt; for example, they were involved in drug trafficking. When General Phao Siryanon was heading the Police Department in the mid-1950s, it was said that he made sure that opium from Yunnan was safely transported from the northern border to Bangkok and loaded on to ships to Hong Kong, Singapore, Saigon, and other commercial centres of Asia. At that time, Yunnan was supplying as much as 75 per cent of the world's opium, and it was said that Phao made huge profits in this illicit trade. He apparently distributed parts of the profits to policemen who needed extra income, but used a large portion of it for his political ends (he was Sarit's rival during Phibul Songkram's time). In addition, the police were running protection rackets for prostitution, smuggling, and gambling in the cities (especially Bangkok).[4]

Police extortion was damaging to business. As explained in Chapter 3, the Chinese became the target of extortion by the police. Since there was no due process of law or any such legal protection introduced from the West in Thailand in the 1950s (under the military government), if a Chinese was charged with being a Communist, it was difficult for him to prove his innocence. The police could arrest the Chinese arbitrarily, and if necessary, deport them as a lesson to other Chinese. It was a show of strength on the part of the government which was concerned about the resistance of the Chinese to assimilation into Thai culture. But the police often abused their powers, and extorted money from Chinese merchants. The vulnerability of Chinese merchants at that time was put dramatically by a Thai newspaper: 'It is the easiest thing in the world to bleed [the] Chinese in our country. . . .'[5]

Police extortion declined in the 1970s and 1980s as Chinese businesses were taken over by new generations who were Thai citizens and integrated into Thai culture, and as the nature of government changed, incorporating more democratic measures. But the reputation of the police did not improve. In the late 1980s, it was said that they were still running protection rackets for prostitution and trafficking in drugs (together with the military), and that they began co-operating with local *chao poh* (godfathers) who were not only involved in illegal prostitution and gambling but also in legal businesses such as real estate development and construction. *Chao poh* killed their business competitors or anyone who stood in the way of their business deals. Killing competitors was not, however, the practice of *chao poh* only. Hired killers were available for a few thousand to several thousand dollars, and if a tough competitor could cost a businessman millions of dollars, it was less expensive to kill him off. In early 1990, the police said that dozens of murders had been sparked off by business conflicts.[6] Still, the extent of such tactics was contained, and the general business climate was not affected.

The police were not even very effective in solving violent crimes. During 1984–8, several thousand murders were committed each year, but suspects were arrested in only slightly over 40 per cent of these cases.[7] The police complained that there were too many murders in Thailand. In the Bangkok Metropolitan area where the largest number of murders was committed, the police did a better job of ferreting out suspects because of public pressure, but they did very poorly in the provinces. In the late 1980s when the government was planning the Southern Seaboard Project, the police undertook a crime study of Nakhon Si Thammarat and Surat Thani (two major provinces in the region). In the former, there were 6,777 murder cases during 1979–88; in 17 per cent of these cases, suspects were arrested; in 14 per cent, they were prosecuted; and in 7 per cent, they were sent to prison. Police performance in Surat Thani was only slightly better.[8]

If murders were too many for the police to handle, thefts were a hopeless case. Even around 1990, many people did not bother to report thefts because the police could not resolve them. However, many others did, and were disappointed. It was said, though, that if private rewards were offered, police performance improved. Under the circumstances, the best form of security was self-protection. In downtown Bangkok, shophouses were usually fitted with iron grilles, and in residential areas, many houses had iron railings with sharp hooks or shards of glass on top of the walls. Some rich ones even had security guards and a burglar alarm.

There were a lot of complaints about the police because people believed that they could do a better job in arresting criminals or reducing the number of crimes; but there were a couple of mitigating factors which could be said for them. First, if they seriously investigated (possibly under political pressure), they often solved the cases. For example, if Japanese tourists were killed, Thai police usually apprehended the culprits to show that they were in control of the situation. Secondly, although police corruption was deplorable, it was mostly restricted to running protection rackets for prostitution and gambling or other 'fringes' of the underworld. It was unusual for the police to be ringleaders of kidnapping and other criminal syndicates, the same problem which was plaguing the Philippines around 1990. Fortunately for the Thai police, the number of violent crimes, which shot up in the 1970s, fell in the mid-1980s, partly because of a rise in income. The number of murders declined from about 12,000 per year in the mid-1970s to 6,000 in 1988.

The peace and order factor did not affect foreign investment adversely. When the economy boomed in the second half of the 1980s, foreign expatriates generally felt it safe to live in the country. Tourists also visited in large numbers, making the tourist industry the country's major foreign exchange earner. Some tourists may have been cheated while shopping (for example, in buying gems), but they generally felt safe to walk in Bangkok or travel in the provinces.

The Crime Outlook in the Philippines

The crime outlook was worse in the Philippines. The conditions in Metro Manila were, however, tolerable until the mid-1980s. But then the situation deteriorated rapidly; foreign expatriates were kidnapped or killed, and numerous incidents of robbery were reported. Heavily guarded banks and armoured vans carrying cash were frequently robbed: in 1991, 18 banks and 32 armoured vans were held up.[9] Bombs exploded at commercial establishments (probably the work of urban guerrillas of the New People's Army and rightist rebels), with 36 explosions occurring during a six-week period around September 1990.

Then many Chinese Filipino businessmen became the targets of kidnappers. In its editorial of February 1992, a Chinese newspaper urged the government to pay more serious attention to the plight of Chinese businessmen as 'the list of preys' had become alarmingly long.[10] Since many victims (or their families) did not report the kidnappings to the police, the exact number of Chinese victims is not clear; but in October 1992, one newspaper reported a cumulative total of 140 cases in the preceding 18 months.[11] It is sometimes reported that victims paid on average ₱6 million (about $220,000 by the 1991 exchange rate), but the real average may be less. The amount of ransom varied from case to case (depending on the ability of the victims' families to pay); in a number of cases the amount was less than ₱1 million.[12] As the deterioration in civil peace became frightening with an explosion of these crimes, the new Fidel Ramos government's first major act was to declare a war on crime. This became a war on the second front (fighting insurgents was the first front).

In the 1980s, when Thailand enjoyed about 10 per cent annual growth in the arrival of foreign tourists, the Philippines experienced no growth in this aspect at all. (Slightly fewer than one million visited the country each year, including the *balikbayan*, Filipino residents abroad returning for a short trip.) Many Japanese tour agents wrote off the Philippines as a tourist destination. Towards the end of the decade, large Japanese companies began shelving their investment projects out of concern for the safety of employees and their families. The reaction of the Chinese victims of kidnapping was usually to scale down their business and start thinking about getting out of the country. The rampant kidnapping affected the whole Chinese business community in Binondo (an area in Manila where Chinese businesses are concentrated). If money was to be made, it had better be done quickly; long-term strategies became unrealistic.

The Philippine Police: Corrupt to the Core

If the Thais did not report thefts to the police, it was because it was a waste of time. In the Philippines, many people did not report even robberies because, it was said, they did not want to be robbed twice: the first time by criminals and the second time by the police. The following report is illustrative of the lack of trust in the police among Chinese businessmen in the early 1990s:

> Five armed robbers held up the Gem Gallery in No. 792, Ongpin St.... They were armed with Uzi machine pistol [*sic*], .38 caliber revolvers and .45 caliber pistols. The armed guards were rendered helpless because of the robbers' superior weapons ... ironically the jewelry store was just a few meters away from the Chinatown police detachment. The jewelry store owner, Jeffrey Ty, refused to file a case.[13]

If the Thai police were corrupt, it was only at the fringes, but the Philippine police were rotten to the core. It was charged that many high-ranking policemen were involved in criminal syndicates undertaking kidnapping, robbery, and car theft (called 'carnapping' in the Philippines). Around 1990, 'hoodlums in uniform' became a serious issue. The early victims of kidnappers went to the police, and discovered that the kidnappers were policemen.[14] After this story spread, kidnap victims stopped reporting to the police. A study by the Philippine National Police (PNP) (probably done in early 1992) showed that 65 per cent of heinous crimes were committed by men in uniform.[15] Vice-President Joseph Estrada, head of the Presidential Anti-Crime Commission, said in late September 1992 that 90 per cent of kidnappers arrested or killed were men in uniform. Among policemen were not only ringleaders of such criminal syndicates, but also drug addicts, rapists, and compulsive killers. One newspaper columnist urged that policemen undergo a psychiatric examination to determine whether or not they are fit for the police force. (They take a test when they apply to join, but it is known to be administered badly.)[16] The situation deteriorated so much that it attracted foreign criminal syndicates (Taiwan's Bamboo Gang, Hong Kong's Triad and 14-K).[17] This was in addition to the over 50 Filipino syndicates extant.[18]

Alfredo Lim, Mayor of Manila and a former police chief, was elected in 1992 on the issue of law and order; he proposes that the only way out of the quagmire is to create an entirely new police force. With the people fed up of corruption in the existing force, there is a great deal of support for Lim's proposal. Many policemen are thugs who used to work for politicians. In the Philippines, most influential persons hire bodyguards, and prefer those who are notorious for being ruthless because they are more effective. When they become politicians, these bodyguards often become policemen with their recommendation. Thugs are said to have a strong urge to be an agent of the law as a badge of social respectability. Once they become policemen, their major concern is to make extra money by moonlighting as thugs.[19] It is said that many policemen are of this ilk. The estimate going around in September 1992 that only about 5 per cent (5,000 out of the 100,000-man force) of them were thugs underestimates the real magnitude of the problem.

Those accused of involvement in kidnapping were not just policemen (belonging to the PNP) but also solidiers in the military and officials in the Department of Justice, especially the National Bureau of Investigation and the Bureau of Immigration and Deportation. The one kidnapping gang busted in late September 1992 involved some in the latter bureau. They had access to files on Chinese businessmen who had applied for naturalization and could select wealthy Chinese businessmen as their targets. A son of a wealthy customs broker was identified as the mastermind of the gang. He told the press that he had six generals in the PNP and four generals in the military protecting him; but he retracted his statement the following day. It is often alleged that high-ranking officers in the military and especially the police were acting as protectors of criminal syndicates. In fact, Vice-President Estrada arrested two high-ranking officers in the PNP, Major Jose Pring, head of the PNP's Anti-Kidnapping Task Force, and Major Timoteo Zarcal, chief inspector of the Criminal Investigation Service Command, on charges of aiding criminals.

Whether high-ranking officers (in the PNP, the military, immigration, or any other government agency) were corrupt or not could be easily found out by investigating their family expenditure and wealth. Their salaries were not high; the starting salary was a few thousand pesos (about $100) per month, and the maximum was around ₱17,000 ($680 in mid-1992). Yet the lifestyle of many of them was luxurious. They bought new cars, which cost at least $10,000; their wives had credit cards; their families went on foreign trips and dined at expensive restaurants; and their children attended private schools. The following report gives a glimpse of their lifestyle:

> The wives of military and police generals had a big bash the other night at the Manila Hotel [a government-owned five-star hotel where state guests usually stay]—supposedly for the benefit of the blind. They called it 'An Unusual Evening.' The generals were resplendent in their bemedalled uniforms; the wives, in their expensive ternos [Filipino women's formal dresses] and evening gowns, glittered from their diamonds and golden ornaments. 'With all the glitter from diamonds and gold, there was no need for disco lights,' a guest remarked, adding, 'The women looked like Christmas trees.'[20]

No government agencies, however, want to investigate the wealth or expenditure of their ranking officers, especially in the PNP. When charges of corruption are hurled against them from outside, they try to cover up for each other. The PNP is probably the most corrupt government agency in the Philippines. While many ranking officers are busy collecting money from criminals for protection, many of their subordinates do not show up in the office for many days, and use officially issued guns to perpetrate crimes. There is a rule that guns are to be handed in when they finish work, but many do not bother, for it is not enforced.

The Philippine Judiciary

The integrity of the judiciary is also suspect. Some judges have been called 'hoodlums in robes', a term recently used by Vice-President Estrada himself. In mid-1992, as part of the efforts to clean up its ranks, the Supreme Court dismissed a judge for pointing a high-powered firearm at a policeman whom he alleged had ridiculed him in public: this was an idiosyncratic case. More troublesome were the judges who could be influenced by money. Many judges in regional trial courts (for example, in Metro Manila) are said to be corrupt. When people entangled in long litigation ask their lawyers how much would be needed to win their cases, they are not asking about the legal fees. In the early 1990s, corruption had besmirched the Court of Appeals too. The Supreme Court did little to remove corrupt judges,[21] some of whom are said to be on the payroll of criminal syndicates.

The Supreme Court does not seem to be rotten to the core (unlike the police), but it is not above criticism. After martial law was declared, people began criticizing its justices. The first round of criticism arose from the decision which upheld the constitutionality of martial law in the mid-1970s. Many who opposed martial law took the case to the court, hoping that it would be ruled unconstitutional, but in their disappointment, they began saying that the majority of the justices who upheld its constitutionality were promised money and perquisites by Marcos. A prominent Filipino lawyer described the attitude of several justices towards martial law: 'Now that you have declared it, I might go along with it, but it depends on what you will give me.'[22] Criticisms especially centred around Enrique Fernando, whom President Ferdinand Marcos had appointed Chief Justice. Then in 1982, a bar examination scandal blew up when apparently some justices had leaked the questions. After this came into the open, all justices resigned, but most of them were later reappointed.[23]

It was not, however, only during martial law that Supreme Court justices were criticized. During the Corazon Aquino administration, people felt that the lifestyle of some justices was too expensive for the salaries they were receiving. (In mid-1992, their pay was around ₱200,000, or $800, per month). In Thailand, though the police are often criticized, one does not hear much about the judges. It is said that although the rich and influential tend to be favoured in civil cases, judges are fair in criminal cases. But even in civil cases, Thai judges seem to be generally fair, and no blatant cases of injustice have been reported.[24] In contrast, in the Philippines, even before martial law, many judges in lower courts were said to be corrupt, and the rich and powerful could get away even with murder.

A basic problem was salaries. Judges' real salaries steadily declined in the post-war period because the government was generally slow in adjusting civil salaries (but they were better paid during martial law). To compensate for the low salaries, many judges were willing to be influenced by the richer and more influential litigants. To make it more lucrative for themselves, they broadened the jurisdiction of the court and began interfering in administrative decisions. Consequently, as early as the mid-1960s, court cases were piling up. Soon after Marcos became President, he deplored the fact that the wheel of justice was turning too slowly. A decade later, Chief Justice Castro warned that 'docket congestion is a large, formidable, and menacing enemy'.[25] In the mid-1950s, after a civil or a criminal case was filed, the judge rendered his decision in at most 6 months, but in the late 1980s, an average case took 3–5 years. The backlog of tax cases was worse: one study showed that even if the judges were to work 50 per cent faster in the Court of Tax Appeals, it would still take them 476 years to catch up.[26]

The delay of justice stemmed from the quality of judges. As judges' salaries declined relative to the incomes of competent lawyers in private practice, the more ambitious and competent of those who passed the bar examination did not enter the judiciary. Furthermore, until recently, the appointment of judges was entirely in the hands of the president, a situation which allowed his political cronies to lobby for their nominees, thus casting aside merit as the basis for appointment. According to the same Filipino lawyer cited above, 'the Philippine judiciary is run mostly by rejects'.[27] Many judges were not fully knowledgeable about procedure and often lost control over their cases.

The decline of the quality of judges has also contributed to the broadening of the court's jurisdiction mentioned above, which, if not motivated by profit, was possibly brought about by wrong prioritization of the cases filed. As if to make up for their deficiencies, judges developed 'a passion for pure law' and got involved in the cases (such as administrative decisions) they could easily refuse to admit into court.[28]

Docket congestion was, however, not only the fault of judges; prosecutors and lawyers too were culpable. Even after a case was filed, proceedings were often delayed because prosecutors were not prepared, or lawyers often wanted an adjournment. It was said that there were about 44,000 lawyers in the country (compared with Thailand's 5,000) and that many of them were the 'world-class champions of delay' (which is profitable for them since they are typically paid by the court appearance rather than by the case). The legal system is partly to blame for the malaise. Essentially, as a copy of American law, Philippine law guarantees many rights to the accused, and defence lawyers can take advantage of them to delay the proceedings. Critics call the Philippine version of due process 'overdue process'.

The penal system is another problem. Despite the rickety judicial system, many criminals end up in prison (especially if they are poor), but prison guards are not doing a good job of keeping them there. It is reported that over 2,700 prisoners escaped between 1987 and 1992. Many of them were serving life terms for rape, murder, and other heinous crimes. It is sometimes suspected that prison guards co-operate with prisoners who are willing to pay to leave the prison for good or for the privilege of temporary freedom so that they can tend to their business, or undertake new money-raising activities (hold-ups and robberies). It was reported that during 1988–90, despite a take-home pay of about ₱40,000 ($1,800) per year, Leon Casanova, a Davao Penal Colony superintendent, made four trips to Japan where one of his sons was studying, bought a brand-new passenger car (costing about ₱400,000), and a couple of jeeps.[29]

Some prisoners have patrons (either in the military or police) who want to use them for special 'missions'. The most notorious of these is Noberto Manero, Jr., who in 1985 killed an Italian priest whom he believed to be a supporter of the Communists. Manero was a leader of the rightist Christian group Ilaga who fought Muslims and Communists in Mindanao and was known for his fearlessness and brutality. (It is said that he sliced and ate the internal organs of the enemies he killed; and that in the case of the Italian priest, he scooped up his brain and proudly showed it to terrified passers-by.)[30] He was originally incarcerated in a maximum security prison in Muntinglupa, but, for some unknown reason, was later transferred to a minimum security detention institution (Davao Penal Colony) where he enjoyed the privilege of going and coming as he pleased. It is argued that if the Bureau of Prisons cannot keep the perpetrators of heinous crimes, the death penalty—abolished under the 1987 Constitution—should be re-imposed.

The Gun Culture in the Philippines

Peace and order deteriorated partly because the Philippine government was lax in controlling the possession of guns. With the Americans as a role model, many Filipinos considered the possession of a gun a democratic right, as guaranteed in the Constitution of the United States. Since security was not good (particularly in the provinces where government forces were inadequate), wealthy people needed guns for their own personal safety as well as to protect their property. In areas threatened by Communist insurgents or Muslim separatists, it was not enough to have guns: wealthy people created their own private army. Some had standing armies of a few hundred well-armed men. Those with a large private army of their own were like warlords, with their own spheres of influence which they controlled like their own 'fiefs'. As long as their supremacy was unchallenged, there was peace and order, but as they often fought each other (for example, in competing for political office), it caused a great deal of violence in the countryside. In addition, they frequently used their forces to increase their control over resources (like agricultural lands), and hence indirectly adding to the violence because many of those who were victimized resisted the injustice and then finding that to be futile, they joined rebel forces or became bandits.

The gun culture has given rise to the violent conditions in the country. Many people settled disputes with guns, whether they were over business deals or personal matters. Incidents of a boy killing another over a girlfriend (or sometimes both of them) are often reported in newspapers in Manila. The killing of people over business deals is less common judging from the dwindling reports in recent years in the Philippines (unlike Thailand), but in earlier years, it was a problem. For example, in 1971, the general manager of Sumitomo Corp., a Japanese trading company, was shot dead in his car (his two Japanese colleagues were wounded); it was suspected that this killing was prompted by conflicts over a business deal.[31] A Japanese textile trader who visited the country for the first time in the 1960s was shocked when he saw Filipino businessmen coming to the negotiating table with pistols on their hips, and demanded that they be left somewhere else.[32] They may not have been carrying pistols as a threat to the Japanese negotiator, but with frequent shootings going on, Japanese businessmen had the impression that the Philippines was similar to the Wild West they had seen in American movies.[33]

Economic Consequences

The prevalence of crime was one of the reasons for Marcos's declaration of martial law in 1972. One often heard then from Japanese businessmen, 'Don't take a taxi even in the daytime. Chances are that you will be robbed by the driver.' This was certainly an exaggerated fear on their part, but the killing and wounding of Japanese traders in 1971 could not help but raise their anxiety. At the same time, there was a mood of general anxiety arising from the political violence and turmoil which had prevailed since the First Quarter Storm of student demonstrations in 1970 (for example, the Plaza Miranda bombing incident in August 1971). Peace and order in the Philippines was certainly the worst among South-East Asian countries up to that time (worse than, for example, in Indonesia which had been shaken by economic chaos until the mid-1960s).[34]

The serious crime problem was neither Marcos's fabrication to justify martial law nor was it a perception confined to the Japanese. It was widely shared by the foreign business community. The American Central Intelligence Agency report around early 1966 stated that the Philippines was beset by 'land hunger in the countryside; unemployment in the cities; and a grinding poverty for the overwhelming majority of the people. The situation was aggravated by widespread violence and lawlessness. . . .'[35] An article in *Fortune*, the business magazine, reported a few years later:

> Like most other characteristics of the irrepressible and altogether likable Filipino people, the lawlessness is flamboyant. It has become a way of life. Much of the countryside is run by warlords . . . ; in the cities there are tens of thousands of armed guards at homes and commercial establishments. The murder rate is the highest in the world, estimated as high as forty-eight per 100,000 population (versus six in the U.S.). Among some recent spectaculars: a provincial vice governor was shot to death at the steps of the provincial capital; bandits aboard an airliner systematically robbed all the passengers, shot and killed one of them just

before the plane landed, and escaped in a getaway car waiting at the end of the runway; and the national water system was robbed of $1,279,000 worth of water through thousands of secret taps on the mains. Justice has become a farce, with some 80,000 cases pending in the courts.[36]

Martial law temporarily arrested the worsening trend of lawlessness, but in the end, it further weakened the law enforcement agencies by corrupting them. As the economy deteriorated at the end of martial law and under the Aquino administration, the crisis worsened. The explosion of crimes during this period was in a way the outcome of the gradual erosion of the legal bureaucracy (the police in particular) since independence. It was a clear manifestation of the Philippine government's inability to govern properly, under either democracy or martial law. The explosion of crimes scared away potential foreign investors and tourists, and caused the flight of badly needed domestic capital.

Given that even the police in Thailand are corrupt, it is not surprising that the Philippine police are also corrupt (in fact, even more so), but what is rather daunting is the corruption of the Philippine judiciary. Not only does the wheel of justice turn very slowly, it is also subject to the influence of the rich and powerful; they can break the law with impunity. The effect of the corruption of the judiciary is not any less deadly to the economy than to the civil peace. When powerful landlords took land away from peasants, there was not much the peasants could do to seek redress in a peaceful manner; the only way left was to join the rebels in a quest for revenge. The corruption of the judiciary may not have been a main cause of rebellions against the government, but it was a contributing factor. When a crook tried to take property away from a small businessman with a fake title or some legal 'gimmicks', there were many judges willing to co-operate with the crook. Thus, the businessman could lose his property to a complete stranger by a court order. Judges might plead that they did not have much choice as the crook was so powerful that he could intimidate them if they did not co-operate. Foreigners engaged in retail trade (including restaurants and many other services) through dummies were easy targets as they were barred from retail trade under the Retail Trade Nationalization Law. The same tactics could also be used for bigger companies, but they could hire lawyers or seek protection from powerful persons. This, however, increased the costs of their operation.

A cynic may argue that, although legal protection of private property is an essential condition for economic development, security of property can be privately arranged. However, this expense is costly, and thus acts as a deterrent to numerous investments which can be carried out only at a lower cost of protection. Moreover, such security may be tenuous, for if the patron dies or loses his influence, the source of protection is gone. For these reasons, the lack of public justice is a barrier to capital accumulation. Thailand faced a similar problem, and businessmen often resorted to private arrangements (for example, by using established business networks), but the Thai judiciary was not so hopelessly corrupt as in the Philippines.

1. Roger Smith (ed.), *Southeast Asia: Documents of Political Development and Change*, Ithaca: Cornell University Press, 1957, p. 40.

2. Joseph Sutton, 'Political and Administrative Leadership', in Joseph Sutton (ed.), *Problems of Politics and Administration in Thailand*, Bloomington: Department of Government, Indiana University, 1962, p. 14.

3. Frank Moore, *Thailand: Its People, Its Society, Its Culture*, New Haven: HRAF Press, 1974, p. 353.

4. Wendell Blanchard, *Thailand: Its People, Its Society, Its Culture*, New Haven: HRAF Press, 1958, p. 198.

5. Quoted in G. William Skinner, *Chinese Society in Thailand: An Analytical History*, Ithaca: Cornell University Press, 1957, p. 303.

6. *Manager* (a business magazine published in Bangkok), 26 March–8 April 1990; *Far Eastern Economic Review*, 17 January 1991; and Saito Chikanori, *Bangkok Taizai Monogatari* [The Story of My Stay in Bangkok], Tokyo: Gakusei-sha, 1990, p. 117.

7. *Statistical Yearbook, Thailand*, Bangkok: National Statistical Office, Office of Prime Minister, 1990, p. 121.

8. Interview with Pol. Maj. Panya Maman, Deputy Superintendent, Research and Planning Division, Royal Thai Police, Bangkok, 5 March 1991.

9. The figures are from Max Soliven's column in the *Philippine Star*, 2 August 1992.

10. *Tulay* (a Chinese Filipino monthly newspaper), 9 February 1992.

11. *International Herald Tribune*, 19 October 1992. The figure comes from *Tulay*.

12. *Tulay* (11 October 1992) estimates the number of kidnap cases at 44 and the ransom paid at ₱150 million (an average of ₱3.4 million per case) in the three-month period after the 11 May 1992 election.

13. *Tulay*, 8 December 1991.

14. The editorial of the *Philippine Star*, 22 July 1992.

15. Quoted in Gemma Luz Corotan's article in the *Manila Chronicle*, 18–24 July 1992.

16. Art A. Borjal's column in the *Philippine Star*, 8 July 1992.

17. *Tulay*, 31 March 1991.

18. It is said that there were over 1,000 criminal groups altogether, with over 6,000 members (Joey Caburnida's report in the *Manila Chronicle*, 27 July 1992).

19. Napoleon G. Rama, 'Coping with Criminality: Why Cops Turn Criminals', *Philippine Panorama* (the weekly magazine of the *Manila Bulletin*), 29 November 1992: 3.

20. Emil P. Jurado's column in the *Manila Standard*, 11 November 1992.

21. Emil P. Jurado's column in *Manila Standard*, 9 November 1992. In a speech delivered during the Philippine Judges Association Conference at Quezon City on 30 July, President Ramos, after quoting a famous judge who said that '[i]t is of fundamental importance that justice should not only be done, but should manifestly and undoubtedly seen to be done', deplored the fact that justice is not yet being seen to be done by a large majority of the Filipino people. The text of the speech was published in the *Philippine Star*, 5 August 1992.

22. Interview with Alfonso Felix, Manila, 20 February 1991.

23. Raul P. de Guzman, 'Towards Redemocratization of the Political System', in Raul P. de Guzman and Mila A. Reforma (eds.), *Government and Politics of the Philippines*, Singapore: Oxford University Press, and Quezon City: College of Public Administration, University of the Philippines, 1988, p. 275.

24. The situation in the late 1950s was described as follows:

'At the present time the Thai judiciary enjoys a good reputation for honesty and competence, although it is often charged that leading politicians and businessmen receive favored treatment' (Blanchard, *Thailand*, p. 182). In one of the conversations the author had with Krirkkiat Phipatseritham, former rector of Thammasat University, he confirmed that roughly the same situation prevailed around 1990.

25. Quoted in Frolian M. Bacungan and Alfred Tadiar, 'The Judiciary', in Raul P. de Guzman and Mila A. Reforma (eds.), *Government and Politics of the Philippines*, Singapore: Oxford University Press, and Quezon City: College of Public Administration, University of the Philippines, 1988, p. 174.

26. Reported in the *Asian Wall Street Journal*, 25 October 1988.

27. Interview with Alfonso Felix, 20 February 1991.

28. The phrase 'a passion for pure law' comes from Beth Day, *The Philippines: Shattered Showcases of Democracy in Asia*, New York: M. Evans and Co., 1974, p. 29.

29. *Sunday Times*, 29 November 1992.

30. Eugene A. Tan's column in the *Business World*, 27 November 1992.

31. Based on the theory that the killing was prompted by business conflicts, a novel was written in Japanese: Fukada Yusuke, *Ennetsu Shohnin*, Tokyo: Bungei Shunju-sha, 1982. The case has not been solved.

32. Kato Mikio of Marubeni told this story to the author in September 1991. A joke going around then in Manila was that you could tell a Filipino couple anywhere in the world: the woman bulged in front and the man bulged behind (Day, *The Philippines*, p. 21).

33. Interview with Osawa Kiyoshi, President of NYK-Fil-Japan Shipping Corporation, Manila, 21 January 1992.

34. Kunio Yoshihara, *Japanese Investment in Southeast Asia*, Honolulu: University Press of Hawaii, 1978, pp. 85–6.

35. Quoted in Raymond Bonner, *Waltzing with a Dictator: The Marcoses and the Making of American Policy*, New York: Times Books, 1987, p. 443.

36. John Mecklin, 'The Philippines: An Ailing and Resentful Ally', *Fortune*, July 1969: 119.

16
Coups D'état

'Peaceful' *Coups* in Thailand

THAILAND has had many *coups*. If a *coup d'état* is defined as an overthrow of the government by violent means, then there has been slightly over 15 *coups* (including unsuccessful ones) since the overthrow of absolute monarchy in 1932. But if it is defined as an overthrow by unconstitutional means, it can only take place when there is a Constitution in place. Defined this way, the first *coup* took place in 1947, and there have been four more successful *coups* since then (in 1957, 1971, 1976, and 1991); in addition, there have been four unsuccessful *coups* (in 1949, 1951, 1981, and 1985). Furthermore, there have been a number of *coup* plots which were not carried out. One such example is the so-called Silent Coup of November 1951 when a group of military officers plotted to abolish Parliament. It is said that it was not carried out because Prime Minister Phibul Songkram objected to it.

The 1947 *coup* set a pattern for the later ones. The Revolutionary Party which usurped power from the King in 1932 consisted of military officers like Phibul and civilian leaders like Pridi Banomyong. In the course of time, the civilian leaders lost their influence, particularly after Phibul took over as Prime Minister in 1938. Under him, Thailand joined Japan in declaring war against the Allies, and the initial Japanese victory in South-East Asia strengthened the hands of the military, for it brought such concrete benefits to the country as the regaining of two west-bank Laotian provinces and north-western Cambodia (including Battambang) from France and four Malay states from Britain. But the tide of the war eventually turned against Japan, and the military government was replaced by a civilian one headed by Khuang Aphaiwong in mid-1994. (Phibul had not abolished Parliament during the war.) With the surrender of Japan in August 1945, the military withdrew from politics, and were replaced by politicians, with the help of the Allies.

Thailand was not, however, treated as a defeated enemy. Its declaration of war against the Allies had not been delivered to the US government because Seni Pramoj, Thai ambassador to the United States, had defied the instruction of the Bangkok government. Seni had instead brought together the Thais in Western countries to form the Free Thai Movement. Establishing contact with civilian leaders such as Pridi in Thailand, the Free Thai Movement fought the Japanese and Thai military under the direction of the Southeast Asia Command, whose headquarters was located in Ceylon (now Sri Lanka). A day after the Japanese surrender, Pridi, in the capacity of Regent, issued a formal statement in the name of the King proclaiming the declaration of war null and void. Seni returned soon after, and became Prime Minister. This series of moves exonerated Thailand from war crimes, and although the military had to move back into their barracks, they went unpunished.

Sir Josiah Crosby, minister in the British Embassy in Bangkok before the war, urged the Allies to crush the Thai military as they were planning to do in Germany and Japan. He argued:

> If the failure of constitutional government in Siam has proved one thing, it is that a relatively powerful army must represent a standing menace to the liberties of the people of any country in which the traditional form of government has been weakened or destroyed without the creation of an effective public opinion to supplement or replace it.... Not until this impediment has been removed will there be a prospect for the application of democratic principles in Siam.[1]

His advice went unheeded, and the military returned to power two years later.

A few factors worked against democracy in Thailand in the early post-war years.[2] First, for people who had been used to swift government decisions, democracy was an inefficient way of making political decisions and a licence for politicians to indulge in corruption. In particular, nothing was done about the worsening inflation. The cost of living index, with 1938 as the base year, went up to 902 in 1945, 1,070 in 1946, and 1,250 in 1947.[3] Government employees, who constituted the bulk of the middle class at that time, suffered under the hyperinflation as their salary increases lagged way behind price increases. Their patience with politicians was wearing thin.

Secondly, King Ananda died of gunshot wounds in June 1946. Although it is said that he was fond of handling guns, and thus may have wounded himself by accident, people began accusing such democratic leaders as Pridi of regicide, because they were suspected of attempting to turn the country into a republic. Although the charge was posssibly false, Pridi, who became Prime Minister in March that year, had to resign two months after the King's death, accepting the responsibility for not being able to clear up the mystery surrounding the death. (Democratic governments did not last long in the immediate post-war years, including the first democratic government of Seni.)

Thirdly, the increasing influence of Communists in the world made the United States and its allies more tolerant of anti-Communist military regimes. The Communists were gaining influence in Asia—China and Indo-China in particular.

After Pridi resigned, Thamrong Nawasawat, a former rear admiral, became Prime Minister. Although Thamrong was a former military officer, he was not a friend of the Army, which had increased its influence under Phibul. He was instead an ally of Pridi. The Army did not like the way they had been treated after the war, and the 1947 *coup* leadership led by Lieutenant-General Phin Chunhawan, Colonel Phao Siryanon, and Colonol Sarit Thanarat forced Thamrong to resign, and asked Khuang, the civilian Prime Minister from mid-1944 till the end of the war, to form a new government. The group could not take over the government directly, partly because they were not sure of foreign reaction to the *coup*. Western powers, which had become worried about the spread of Communism and more appreciative of the ability of a military government to stop it, did not react negatively to the *coup d'état*. Several months later, they replaced Khuang with Phibul. There was no strong reaction from pro-democracy forces against the return of the military to politics: the roots of democracy were too shallow.

This time, Phibul did not have the absolute power he had before and during the war. The *coup* leaders needed Phibul because they did not have a dominant leader in the group. In a way, they shared power with Phibul. But the group was not a solid one, and they started quarrelling with each other. Phin retired in 1954, and after that, Phao (Phin's son-in-law) and Sarit competed for supremacy. The 1957 *coup* was the overthrow of Phibul as well as the elimination of Phao by Sarit. With Phao heading the police, which under him was akin to a fourth branch of the armed forces, Sarit's victory also meant the victory of the army in the power struggle. The Navy had lost influence earlier—having participated in two failed *coups* (in 1949 and 1951)—and joined hands with Pridi's civilian group. The Navy's grudges were related to the overthrow of their leader Thamrong in the *coup* of 1947.

Sarit abolished Parliament, but did not rule out reinstating Parliament sometime in the future. The pattern of *coups* after this was to dissolve the existing Parliament and promise a new Constitution, under which a new Parliament was to be elected. The opening of a new Parliament would weaken the power of the military, and in order to reassert their power, they carried out another *coup*, thus starting a cycle again. But over time, the interval between a *coup* and a new Parliament became shorter, and the new Parliament lasted longer. (The Parliament elected under the Constitution of 1978 lasted until February 1991. This was as a result of the growth of democratic forces.) The only exception to this pattern was the Parliament opened under the Constitution of 1974, which was not drafted by a *coup* government. In October 1973, the Thanom Kittikachorn–Prapart Charustien government was brought down by democratic forces led by students. This was the first indication that democratic forces were growing in the country, and that it was not possible for the military to revert to the style of government in the 1950s and 1960s which allowed them to run the country in the way they liked.

The *coups* did not affect the economy; in fact, their economic results were usually positive. The *coup* of 1947 indirectly stopped the ongoing inflation because the government budget was brought under control after the *coup*. The *coup* of 1957 strengthened the economic bureaucracy, opened up the country to foreign investment and saw the implementation of the first of the Development Plans. The economic effects of the *coup* of 1971 were not clear cut. Its purpose was the abolition of the Parliament convened under the Constitution of 1968. The government leadership remained with Thanom and Prapart after the *coup*; it was their *coup* against their own government, supported by the Army. The *coup* of 1976 was more controversial in that it smashed the growing democratic forces, but it was welcomed by people in business because leftist influences had been getting stronger, as reflected in the increase in industrial and agrarian disputes. It was also the time when the Communists were gaining power in Indo-China, and people were worried about the possibility of their take-over of the country. For these as well as many other people, the return of the military to power was welcomed.

The most recent *coup* (1991) was unpopular, but people had been fed up with widespread corruption among politicians; thus, their reaction to the *coup* was not strong. But with the increased strength of democratic forces, the military could not form a government by appointing their leader as prime minister. They instead chose Anand Panyarachun, former Under-Secretary of the Ministry of Foreign Affairs, as interim Prime Minister. Anand, together with the Members of Parliament (appointed by the *coup* leadership), undertook various reforms to strengthen the economy, such as trade liberalization, the creation of the Securities and Exchange Commission, and the replacement of business taxes with value-added taxes. The Anand government was favourably received by the business community.

Take-overs of the government went smoothly in all *coups*. The *coups* of 1947 and 1991 entailed little violence because the military were unified and did not face popular opposition. In the *coup* of 1976, the military (together with the police and armed civilian groups) smashed student groups in Thammasat University, the centre of student activism, and a large number of students died. (Thirty-nine students died on the day the military moved into the campus, 12 more died later, and 137 were wounded.) The attack on the students was completed in a matter of hours, and the scene of violence was restricted to the university campus located along the Chao Phraya River, far from the business centres. The only successful *coup* which might have resulted in large-scale violence was the one in 1957, but the Sarit group overwhelmed the opposition quickly and let Phao and Phibul leave the country for exile abroad.

There were four failed *coups* against the Army's leadership, and these entailed more violence than the successful ones, though the level of violence was still low. The first two in 1949 and 1951 were perpetrated by politically motivated naval officers (who were disgruntled with the government) together with the Pridi civilian group against the Phibul government. They were easily overwhelmed by the Army. The other two failed *coups* took place in 1981 and 1985. They were planned and carried out by certain groups in the Army, and could have had devastating effects on the economy if their leaders had decided to fight it out. But they also ended with little violence.

The *coup* of 1985 was planned by a group in the Army disgruntled over promotion and other service conditions. The motivation behind the *coup* of 1981 was different, and was more menacing to political stability than the *coup* of 1985. A certain group became unhappy with the way the political situation had been moving under the 1978 Constitution, and wanted to abolish Parliament and set up a military dictatorship. They were particularly unhappy with 'monopoly capitalists' (especially bankers) who were gaining influence under democracy and using it, in the group's view, to pursue monopoly profits while many people were suffering from poverty.

The 1981 *coup* was led by the Young Turks, whose most prominent leader at this time was Colonel Manoon Ruperkachorn, who had participated in the *coup* of 1976, engineered the one in 1977, installing Kriangsak Chomanan as Prime Minister, and then replacing him with Prem Tinsulanonda in 1980. The *coup* leaders took control of the First Army in Bangkok, and demanded that Prime Minister Prem (who was also Army Commander at this time) lead a *coup* against his own government. Prem refused, and with the King escaped to Nakhon Ratchasima where the Second Army's headquarters is located. The King's move was a clear sign of disapproval of the *coup* and support for Prem. Soon after this, the Third and Fourth Armies sided with Prem, and it also became difficult for the *coup* leaders to mobilize even the divisions of the First Army in the Bangkok area, let alone those outside it. The *coup* collapsed a few days later. (The First Army covers the Central Region, the Second Army the North-eastern, the Third Army the Northern, and the Fourth Army the Southern.)

The fact that two *coups* were attempted against the Army's top leaders shows that there have been problems within the Army bureaucracy. The fall of the Thanom–Prapart government is also said to have been brought about by a split in the Army. A certain group in the Army (led by General Krit Sivara) was getting upset over the possibility of Narong, the son of Thanom and son-in-law of Prapart, succeeding them. Narong was being groomed as their successor, but he was not well liked in the Army because of his arrogance and extensive involvement in corrupt dealings. Such instances of disunity notwithstanding, it is impressive that the Army could minimize infighting in its over 50-year history of political involvement.

Since the early 1960s, the growing economy has increased the number of sinecures Army leaders can occupy during their service or after retirement, enabling them to control a greater amount of the budget. Their control of expanding resources has undoubtedly contributed to the easing of tension within the Army bureaucracy. But discipline was also a contributing factor; in particular, the mandatory retirement age of 60 was generally observed, and the chances for promotion were there for younger officers as they got older. (To ease the aspirations for promotion, the Thai military may have become a little top heavy.) There was also a strong *esprit de corps* among Army officers. All graduating from the Chulachomklao Military Academy, they shared a number of values, and there was extensive communication between officers of different graduating classes and those in different Armies. This was helped by the practice of rotating officers from one Army to another. This, of course, does not mean that there were no factions in the Army.

The most serious cause for factionalism was based on graduating classes, and such a split was the basis for *coups*. But the redeeming feature in all their differences is that when *coups* did not succeed (as in 1981 and 1985), their leaders surrendered without fighting. Because of certain grievances, they staged *coups*, hoping that they would be supported by the rest of the Army. However, if they failed to gain support, they were willing to talk matters over with their fellow officers or superiors, and eventually surrender. If the king was on the other side (as in 1981), their cause was almost hopeless. The split in the Army was not so deep that *coup* leaders would want to fight it out.

Recent but Bloody *Coups* in the Philippines

The history of *coups d'état* in the Philippines is shorter and confined to more recent years; but when they occurred, they involved a large number of soldiers, caused many casualties, and rocked the economy to its foundations. Until the early 1970s, the military did not get involved in politics. Their major function was to fight insurgents; in the 1950s, they crushed Huk rebels, and in the early 1970s, they were fighting newly constituted Communist insurgents and newly emerged Muslim separatists in Mindanao. But after President Ferdinand Marcos declared martial law, he brought the military out from the barracks and into the corridors of power. Marcos needed them to back him up, and increased their personnel and budget as well as their privileges and perquisites. The military certainly liked their upgraded status.

Nepotism and corruption were the two major problems that cropped up within the military bureaucracy. Already before martial law, a number of officers had got fed up with Marcos's blatant interference and favouritism in matters of promotion, such as the one of Ver, his former driver and fellow Ilocano, to General in 1971. In the eyes of the graduates of the Philippine Military Academy, Ver was 'an integree [an ROTC reservist integrated into active duty], an outsider who had started as a non-commissioned officer'.[4] Furthermore, 10 years later, Marcos made him Chief of Staff. Soon after this, a movement started in the military to reform itself (Reform the Armed Forces Movement, RAM), and over time, its leaders came to believe that the only way to reform the military was to remove Marcos.

Even Arturo Aruiza, Marcos's close military aide who fled to Hawaii with him and stayed until his death in 1989, could see that Ver had become a liability to the Marcos administration:

> Under Gen. Fabian C. Ver, many retireable high-ranking officers who should have been let out to pasture were still being extended in the service, so long as they were known to be loyal to Ver and the President. This froze the upward movement of younger men, who were capable, ambitious, and professional. Graft and corruption among the officers flourished, contributing to the low state of morale in the rank and file, and fueling among the more decent officers, a deep anger.[5]

Aruiza further states that Ver 'grew rich, very rich' by abusing the power vested in him by Marcos and that 'his name was invoked whenever smuggling and gambling flourished'.[6] As to Ver's favouritism in the promotion of officers, he states:

> Ver protected and promoted his boys, among them his three sons: Rexor, Irwin, and Wyrlo, who made it to Lt. Colonel, Colonel, and Major respectively. Irwin's rise was particularly meteoric and galling. He was the middle son but without doubt his father's favorite, and his promotion was disgusting to the officer corps.[7]

RAM leaders (such as Lieutenant-Colonel Gregorio Honasan) had planned to stage a *coup* in February 1986, soon after the presidential election. But when they thought that their plot had been leaked to the Ver side, they quickly dropped their plan, and joined the revolt of Juan Ponce Enrile (Minister of National Defense) and Fidel Ramos (Vice-Chief of Staff) against Marcos in Camp Aguinaldo (located along Epifanio Delos Santos Avenue, commonly known as EDSA). This led to the so-called EDSA Revolution which brought down Marcos and installed Mrs Corazon Aquino as the new President. Under the new administration, some RAM leaders viewed their task as having been accomplished and hence left the movement, but many stayed on and kept the movement alive. Then in December 1989, RAM staged the most serious *coup* the Philippines had ever seen. A total of 2,911 rebel troops (469 officers, 70 officer candidates, and 2,372 enlisted men) fought government forces; 99 were killed, and 570 were wounded. Total damage was estimated to be around ₱1 billion ($46 million).[8]

The *coup* of December 1989 lasted about a week. The rebel soldiers bombed Malacanang (the President's office) and military establishments, succeeding in taking some of them (for example, Villamor Air Base and Sangley Point), but the forces loyal to the government successfully resisted their attack in such key military establishments as Camp Aguinaldo. The trend of the fighting eventually began to turn against the rebels, and the crack Scout Rangers on the rebel side retreated from Fort Bonifacio (which they had taken earlier) to the nearby business town of Makati, as the strategy changed to one of prolonging the mutiny. They occupied its first-class hotels, large condominiums, and office buildings. Hotel guests and condominium residents were trapped, and their lives endangered. Makati was paralysed, and foreign residents in nearby residential areas panicked. The *coup* received extensive coverage from the international media, and the image of the Philippines as an unstable country was fixed in the minds of tour agents and investment decision-makers. After the *coup*, hotel occupancy in Metro Manila plunged to a low 40 per cent;[9] and a number of foreign investment projects were shelved (for example, Sony's investment plan). Reflecting the worsening economy, the booming stock prices before the *coup* plummeted (from 1,400 points in November 1989 to 654 in 1990).

There had been a few *coup* attempts before December 1989. The first was the Manila Hotel Incident of July 1986, only several months after

Aquino became President. It was the attempt of Marcos loyalists, civilian as well as military, to establish a new government with the support of the people, as Aquino's supporters had done to Marcos in February. However, there was no such popular support, and the rebel group, isolated in the hotel, capitulated in two days. There were no casualties, and property damage (mainly to the hotel) was minimal, but this conveyed the impression to the world that Aquino's presidency was far from stable.

After this, Marcos loyalists (led by Brigadier-General Jose Maria Zumel) staged a few more *coups*. The one in January 1987 resulted in a small number of casualties, but the rebels were quickly overcome. It was a small group, but because they occupied a television station for a few days, it attracted some attention from the media. Marcos loyalists staged one more *coup* a few months later, but this met a fate similar to that of the January *coup*. After this, they did not plot a *coup*, but remained disgruntled under the new administration. In December 1989, many of them participated in the *coup* initiated by the RAM group.

In August 1987, RAM surfaced as the major rebel group; by mobilizing over 1,000 soldiers, it launched simultaneous attacks on military establishments and Malacanang. The rebel soldiers led by Honasan tried to capture Malacanang, but they failed; several men were killed or wounded. On the way back to their camp (Aguinaldo), they spotted the convoy of Aquino's son (Benigno 'Noynoy' III), who was rushing to Malacanang after hearing news of the attack; they wounded him and killed his bodyguard. They also shot at jeering civilians, killing 11 and wounding 54. The rebels were overwhelmed by government forces in one and a half days, but this rebellion had become the bloodiest so far, with some 53 people dead and more than 200 wounded.[10] Over 2,000 soldiers were involved in this *coup*. Because of the scale of the *coup* and the large number of casualties, the *coup* attracted considerable attention from the international media, and contributed further to the notoriety of the Philippines as a politically unstable country. After the *coup* was foiled, one journalist wrote that 'the President hid under the bed while the firing was going on—perhaps the first commander-in-chief of the Armed Forces of the Philippines to do so'.[11] This turned out to be false (her bed was so low that none could have hidden underneath it); but it tarnished the image of the President.[12]

The *coups* were bad enough, but *coup* leaders, in order to give legitimacy to the *coups*, tried to cause social chaos by terrorism and sabotage before the events. Before the intended (but not carried out) *coup* of November 1986, Rolando Olalia, the leader of the radical trade union Kilusang Mayo Uno, was abducted, and his mutilated body was found soon afterwards. It was probably a provocation aimed at the anti-military labour and various other groups. They blamed the military for the murder of Olalia, and staged a nation-wide protest. On the day of the *coup* of April 1987, the premises of two multinational firms (Colgate–Palmolive and Unilever's subsidiary, Philippine Refining Co.) were bombed. Shortly before the *coup*, a spate of bombings rocked Manila.

Certainly not all bombings and acts of sabotage in Metro Manila during the Aquino presidency were the acts of NPA urban guerrillas.[13]

The *coups* were unavoidable in the transition from dictatorship to democracy. There were Marcos loyalists in the military who lost their privileges and perquisites and felt discriminated against under the new presidency. They wanted to bring Marcos back as President, but did not have the support of the people. Although, over time, many people became disillusioned with the Aquino administration, they were not yet ready to accept a *coup d'état*. By mid-1987, Marcos loyalists had lost the capacity to stage a *coup* on their own, and after his death in Hawaii in September 1989, they lost their cause too. They represented the first *coup* group.

The second *coup* group was RAM led by Honasan. Undoubtedly, its leaders were not happy with Aquino and wanted to overthrow her. In many ways, they represented the genuine grievances of the military under Aquino. They had ties with civilian leaders who felt the same way, and obtained financial assistance from them. Many RAM leaders (including Honasan) were called 'Enrile's boys', because they had worked for him in the Ministry of National Defense during the Marcos period. It is widely believed that at that time, Enrile used his personal funds to give them privileges and perquisites because he needed them as an insurance against Ver, who would have been more than glad to get rid of him. Even after the new administration was installed, Honasan and other RAM leaders stayed with Enrile in the (now) Department of National Defense. They became dissatisfied with Aquino's handling of the government, and planned a new *coup*. But Ramos, Chief of Staff, did not go along with it (the code name was 'God Save the Queen'); and without his support, it was not carried out. But Enrile was implicated in the plot, and Aquino asked him to resign. His forced resignation must have made RAM leaders more determined than ever to get rid of Aquino.

Ramos remained loyal to Aquino, but Enrile and other Marcos allies were against her. The EDSA Revolution was instigated by Enrile and Ramos, but its success depended crucially on citizens' groups who flocked to EDSA in support of their revolt. The latter included business leaders such as Jaime Ongpin who became the first Secretary of Finance under Aquino, and also included other critics of Marcos with leftist ideologies and anti-military views. Some of their leaders were included in the new Cabinet. *Coup* leaders had a large number of followers in the military because these leftist secretaries were soft on Communist insurgents and trade union leaders, and attacked the military for human rights violations (while forgetting those committed by the insurgents). The critics of the military had been persecuted by the armed forces during martial law, and were naturally antagonistic towards those who occupied high positions in the military under Marcos. If the whole military had gone against Aquino then, the November 1986 *coup* would have succeeded. Thus, the military was split into factions, and the disgruntled ones 'exploded' from time to time. In the meantime, the President took measures to placate the military, such as increasing their salaries and firing leftist secretaries. By early 1990, the Aquino administration had become more rightist than a few years earlier, and rebel forces seemed to have run out of steam. There were no more *coups* after December 1989.

There was nevertheless a sense of camaraderie among the soldiers; there were friends and classmates on opposing sides. But factionalism, intensified by the different alignments of military officers with the Aquino administration, became serious enough to smother the sense of camaraderie, and they killed fellow soldiers and officers on the opposing side. Many of the *coup* plotters of December 1989, including Honasan, still remain at large, but the military appear to have finally adjusted to a democracy.

But democracy may not prevail in the Philippines. With a worsening economy, people will lose confidence in democracy, thus creating a basis for another *coup*, this time possibly a successful one. But this will not come in the near future, since the support base for democracy is still strong. But there is no guarantee that the situation will remain favourable for democracy. A *coup* may yet be staged in the future, and if it is, it will be undertaken by a new generation of military leaders. Honasan and his followers are passing into history.

1. Quoted in Likhit Dhiravegin, *Thai Politics: Selected Aspects of Development and Change*, Bangkok, Tri-Sciences Publishing House, 1985, p. 288.

2. The most readable account of politics in the immediate post-war years is Judith A. Stowe, *Siam Becomes Thailand*, London: Hurst & Co., 1991.

3. James Ingram, *Economic Change in Thailand, 1850–1970*, Stanford: Stanford University Press, 1971, p. 164.

4. Arturo Aruiza, *Ferdinand E. Marcos: Malacanang to Makiki*, Quezon City: ACAruiza Enterprises, 1991, p. 47.

5. Ibid., p. 41.

6. Ibid., p. 85.

7. Ibid., p. 86.

8. *The Final Report of the Fact-finding Commission*, Manila: Bookmark, 1990, pp. 376–8 and 437. This is the report of the Commission set up by the Philippine Congress in January 1990 to investigate the *coup* of December 1989. It also looked into the previous *coups*, and reported its findings. A less authoritative but more readable account of *coups* is given by Criselda Yabes, *The Boys from the Barracks: The Philippine Military after EDSA*, Pasig: Anvil Publishing, Inc., 1991.

9. *Final Report*, p. 378.

10. Ibid., p. 200.

11. Luis Beltran's column, 'Straight from the Shoulder', *Philippine Star*, 21 October 1987.

12. The President sued the journalist and the publisher of the newspaper. In October 1992, the Manila Regional Trial Court convicted the two of libel. The case is now pending at the Court of Appeals.

13. In the morning (30 June 1992) of newly elected President Ramos's inauguration ceremony, four bombs exploded in Metro Manila, three of which were at the branches of Banco de Oro in Quezon City. It is believed that these were the acts of the RAM group. It is said that Henry Sy, the major shareholder of Banco de Oro (as well as the Shoemart chain of department stores), had refused a demand from the rebels to make a financial contribution to their cause (the amount is not known, but believed to be large). The bombings are believed to be their retaliation for his non-co-operation. The rebel group may have made similar demands on others, but the Sy case is the only one which has come out into the open.

17
The Underlying Factors in Maintaining Peace and Order

The Philippines: A Divided Nation

National Division

WHY did the Philippines have more problems upholding peace and order than did Thailand? As have been discussed so far, the different aspects of peace and order (Communist insurgency, Muslim rebellion, crime, and *coup d'état*) arose from various reasons, but one overall cause is the fact that the Philippines is a more divided country.

The reason is mainly historical. Unlike Thailand, there was no Filipino kingdom which shaped the history of the country. The country was created by the Spaniards, and maintained as a colony for a little over 300 years. In a way, the Philippines was created and managed as a 'joint venture' of the Spanish king and the Catholic Church. At the end of the nineteenth century, the Americans took over the country, and tried to implant American ideals; they set up public schools and taught English to Filipinos. Through English education, they were also exposed to American popular culture, such as Hollywood movies. Filipinos sometimes ask rhetorically, 'How could we be a nation after having lived in a covenant for 350 years and in Hollywood for 50 years?' But it is not just the different colonial influences which have divided the country; it was also the 'incompleteness' of colonization—many traditional cultures remained, and coexisted with foreign cultures which were introduced into the country by the colonial masters.

Language

The country is divided in a number of ways. Some 80 languages are spoken as the mother tongues of various ethnic groups in the Philippines today. Of these, 8 may be considered major languages. They are: (i) Tagalog, spoken around Manila; (ii) Ilocano and (iii) Pangasinan in northern Luzon; (iv) Pampango in central Luzon; (v) Bicol in southern Luzon; (vi) Waray in the eastern Visayas; (vii) Cebuano in the central Visayas and Mindanao; and (viii) Hiligaynon in the western Visayas. There have been attempts since the mid-1930s to create a national language, but they have not been quite successful. English has been used as the major language of government and business in the past several decades.

Religion

The Philippines is also split religiously, though not as extensively as in the case of language. The dominant religion is Catholicism. It is not, however, as dominant as Buddhism is in Thailand where 94 per cent of Thais are Buddhists. Only 84 per cent of Filipinos are Catholics; the remaining are Protestants, followers of the Philippine Independent (or Aglipayan) Church and Iglesia ni Kristo (both Christian denominations born in the Philippines), Muslims, Buddhists, and others. Among the minority Christian groups, the followers of Iglesia ni Kristo are particularly noticeable. They account for only a small percentage of the population (about 1 per cent), but their influence is felt far out of proportion to their size because of their unified action. For example, they take a political stand on issues and organize demonstrations, or support a particular candidate for political office. In Thailand, the only major non-Buddhist group is the Muslims, who account for about 4 per cent of the population, with slightly over 1 per cent living in Buddhist-dominated areas, and a little less than 3 per cent in the four provinces bordering Malaysia where they constitute a majority.

The Catholic Church is not as unified as Thai Buddhism is. On the one hand, the conservative clergy believe that religion and politics do not mix, and that the Church risks its credibility by getting involved in political issues. On the other hand, the progressive clergy do not want the Church to confine its role to religious matters, and especially argue that if many people do not have enough to live in a manner appropriate to the dignity of children of God, the Church should play a political role. The schism began appearing after the Second Vatican Council was concluded in the mid-1960s, and became more serious after liberation theology (born in Latin America as a reaction to the Second Council) spread to the Philippines in the early 1970s. There are also different sects within Thai Buddhism, but compared with the Catholic Church of the Philippines, the Thai *sangha* (group of priests) is a unified group. This unity is related to the fact that Thai priests do not concern themselves with temporal matters (which are potentially divisive). For example, the Supreme Patriarch of the Thai *sangha* rarely comments on secular issues. If the Thai mass media pay any attention to him, it is usually when he undertakes a religious ceremony.

In contrast, Catholic priests often comment on social and political issues and sometimes take a strong stand on them. Since the Catholic Church in the Philippines consists of dioceses individually managed by a bishop, there is no one comparable to the Supreme Patriarch of the Thai *sangha*. Among the bishops, the most visible is the Archbishop of Manila, Cardinal Sin. He comments on a wide range of social and political issues and attracts the attention of the mass media. Many people think that he represents the views of the Church in the Philippines, but his administrative authority does not extend beyond the Manila archdiocese; he is only one of many bishops in the Philippines. However, Cardinal Sin is not the only one who takes a strong stand on social and political issues; in fact, many bishops and priests do, and are also active in various social movements.

The Church's involvement has also become a source of division in Philippine society because not all who identify themselves as Catholics agree with the Church on social issues. Some critics say that the Church is too involved in secular affairs. For example, the progressive clergy take a strong stand on the human rights issue, being especially critical of the violations of human rights by the military, thus antagonizing the rightists (especially the military), who feel that the Church is soft on violations by the Communists. Not surprisingly then, among the rightists, there is deep resentment against the progressive clergy. The Church's stand against the use of contraceptives has also split society into those who favour the Church's position and those for a strong family planning programme. The latter, who believe that the population increase is a major cause for the rise of poverty and many other ills in the country, feel bitter about the Church's obstruction of progress.

The Church has been influential in shaping public opinion and putting pressure on the government not to do anything to undermine its (the Church's) position. It is not only the strongest religious organization, but also the most effective civic body. In the field of education, for example, the Catholic Church runs 17 universities, 151 colleges, and almost 400 secondary schools with a total enrolment of more than 670,000 students. Many of the country's brightest students are educated at such Catholic tertiary institutions as Ateneo de Manila University and De La Salle University.[1] Some of the Church's lay members, especially those in Opus Dei, are active in education and writing, and have filled influential government positions (for example, Jesus Estanislao, former Secretary of Finance, is an Opus Dei member). During the Aquino administration, Church-affiliated people became so influential that they became known as the 'Council of Trent'.

Landownership

As pointed out in Chapter 13, there is great inequality in land distribution in the Philippines. In Thailand, however, small landholdings are the dominant pattern. In the mid-1970s when there was some land consolidation with commercialization of the rural sector, even the largest holding did not exceed a few hundred hectares.[2] In 1948, 65 per cent of Philippine rural households did not have their own lands, but worked as tenants or agricultural labourers. In 1955, there were 13,859 owners holding more than 50 hectares each, and of these, 221 held more than 1000 hectares each.[3] Even today, Hacienda Luisita (owned by the Cojuangco family, from which former President Aquino comes), with its more than 6000 hectares, stands as a symbol of inequity in central Luzon. Racehorses and fighting cocks are raised on the hacienda, and it is said that the daily expenses of keeping these animals exceed the yearly income of a peasant.[4]

Education

The country is also culturally handicapped by a lack of a national language. English has been the dominant language of instruction in schools, although the Tagalog-based Filipino language (formerly called Pilipino) has made some inroads into primary and secondary education since the late 1960s.[5] English education has produced a small cultural élite (at most 10 per cent of the population),[6] many of whom have studied abroad, particularly in the United States, and are probably better-educated than their counterparts in other South-East Asian countries. However, the large majority of Filipinos are poorly educated with only a limited, or practically no, knowledge of English. Proficiency in English and the level of education are highly correlated in the Philippines because it is the dominant language through which knowledge is transmitted. (In recent years, however, the situation has begun changing with the increasing use of Tagalog in the mass media.) As a result, to put it strongly, the cultural élite live in the modern world, while the masses inhabit the traditional world where 'feudal' relations remain strong and ignorance is appallingly deep.

As Westernized (that means Americanized) as they are through English education, the cultural élite cannot be well integrated with the rest of Philippine society. A nationalist Filipino historian wrote of their alienation:

> The Western orientation of local education assures that they fit into an American environment. For many Filipinos who go to an American university to study, there is absolutely no 'culture shock.' They are at home, in fact they feel they have found a better home. The culture shock occurs if and when they come back. All at once they cannot stand the heat, the stupidity, the filth, the poor working conditions, everything. They return unprepared to work for or even to understand their own people.[7]

Some critics go further, saying that the cultural élite are not using their influence and position for national development because, blinded by the American model, they do not understand what is truly good for the country. Recently, a prominent Filipino newspaper columnist wrote:

> ... since time immemorial we have sought to imitate the Western model, the American model for national progress. It has not brought us anywhere. We didn't have the culture to absorb such models. Our culture was feudal and pastoral, a village culture overlaid with an elite that aped the Spaniard and the American and borrowed everything shallow and superficial from the West. It was and remains an elite at the top that is an appendage of New York and the Bronx, not of Asia. It is a bought elite, a parasitic elite, a mercenary elite and not a transforming, creative elite.[8]

The élite themselves are not by any means a unified group. On the language issue, some want to retain English as the best way to develop and modernize the country, while others reject it and argue that a national language is essential for mass-based education. On the economic issue, the élite are split into those who have imbibed conservative business philosophy and those who have taken to liberal and socialist economic ideas. The latter argue for foreign debt repudiation, increased minimum wages, more effective land reform, and increased subsidies to government corporations which provide basic services (such as electricity) or directly help the poor (such as the National Food Authority which buys rice and corn at higher prices and supplies them to consumers at lower prices). They are pro-labour, pro-peasant, and pro-poor, and some of them support the Communist Party. They are also severe critics of the International Monetary Fund and the World Bank which try to impose market discipline on the Philippine economy. Not surprisingly, both institutions' position is usually supported by the conservative group who have dominated government policy in the past few years. There are leftists and economic liberals in Thailand also, but they have been a weaker force by far. Philippine democracy tends to produce populist politicians, and because conservative traditions have been weak, the leftists and liberals have been a much greater political force.

Exacerbating Factors in Post-war Philippines

Many of these language, religious, and educational differences have existed in the Philippines since the colonial period, but peace and order still prevailed then. New developments occurred subsequently which exacerbated these divisions. One is political change (in particular, the Pacific War and political independence), and another is the population increase. The first weakened the government structure which maintains peace and order; the second intensified conflicts; and both affected the civic and moral values which work to reduce differences. The Communist insurgency and the Muslim rebellion were the crises which exploded and were prolonged by the weakened military organization, while the crime increase was caused by the decline of moral and civic values and aggravated by the weakened police structure, and *coups d'état* were the conflicts which exploded within the military.

The Pacific War

The Pacific War affected the Philippines and Thailand very differently, not only in terms of the damage and casualties it caused but also in its effects on peace and order. In Thailand, the Japanese intrusion did not change the administrative structure of the country. It enhanced the power of the military regime under Phibul Songkram, and delivered to the country such concrete benefits as the regaining of lost territory. After the war, the military went back to their barracks, but because Thailand was not treated as an enemy country by the Allies, the might of the military remained intact. A couple of years later, through a *coup d'état*, they made a comeback; Phibul became Prime Minister again; and the post-war transition was 'completed'.

The Japanese invasion fundamentally changed the Philippine government. The Japanese military ran the country through a Philippine government. The government's legitimacy was, however, questionable, and guerrilla groups sprung up to fight the Japanese. The Hukbalahap was one of these groups, and with their support, tenants began taking over land from their landlords: the war was good for them. But with the defeat of Japan, the landlords who had suffered during the war wanted to restore the pre-war situation, thus causing the Huk rebellion which devastated many parts of central Luzon.

The Population Increase

The population increase also had differential effects on both countries. With the introduction of DDT (which kills malaria-causing mosquitoes), invention of new medicines (such as antibiotics), and other medical progresses, the death-rate declined dramatically in the post-war years, causing a sharp rise in the population. Both Thailand and the Philippines experienced a 3 per cent increase in population per annum in the 1950s, though the rate of increase declined at a different pace in the following decades. (In Thailand, the decline was more pronounced in the 1980s.) This population increase brought about a massive migration of people from rural areas to cities, raising the level of urbanization to an unprecedented level. In the early 1990s, Metro Manila has slightly over 15 per cent of the total population, a large increase from about 5 per cent in the late 1930s; the Bangkok Metropolitan area has experienced a similar increase in the same period.

Thailand absorbed its population increase better. First of all, it had more land which could absorb the increasing population in rural areas. In the North-east in particular, the area under cultivation expanded in the 1950s and 1960s. Secondly, agriculture diversified, and new agricultural exports such as maize, tapioca, and sugar emerged, which enabled the rural people to increase their income. The whole Thai economy grew at a healthy rate over the 40-year period (1951–91) under study in this book, thus absorbing surplus rural population into gainful employment in cities (the Bangkok area in particular), and at the same time, strengthening the economy of regional cities to which rural areas became increasingly linked through commercial transactions (like the production of food for these cities and people working part-time there).

In the Philippines, however, there was little room for increasing the area under cultivation; there was little diversification in agricultural exports; and the whole economy tended to flounder. Urban absorption of labour was weak, and real wages went down during the 40-year period (especially after the early 1960s). In rural areas, a similar phenomenon took place. There was surplus labour pressing down on wages and pushing up land rent, while with little diversification, the products (sugar, rice, coconuts, etc.) whose prices were declining in real terms continued to be produced. The outlook for sugar and coconuts worsened in the 1980s when nominal prices fell. The overall result was a sharp increase in poverty in both rural and urban areas. According to the government's estimate, the incidence of poverty peaked in 1985 when it reached 62 per cent. In a few years, it declined, but has been hovering around 50 per cent.[9] Poverty became, in turn, the hotbed of crime and Communist insurgency.

The population increase had another consequence. Christian Filipinos migrated from the Visayas and Luzon to Mindanao where there was more agricultural land, thus giving rise to conflicts with indigenous Muslims there. But this migration had been going on since the American period, and if there was anything new to it, it was the increasing rate of migration—it reached the level where conflict was inevitable. To explain the rise of violence there in the post-war years, a few new developments have been considered. One, with independence Christian Filipinos became the rulers of Mindanao, replacing the Americans. Already in the late 1930s, there were many Filipino officials in Mindanao, but they worked under the Americans, in whom Muslim leaders had had greater trust. Later, with the rise of the international Islamic movement starting around 1970, and funded by the oil money of the Middle East, the Moros became more conscious of their rights, and if they wanted to fight, they could get assistance from abroad easily. The Philippine declaration that Sabah is part of its territory aggravated the Moro–Christian Filipino conflict in Mindanao by prompting the Malaysian government to help the Moro fighters.

In Thailand, the problem of Muslim separatism was contained partly because having been an independent country, the question of legitimacy did not arise there as it did in the Philippines. In the southern provinces where Muslims are a minority, they are more willing to accept the central government than Muslims in Mindanao under similar circumstances. Even in the four provinces where Muslims are a majority, their general attitude towards the Thai government is much less hostile than that of their counterparts in Mindanao towards the Philippine government. Muslims accepted Thai rule many centuries ago, and despite various grievances, this historical fact has had a dampening effect on radical Muslim separatists. In the Philippines, the Christian Filipinos were new 'colonizers' to the Muslims; thus, there was greater legitimacy for the Muslim struggle against the government in Manila.

Political Decay

Independence unleashed numerous other problems, for example, that of political decay. As Francis Sayre pointed out (see p. 129), if the masses are not well educated, democracy does not work. In the Philippines, the problem was not simply buying votes with money or getting support with patronage; powerful politicians (especially at the local level) used 'goons' and guns to get 'elected'. Once in office, they bent rules and broke them with impunity. In the beginning, they were more constrained in what they did, but as they found out that they could get away with many things, they got bolder, and the government increasingly became an institution to serve their interests. High stakes were involved in getting elected to political office, because successful candidates could quite freely use government powers and resources to enhance their interests. 'All political offices,' Claro Recto observed, 'are the open sesame to wealth and influence.'[10] Politicians spent a large amount of money on their election campaigns (and even resorted to violence). For example, in the 1957 presidential campaign, the Philippines spent nearly four times as much, in proportion to per capita income, as was spent in the American presidential campaign of 1956.[11]

As unscrupulous politicians gained more power, corruption spread in the bureaucracy. In the process, it lost the ideals and traditions of public service which had been nurtured during the American period. In particular, corruption pervaded the police, military, and judiciary. Judges could be bought; and military leaders and policemen perpetrated crimes. There were also plenty of corrupt officials in other government agencies. Those in internal revenue, immigration, and customs were particularly notorious. In all agencies, government officials used whatever powers they had for their own benefit. For example, many of them kept 'sitting on' papers since the higher the pile of papers was, the more money people were willing to pay in order to get their transaction moving. They stood in the way of things, instead of facilitating them. It is said that even firemen went to the house whose owner paid them most, and negotiated for payments while houses were burning; or that if they went into a house voluntarily, they were stealing instead of putting out the fire.[12]

Marcos's Misrule

The government exacerbated national division by making itself a source of conflict. A good example is Ferdinand Marcos's misrule of the country. Martial law was a factor in the escalation of Muslim violence in Mindanao. His proclamations under martial law that private armies disarm were to Muslims a Christian Filipino trick to subjugate them, and for those who refused, one natural choice was to join the Muslim rebels. It was after his declaration of martial law that the Moro National Liberation Front (MNLF) surfaced, and conflicts in Mindanao mushroomed into a civil war. In fairness to Marcos, however, it should be added that his subsequent measures, which could be implemented only with martial law, removed some Muslim grievances and undercut the strength of the MNLF. But violence remained a serious problem.

Martial law also affected the Catholic Church. The proclamation came soon after liberation theology was introduced into the Philippines, and the government's crackdown on leftist Church activists drove the radical clergy underground. In the beginning of martial law, the stand of a majority of the Catholic clergy was one of critical collaboration, but as an increasing number of human rights violations were reported and crony capitalism became rampant, more clergymen became critical of Marcos and gave their support to the leftist movements fighting him, including the Communist Party. This was accentuated by a number of Western missionaries (belonging to international religious orders) who entered the country and took a very strong stand against Marcos and for 'oppressed' people. The support of Communist insurgents by the leftist Catholic clergy gave the rebels legitimacy (especially in the areas where they worked together, such as Negros and Mindanao), and contributed to the growth of Communist insurgency.

Martial law also antagonized pro-democracy people, pushing many of them (especially the leftists who did not go as far as to join the Communist Party) into activities to oppose Marcos. As the martial law regime decayed, their fears proved correct, and they were joined by the liberals who had become disillusioned with Marcos. This leftist-liberal coalition eventually became an important pillar of the EDSA Revolution in 1986. Many of them were 'internationalists', belonging to leftist or liberal international groups of one hue or another and supported by them morally and financially. They were pro-peasant, pro-labour, and anti-military. After the EDSA Revolution, some of them were brought into the Aquino Cabinet (for example, Executive Secretary Joker Arroyo and Labor Secretary Augusto Sanchez, both of whom are human rights lawyers), and ran into conflict with the military. In Thailand or any other country where government has worked decently, the leftist-liberal group is marginalized, but in the Philippines, it was the confusing transition from Marcos to Aquino (and the latter's political inexperience) which brought some of them to Cabinet positions.

From the viewpoint of the military, if these leftists and liberals were not 'reds', they were definitely 'pinkos' who, like the leftist clergy of the Catholic Church, contributed to the growth of the Communist Party. *Coups d'état* during the Aquino administration were, in some respects, a reaction against them. After each major *coup*, the military's influence paradoxically rose. To forestall another *coup* and to obtain their (the military) support if it occurred, President Aquino needed the 'constitutionalists' under General Fidel Ramos who had sided with her during the previous *coups*. In return, she accepted their demands, such as putting national security matters under their control, and removing leftist Cabinet members. Another factor in the military's favour was the collapse of peace negotiations with Communist and Muslim insurgents; after this failure, Aquino needed a strong military to fight them.

Coups were also the result of strong factionalism within the military. Soon after he became President in 1966, Marcos gave key appointments in the armed forces to fellow Ilocanos. One of these was the appointment of Colonel Fabian Ver as Commander of the Presidential Security Command. It was the beginning of Ver's rise in the military. A few years later, Ver became General, and in the early 1980s, Chief of Staff. During martial law, there were non-Ilocano officers who fared well, but Marcos depended heavily on Ilocanos because he felt that he could count on their sense of tribal loyalty. It was as if Marcos was afraid of the more cosmopolitan non-Ilocanos, especially the Tagalogs. The Ilocanos are somewhat like the Chinese. They are frugal and hardworking, but are often ridiculed as *probinsiayano* (country bumpkins) by the Tagalogs and Visayans. The creation of Marcos loyalists, in turn, gave rise to a reform-minded group—the Reform the Armed Forces Movement (RAM)—who were fed up with the breakdown of the merit system and the spread of corruption in the military. The EDSA Revolution was initiated by the RAM group.

When Marcos fled the country, Ver and some Marcos loyalists went with him, but most of them were left in the military under the new administration. President Aquino immediately removed many overstaying generals, but a strong Marcos faction remained. In retrospect, one can say that the military were split into Marcos loyalists, the RAM group under Gregorio Honasan (which did not disband even after Marcos's downfall), and constitutionalists under General Ramos. Being unhappy under the new President, Marcos loyalists first staged *coups* to try to bring Marcos back to power (but all these failed). Then the RAM group struck, first in August 1987 and then in December 1989. In the latter *coup*, Marcos loyalists joined hands with RAM to stage the bloodiest *coup* the country has ever experienced. (RAM was formed to fight Marcos loyalists towards the end of his rule, but by 1989, their grievances against the Aquino government had superseded their animosity towards each other). Military critics say that the rebels are a spoiled lot who were pampered by Marcos and do not want to go back to the barracks, having had a taste of power under him.

Thailand: A Tradition of Functional Government

Thai politics was dominated by the military for most of the 40-year period, but compared with the Philippine situation, government authority was more acceptable to the people, and the bureaucracy was more effective (particularly in maintaining peace and order). This may be related to the fact that Thailand had an established tradition of governing. During the period of absolute monarchy, the king made efforts to keep the peace in the country. This was necessary; otherwise, he would lose 'his' country. For internal peace, he needed the civil bureaucracy to 'protect [the] people's welfare', and the military bureaucracy to suppress rebellion if it occurred. The military bureaucracy was also needed to defend the country against foreign aggression (especially from the Burmese during the first half of the nineteenth century and from Western imperialists later on). It was necessary for the king then to take measures to attract—and keep—competent personnel into the civil bureaucracy and able and strong men into the military. Fortunately (it was an accident of history to some extent), all Chakri kings were rather competent during the period of absolute monarchy, and carried out reforms to strengthen the bureaucracy.

The Revolution of 1932 changed the nature of the government, but it did not lead to an overhaul of its structure. What emerged was a 'bureaucratic polity', sovereignty controlled by the bureaucracy—the real power of government was transferred from the king to bureaucratic leaders.[13] Between the two bureaucracies, it was the military which had the ultimate power. Since the early 1980s, the military has shared power with politicians, but one can as a whole characterize the government of the 40-year period as military-dominated. The military enjoyed greater privileges and strengthened its bureaucracy by attracting capable Thais into its academies. There was no political meddling in the matter of promotion, as happened in the Philippines, and no decline of morale due to the loss of privileges as took place in the Philippines under President Aquino. Even without political interference, the Thai military developed problems of disunity, corruption, and low morale, but it is to their credit that they did not become serious. As a result, the military could combat insurgents effectively. At the same time, they did not antagonize the residents affected by the fighting, thus not pushing them to the side of the insurgents. In contrast, the Philippine military suffered from low morale, poor discipline, and poor combat capability.

The military-dominated government of post-war Thailand was sympathetic towards the civil bureaucracy too, for the military needed them to run the country well (for good management of the country was in a sense the military's legitimacy). This enabled the bureaucracy to also enjoy privileges (including some degree of corruption in most ministries, though probably not including the Ministry of Justice), which in turn enabled it to attract competent university graduates. There was little political interference in the bureaucracy (until the mid-1980s), which was essentially an autonomous body. The Ministry of the Interior, which has charge of local administration, and the Ministry of Justice, the judiciary, attracted, for many years, the best students from the law and political science faculties of the top Thai universities. Once they entered the ministries, they worked hard, and competed for promotion. If they were assigned to the provinces by the Ministry of the Interior, their job was to work for provincial development and contribute, in general, to 'the welfare of people' there, including the preservation of peace and order. In the Ministry of Justice, judges were to settle disputes without undue delay. The absence, and later the low degree, of political interference helped, rather than hinder, both ministries in performing their tasks.

In Thailand, top priority was given to strengthening the government structure. Thai leaders believed that without it there would be no nation, and that the viable private structure, such as the market economy, would only emerge under it. The government structure consisted of the king, the military bureaucracy, and the civil bureaucracy. In the Philippines, however, the principle of government was different: power was vested with the people. The executive (the president) and the legislature were elected by them, and the bureaucracy existed to serve them. The theory was that an effective government structure could be built and maintained by popular sovereignty. Under different circumstances, the Philippine system might have worked; instead, there was, as pointed out above, decay of the government structure (which had been relatively strong under American tutelage).[14] In particular, the judiciary, the police, and the military became so corrupt that in the early 1990s, the press began referring to 'hoodlums in uniform' and 'hoodlums in robes'. These labels may exaggerate the problems the Philippine government was facing, but there was a general feeling that the whole bureaucracy had gone astray, not just the agencies related to the maintenance of peace and order.

Civic and Moral Values

Inculcating National Consciousness in Thailand

A country usually emphasizes civic and moral education in order to promote national integration and to inculcate among the people values that will maintain the peace. In this task, Thailand has a big advantage over the Philippines: the former has a national language. In earlier years, there were greater dialectal variations (in tonal patterns, and consonant and vowel sounds) in spoken Thai; and various minority groups did not speak Thai, or if they did, they did so poorly (in the case of Chinese and Muslim schools, the medium of instruction was their own language). However, in the early post-war years, the Thai government began imposing the use of the Thai language on all schools (though for Muslim schools, some exceptions were made for the lower grades).

By adopting officially approved textbooks, the government spread the central (or Bangkok) Thai dialect as standard Thai. This effort went hand in hand with improvements in land transportation (which increased mobility) and development of the mass media (especially television). As a result, standard Thai spread and is understood by the bulk of the population today. One difficult task, however, was to teach the Thai script to enable schoolchildren to read and write. First, they had to be taught Thai alphabets, and then rules concerning how they should be pronounced individually or in combination. But this task was not too demanding (compared with, for example, Chinese or Japanese) since the number of Thai alphabets is limited and the rules on the combination of two or three alphabets are relatively few.

The Thai government emphasized the importance of education particularly after Sarit Thanarat became Prime Minister, and in successive National Development Plans, an increasing amount of the budget was allocated to it. The objective was not only to impart knowledge as the bulk of children did not go beyond elementary schools, and for them, the government's other primary objective was to instil moral and civic values. (Many Thai liberals feel that there was too much emphasis on this.)

Civic education centres around the king. Schoolchildren are taught about the present king, other Chakri kings, and their predecessors (Ayutthaya and Sukhothai kings). They learn of the kings' exploits and their contributions to the Thai nation. (As warrior kings, they are the heroes who conquered another kingdom or defended the country from foreign invasion.) This is reinforced with the national holidays proclaimed in honour of them: Chulalongkorn Day, King's Birthday, Queen's Birthday, and Chakri Day (Rama I is most honoured as the founder of the Chakri dynasty). As these holidays approach, children are taught about the respective kings honoured, and participate in various events sponsored by the government or civic groups. All this is to implant in the minds of children the belief that the king is the guardian of the nation. From those whom education does not convince of the sanctity of the king, the law protects him through the provision of lese-majesty.

The material taught in schools is reinforced by various reports in the press and on television about King Bhumibol's activities all over the country. Since he lives in the provinces about several months a year, people there feel closer to him. He maintains residences at Chiang Mai in the North, Sakon Nakhon in the North-east, Hua Hin on the Gulf of Thailand, and Narathiwat in the South. He also presides over numerous ceremonies; for example, in graduation ceremonies, he personally hands out diplomas to graduating students. (The number of students who have received diplomas from the king is said to have exceeded 500,000.) For many ordinary people, it is often through the symbolism reposed in the king that they perceive the Thai nation.

Civic education, however, is more than just teaching about the king. Students are also taught that all people living within the national territory constitute one nation. In an effort to forge unity, they study national geography so that people, cities, and landscape (rivers, mountains, etc.) in other provinces become familiar to them. They are also taught their national heritage, such as history, music (songs in particular), and literature (plays, stories, maxims, poems, novels, some of which glorify Thai heroes who defended the country from foreign aggression or brought honour to the nation), so that they know they share many things in common, thus enabling them to transcend geographical or class differences and to develop at the same time a sense of pride in their country. Thailand enjoys the advantage of having an independent history of several centuries, during which time, there was cultural development (largely under the patronage of kings until 1932). When people from different provinces meet, because they speak the same language and have a shared knowledge, the sense of belonging to the same nation is reinforced.

Some Thais, however, did not develop a strong sense of loyalty to the existing order. As discussed in Chapters 13 and 14, a number of peasants and intellectuals joined the Communist Party, and Thai Muslims in southern Thailand felt alienated and joined the rebellion. Moreover, many Thais migrated to the United States (especially in the 1960s). There were 91,000 Thais in the United States in 1990, according to the US population census. A large percentage of them live in Los Angeles where there are a few Thai newspapers and even a Thai radio programme. Many of them are professionals, including medical practitioners (about 1,500 Thai doctors were practising in the United States around 1980).

Overall, however, civic education has not been without effect. According to one study on the national consciousness of 294 local leaders (village and sub-district leaders, *phu yai baan* and *kam naan*) in 1984, 82 per cent were happy being Thai and 94 per cent would like to be born Thai in the next life. These leaders were not well educated: 69 per cent had schooling of 4 years or less, and another 11 per cent, 5–7 years. In schools they were taught about Thai heroes and their exploits in history, and developed the sense that Thailand is a great nation (62 per cent said that it is). The study concluded that Thai education was rather successful in inculcating national pride in the hearts and minds of the Thai people.[15]

The Philippines: A Weak Sense of National Consciousness

In the Philippines, the president is the head of state, and as a secular person with secular power, he is often vilified by critics. Presidents are changed periodically. Before Marcos, the presidential term of office was 4 years, and no one had served two full terms. Starting with Aquino, the term has been extended to six years, but the president cannot serve more than one term. Marcos was President for about 20 years, and he is the most criticized president in Philippine political history. His name has entered the Guinness Book of World Records as the biggest alleged thief in the world; his rule is characterized as a kleptocracy. His eldest daughter, Imee Marcos Monotoc, once called Malacanang (the President's office) a snake pit. In October 1992, after the flood brought about by a typhoon, a few real snakes came out into the open and were caught. Following this, people began setting loose various gibes regarding 'two-legged snakes'. With this sort of attitude prevailing, civic education cannot effectively focus on the president as it can on the king in Thailand. In the early post-war years when the country was still fresh as an independent nation, the president commanded a great deal of respect from the people, but over time, as corruption pervaded the political system, he became a weak symbol of national unity.

Philippine schools generally did a poor job of imparting civic education. One problem was in the use of English, which is too complicated a language for the majority of Filipino children to learn. Without a good knowledge of the medium of instruction, students could not absorb the material and develop their intellectual capability well. To compound the problem, the quality of instruction declined, a decline most clearly reflected in the deterioration of the English proficiency of students. The average high school graduate from a public school in the early 1990s does not read and write English better than a fourth grader of a generation ago.[16]

Another big problem was the decline of the quality of teachers in public schools. As the real wages of teachers deteriorated over time, more and more qualified people chose not to enter the teaching profession, while many competent teachers resigned to go into the private sector or overseas. The government did not increase the education budget to match the population and price increases.[17] The inadequate budget also resulted in a shortage of school buildings, so that children were divided into morning and afternoon sessions in many areas. As a result, the number of hours children spent in school declined. However, those who could go to school were fortunate; many remote areas did not even have schools. As recently as 1992, about 10 per cent of children did not have a school to go to.[18]

According to one study conducted in Metro Manila in the early 1980s among 207 grade school students, 194 (94 per cent) of them would rather be citizens of another country. The study also showed that they did not identify with or value the country's historical traditions primarily because they had little knowledge of the subject.[19] The majority of Filipinos have difficulty identifying such prominent figures in modern political history as Claro Recto, Sergio Osmena, and Quintin Paredes; many do not even know Manuel Quezon, President of the Commonwealth; and only if they are pressed, will they cite public places named after him (such as Quezon Bridge in Manila).[20] Schools have been doing a poor job in inculcating a sense of pride and togetherness among Filipinos. The better educated share many values in common, but not with the poorly educated masses, who are, in turn, divided among themselves, often along ethnic and kinship lines.

A large number of Filipinos have left the country for greener pastures abroad. In 1990, there were 1.4 million Filipinos in the United States according to the US population census. Many of them are professionals (doctors, engineers, business executives, accountants, professors); there were about 15,000 Filipino doctors working in the United States then. Unlike the non-professionals who go abroad under contract (overseas contract workers), the professionals are not likely to come back, and since they have a family there, their remittances are limited. (In the first eight months of 1992, $1.16 billion was remitted from abroad, out of which only $10 million came from Filipino residents abroad. The rest came from overseas contract workers who number close to a million.) In addition, it is said that there are a large number of people (including some so-called nationalist politicians and their families) who are waiting for opportunities to emigrate or who have the 'green cards' (denoting permanent resident status in the United States) or American citizenship and will leave the country at an opportune time.

The United States is also a preferred place for Filipinas to give birth in. Professionals often want to have their children born in the United States when they are studying, temporarily assigned, or even travelling there, and if they have to return, wives are left behind if they are pregnant. If wives become pregnant in the Philippines, many make the trip to the United States especially to give birth. Children born there can acquire American citizenship (which is based on the principle of *jus soli*). One American volunteer working at the Smokey Mountain squatter colony (where there is a huge heap of garbage) in Manila says, 'This is a country where the national ambition is to change your nationality.'[21] One prominent Filipino novelist observes, 'To most [Filipinos], America is their second country. Indeed, if a referendum were held today on whether to become the 51st state, I am sure it would pass overwhelmingly.'[22]

One hastens to add, however, that there are a large number of well-educated Filipinos who are at least as committed to the country as their counterparts in Thailand. But the fact that a large number are not loyal (as reflected in their willingness to migrate) is a handicap in building Filipino nationhood. The Philippines needs them as civic leaders; instead, by leaving, they are in effect saying that the country is not worthy of their commitment.

Religious Influence

As an incentive for people to observe the law, the social system should be fair. If not, it becomes morally justifiable for the underprivileged (say, the poor) to break the law as a means to get even with the privileged. How can underprivileged people, who constitute a majority, be convinced to accept the existing social system and believe that to rebel against it is a sin. In Thailand, the hope is held out to them that if they try, their status will improve (not necessarily in their present life). This is greatly helped if the privileged show compassion for the underprivileged.

In Thailand, Buddhism teaches that by accumulating merit (*bun*) in their present life, all people can improve their status in the next life and that they have to accept their present status as the result of their accumulation of merit in the previous life. Thai Buddhism regards acts which help society to function smoothly (such as respecting authority) as merits, while anti-social acts (such as breaking social rules and rebelling against authority) are regarded as sins (*bahp*). This teaching may not have worked without an economic basis, but fortunately, since most peasants owned the lands they cultivate and were assured of basic economic necessities, such teaching was widely accepted, and minimized the penetration of anti-establishment, rebellious values into society.

The Thai government has relied heavily on Buddhism in imparting moral education in schools. In Thailand, there is no separation of church and state; on the contrary, Buddhism is an important part of the state. For example, the land on which Buddhist temples stand belongs to the state. Buddhist priests belong to the *sangha*, which is, in turn, under the jurisdiction of the Department of Religious Affairs in the Ministry of Education, and the king appoints the Supreme Patriarch of the *sangha*.

All students beyond the fourth grade in elementary schools use officially approved textbooks on Buddhism, which extol such values as moderation and peacefulness; respect for parents, elders, and the superior (through *wai*, for example);[23] and cultivation of merit (such as showing compassion to fellowmen). Some of these virtues are in accordance with Buddhist teachings. One example is to 'make' merit (*tham bun*) to improve one's own individual karmic status, and another is to accept the present social order and respect those who are higher in status because they owe their positions to the karmic law. But a number of virtues (such as respect for one's parents and elders) which appear in the textbooks on Buddhism are not directly related to the religion, so the course is also on morals beside religion.

In earlier years when there was a shortage of teachers and an inadequate budget for building schools, priests were teachers and temples were schools. Today, however, with the increase in secular teachers and the construction of numerous schools in the past few decades, such arrangements are few. But a school building is often erected in a temple compound or attached to it, and the priest watches over the moral upbringing of the schoolchildren. He can perform this role because he interacts with villagers in various ways and often acts as their leader;

Catholic priests play a similar role in the Philippines. But because Buddhism has been supported by the state over centuries, there are more temples and priests per person, making it more effective in penetrating the lives of the people. (There was 1 Catholic priest per 8,705 believers in the Philippines in 1983, whereas in Thailand the ratio was 1 to about 1,600 in 1976.)[24]

In the Philippines, the separation of church and state made moral education difficult. Morality is derived, directly or indirectly, from religion, and a religious institution often assumes the role of moral custodian, but in the beginning of the American period, the Catholic Church, the dominant religious (as well as educational) institution, was left out of the public school system. The Americans tried to build the school system almost completely anew, secularizing education and also changing the medium of instruction from Spanish to English. They believed that the Catholic Church was a feudal institution which would work against the implanting of democratic ideals in the minds of the newly colonized Filipino people, and that social morality could be inculcated in children without its help. In retrospect, this was too bold an attempt, and it did not succeed because the Americans soon lost enthusiasm for their new colony; but social morality was not a problem during the American period.

It was after independence that the country began facing all kinds of problems. As the government failed over the years to allocate adequate funds, the quality of public education declined, and as in civic education, schools did a poor job with moral education. If many children left school with a poor understanding of national institutions (without even knowing who Manuel Quezon is), the chances are that they also left school without a strong sense of right and wrong. The erosion of moral values was also exacerbated by the weakening of religious influence, which was partly the result of the global trend of secularism, but it can also be attributed to the rise of the population to priest ratio. Since the Catholic Church was unable to ordain more priests to the rising population, the number of villages without a resident priest increased, or in the village with a resident priest, the priest had to serve a larger number of people.

The Decline of Moral Values in the Philippines

The state of morality in Philippine society is reflected in the goings-on among socialites. Robin Padilla, a popular movie star, is now accused of drug addiction, involvement in a hit-and-run accident, and illegal possession of firearms. Movies stars are role models for many young people, but they often set a bad example. The police suspect altogether 87 movie stars of drug addiction or abuse.[25] In private schools where students come from relatively well-to-do families, students or their parents often present gifts to teachers and invite them to meals to get better grades. In public schools, it is said that some teachers obtain their jobs with fake certificates. Many doctors are willing to issue any certificates (for example, death certificates) if enough money is offered.

Journalists are also willing to write anything if the price is high enough. Freedom of the press is not contributing to the strengthening of democracy or to the eradication of corruption. Some well-known journalists who write a column in an op-ed page are accused of using it as a weapon for extortion. Sports officials are also sometimes accused of cheating in international competition (for example, the Little League baseball controversy in September 1992) or choosing the athletes they favour to represent the country.[26] Many business leaders unconscionably evade taxes or pilfer electricity and water, and send money abroad (capital flight) even though it is badly needed in the country for creating jobs.

Trusting relations are difficult to establish because cheating pervades society, and people are unduly contentious. A good example of this is the disputes over election results. Those defeated often contest the results announced by the Commission on Elections, supposedly an autonomous government body. In the past, commissioners were corrupt (especially during Marcos's time), and private watchdog bodies (the best known is the National Movement for Free Elections) have been active in monitoring the past several elections. At the national level, the most divisive are those disputes over the results of presidential elections. This trend started immediately after independence. In the 1949 presidential election, the opposition candidate (Jose P. Laurel) never conceded defeat to the winner (the incumbent President Elpidio Quirino).

After the most recent presidential election of May 1992, the runner-up (Miriam Santiago) is contesting the results. She has asked the Supreme Court to reopen ballot boxes and recount votes in several Metro Manila towns and provinces where she feels that she was cheated. The court asked for ₱10 million (about $400,000) from her as part of necessary expenses, with which she complied. The case is still with the court. Unlike the presidential election of February 1986, it is generally believed that the commissioners were honest in the 1992 election, but there may have been fraud in counting and compiling votes at the local level. It took more than a month after the election for the winner to be proclaimed, but even this slow, cautious procedure did not satisfy the runner-up. Several months later (November 1992), there was an American presidential election. Within a few hours of the polls closing, President George Bush conceded defeat. Many Filipinos were impressed with the workings of American democracy, but a couple of months earlier (September), Thailand had also accomplished an election feat (which was hardly noticed in the Philippines). In its parliamentary election, all the results were out in less than a day. In the Philippines, it takes time to announce election results, and they are frequently contested because cheating has undermined the moral fabric of society. A Filipino Jesuit priest self-contemptuously calls the Philippines a nation of cheats.[27] Recently, the Catholic Church has become increasingly concerned with the spread of corruption and fraud in society.[28]

Values and Institutions

If one is too preoccupied with the institutional structure, the tendency is to forget that moral and civic values also count in the performance of the government bureaucracy. These values may not eliminate corruption, but can work to mitigate it. They engender the public spirit which motivates government leaders to exercise their power for the welfare of the people. Without these values, despite all institutional constraints, government power will be abused. Corruption in and abuse of power by the Philippine judiciary, police, and military (against their own citizens) stem from the lack of a public spirit and the tenuousness of national integration. For example, the corruption of the judiciary reflects the lack of a public spirit on the part of judges and their obsession with money and wealth; and the prevalence of human rights violations in rural areas by the military made them akin to foreign invaders (consider, for example, the atrocities committed by Charlie's Angels under Colonel Carlos Lademora in Mindanao against suspected MNLF and NPA supporters).

From the top to the bottom of Philippine society, almost everyone seemed to be pursuing his personal objectives with little regard to the social rules. The religious organizations (the Catholic Church in particular) used to be a restraining influence, but it became weaker in recent years as the world became increasingly secular and materialistic. The police were formerly a deterrent, but with the spread of corruption within the force, they ceased to be effective. The heads of government agencies used to set an example for their subordinates by disciplining those who broke the rules, but because they became corrupt, institutional discipline broke down. People used to be a deterrent to corrupt politicians by voting them out at election time, but politicians got smarter and the electorate became more gullible as a large number of poorly educated people began voting. The corrupt grew more corrupt, and the unscrupulous became more ruthless.

The Nation and Institutions

It is traditions which make a nation out of a country. The Philippines has existed as a political entity for about four centuries, but unlike Thailand, it was maintained and nurtured by foreign powers. In 1946, when the country gained independence, the traditions that had kept the Philippine nation cohesive were synthetic in some ways. For example, the democratic system had not grown out of the people's political consciousness and could not function effectively.

During the American period, English was developed as the *de facto* national language, and the necessary traditions were built upon it. But after independence, as a result of government neglect, public education deteriorated, and English ceased to be the language of the majority of Filipinos. Tagalog-based Filipino has been evolving as the national language, but it has not yet replaced English as the dominant language in education as well as in government and business. This linguistic situation, together with the decline of public education, has produced a large group of poorly educated Filipinos.

The country has also produced a small, English-educated, cosmopolitan élite (most of whom had attended private elementary and secondary schools). The élite and the poorly educated majority share few common traditions. Both groups are also split among themselves. The poorly educated are split along ethnic and kinship lines largely because education has failed to integrate them into a nation, while the élite are split on major issues confronting the country. Possibly because Philippine traditions are weak, the people have taken to Western ideas, which are conflicting (ranging from conservative to Communist); as there are no strong traditions to discern between them, the Philippine élite do not therefore have a dominant ideology.

The deterioration in public education also led to the decline of social morality in the Philippines. But the weakness of the religious institution was another contributing factor. Unlike Thailand where there is a national religion, in the Philippines, all religions have to be privately supported because of the separation of church and state. This separation left the Catholic Church out of public schools, thus weakening religious influence on the people. The Church, the dominant religion of the country, could not expand the clergy fast enough to match the population increase, as a result of which the ratio of population to priest rose, thus further reducing the impact of the Church.

Furthermore, because of strong cultural ties with the United States through the visual and print media, Filipinos were exposed to the American way of life. It was an unattainable dream for many Filipinos, which they nevertheless clung to; in the process, materialistic values were strengthened to the detriment of religious and moral values. While religious influence waned, moral education was poorly conducted in schools. As a result, many people became willing to break the law in pursuit of material enhancement.

Many of those who did not break the law left the country for greener pastures abroad. Over a million of them emigrated to the United States in the post-war period. Their English education was an excellent preparation for emigration. A number of Thais also left for the United States, but only about one-tenth that of Filipino emigration. Besides, the Thai professional brain drain was much more limited. In the Philippines, in contrast, emigration to the United States became the norm for the country's best and brightest: the Philippines was not worth staying for. If they stayed, they wanted to enrich themselves quickly to compete with those who had left the country. They paid little attention to the plight of the poor masses and resorted to all sorts of legal and illegal 'gimmicks'. As a result, the sense of common destiny faded, in turn eroding the basis for civic and moral values.

Civic and moral values were also destroyed by economic inequity. In villages, the relationship between landlords and landless peasants was confrontational (if not openly, at least psychologically). Landless peasants felt that the unfair economic system (letting landlords get an undue share) made it morally justifiable to cheat landlords and the government (which they thought was the landlords' agent) as a means to get even with them. Many landlords felt no particular responsibility towards landless peasants and did their best to protect their own economic interests.[29] In Metro Manila and other cities also, many poor people felt the same way about the economic system as landless peasants did, and did not feel it morally wrong to squat on other people's land, especially if it was vacant. Nor did they feel inhibited from cheating or stealing from their rich employers. The latter, in turn, felt no particular responsibility towards their employees, and often underpaid their workers (ignoring the minimum wage law). The frailty of social harmony was a poor environment for moral and civic values to take root.

Civic and moral values faded as the Philippine political institution decayed. In the pre-war period, as a whole it worked better than in Thailand, though government power was too decentralized and social discipline too weak, as reflected in the large number of rural unrests and industrial disputes. The American presence and the modernization of the government institution under its tutelage made the Philippines probably the best-run country in the region at that time. In the post-war period, however, the Philippine government had to be maintained and improved upon by the Filipinos themselves. In this, they did not succeed; for democracy started malfunctioning as politicians bought votes or resorted to 'goons' and guns to get elected. In 1972, President Marcos declared martial law to impose order, but the results were even more disastrous. He elevated the art of corruption to that of a kleptocracy. In the meantime, people began losing confidence in government leaders. Instead of demonstrating moral leadership, they used their powers unscrupulously to enhance their own private interests. Instead of uplifting moral and civic values, they became the social cancer which undermined the fabric of the nation.

National division, the decline of civic and moral values, and the decay of the government structure were interrelated problems. The first was the source of conflicts in the nation, the second weakened the nation's ability to resolve them, and the third aggravated the crisis. The Muslim insurrection, Communist insurgency, and *coups d'état* were the conflicts which exploded, and the first two were prolonged because of the weakness of the military structure. Crimes were, unlike the others, not a rebellion against the government. They were individual acts following the erosion of civic and moral values and compounded by the weakness of the police force.

Having imbibed American democratic and egalitarian values during the colonial period which were reinforced through strong cultural ties with the United States in the post-war period, many among the Filipino élite believed that democracy would enable the government to perform its tasks well, including that of maintaining peace and order. But the result has been far from their expectation. Their belief in democracy might be right given the Philippine setting, since authoritarian government under Marcos did not work. But because of exacerbated national division and the decline of civic and moral values, Philippine democracy has not worked well. Judging from the chaos in recent years, one might go as far as to say that the Philippine political situation is lurching towards anarchy.

In contrast, peace and order has been maintained much better by an authoritarian government in Thailand. Thailand is, of course, a more unified country, and because of the advantage of a national religion and other traditional institutions, civic and moral values are stronger (or at least has not declined as fast as in the Philippines). What made the difference then is the viability of a country as a nation. The deterioration of peace and order in the Philippines was the manifestation of the malaise of all of its institutions, not just the political one. The Philippines, as a nation, was structurally flawed, and this constitutes the basic explanation for various governmental malfunctions, resulting in the lack of peace and order.

1. David Timberman, *A Changeless Land: Continuity and Change in Philippine Politics*, Singapore: Institute of Southeast Asian Studies, and Metro Manila: Bookmark, 1991, p. 273.

2. Harry T. Oshima, *Economic Growth in Monsoon Asia: A Comparative Survey*, Tokyo: University of Tokyo Press, 1987, p. 214.

3. Dante Simbulan, 'A Study of the Socio-economic Elite in Philippine Politics and Government, 1946–1963', Ph.D. thesis, Australian National University, 1965, pp. 82–5.

4. Victor Corpus, *Silent War*, Quezon City: VNC Enterprises, 1989, p. 186.

5. Realizing the problem, the government started using vernaculars in the first two years of primary education in the late 1960s, and more recently, began making determined efforts to unify teaching by using Filipino. According to a survey in 1989, Filipino was understood by 92 per cent of the population. This percentage was given by Fe Aldave Yap, Director of the Institute of Philippine Language, Department of Education, in *Solidarity*, October–December 1990: 83.

6. According to the same survey of 1989, 51 per cent said that they could speak English, but the level of their mastery of English seems to have been generally low. Those who have mastered English and are comfortable in speaking, reading, and writing it probably do not exceed 10 per cent of the population.

7. Renato Constantino, 'Brain Drain Within', *Manila Chronicle*, 23 February 1971.

8. Teodoro Benigno's column in the *Philippine Star*, 2 November 1992.

9. A leftist research organization, Ibon Databank, estimates that 47 million Filipinos, about 80 per cent of the population, lived below the poverty line in 1992. The poverty line income is defined as about ₱5,600 per month for an average family of six. Ibon's estimate of poverty incidence was 70 per cent in 1991. (The government's estimate of poverty incidence, which seems to be around 53 per cent, uses ₱4,800 per month for a family of six as the poverty line.) Reported in the *Philippines Free Press,* 17 October 1992, p. 2.

10. Renato Constantino (ed.), *Recto Reader: Excerpts from the Speeches of Claro M. Recto*, Manila: Karrel, 1965, p. 143.

11. Lucien Pye's estimate, quoted in Simbulan, 'A Study of the Socio-economic Elite', p. 271.

12. A Chinese interviewee tells a story about the Chinese community starting a fire brigade because of the difficulties they had with Filipino firemen. He also narrates an incident at the Regent Hotel when it burnt down (Marilies von Brevern, *Once a Chinese, Always a Chinese*, Manila, privately published, 1988, pp. 14–15.

13. See Fred W. Riggs, *Thailand: The Modernization of a Bureaucratic Polity*, Honolulu: East–West Center Press, 1966.

14. According to Joseph Ralston Hayden, *The Philippines: A Study in National Development*; New York: Macmillan Co., 1942, p. 123, already in the pre-war period, the civil bureaucracy was little more than a Nacionalista electioneering machine. He was exaggerating the situation, but there is no doubt that politicization of the bureaucracy started then.

15. Likhit Dhiravegin, *Thai Politics: Selected Aspects of Development and Change*, Bangkok: Tri-Sciences Publishing House, 1985, pp. 398–9.

16. Rosalinda Orosa's column in the *Philippine Star*, 1 December 1992.

17. According to Alejandro N. Herrin's study in *An Assessment of Population, Health and Education Policies in the Philippines, 1986–1988*, Working Paper Series No. 90–10, Makati: Philippine Institute for Development Studies, January 1990, despite the population increase, the share of education expenditure in the national government budget declined from about 25 to 11 per cent between the late 1960s and the mid-1980s. In the mid-1960s, the share of education budgets was about 29 per cent. See also *Edgardo J. Angara: Views & Comments*, Quezon City: Friends of Edgardo J. Angara, 1984, pp. 106–7.

18. The figure, given by Education Secretary Armand Fabella, is reported in the *People's Journal*, 21 October 1992.

19. Maria Luisa Canieso-Doronila, *The Limits of Educational Change: National Identity Formation in a Philippine Public Elementary School*, Quezon City: University of the Philippines Press, 1989, pp. 74 and 82.

20. Interview with Alfonso Felix, Manila, 20 February 1991. Felix is a lawyer as well as President of the Historical Conservation Society.

21. James Fallows, 'A Damaged Culture', *Atlantic*, November 1987: 58.

22. F. Sionil Jose, 'Base Realities', *Asian Wall Street Journal*, 24 November 1992.

In the early 1970s was born a political movement called the Philippine Statehood, U.S.A. which sought admission of the Philippines into the United States. It claimed a membership of six million. In the 1981 presidential election, Bartolome Cabangbang ran against Marcos on the statehood platform, and won 4 per cent of the total national vote. For the birth of the movement, see Lewis E. Gleeck, *President Marcos and the Philippine Political Culture*, Manila, privately published, 1987, pp. 108–9.

23. The Thai *wai* is not just 'hello'. Who *wai* whom, who *wai* first, and exactly how one places the hands in relation to the head are determined by his rank in the social hierarchy.

24. The Philippine ratio is from James H. Kroeger, 'Human Promotion as an Integral Dimension of the Church's Mission of Evangelization: A Philippine Experience and Perspective since Vatican II—1965–1984', Ph.D. thesis, Pontificia Universitas Gregoriana (Vatican), 1985, p. 65. In Thailand, there were 213,175 monks and 25,702 temples (Niels Mulder, *Inside Thai Society: An Interpretation of Everyday Life*, Bangkok: Editions Duang Kamol, 1990, p. 114).

25. The Philippine National Police Narcotics Command lists 87 movie stars, including Padilla, as drug users (*Manila Standard*, 15 November 1992).

26. The Zamboanga Little League team won the Little League International title of the World Series, but was later stripped of it on charges that the team included overaged boys, and that some players had come from other areas like Metro Manila. According to the Little League rules, a team should be a local one.

27. Fr. Alfeo G. Nuda's column in the *Daily Globe*, 7 November 1992. If the country has to change its name (a new bill was submitted to Congress to change the name of the country to Filipinas), Fr. Nuda proposes *Islas de los ladrones*. It means literally the Islands of Thieves, but what he really means is that the country is full of cheats. Earlier in the column, he argues that cheating is a form of theft.

28. For example, at a mass marking the first anniversary of the Parish Pastoral Council for Responsible Voting at St. Paul College in Quezon City, Cardinal Sin warned that Philippine society may collapse unless 'we apply the antidote of honesty and responsibility' (*Philippine Daily Inquirer*, 8 November 1992).

29. For an analysis of life in a village in central Luzon where contending beliefs about what is just undermine social rules, see Benedict Kerkvliet, *Everyday Politics in the Philippines: Class and Status Relations in a Central Luzon Village*, Quezon City: New Day Publishers, 1991, Chapters 5 and 6.

18
Putting It All Together

Summing Up

In the early 1950s, the Philippines was more advanced economically than Thailand. Philippine agriculture was earning more foreign exchange, by exporting such cash products as sugar and coconuts mainly to the United States, than Thai agriculture, which was exporting rice to neighbouring countries. Thai industrialization had barely started, while Philippine industrialization was moving rather rapidly with import substitution, in such areas as textiles. Philippine banks were more professionally run and their ownership was structured in a more modern manner than Thai banks which were family-controlled and run in the traditional Chinese way. The Philippines was also enjoying twice as high per capita gross national product (GNP) as Thailand. When these factors were weighed together with its large, educated manpower and long experience in democracy, it appeared that the Philippines had a much better chance to develop than Thailand.

In the following two decades, however, it was the Thai economy which did better. By the early 1970s, Thailand had caught up with the Philippines. In the decade under martial law, however, the Philippine economy performed as well as the Thai economy, though in retrospect this was made possible by borrowing heavily from abroad. In the early 1980s when the Philippines could no longer borrow to maintain its economic growth and faced the second oil shock, the economy began to stagnate. In the middle of the decade, as the country began facing serious political instability, the economy declined, and has not gone back to a steady growth path since then. Although Thailand also faced the parallel difficulties created by the second oil shock, it undertook reforms to restructure its economy. These reforms were particularly useful in capturing a large percentage of the investment from Japan and Taiwan, which was prompted by the appreciation of their currencies after 1985. During 1987–91, the Thai economy grew at 10.5 per cent per annum, and in the final year, Thai per capita GNP became a little more than twice Philippine per capita GNP.

Three major reasons were offered in this book for the better performance of the Thai economy *vis-à-vis* the Philippine economy. First, the Thai government's more positive attitude towards the Chinese and foreign capital made Thailand much less discriminatory towards the

Chinese and more open to foreign investment, especially East Asian investment, which became the dominant foreign investment in the 1980s. In Thailand, although there were some attempts in the early 1950s to replace Chinese capital with Thai capital, this policy was soon discarded and the Chinese were given a free hand in the economy. Thailand also welcomed foreign investment as a means by which to catch up with other countries, especially in the manufacturing industry.

In contrast, the Philippines discriminated against the Chinese and restricted foreign investment, especially non-American investment. The Retail Trade Nationalization Law of 1954, which restricted retail trade to Filipinos and 100 per cent Filipino-owned corporations, caused great damage to Chinese distribution networks. Many Chinese traders were replaced by less efficient Filipino traders and government corporations. In foreign investment, the Philippines was open to American capital under the Laurel–Langley Treaty which granted their former colonial masters national treatment, but because the treaty was to expire in 1974 (and the rights acquired under the treaty were uncertain after that) and there was a great deal of government intervention in the market economy (such as foreign exchange and import controls), not much American investment came to the Philippines either. Japanese and other foreign investors were virtually shut out until martial law began. Under martial law, the Philippine government became less restrictive, but it was only around 1985 that it became seriously interested in attracting foreign investment. But at this time, the poor state of the economy and the deterioration of peace and order were deterrents to foreign investment.

Secondly, there is more government involvement in the market economy in the Philippines than in Thailand. The Philippine government was populist, an attitude reflected in its minimum wage legislation, whose history goes back to the early 1950s. To appease workers, the Philippine Congress tended to set minimum wages at a rather high level. Even after Philippine income fell below Thai income, Congress set minimum wages higher than did the Thai government (which also began setting minimum wages in the early 1970s under populist pressure).

The Philippine government was also interventionist. The most blatant example of this tendency was the exchange control started in the late 1940s. By the early 1960s, the problems had mounted, and it was abolished, but several years later, import control was instituted, and in the next decade, many goods faced import restrictions. In Thailand, foreign exchange was available almost freely to importers, and the number of goods which came under import control was much smaller. Although there were tariff barriers, the absence of exchange and little import control subjected Thai industry to greater import competition. Together with a positive foreign investment policy, this factor made Thailand a more open economy than the Philippines.

Both the Philippines and Thailand set up government corporations, but those in the Philippines were subject to more abuse, often becoming money-making machines for their executives, politicians, and their cronies. Both Thai Airways International and Philippine Airlines (PAL) were government corporations (in the case of PAL, since 1977), but the former was a much better-run company than the latter. Thai Airways made profits and expanded its routes and fleet, but PAL suffered losses and became the last airline an international traveller would take when there was a choice.

In finance, the Philippine National Bank (PNB) and the Development Bank of the Philippines (DBP) dominated the banking sector, especially in the early 1980s, but they suffered huge losses in the mid-1980s (₱117 billion), having given large 'behest' loans to Marcos's cronies. The Thai government bank, Khrung Thai Bank, had problems, but its losses were much smaller, and the government is prosecuting the head of the bank (Tamchai Kambhato) who is responsible for these losses. (Tamchai was sentenced to 20 years in prison by the lower court.) In contrast, no executives of the DBP and the PNB have been brought to court in the Philippines.

Government intervention was desirable when the purpose was to build public confidence in banking institutions. Effective financial intermediation was essential for economic growth, and this required that the public develop confidence in banking instituions (otherwise, they would not deposit money with them). In the beginning, the task was more difficult for Thailand since its banks were mostly Chinese-owned and run in the traditional way. But the Bank of Thailand did a fairly good job of building public confidence in the banking system. The Bank had commercial banking laws passed and made banks adhere to the Bank's regulations (backed by those banking laws). These regulations were intended to modernize banks and make them less susceptible to large losses. In several cases, the Bank had to take over banks and either restructure their capital or merge them with healthy banks. On the whole, the Bank was rather effective in these tasks largely because of its strength as a bureaucracy: it attracted competent people and was virtually free from corruption.

In contrast, the Central Bank of the Philippines was a 'damaged' institution. By the early 1990s, it had accumulated losses of a few hundred billion pesos; it was infested with corruption (for example, in the administering of foreign exchange and import controls); and it faced numerous lawsuits, some of which successfully challenged its decisions. (In December 1991, the Supreme Court annulled the Central Bank's closure of Bonco Filipino in 1985.)

In Thailand, bank deposits increased rapidly, starting in the early 1960s. The ratio of bank deposits to GNP, which can be taken as an indicator of banking development, increased to about 80 per cent in the early 1990s. In the Philippines, however, though the ratio increased somewhat over time, it was still below 30 per cent in 1991. This disparity is at least partly attributable to the difference in the effectiveness of the two central banks.

Thirdly, the Thai government maintained peace and order better than did the Philippine government. Foremost, the Philippines faced a more serious Communist insurgency, from the late 1940s to the mid-1950s in central Luzon, and then from the early 1970s onwards in various parts of the country. The Communist insurgency created a great deal of confusion and uncertainty and was a deterrent to investment in the affected areas. It can be regarded as one factor for the lacklustre agricultural performance in the Philippines. In the 1980s, Communist urban guerrillas began threatening peace and order in Metro Manila by kidnapping businessmen for ransom and bombing commercial and public buildings, while Communist-infiltrated unions (especially those under the Kilusang Mayo Uno) increased their influence among workers, making it difficult for the management to control wage increases and impose industrial discipline, especially in multinational companies.

There were a few other peace and order problems in the Philippines. Moro–Christian Filipino conflicts started in Mindanao soon after the Philippines gained independence, but it was in the early 1970s that the situation escalated into a civil war. In a few years, however, President Marcos managed to appease certain segments of the Muslim population, and the level of violence declined somewhat, but fighting went on. Muslim rebels not only fought with the military but also resorted to terrorist activities and to kidnapping wealthy people and their families for ransom. (Although the latter activity is denied by Muslim rebels and attributed to their breakaway factions, they were responsible for some cases as they needed money to fight for their cause. International assistance has been dwindling since the mid-1980s.)

In Metro Manila, the general crime situation was already bad in the 1960s, but it deteriorated rapidly in the 1980s and became a serious problem towards the end of the decade. Corruption in the police force and the judiciary became so serious that people began referring to 'hoodlums in uniform and robes'. The sharp increase in kidnappings of Chinese businessmen and their families which started around 1990 affected not only the Chinese business community but also Filipino as well as foreign investors. In the second half of the 1980s, there were a series of *coups* in the Philippines which showed the world the political instability of the country. The one in December 1989 spilt over into Makati—the country's business centre which also has plush residential areas and condominiums—and threatened the personal safety of many businessmen and their families.

Peace and order posed a much less serious problem in Thailand. The Communist insurgency was restricted largely to border provinces. It became serious in the mid-1970s, but only for several years. The Muslim rebellion was more long-lasting than the Communist insurgency, but it was restricted to a few small provinces in the South and the level of violence was much lower than that in Mindanao. Thailand has had more *coups d'état* than the Philippines, but none of them has affected the economy. Most *coups* were carried out smoothly without any fighting. The only significant exception was the *coup* in 1981, but even then it was over in a few days, and the number of casualties was very small; ordinary citizens were hardly affected.

The crime situation was not good, but the number of violent crimes, such as murders, declined after hitting a peak in the mid-1970s. The Thai police were generally regarded as corrupt and ineffective, but they were less corrupt and more effective than their Philippine counterparts, who often could not even solve important cases, but the Thai police could (though they ignored most of the less important cases). The Thai police were corrupt at the fringes, while the Philippine police were rotten to the core. In the Thai police force, if there was any high-level corruption, it was mostly related to drug trafficking (for export, not for domestic use), prostitution, and gambling—areas which did not affect internal peace and order directly. In the Philippines, in the early 1990s, a number of high-ranking police officers were charged with masterminding criminal syndicates (which carried out kidnappings, car thefts, and other criminal activities) or protecting them.

Why was the Thai government more positively inclined towards the Chinese and foreign capital, more cautious in getting involved in the market economy, better in performance when the government did get involved, and more successful in maintaining peace and order than the Philippine government? Broadly speaking, one reason is that Thailand was never colonized, whereas the Philippines gained political independence only in 1946. During the period of absolute monarchy, Thailand was woven into a nation by the care and efforts of kings, and it developed the bureaucracy to maintain internal stability and protect the country from foreign invasion. After the Revolution of 1932, the military took over the government from the king, inheriting a fairly solid national structure to build on. The country was linguistically and religiously integrated; there were no regional groups which could oppose the Bangkok government, except the Muslims in the South; and although the bureaucracy was far from modern, it was blessed with a strong bureaucratic tradition (including the supremacy of government officials over people) which could be used to run the country peacefully and effectively. Because the country was independent, its underdevelopment was its own problem, and was not attributed to the Chinese and foreign capital, as was typically done in newly independent countries (such as the Philippines). In the pre-war period, ordinary Thais were engaged in agriculture, while the more-educated ones were in the government bureaucracy, and the Chinese and foreign capital in the modern sector of the economy. This economic apportionment was largely maintained in the post-war years, since it had worked earlier.

Having usurped power from the king, the military needed legitimacy for its action. Initially, political legitimacy was sought from the newly created Parliament. Military leaders (such as Phibul Songkram) formed a government at the request of the majority of its members (who were in turn supported by the military). When Sarit Thanarat took over the government in 1958, he abolished Parliament, and thus needed new legitimacy for his government. He restored the king (Bhumibol) as the sovereign of the country without actual power; a fiction was created that the king had delegated power to Sarit. A new task he set for himself and his government was economic development, especially the uplifting of the standard of living in rural areas. There was also the problem of Communist insurgency, which was gaining ground in neighbouring countries. Communism was a threat to the very foundation of the country's socio-political structure; it had to be defeated by all means. As economic development was a very important means by which to do that, it became an even more important national goal. During Phibul's times, because Parliament was kept open, the need for legitimacy was less keenly felt, but even then, there were efforts to modernize education for national development. It was, however, after Sarit came to power and abolished Parliament that the country was geared up to promote economic development.

The Thai political situation evolved in the following decades in favour of economic growth. The military could easily have become corrupt and therefore a minus factor, but political pressure was brought to bear on them to perform. One source of pressure was from the growth of democratic forces. Economic development required better-educated manpower, and the government allocated more money to education, especially to tertiary education. Educational progress created a more politically conscious public. The military government faced their challenge for the first time in 1973 when students organized a protest movement, and as a result, the Thanom Kittikachorn–Prapart Charustien government fell. A few years later, however, the military made a comeback. But the political environment had changed; they had to accommodate democratic forces which had become stronger, soon reopening Parliament. After this, they had to share power with politicians, but they did not give up the defence and interior portfolios; they gave the finance portfolio and a few other key economic positions to technocrats in most of the following years.

The rise of democratic forces was greatly facilitated by the assimilation of the Chinese into Thai society. Over time, Chinese businesses were gradually taken over by second- and third-generation Chinese who were well assimilated into Thai society, and they became heavily involved in politics as financial contributors or by running for political office themselves. In the late 1980s, the power of the military was greatly constrained, and even after they carried out another *coup* in February 1991, they had to appoint a civilian prime minister.

Another constraint on the military was King Bhumibol. He was young and powerless when he returned in 1950 from an extended stay in Switzerland as a student. He could have remained a politically ineffective king, but two factors changed that. Sarit, who had replaced Phibul, needed the king as a source of legitimacy, as pointed out above. At this time, the young king was inexperienced in politics, and was not an effective constraint on the military, but Sarit died several years later, while the king remained a visible symbol of the country in the following years. Fortunately for the country, he was—and is—intelligent, morally upright, and dedicated to the welfare of the country, so that he became greatly respected by and beloved of the people. As time passed, he became a fatherly figure to many Thais. This made it difficult for military leaders to go against his will, which was often interpreted as the people's will, and it was only by managing the country well that they could remain in power.

The Philippines was organized quite differently. It was an artificial political unit created by the Spaniards and maintained by the Americans. The country was poorly integrated linguistically and socially (with a small minority of extremely rich people and a large majority of poor people). In Mindanao, many Muslims never submitted to the Christian Filipinos. In the pre-war period, despite these divisions, the country was kept together, peace and order were maintained, and the government did not interfere in the market economy much, primarily because of a relatively strong, market-friendly colonial government. But after independence, the government gradually weakened, yet diversified its functions (especially the economic ones).

The government disintegrated because democracy did not work and because Marcos's authoritarian government which replaced it was a political disaster. As the Philippines's last High Commissioner in the pre-war period, Francis Sayre, told King Rama VI in Thailand when he was his adviser, it was difficult for democracy to work in a developing country such as the Philippines where the majority of voters were poorly educated and did not understand public issues: they were in no position to vote for the right candidate, considering the long-term interest of the country. In the early post-war years, the quality of public education was still relatively high and many poor and badly educated people did not register to vote, but it deteriorated over time as the electorate expanded. (The percentage of the population who voted increased from about 10 to about 33 per cent between the early 1930s and the early 1960s.) The fact that the country was divided linguistically, ethnically, and socially made it more difficult for democracy to work.

The people had some leverage in democracy, and so politicians had to promote their interests. Various government interventions in the market economy came about for this reason. For example, Filipino traders organized to lobby for retail trade nationalization, while workers organized to lobby for minimum wage legislation. It was good politics to sponsor a bill for retail trade nationalization because, by doing so, politicians could get the support of a large number of Filipinos who would benefit from such legislation. If they were challenged on the merit of such a measure, they could easily justify it by parroting the nationalistic rhetoric which had gained currency in the early post-war years. The argument that such a measure would harm the country in the long run could not become a political force under such a circumstance.

National politicians needed financial backers to pay the ever-increasing campaign costs and the political brokers who could deliver large blocks of votes in various parts of the country. These supporters wanted something in return from their candidates who got elected. What they wanted varied according to the nature of the business they were in or wanted to start. Typically, they wanted loans from government financial institutions, protection from imports and foreign investors, business licences, concessions, and government contracts. Sometimes, they wanted government barriers (set up by an earlier administration) to be removed. Local politicians played essentially the same role as national politicians, though the former depended greatly on the latter for the resources of patronage they could distribute. From the viewpoint of both national and local politicians, the more government intervention there was the better, since political office could be used to deliver more patronage or to advance their (or their families') economic interests. Under this circumstance, none questioned seriously whether certain measures would harm the market economy in the long run. Long-term interest did not matter to them, since they would not be around when the measures they sponsored started to harm the country.

The bureaucracy did not support the market economy, either, because it was a heavily politicized and weak institution. The government became a huge employer by creating a large number of posts in the bureaucracy which were filled by political appointees or politically supported people. People came to politicians for jobs; a job offer was the patronage expected of politicians. Since the number of unemployed was increasing, the politicians placed many people into the government bureaucracy. Some resigned with a change in administration, but many stayed on, and were later fully integrated (it was bad politics for the new administration to force them to leave).

Then with martial law, the bureaucracy lost its independence completely. There had been a great deal of political interference in recruitment and promotion before martial law, but after that, Marcos freely interfered. His henchmen were appointed heads of many government agencies. After his fall, attempts were made to make the bureaucracy independent again, but the many high-ranking officials during the Marcos period who had to resign were replaced by a large number of new political appointees. With the extensive political interference, morale in the bureaucracy flagged, and salaries declined in real terms as it became bloated with overemployment and the government could not increase nominal salaries to match price increases because of budget constraints. The result was the spread of corruption, and government officials began using whatever power they had to make extra money: the government bureaucracy became a road-block to the market economy rather than its promoter.

In summary, it is tempting to say that the Thai economy performed better than the Philippine economy because Thailand was more of an *echt* nation than the Philippines was. Although this may be correct as a sweeping generalization, it cannot be supported by simply pointing out that Thailand has a history of independence, whereas the Philippines was a colony of Spain for 300 years and of the United States for 40 years and became independent only after the Pacific War. More important are the developments during the history of independence in Thailand and the type of legacy inherited from colonial times by the Philippines. The Philippines was more economically advanced than

Thailand in the early 1950s; hence, the changes which took place thereafter are very important in understanding the reversal in fortunes. Even though the Philippine advantage then was artificial, close attention has to be paid to historical developments in the following four decades. The same can be said of Thailand; there was no assurance in the early 1950s that it would overtake the Philippines in the way that it has. If Thailand was more of an *echt* nation than the Philippines was, it is because the Thai political institution became more supportive of economic growth in the post-war period. To explain why this is so, a complexity of developments has to be taken into account, something which this book has tried to do. It is not unrelated to Thailand's history of independence, but this is not a sufficient explanation.

Government Failure

It is the central tenet of free market economists that the economy performs best if it is left to the private sector. Hence, they urge the government to deregulate and privatize the economy. But it cannot be stated categorically that government intervention does not work, for in Japan, South Korea, Taiwan, and Singapore, there was extensive government intervention, yet their economies performed well. The reason why government intervention impairs economic performance in many developing countries is that it tends to be directed towards enhancing the economic interests of particular groups, including those of politicians and bureaucrats, at the expense of the overall national interest.

Free market economists might argue that even in countries where the economy performed well with government intervention, the performance would have been better with less intervention. Certainly, in such countries, there were plenty of examples showing that government intervention resulted in the promotion of the economic interests of particular groups. But whether or not the negative effects outweighed the positive effects of government intervention is a moot question. The question essentially boils down to the type of government prevailing in the country.

There is another facet to government–market economy relations. Even if government intervention in the market economy is undesirable, the economy still needs the government to perform certain tasks. In modern times, it is the government which has sole control of the money supply. Because there are no artificial constraints (such as the formerly used gold standard), the government may increase the money supply and cause monetary instability, or it may borrow from abroad and squander it, leaving a huge burden of debt to successive governments (thus reducing the government budget to provide public goods in the future). The modern government has the power to issue and borrow money, and it is required to judiciously exercise this power.

There is a broad category of goods called public goods, which by their nature is best supplied by the government. If goods (and services) are divisible, and if consumers can enjoy them only by payment, the market can supply them. But there are certain goods which the market economy needs and yet cannot supply (efficiently) because they are jointly consumed (for example, national defence) or because it is too expensive to charge individual consumers (for example, ordinary roads). Peace and order is also such a good. Although it can be privately arranged (a typical example is a company hiring security guards or private citizens jointly hiring guards in a restricted residential area), it is an inefficient arrangement (costly to the economy) if everyone does so.

In modern times, the public goods sector has been rapidly expanding. Besides national defence, peace and order, roads, and other public works, there are a number of other expensive public goods. Litigations are increasing, and their adjudication is another public good. Despite the clamour for deregulation among free market economists, complete deregulation is impossible. For example, the government is expected to regulate airlines (to some extent), so that air travel is safe; medical doctors and pharmacists have to be licensed, so that quack doctors or pharmacists do not endanger people's lives; and food producers, drink makers, and restaurants have to be inspected, so as to safeguard public health. Taxis are also licensed, partly for the safety of passengers. It is also the government which is expected to take precautions against the onset of contagious diseases and to stem its spread before it begins to seriously affect public health.

There are, however, a number of goods which the government supplies, but they are not public goods. For example, the telephone service and electric power supply are not public goods. Toll roads are a borderline case: they can be regarded as a public good, and users' fees can be considered their partial contribution to the cost of building and maintaining them; or they can be considered private goods, heavily subsidized by the government. The difficulty in considering them as purely private goods lies in the fact that it is only the government which can exercise the right of eminent domain in the matter of road construction (without this right, the cost of road construction can become prohibitive); therefore, the government usually undertakes it. In some countries, they are treated like ordinary roads, with no fees imposed on their use. This makes toll roads more of a public good than a 'private' good.

A further complication is that there are certain public goods which the government pays private companies to supply. In the future, the government is expected to expand the scope for this type of 'privatization'. A good example is garbage collection where price discrimination is not applied because those who cannot pay for it may dump it at a public place, thus posing a public hazard. It is best to regard garbage collection as a public good, but the government often pays private companies to perform this service. Even business establishments which have a lot of garbage to dispose of often arrange with a private company to collect them.

Education is a peculiar good. Like garbage collection, education can be provided by the market, which is the main reason for the existence of private schools. But like garbage collection, if those who cannot pay tuition fees are deprived of an education, they may become a public hazard. Education has an investment aspect which benefits (economically) those who receive it, and it also has a public good aspect. As discussed in Chapter 17, moral and civic education is necessary for maintaining peace and order, and it can be useful also for providing other public goods. At the very least, primary education is necessary for this purpose. Children who receive primary education develop basic language skills and broaden their intellectual horizon, and may be more motivated and more capable in responding to market opportunities than those who do not receive any education. Primary education therefore has an investment aspect, but it cannot be neatly separated from moral and civic education, which is imperative for peace and order and other public goods.

Thailand has done a better job also in nurturing its children in primary schools, and through its effects on human capital formation, education may have contributed to higher productivity (for example, through the better response of peasants to market opportunities). Filipinos often say with great pride that their country has the largest pool of educated manpower in South-East Asia. The Philippines may have the largest 'exportable' pool because of its English education, but it is equally true that it has large poorly educated masses. Thailand has a larger percentage of people who can understand television news broadcast from the capital, who read newspapers daily, and who buy books and magazines. Particularly impressive in recent years is the growth of newspaper readership in the country (especially in the provinces) and the proliferation of books and magazines published in Thai. For example, one newspaper (*Thai Rath*) increased its circulation from about 100,000 to 1,000,000 between the mid-1960s and early 1990s. Such an increase in circulation was made possible partly by increased income, but it also showed a growing number of functionally literate people in the country. (In Khon Kaen, the central city of the North-east, about 450 kilometres from Bangkok, the *Thai Rath* is available in the morning of the same day.) In book publishing, Thailand was publishing about 10 times as many books as the Philippines in the late 1980s.

Part III discussed peace and order problems and showed that Thailand handled them better compared to the Philippines. Some of the crises in the Philippines arose from the country's national divisions (for example, the lack of a national language); thus, the inability of the government to tackle them is not necessarily a reflection of its incompetence. But many problems were related to the corruption of government agencies (the police, military, and judiciary), which in turn affected peace and order. In general, the Thai government has done a better job of providing public goods and services than has the Philippine government. This is also reflected in the extensive road network the Thai government built (discussed in Chapter 12 in connection with distribution channels). Needless to say, the Philippine record of road construction is not as good.

The Thai government has also logged a better record of maintaining monetary and foreign exchange stability than has the Philippine government. Although the latter managed to keep the rate of inflation in the 1950s lower through foreign exchange control than did the Thai government, in the following decades, the Philippine rate of inflation was consistently higher. The exchange rate of the peso declined from ₱2 to about ₱27 per dollar in the 40-year period, while the exchange rate of the baht depreciated only slightly (from about B20 to B25 per dollar). The monetary instability in the Philippines caused a great deal of uncertainty for investors and also resulted in capital flight.

While the Philippine government borrowed recklessly from abroad and squandered much of it on unproductive (or poorly conceived) projects, thus causing huge debt burdens in the 1980s, the Thai government was able to avoid the financial crisis experienced in the Philippines and other developing countries. There were people in the Thai government (including government corporations) who wanted to increase borrowings from abroad and benefit from it, and they succeeded in doing so to some extent, but the government was able to create checks on foreign borrowings and stop the further accumulation of foreign debts. The conservative monetary and fiscal policy set down by British Financial Advisers in the pre-war period was modified in the post-war period, partly because of the bigger government role in the economy and partly because of political pressure, but the conservative spirit was kept alive by the Bank of Thailand and its allies in the government (the Ministry of Finance, the National Economic and Social Development Board, and the Budget Bureau).

The better performance of the Thai government is not only in supplying public goods and fulfilling monetary and fiscal responsibilities. As discussed in Chapter 6, the Thai government also successfully nurtured public confidence in banking institutions, and when it was directly involved in the market economy through government corporations, it did a better job of managing them. As reflected in the contrast between Thai Airways International and Philippine Airlines, Thai government corporations tended to perform better than Philippine ones.

If one argues, however, that the Thai government should not have been involved in the market economy, this author falls back on the more proper sphere of government activity: there is a correlation between government performance in corporations and in fulfilling its responsibilities in its proper sphere. It is the latter which only the government can undertake, and how well it does here greatly affects the market economy. If the government does not perform well there, then there is government failure.

The Philippines has had many instances of government failure—far more than Thailand did. The Philippines is poorly integrated as a nation (thus, giving rise to insurgency, for example); its people were not well disciplined (partly because of the decline of public education and partly because of the weakening of religious influence); and democracy (and martial law) had politicized the government bureaucracy and weakened it. The decline of the bureaucracy created all sorts of problems. For example, the government could not collect taxes well to pay for public goods, could not provide public goods efficiently because of corruption and incompetence, and could not punish many of the people who broke the law. Partly because of such instances of government failure, the Philippine economy performed poorly. As argued earlier, for the economy to perform well, the government must provide public goods, maintain monetary stability, and fulfil its fiscal responsibility. The government cannot be done away with by preaching deregulation and privatization; it is an essential partner of the market economy. To promote economic growth, improving government performance is as equally important as improving the performance of the market economy.

Looking to the Future

This book is about what happened in the Philippines and Thailand and why they respectively suffered and enjoyed a reversal in fortunes, and from what has been discussed, the future cannot be predicted very well. Economics is not an exact science (this is true of all social sciences). When it develops further with more accumulation of data, the ability to predict the future may improve, but not to the level of the natural sciences, because causal relations among socio-economic variables cannot be specified precisely. Even in analysing past events, the best that can be done is to develop plausible explanations for these events. This book offers a personal thesis, and does not exclude the possibility that another who asks the same question about the Philippines and Thailand will come up with different explanations. Which is more correct cannot be neatly decided. Only time can decide: the one which is more plausible will remain, while the less plausible one will fade away. Critics may accuse this author of not utilizing the body of knowledge available fully as well as competently. Be that as it may, differences in explanations are partly due to the limitations of economics at the present stage.

Furthermore, factors which were relevant in the past may not figure in the future; after all, society has the ability to solve problems. For example, the negative attitude towards the Chinese and foreign capital in the Philippines (Part I) ceased to be very important in the mid-1980s. In Chapter 9, it was pointed out that such government interferences as foreign exchange and import controls caused a great deal of inefficiency. However, in the 1980s, especially during the second half, the Philippine government eliminated many of these controls, and in August 1992, the government implemented full liberalization of foreign exchange. Clearly, some of the problems highlighted in Chapter 9 no longer exist.

If economics has limitations and factors affecting economic growth are changing, it is extremely difficult to predict the future. Nevertheless, this author will try to forecast performance in the next few decades, not out of confidence in his predictive ability, but out of a desire to further clarify what he thinks are the important trends in the future course of socio-political evolution in the Philippines and Thailand.

The first question to settle is whether the Philippines will remain as it is or split. Since such names as the Republic of Mindanao and the Republic of Cebu are sometimes heard, the possibility of a breakup cannot be completely ruled out. After all, the Philippines is not yet a nation-state; it is still too divided to qualify as one. But the probability of splitting up is not large: the élite who dominate the state appear united in keeping the country together, having been educated in English and imbibed the notions of Filipinos and the Filipino nation (though they are divided on policy issues); and the spread of the Tagalog-based national language, Filipino, has been increasing inter-ethnic communication. But if the national economy continues to stagnate because of the policy emanating from Manila, centrifugal forces can set in. If other South-East Asian economies boom while that of the Philippines stagnates due to central policy, it will be tempting for southern regions to secede. As for Thailand, the possibility of the country breaking up is very small. In the worst-case scenario, the four provinces in southern Thailand where Muslims concentrate may split off; even then, Thailand remains essentially as it is, since they account for only 2.6 and 2.8 per cent of the country's territory and population respectively.

If the Philippines loses a large part of its present territory (maintaining the Republic of the Philippines as the name for the remaining entity), the basis for prediction disappears or has to be substantially altered. Assuming that the country will remain as it is, this author offers his prediction for the next few decades (say, the next 40-year period from 1992 to 2031). The Philippine economy will not be able to get on a rapid growth trajectory; its average growth rate of GNP will be at most 5 per cent, or a few per cent growth in terms of per capita GNP. At worst, per capita GNP will not grow at all, or even decline. The Thai economy will, however, perform at least as well as that of the Philippines. Thus, for the Philippines to catch up with Thailand in that time span is very unlikely. The chances are that the absolute difference in per capita GNP between the two countries will widen. (The absolute difference was slightly over $800 in 1991.)

The relative standing of the two countries will depend partly on events in Thailand. Undoubtedly, one big problem is how the Thai military will retreat from politics. As the political upheaval of May 1992 indicated, the military may not voluntarily step down from its position of power. Blamed for the massacre of pro-democracy demonstrators at that time, the military are keeping a low profile now, but they may try to exert greater influence again. The outcome of competition between democratic forces and the military is far from certain. Even if democratic forces win, whether or not democratic excesses can be avoided is another uncertainty. With little experience in democracy in the past, the political situation may become unstable, and government effectiveness may decline. Another problem, which is sometimes privately discussed, is who will succeed the present king. In this modern era of democracy, the monarchy is not an assured institution. If the monarchy is lost for some reason, this will set off fundamental socio-political changes, and the country will have to go through politically turbulent periods even if it can eventually reach a workable equilibrium. If the monarchy is maintained, a lacklustre monarch will cease to be a political asset.

Despite these problems, the odds are good that the Thai government will provide a better environment for economic growth than its Philippine counterpart. The factors which combined to plague the Philippine government in the past will continue to operate, though some may become irrelevant in the future, but in the case of the factors having a fundamental bearing on government performance, progress will be slow, and many of them will remain valid in the next few decades. The reference is to such factors as social integration, linguistic integration, and governing tradition—the administrative structure and its functional capability. These are deeply embedded in the nation, the result of historical evolution over centuries. Thailand will continue to enjoy advantages in these areas.

Certainly, when the economy improves, government performance too is enhanced because many of the causes giving rise to poor government performance are economic ones (for example, corruption due to low salaries in government service). If the economy stagnates or declines, the reverse is true. The chances are good that the Thai economy will continue to grow and that it will have positive effects on government performance, and vice versa. In the Philippines, the economy will also grow, but with the present rate of growth (almost zero growth on per capita basis), it will take some time before income becomes high enough to have substantive effects on government performance.

This author is reasonably confident about his prediction that the performance of the Philippine government will not improve greatly, which is based on an extrapolation of the past performance of democracy. But a drastic upheaval in the form of government will affect the basis of the prediction. The change referred to is not, for example, from the present presidential system to the parliamentary system, which has considerable support even now. This change might improve the situation a little since the present division of powers between the executive and legislative branches makes government decision-making slow and difficult. But even the parliamentary system may not work very well. The drastic development this author has in mind is the rise of another authoritarian government.

Marcos's authoritarian government was worse than democracy, and another one may give rise to similar results, but rise it may again if the economy stagnates or declines under democracy and the people get fed up with politicians, as they were in 1972 when Marcos declared martial law. Moreover, there was little resistance to it at that time. The next time around, since the previous one did not work, there may be more resistance, but one cannot rule out its possibility. The majority of Filipinos will support authoritarian government if it improves their living conditions (in the early 1990s, about half the population are weighed down by poverty; and the rate of unemployment, which is about 9 per cent, becomes much higher if underemployment is included—a reliable estimate of it is not available). The roots of democracy are shallow, after all. If authoritarian government arises but fails to improve on the previous performance, this prediction still remains correct.

What will prove the prediction wrong is the rise of a better authoritarian government. But is this possible? It will be under certain conditions. One likely scenario is that the military will take over power. The military has a national organization which can both administer the country and suppress opposition to the abolition of democracy. (The other effective organization is the Catholic Church, but as a religious body and in view of its commitment to democracy, it is unlikely to take over power by unconstitutional means.) But if the military leadership is divided, controls government largely for their personal benefit, or promotes government intervention in the economy by subscribing to inward-looking nationalism, the results will be worse than under democracy; it will be a repetition of what happened under Marcos. For the military government to work, there has to be a central figure, like Suharto in Indonesia (or a small cohesive group); he has to be relatively young so that can he stay in power for a few decades (to prevent the destabilizing succession problem for at least a few decades); he should promote trade liberalization and encourage foreign investment (unlike the nationalistic, anti-foreign investment policy of the Reform the Armed Forces Movement under Gregorio Honasan); and he should restrict government activity to the public goods sector and strengthen the bureaucracy to undertake such activity effectively (the motto for administration must be 'Specialize and Strengthen').

Another possible scenario involving the military is for an elected president to tie up with it, as Marcos did in 1972. In this case, the president may not be young, and the transfer of power to his successor will create uncertainty about the future. If this problem can be overcome, this scenario becomes a feasible alternative. But as in the first scenario, the other conditions, although difficult, have to be met if an authoritarian government is to work. If they can be achieved, an authoritarian government can change the fundamentals of the country on which the prediction is based.

It is best, of course, if the Philippines can develop a growth-friendly democracy, but the chances for that are slim, given the social, religious, ethnic, and linguistic divisions and the presence of the largely uneducated, poor masses. But there are some flickers of hope. One is the federal system of government. Those who advocate independence for Mindanao or the Visayas feel that there is too much concentration of political power in Metro Manila and that the regions cannot take the initiative in improving their individual economy. The major problem of government is that as a monopoly, there is no competitive pressure on what it does, but under a federal system, regional governments have to compete with each other to make their areas attractive for people and business. However, for this system to work, the federal government must be much weaker than, for example, that of the United States. Without devolution of the power to determine trade, foreign investment, and monetary policy, there will not be enough competition among regional governments. If such devolution of power is carried out, the federal system of government may be a solution to Philippine economic ills.

Another hope lies in the ASEAN Free Trade Agreement (AFTA), which plans to cut tariffs to a maximum of 20 per cent by the end of 1997 and to 5 per cent by the end of 2007. The important feature of the agreement is that it constrains domestic economic policy. If the Philippines stays with AFTA, government intervention in the economy will decline or be substantially reduced, and there will be greater pressure on the government to fulfil its responsibilities in its proper sphere, for it will be mostly there where government action is needed. The Filipinos may increasingly scrutinize their government's performance in relation to those of other ASEAN countries, thus imposing greater rationality on their own government.

The Philippines has suffered from the way the nation is organized. For those familiar with Thailand, which has strong traditions of its own, the Philippines may appear to be an ersatz nation. In the future, if the two countries continue to evolve separately, the odds are that Philippine economic performance will remain poor, as in the past. But if there is greater interdependence in the ASEAN community, as expected to be realized in AFTA, some of the factors which plague the Philippine government will not be relevant anymore, for its performance will no longer be determined by national factors alone. The nation itself is a crucial determinant of economic growth at a time when it enjoys virtual sovereignty, but as it is undermined by greater international linkage, it will decline in importance. However, there are many obstacles to ASEAN becoming an economic community. Whether or not they will be successfully overcome in the next couple of decades remains to be seen.

The Comparative Approach to Economic Development

In trying to understand a country's development, a comparative approach is unavoidable. If the country has succeeded in developing, one will ask why it has succeeded and try to understand the reasons by comparing its economic records with those of a country which has not succeeded; or one can pool the economic records of successful and not so successful countries, and compare the two. Many of the stylized facts in economic development come from such comparison.

In this book, a different kind of comparison is attempted. As shown in Figure 1.2, the nation is considered to be a set of interrelated institutions. Thus, the economy becomes a subset of the nation, and how the economy performs is influenced by how the nation is structured. In particular, the government is focused on as another subset, and it is argued that the relations between the government and the economy were differently structured in the Philippines and Thailand, and that the government also differed in effectiveness because of the way it evolved in the past and also during the course of the 40-year (1952–91) period under study. The Thai evolution is distinguished by the modernization of a traditional (authoritarian) government, whereas the Philippine evolution is characterized by the decay of a modern democratic government implanted by idealistic Americans who came to the country on a mission of 'manifest destiny'.

Economists tend to think that development is a matter solely of the economy which can be analysed with neo-classical economics, but if the economy is a subset of the nation, neo-classical economics is then far from being an adequate tool for understanding the problems of economic development. One might argue that the task of economists is to make the most of neo-classical economics (the dominant tool in economics), but development economists should address themselves to the question of development (particularly long-term growth), and if this requires them to go beyond neo-classical economics, they must do so. To leave such analysis to other disciplines will weaken the field of economics (through invasion by other disciplines) as well as lay economists open to the accusation of intellectual negligence, especially since they maintain that they are concerned with development problems.

Neo-classical economics does not help to understand, for example, why one policy works in one country but not in another. An import substitution policy worked in such countries as Japan and South Korea, but failed miserably in many others. To preach simply outward-oriented policy as a panacea for the problems of developing countries ignores important aspects of development. The countries which succeeded in import substitution had an effective government (capable and not dominated by vested interests) and had a flexible (or dynamic) economy. Then, the next question to ask would be how the differences in the effectiveness of government and the flexibility of the economy have come about. This question cannot be answered without understanding how the nation is made up and how its institutions evolved over time.

The nation is shaped as the economic or other institutions evolve, but if the time span is a few decades, the nation changes much more slowly than the economy (primarily because cultural and kinship institutions change slowly). A successful developing country usually 'dynamizes' its economy by adjusting government policy when appropriate (as done by Sarit Thanarat in Thailand, by Park Chung Hee in South Korea, or by Deng Xiaoping in China). In some nations, this worked because other institutions, which could be supportive of economic dynamism, were given a chance to prove their usefulness to the economy.

With a broader perspective, the problems of development can be better identified, and in that way, a more realistic approach to development can be developed. It is a fallacy to think that developing countries face the same problems and travel the same path. Yet, an import substitution policy tends to be written off because it requires the government to interfere in the market economy (which contradicts the now-dominant deregulation doctrine). When it comes to the question of the best political system, democracy is argued to be the ideal system. Yet, as this book has shown, authoritarian government was not harmful to Thai economic growth, and the chances are that democracy would have dampened it. Everyone agrees that the ultimate goal of development is democracy and high income (economic liberation), but the path to these goals varies by country, for a developing country that practises full democracy (in form) could still fail in its pursuit of economic development. The Philippine experience is an example of that.

Economics is divided into different sub-disciplines such as international trade, monetary economics, human resource economics, public economics, etc. As a result, economic development is hardly tackled as an integrated problem. Trade specialists, for example, look at economic development from the angle of international trade alone and argue for outward-oriented policy. But development problems are much broader than that. International trade is only one loop of the development mechanism. There are other loops linked to it and how well they function affects trade performance. Development economics has to integrate the various sub-disciplines in focusing on how to sustain economic growth, but at the same time, it has to delve into how the performance of the economy is linked to that of other institutions. More needs to be done than just bringing in institutions as an escape hatch, as done by some 'enlightened' neo-classical economists when they are at the end of their tether in explaining different economic performances in a comparative study.

This task cannot be accomplished in general terms. The best starting point is to compare two relatively similar countries which differed in economic performance. For example, Argentina and Australia, two countries which had similar incomes by exporting agricultural products in the pre-war period, but differed greatly in post-war economic performance; or Brazil and South Korea, a pair which were successful in their export-oriented policy until around the early 1970s, but whose performance took divergent paths in the following years. Without undertaking an in-depth comparative study, the results will be mere observations on changes in economic variables or policy. If such changes are important for understanding comparative economic performance, why they came about or had to come about have to be understood.

This study was undertaken as an in-depth comparative study of the Philippines and Thailand, but further analysis is needed to examine the structure of the economy in detail (for example, how land tenure affected land productivity). It should also scrutinize external debt in the Philippines explicitly as a case of government failure and also take up the question of national language and its effect on communication within an organization, such as the government bureaucracy (how it works has repercussions on the economy). This study has focused on the relations between the economy and the government, and on the structure of the latter as long as it influenced the performance of the former, although other institutions (in particular, religions and schools) were also highlighted.

For a fuller understanding, the most urgent task is to look into cultural and kinship institutions in greater detail. It is these institutions which nurture, discipline, and educate children who join the labour force when they grow up. A comprehensive study requires greater efforts to delve into the structure of these institutions and their interactions with the government and the economy, but unfortunately, the task remains essentially undone. This study set a more modest target, and focused on the government and its relation with the economy. Even to untangle the relations between the two and the rationale underlying them was difficult enough. Yet it is far from a complete picture of institutional influence on economic performance. This requires a deeper study of institutions and their interactions in the Philippines and Thailand. At the same time, other pairs of countries should be examined to broaden understanding of the institutional underpinning of economic growth. This comparative study of the Philippines and Thailand is barely enough to build a general theory, but is offered as a modest beginning in that direction.

Appendices

APPENDIX 1

Philippine Administrations

Spanish Administration, 1565–1898

American Administration, 1898–1946

Name	*Tenure*
Military Governors	1898–1902
Governors-General	
William Taft	1901–4
Luke Wright	1904–6
Henry Ide	1906
James Smith	1906–9
Cameron Forbes	1909–13
Francis Harrison	1913–21
Leonard Wood	1921–7
Henry Stimson	1928–9
Dwight Davis	1929–32
Frank Murphy	1933–5
High Commissioners	
Frank Murphy	1935–7
Paul McNutt	1937–9
Francis Sayre	1939–42
Paul McNutt	1945–6

Philippine Presidents, 1935–

Name	*Tenure*
Commonwealth Period	
Manuel Quezon (from February 1942, the government in exile)	1935–44
Sergio Osmena	1944–6
Second Republic Period	
Jose Laurel	1943–5
Independence Period	
Manuel Roxas	1946–8
Elpidio Quirino	1948–53
Ramon Magsaysay	1954–7
Carlos Garcia	1957–61
Diosdado Macapagal	1962–5
Ferdinand Marcos (authoritarian rule after September 1972)	1966–86
Corazon Aquino	1986–92
Fidel Ramos	1992–

APPENDIX 2

Thai Administrations

Chakri Kings, 1782–

Name	*Reign*	*Title*
Yodfah	1782–1809	Rama I
Lertlah	1809–24	Rama II
Nang Klao	1824–51	Rama III
Mongkut	1851–68	Rama IV
Chulalongkorn	1868–1910	Rama V
Vajiravuhd	1910–25	Rama VI
Prajadipok	1925–35	Rama VII
Ananda Mahidol	1935–46	Rama VIII
Bhumibol Adulyadej	1946–	Rama IX

Prime Ministers, 1932–

Name	*Tenure*
Manopakon	1932–3
Phahon Phonphayuhasena	1933–8
Phibul Songkram	1938–44
Khuang Aphaiwong	1944–5
Tawi Bunyakhet	1945
Seni Pramoj	1945–6
Khuang Aphaiwong	1946
Pridi Banomyong	1946
Thamrong Nawasawat	1946–7
Khuang Aphaiwong	1947–8
Phibul Songkram	1948–57
Phot Sarasin	1957
Thanom Kittikachorn	1958
Sarit Thanarat	1958–63
Thanom Kittikachorn–Prapart Charustien	1963–73
Sanya Dharmasakti	1973–5
Kukrit Pramoj	1975–6
Seni Pramoj	1976
Thanin Kraivichien	1976–7
Kriangsak Chomanan	1977–80
Prem Tinsulanonda	1980–8
Chatichai Chunhawan	1988–91
Anand Panyarachun	1991–2
Chuan Leekpai	1992–

Bibliography

General

Asian Development Bank, *Key Indicators of Developing Asian and Pacific Countries*, Manila, various years.

Bennett, M. K., 'International Disparities in Consumption Levels', *American Economic Review*, September 1951.

Binder, Leonard et al., *Crises and Sequences in Political Development*, Princeton: Princeton University Press, 1971.

Boulding, Kenneth E., *Three Faces of Power*, Newbury Park: Sage Publications, 1989.

Clad, James, *Behind the Myth: Business, Money & Power in Southeast Asia*, London: Unwin Hyman, 1989.

Cole, Arthur, 'Entrepreneurship and Entrepreneurial History', in Joseph T. Lamble and Richard V. Clemence (eds.), *Economic Change in America: Readings in the Economic History of the United States*, Harrisburg: Stackpole Co., 1954.

Donald, David, 'An Excess of Democracy: The American Civil War and the Social Process', An Inaugural Lecture, Oxford at the Clarendon Press, 1960.

Easton, D., *A Systems Analysis of Political Life*, Chicago: University of Chicago Press, 1965.

Friedman, Lawrence M., *The Republic of Choice: Law, Authority and Culture*, Cambridge: Harvard University Press, 1990.

Geertz, Clifford, 'Patrimordial Sentiments and Civil Politics in the New States', in Clifford Geertz (ed.), *Old Societies and New States*, New York: Free Press of Glencoe, 1963.

_____, *Peddlers and Princes*, Chicago: University of Chicago Press, 1963.

Golay, Frank H. et al., *Underdevelopment and Economic Nationalism in Southeast Asia*, Ithaca: Cornell University Press, 1969.

Hara, Katsuro, *Nankai Ikken* [A Glance at the South Sea], reprinted Tokyo: Chuo Koron-sha, 1979.

Hart, Gillian et al. (eds.), *Agrarian Transformation: Local Processes and the State in Southeast Asia*, Berkeley: University of California Press, 1989.

Huntington, Samuel P., *Political Order in Changing Societies*, New Haven: Yale University Press, 1968.

International Institute for Strategic Studies, *The Military Balance 1992–1993*, London: Brassey's, 1992.

International Monetary Fund, *International Financial Statistics Yearbook 1992*, Washington, DC.

Jacoby, Erich, *Agrarian Unrest in Southeast Asia*, 2nd edn., Bombay: Asia Publishing House, 1961.

Lipset, S. M., *Political Man*, London: Heinemann Mercury Books, 1966.

_____, 'Some Social Requisites of Democracy: Economic Development and Political Legitimacy', *American Political Science Review*, 53 (1959).

McAlister, John (ed.), *Southeast Asia: The Politics of National Integration*, New York: Random House, 1973.

Mackie, J. A. C., 'Overseas Chinese Entrepreneurship', *Asian-Pacific Economic Literature*, May 1992.

1950–1983 Commodity Trade and Price Trends, Baltimore: Johns Hopkins University Press, n.d. [1985].

Oshima, Harry T., *Economic Growth in Monsoon Asia: A Comparative Survey*, Tokyo: University of Tokyo Press, 1987.

Pernia, Ernesto, *Economic Growth Performance of Indonesia, the Philippines and Thailand: The Human Resource Dimension*, Report No. 48, Economic and Development Resource Center, Asian Development Bank, January 1990.

Purcell, Victor, *The Chinese in Southeast Asia*, reprinted Kuala Lumpur: Oxford University Press, 1980.

Rossa, Alberto (comp.), *The Theology of Liberation*, Manila: Historical Conservation Society, 1967 and 1986.

Shaplen, Robert, *Time out of Hand: Revolution and Reaction in Southeast Asia*, London: A. Deutsch, 1969.

Skinner, G. William, 'Report on the Chinese in Southeast Asia', Southeast Asian Program, Cornell University, 1950.

Smith, Roger (ed.), *Southeast Asia: Documents of Political Development and Change*, Ithaca: Cornell University Press, 1957.

Steinberg, David Joel (ed.), *In Search of Southeast Asia: A Modern History*, Revised edn., Honolulu: University Press of Hawaii, 1987.

Stiglitz, Joseph E. et al., *The Economic Role of the State*, Oxford: Basil Blackwell, 1989.

Studenski, Paul, *The Income of Nations, Measurement and Analysis: Past and Present*, New York: New York University Press, 1958, pp. 229–30.

Tate, D. J. M., *The Making of Modern South-East Asia*, 2 vols., Kuala Lumpur: Oxford University Press, 1971 and 1979.

Tilly, Charles, 'War Making and State Making as Organized Crime', in Peter Evans et al. (eds.), *Bringing the State Back In*, Cambridge: Cambridge University Press, 1985.

Tyler, Tom R., *Why People Obey the Law*, New Haven: Yale University Press, 1990.

UN ECAFE, *Economic Survey of Asia and the Far East, 1961*, Bangkok, 1962.

United Nations Development Programme, *Human Development Report 1991*, New York: Oxford University Press, 1991.

Yoshihara Kunio, *Japanese Investment in Southeast Asia*, Honolulu: University Press of Hawaii, 1978.

_____, *Sogo Shosha: The Vanguard of the Japanese Economy*, Tokyo: Oxford University Press, 1982.

Wu, Yuan-li and Wu, Chun-hsi, *Economic Development in Southeast Asia: The Chinese Dimension*, Stanford: Hoover Institution Press, 1980.

The Philippines

Abueva, Jose, 'Ideology and Practice in the "New Society"', in David Rosenberg (ed.), *Marcos and Martial Law in the Philippines*, Ithaca: Cornell University Press, 1979.

Agoncillo, Teodoro A. and Guerrero, Milagros C., *History of the Filipino People*, 5th edn., Quezon City: R. P. Garcia Publishing Co., 1977.

Agpalo, Remigio E., *The Political Process and the Nationalization of the Retail Trade in the Philippines*, Quezon City: Office of Coordinator of Research, University of the Philippines, 1962.

Alonzo, Ruperto, 'Public Finance in Philippine Development', in Dante Canlas and Hideyoshi Sakai (eds.), *Studies in Economic Policy and Institutions: The Philippines*, Tokyo: Institute of Developing Economies, 1990.

Amyot, Jacques, *The Manila Chinese: Familism in the Philippine Environment*, IPC Monographs No. 2, Quezon City: Ateneo de Manila University, 1973.

Appleton, Sheldon, 'Overseas Chinese and Economic Nationalism in the Philippines', *Journal of Asian Studies*, February 1960.

Aquino, Belinda A., *Politics of Plunder: The Philippines under Marcos*, Quezon City: Great Books Trading, 1987.

_____ (ed.), *The Failed December Coup: View from the UP Community*, Quezon City: Office of the Vice President for Public Affairs, University of the Philippines, March 1990.

The Aquino Administration: Record and Legacy (1986–1992), Quezon City: University of the Philippines Press, 1992.

Aruiza, Arturo, *Ferdinand E. Marcos: Malacanang to Makiki*, Quezon City: ACAruiza Enterprises, 1991.

Averch, H. A. et al., *The Matrix of Policy in the Philippines*, Princeton: Princeton University Press, 1971.

Bacungan, Frolian M. and Tadiar, Alfred, 'The Judiciary', in Raul P. de Guzman and Mila A. Reforma (eds.), *Government and Politics of the Philippines*, Singapore: Oxford University Press, and Quezon City: College of Public Administration, University of the Philippines, 1988.

Bautista, Romeo, 'The 1981–85 Tariff Changes and Effective Protection of Manufacturing Industries', *Journal of Philippine Development*, 8, 1–2 (1981).

Bello, Walden et al., *Development Debacle: The World Bank in the Philippines*, San Francisco: Institute for Food and Development Policy, 1982.

Benigno, Teodoro, *Here Is the Score*, Manila: Philippines Today Inc., 1990.

Bentley, G. Carter, 'People Power and After in the Islamic City of Marawi', in Benedict J. Kerkvliet and Resil B. Mojares, *From Marcos to Aquino: Local Perspectives on Political Transition in the Philippines*, Quezon City: Ateneo de Manila University Press, 1991.

Bonner, Raymond, *Waltzing with a Dictator: The Marcoses and the Making of American Policy*, New York: Times Books, 1987.

Boyce, James K., *The Political Economy of External Indebtedness: A Case Study of the Philippines*, Makati: Philippine Institute for Development Studies, n.d. [1990].

A Brief History, Manila: Manila Electric Co., 1976.

Brillantes, Alex Bello, Jr., *Dictatorship & Martial Law: Philippine Authoritarianism in 1972*, Quezon City: Great Books Publishers, 1987.

Briones, Leonor, 'The Philippine Debt Burden: Who Borrows, Who Pays', in *International Debt Crisis: Focus on the Philippines*, Manila: International Studies Institute of the Philippines, University of the Philippines, 1984.

Broad, Robin, *Unequal Alliance, 1979–1986: The World Bank, the International Monetary Fund, and the Philippines*, Quezon City: Ateneo de Manila University Press, 1988.

Canieso-Doronila, Maria Luisa, *The Limits of Educational Change: National Identity Formation in a Philippine Public Elementary School*, Quezon City: University of the Philippines Press, 1989.

Canlas, Mamerto et al., *Land, Poverty and Politics in the Philippines*, London: Catholic Institute for International Relations, 1988.

Carino, Ledivina, *Bureaucracy for Democracy: The Dynamics of Executive–Bureaucracy Interaction during Governmental Transitions*, Quezon City: College of Public Administration, University of the Philippines, 1992.

Castro, Amado, 'Philippine Export Development, 1950–65', in T. Morgan and N. Spelstra (eds.), *Economic Interdependence in Southeast Asia*, Madison: University of Wisconsin Press, 1969.

Chafee, Frederic et al., *Area Handbook for the Philippines*, Washington, DC: US Government Printing Office, 1969.

Chapman, William, *Inside the Philippine Revolution*, New York: W. W. Norton & Co., 1987.

Che Man, W. K., *Muslim Separatism: The Moros of Southern Philippines and the Malays of Southern Thailand*, Singapore: Oxford University Press, and Quezon City: Ateneo de Manila University Press, 1990.

Clarete, Ramon and Roumasset, James, *An Analysis of the Economic Policies Affecting the Philippine Coconut Industry*, Working Paper No. 83–08, Makati: Philippine Institute for Development Studies, 1983.

Coates, Austin, *Rizal: Philippine Nationalist Martyr*, Hong Kong: Oxford University Press, 1968.

Constantino, Renato, 'Brain Drain Within', *Manila Chronicle*, 23 February 1971.

_____ (ed.), *Recto Reader: Excerpts from the Speeches of Claro M. Recto*, Manila: Karrel, 1965.

Constantino, Renato and Constantino, Letizia, *Demystifying Aquino*, Quezon City: Karrel, Inc., 1989.

_____, *The Philippines: The Continuing Past*, Quezon City: Foundation for Nationalist Studies, 1978.

_____ (eds.), *Southeast Asian Perceptions of Japan*, Tokyo: Zensei Publishing Co., and Quezon City: Karrel, Inc., 1991.

Corpus, Victor, *Silent War*, Quezon City: VNC Enterprises, 1989.

Corpuz, Onofre D., *The Bureaucracy in the Philippines*, Quezon City: Institute of Public Administration, University of the Philippines, 1957.

_____, 'Notes on Philippine Economic History', in G. P. Sicat et al. (eds.), *Economics and Development*, Quezon City: University of the Philippines, 1965.

_____, *The Philippines*, Englewood Cliffs, New Jersey: Prentice-Hall, 1965.

Cuaderno, Miguel, *Guideposts to Economic Stability*, Manila: Central Bank of the Philippines, 1955.

_____, *Problems of Economic Development*, Manila, privately published, 1964.

Day, Beth, *The Philippines: Shattered Showcases of Democracy in Asia*, New York: M. Evans and Co., 1974.

De Dios, Emmanuel S. (ed.), *An Analysis of the Philippine Economic Crisis*, Quezon City: University of the Philippines Press, 1984.

De Guzman, Raul P., 'Towards Redemocratization of the Political System', in Raul P. de Guzman and Mila A. Reforma (eds.), *Government and Politics of the Philippines*, Singapore: Oxford University Press, and Quezon City: College of Public Administration, University of the Philippines, 1988.

De Guzman, Raul P. and Reforma, Mila A. (eds.), *Government and Politics of the Philippines*, Singapore: Oxford University Press, and Quezon City: College of Public Administration, University of the Philippines, 1988.

De la Costa, H., *Readings in Philippine History*, Manila: Bookmark, 1965.

De Quiros, Conrado, 'The Wisdom of Democracy', *Far Eastern Economic Review*, 2 November 1989.

De Villa, Renato S., 'National Defense and Security', in *The Aquino Administration: Record and Legacy (1986–1992)*, Quezon City: University of the Philippines Press, 1992.

Dohner, Robert and Intal, Ponciano, 'The Marcos Legacy: Economic Policy and Foreign Debt in the Philippines', in Jeffrey Sachs and Susan Collins (eds.), *Developing Country Debt and Economic Performance*, Chicago: University of Chicago Press, 1989, Vol. 3.

Doronila, Amando, *The State, Economic Transformation, and Political Change in the Philippines, 1946–1972*, Singapore: Oxford University Press, 1992.

_____, 'The Transformation of Patron–Client Relations and Its Political Consequences in Postwar Philippines', *Journal of Southeast Asian Studies*, March 1985.

Edgardo J. Angara: Views & Comments, Quezon City: Friends of Edgardo J. Angara, 1984.

Ellison, Katherine, *Imelda: Steel Butterfly of the Philippines*, New York: McGraw-Hill Book Co., 1988.

Fabros, Wilfredo, *The Church and Its Social Involvement in the Philippines, 1930–1972*, Quezon City: Ateneo de Manila University Press, 1988.

Fallows, James, 'A Damaged Culture', *Atlantic*, November 1987.

_____, 'The Ilocos: A Philippine Discovery', *Atlantic*, May 1991.

Felix, Alfonso, 'Of Bribes and Men', in Lewis Gleeck, *The Rise & Fall of Harry Stonehill in the Philippines*, Manila: Author, 1989.

The Final Report of the Fact-finding Commission, Manila: Bookmark, 1990.

Forbes, W. Cameron, *The Philippine Islands*, Cambridge: Harvard University Press, 1945.

Friend, Theodore, *The Blue-eyed Enemy: Japan against the West in Java and Luzon, 1942–1945*, Princeton: Princeton University Press, 1988.

George, T. J. S., *Revolt in Mindanao: The Rise of Islam in Philippine Politics*, Kuala Lumpur: Oxford University Press, 1980.

Gleeck, Lewis E., *President Marcos and the Philippine Political Culture*, Manila, privately published, 1987.

_____, *The Rise & Fall of Harry Stonehill in the Philippines*, Manila, privately published, 1989.

Golay, Frank, *The Philippines: Public Policy and National Economic Development*, Ithaca: Cornell University Press, 1961.

_____, 'Taming the American Multinationals', in Norman G. Owen (ed.), *The Philippine Economy and the United States: Studies in Past and Present Interactions*, Ann Arbor: Center for South and Southeast Asian Studies, University of Michigan, 1983.

Gonzalez, Andrew, *Language and Nationalism: The Philippine Experience Thus Far*, Quezon City: Ateneo de Manila University Press, 1980.

_____ (ed.), *The Role of English and Its Maintenance in the Philippines*, Manila: Solidaridad Publishing House, 1988.

Goodno, James B., *The Philippines: Land of Broken Promises*, London: Zed Books, 1991.

Gowing, Peter, *Muslim Filipinos: Heritage and Horizons*, Quezon City: New Day Publishers, 1979.

Grossholtz, Jean, *Politics in the Philippines*, Boston: Little, Brown and Co., 1964.

Guideposts to Economic Stability and Progress: A Selection of the Speeches and Articles of Miguel Cuaderno, Sr., Governor of the Central Bank of the Philippines, Manila: Central Bank of the Philippines, 1955.

Haddad, Maurice, 'The Industrialization of the Philippines', Ph.D. thesis, Australian National University, 1966.

Hawes, Gary, *The Philippine State and the Marcos Regime: The Politics of Export*, Ithaca: Cornell University Press, 1987.

Hayden, Joseph Ralston, *The Philippines: A Study in National Development*, New York: Macmillan Co., 1942.

Herrin, Alejandro N., *An Assessment of Population, Health and Education Policies in the Philippines, 1986–1988*, Working Paper Series No. 90–10, Makati: Philippine Institute for Development Studies, January 1990.

Hill, Hal and Jayasuriya, Sisira, *The Philippines: Growth, Debt and Crisis*, Working Paper No. 85/3, Development Studies Center, Australian National University, Canberra, 1985.

'A History of Philippine Airlines', n.d. [1989].

'How the Coco Levy Worked', *Philippine Daily Inquirer*, 26–28 April 1992.

'IBON Primer on the Philippine Coconut Industry', Manila: IBON Databank Phils., Inc., n.d. [1979].

Ileto, Reynaldo C., *Pasyon and Revolution: Popular Movements in the Philippines, 1840–1910*, Quezon City: Ateneo de Manila University Press, 1979.

Inter-Agency Working Group on Foreign Investments, 'Study of Private Foreign Investments in the Philippines (as of December 31, 1970)', n.d.

Jayme, Vicente, 'The Philippine Business and Economic Outlook', Manila, Speech delivered at the 19th IAFEI World Congress, Manila, 17 October 1988.

Jensen, Khin Khin Myint, 'The Chinese in the Philippines during the American Regime: 1896–1946', Ph.D. thesis, University of Wisconsin, 1956.

Joaquin, Nick, *The Aquinos of Tarlac*, Mandaluyong: Cacho Hermanos, 1983.

_____, *Jaime Ongpin: The Enigma*, Makati: Jaime V. Ongpin Institute of Business and Government, 1990.

Jocano, L. Landa (ed.), *The Philippines at the Spanish Contact*, Manila: MCS Enterprises, 1975.

Jones, Gregg R., *Red Revolution: Inside the Philippine Guerrilla Movement*, Boulder: Westview Press, 1989.

Karnow, Stanley, *In Our Image: America's Empire in the Philippines*, New York: Random House, 1989.

Katayama, Yutaka, 'Gendai Firipin no Kokyu Kanryo Nin'yo ni Mirareru Chiiki Shugi' [Regionalism in the Recruitment of High-ranking Government Officials in the Modern Philippines], *Kikan Gyosei Kanri Kenkyu*, 36 (25 December 1986).

_____, 'Marcos Seiken no Gyosei Kanryo Seido', *Kokusai Mondai*, 1 (1987).

Kerkvliet, Benedict J., *Everyday Politics in the Philippines: Class and Status Relations in a Central Luzon Village*, Quezon City: New Day Publishers, 1991.

_____, *The Huk Rebellion: A Study of Peasant Revolt in the Philippines*, Berkeley: University of California Press, 1977, and Quezon City: New Day Publishers, 1979.

_____, 'Understanding Politics in a Nueva Ecija Rural Community', in Benedict J. Kerkvliet and Resil B. Mojares (eds.), *From Marcos to Aquino: Local Perspectives on Political Transition in the Philippines*, Quezon City: Ateneo de Manila University Press, 1991.

Kerkvliet, Benedict J. and Mojares, Resil B., 'Themes in the Transition from Marcos to Aquino: An Introduction', in Benedict J. Kerkvliet and Resil B. Mojares (eds.), *From Marcos to Aquino: Local Perspectives on Political Transition in the Philippines*, Quezon City: Ateneo de Manila University Press, 1991.

Kessler, Richard J., *Rebellion and Repression in the Philippines*, New Haven: Yale University Press, 1989.

Kroeger, James H., 'Human Promotion as an Integral Dimension of the Church's Mission of Evangelization: A Philippine Experience and Perspective since Vatican II—1965–1984', Ph.D. thesis, Pontificia Universitas Gregoriana (Vatican), 1985.

Lamberte, Mario, *The Development Bank of the Philippines (DBP) and the Financial Crisis: A Descriptive Analysis*, Staff Paper Series No. 84–07, Makati: Philippine Institute for Development Studies, November 1984.

Lande, Carl H., 'Introduction: Retrospect and Prospect', in Carl H. Lande (ed.), *Rebuilding a Nation: Philippine Challenges and American Policy*, Washington, DC: Washington Institute Press, 1987.

Larkin, John A., *The Pampangans: Colonial Society in a Philippine Province*, Berkeley: University of California Press, 1972.

Laurel, Jose P., *Forces That Make a Nation Great*, Manila: Bureau of Printing, 1944.

Lichauco, Alejandro, *Nationalist Economics*, Quezon City: Institute for Rural Industralization, 1988.

Macapagal, Diosdado, *A Stone for the Edifice: Memoirs of a President*, Quezon City: Mac Publishing House, 1968.

McCoy, Alfred W., *Priests on Trial*, Ringwood, Victoria: Penguin Books Australia, 1984.

_____, 'The Restoration of Planter Power in La Carlota City', in Benedict J. Kerkvliet and Resil B. Mojares (eds.), *From Marcos to Aquino: Local Perspectives on Political Transition in the Philippines*, Quezon City: Ateneo de Manila University Press, 1991.

Manapat, Ricardo, *Some Are Smarter Than Others: The History of Marcos' Crony Capitalism*, New York: Aletheia Publications, 1991.

Manglapus, Raul S., *Japan in Southeast Asia: Collision Course*, New York: Carnegie Endowment for International Peace, 1976.

Manila Electric Co., *66 Years of Service*, Manila, 1969.

May, Glenn Anthony, *Battle for Batangas: A Philippine Province at War*, New Haven: Yale University Press, 1991.

_____, *Social Engineering in the Philippines: The Aims, Execution, and Impact of American Colonial Policy, 1900–1913*, London: Greenwood Press, 1980.

Mecklin, John, 'The Philippines: An Ailing and Resentful Ally', *Fortune*, July 1969.

9Mijares, Primitivo, *The Conjugal Dictatorship of Ferdinand and Imelda Marcos I*, San Francisco: Union Square Publications, 1986.

Miranda, Felipe and Ciron, Ruben, 'The Philippines: Defence Expenditures, Threat Perception and the Role of the United States', in Chin Kin Wah (ed.), *Defence Spending in Southeast Asia*, Singapore: Institute of Southeast Asian Studies, 1987.

Munro, Ross, 'The New Khmer Rouge', *Commentary*, December 1985.

National Economic and Development Authority, *Regional Development Information: Region XII*, Metro Manila, 1978.

Nemenzo, Francisco, 'Rectification Process in the Philippine Communist Movement', in Lim Joo-Jock (ed.), *Armed Communist Movements in Southeast Asia*, Aldershot: Gower, 1984.

Noone, Martin, *The Life and Times of Michael O'Doherty*, Manila: Historical Conservation Society, 1989.

Onorato, Michael (interviewer and ed.), 'Salvador Araneta: Reflections of a Filipino Exile', Oral History Program, California State University, Fullerton, 1979.

Pante, Filologo and Medalla, Erlinda, *The Philippine Industrial Sector: Policies,*

Programs and Performance, Working Paper Series No. 90–18, Makati: Philippine Institute for Development Studies, July 1990.

Papers on the Tripoli Agreement: Problems and Prospects, Manila: International Studies Institute of the Philippines (Faculty of Law), University of the Philippines, 1986.

Paredes, Ruby (ed.), *Philippine Colonial Democracy*, Quezon City: Ateneo de Manila University Press, 1989.

Paterno, Vicent, 'Statement to the Foreign Investments Committee of the Constitutional Convention', 17 January 1972.

Pertierra, Raul, *Religion, Politics, and Rationality in a Philippine Community*, Quezon City: Ateneo de Manila University Press, 1988.

Poole, Fred and Vanzi, Max, *Revolution in the Philippines: The United States in a Hall of Cracked Mirrors*, New York: McGraw-Hill Book Co., 1984.

Porter, Gareth, *The Politics of Counterinsurgency in the Philippines: Military and Political Options*, Philippine Studies Occasional Paper No. 9, Honolulu: Center for Philippine Studies, University of Hawaii, 1987.

Power, John and Sicat, Gerardo, 'The Philippines: Industrialization and Trade Policies', in John Power and Gerardo Sicat (eds.), *The Philippines and Taiwan*, London: Oxford University Press, 1971.

Preliminary Estimates of Philippine Property War Damages and Losses, Report of the Technical Committee to the President of the Philippines, Washington, DC, March 1945.

Quirino, Carlos, *History of the Philippine Sugar Industry*, Manila: Kalayaan Publishing Co., 1974.

Rama, Napoleon G., 'Coping with Criminality: Why Cops Turn Criminals', *Philippine Panorama*, 29 November 1992: 3.

Ramos, Elias T., *Dualistic Unionism and Industrial Relations*, Quezon City: New Day Publishers, 1990.

Regional Development Information: Region XII, Metro Manila: National Economic and Development Authority, 1978.

Reinah, David, 'Philippine Sugar Industry Market Considerations and United States Policy', in Carl H. Lande (ed.), *Rebuilding a Nation: Philippine Challenges and American Policy*, Washington, DC: Washington Institute Press, 1987.

Report of the Joint Preparatory Committee on Philippine Affairs, 4 vols., Washington, DC: US Government Printing Office, 20 May 1938.

Reyes, Edna and Sanchez, Ma. Teresa, *An Assessment of Labor and Employment Policies in the Philippines, 1986–1988*, Working Paper Series No. 90–09, Makati: Philippine Institute for Development Studies, January 1990.

Romulo, Beth Day, *Inside the Palace*, New York: Feffer & Simons, 1987.

Rossa, Alberto (comp.), *The Theology of Liberation*, Manila: Historical Conservation Society, 1986.

Sanvictores, Gerardo, 'Economic Development Policies and Japanese Investments in the Philippines', in Aiichiro Ishii et al. (eds.), *National Development Policies and the Business Sector in the Philippines*, Tokyo: Institute of Developing Economies, 1988.

Saulo, Alfred, *Communism in the Philippines: An Introduction*, Quezon City: Ateneo de Manila University Press, 1990.

Sayre, Francis B., *Glad Adventure*, New York: Macmillan Co., 1957.

Schumacher, John, *Readings in Philippine Church History*, Quezon City: Loyola School of Theology, Ateneo de Manila University, 1979.

_____, *Revolutionary Clergy: The Filipino Clergy and the Nationalist Movements, 1850–1903*, Quezon City: Ateneo de Manila University Press, 1981.

Seagrave, Sterling, *The Marcos Dynasty*, Sevenoaks (Kent): Hodder and Stoughton, 1988.

See, Teresita Ang, *The Chinese in the Philippines: Problems and Perspectives*, Manila: Kaisa Para Sa Kaunlaran, 1990.

Seidman, Samuel, 'Enterprise and Entrepreneurship in the Philippine Republic, 1949–1959', Ph.D. thesis, New York University, 1963.

Seifu Haken no Firipin Keizai Shisatsu-dan Hokokusho [The Report of the Government-sponsored Mission to the Philippines], Tokyo: Federation of Economic Organizations, 1971.

Semana, Caridad C., 'Some Political Aspects of Philippine Economic Development after Independence', Ph.D. thesis, Harvard University, 1965.

Shaplen, Robert, 'Letter from Manila', *New Yorker*, 8 June 1963.

———, 'Letter from the Philippines', *New Yorker*, 4 February 1985.

A Short Story of the National Power Corporation, 1936–1986, Quezon City: National Power Corp., 1986.

Simbulan, Dante, 'A Study of the Socio-economic Elite in Philippine Politics and Government, 1946–1963', Ph.D. thesis, Australian National University, 1965.

Simons, Lewis M., *Worth Dying For*, New York: William Morrow and Co., 1987.

'The Solidarity Seminar on the Mindanao Problem', *Solidarity*, 110 (January–February 1987).

Steinberg, David Joel, *The Philippines: A Singular and a Plural Place*, Boulder: Westview Press, 1990.

Sturtevant, David R., *Popular Uprisings in the Philippines, 1840–1940*, Ithaca: Cornell University Press, 1976.

Swinerton, E. Nelson, *Philippine Higher Education*, New York: Praeger, 1991.

Tan, Edita, *The Structure and Growth of the Philippine Financial Market and the Behavior of Its Major Components*, Working Paper No. 81–94, Makati: Philippine Institute for Development Studies, June 1981.

Tapia, Cesar, 'The Moro National Liberation Front', *Solidarity*, 110 (January–February 1987).

Theunissen, Joop, 'Linkage and Alternatives: The Philippine Sugar Industry in the 1990s', Discussion paper, Tilburg University, July 1989.

Thompson, W. Scott, *Unequal Partners: Philippine–Thai Relations with the U.S., 1965–75*, Lexington, Mass.: Lexington Books, 1975.

Timberman, David, *A Changeless Land: Continuity and Change in Philippine Politics*, Singapore: Institute of Southeast Asian Studies, and Metro Manila: Bookmark, 1991.

Tinio, Rolando S., *A Matter of Language*, Quezon City: University of the Philippine Press, 1990.

Turner, Mark et al. (eds.), *Mindanao: Land of Unfulfilled Promise*, Quezon City: New Day Publishers, 1992.

Vellut, J., 'Japanese Reparations to the Philippines', *Asian Survey*, October 1963.

Von Brevern, Marilies, *Once a Chinese, Always a Chinese*, Manila, privately published, 1988.

Weightman, George, 'The Philippine Chinese: A Cultural History of a Marginal Trading Community', Ph.D. thesis, Cornell University, 1959.

Wickberg, Edgar, 'The Chinese Mestizo in Philippine History', *Journal of Southeast Asian History*, March 1964.

Wideman, Bernard, 'Philippine Airlines: A Presidential Landing', *Insight*, July 1978.

Wise, William, 'The Philippine Military after Marcos', in Carl H. Lande (ed.), *Rebuilding a Nation: Philippine Challenges and American Policy*, Washington, DC: Washington Institute Press, 1987.

Wolters, Willem, *Politics, Patronage and Class Conflict in Central Luzon*, Quezon City: New Day Publishers, 1984.

Wurfel, David, *Filipino Politics: Development and Decay*, Ithaca: Cornell University Press, 1988.

Yabes, Criselda, *The Boys from the Barracks: The Philippine Military after EDSA*, Pasig: Anvil Publishing, Inc., 1991.

Yamamoto Munesuke, *Negurosu: Nageki no Shima* [Negros: An Island of Grief] Tokyo: Dai-san Shobo, 1991.

Yap, Josef et al., *Central Bank Policies and the Behavior of the Money Market: The Case of the Philippines*, Working Paper Series No. 90–24, Makati: Philippine Institute for Development Studies, November 1990.

Yoshihara Kunio, *Philippine Industrialization: Foreign and Domestic Capital*, Singapore: Oxford University Press, and Quezon City: Ateneo de Manila University Press, 1985.

Youngblood, Robert L., *Marcos against the Church*, Ithaca: Cornell University Press, 1990.

Zaide, Gregorio F., *The Philippine History & Government*, Manila: Modern Book Co., 1980.

Zobel, Enrique, 'Philippine Agriculture in the Year 2020: An Endangered Sector', *Manila Bulletin*, 6 July 1992.

Thailand

Abonyi, George and Bunyaraks Ninsananda, *Thailand: Development Planning in Turbulent Times*, Asia Papers No. 3, University of Toronto–York University Joint Centre for Asia Pacific Studies, n.d.

Akagi, Osamu, *Thai no Seiji Bunka*, Tokyo: Keiso Shobo, 1989.

Ammar Siamwalla and Suthad Setboonsarng, *Trade, Exchange Rate, and Agricultural Pricing Policies in Thailand*, World Bank Comparative Studies, Washington, DC: World Bank, 1989.

Amnuay Viravan, 'Thailand into the 1990s: The Emergence of Asia's Fifth Tiger?', Paper presented at the Southeast Asian Studies Center, University of Michigan, 15 March 1988.

Anan Ganjanapan, 'Conflicts over the Deployment and Control of Labor in a Northern Thai Village', in Gillian Hart et al. (eds.), *Agrarian Transformation: Local Processes and the State in Southeast Asia*, Berkeley: University of California Press, 1989.

Anderson, Benedict R. O'G., 'Studies of the Thai State: The State of Thai Studies', in E. B. Ayal (ed.), *The Study of Thailand*, Athens: Ohio University, 1978.

Anderson, Benedict R. O'G. and Ruchira Mendiones, *In the Mirror: Literature and Politics in Siam in the American Era*, Bangkok: Editions Duang Kamol, 1985.

Anek Laothamatas, *Business Associations and the New Political Economy of Thailand: From Bureaucratic Polity to Liberal Corporatism*, Boulder: Westview Press, and Singapore: Institute of Southeast Asian Studies, 1992.

Anuman Rajadhon, *Fun Khwan Lang* [Biography of Phraya Anuman Rajadhon], 3 vols., translated into Japanese by Mori Mikio, Tokyo: Imura Bunka Jigyosha, 1981–6.

Aoki, Tamotsu, *Tai no Soin nite*, Tokyo: Chuo Koron-sha, 1976.

Arunee Sopitpongstorn, *Kiarti Srifuengfung: The Boy from Suphanburi*, Bangkok: Sri Yarnie Corp., 1991.

Bangkok Bank, 'Public Debt: Is Thailand Going Bankrupt?', in Vichitvong na Pombhejara (ed.), *Readings in Thailand's Political Economy*, Bangkok: Bangkok Printing Enterprise, 1978 (originally appeared in *Bangkok Bank Monthly Review*, May 1977).

Batson, Benjamin A., *The End of the Absolute Monarchy in Siam*, Singapore: Oxford University Press, 1984.

______, 'The Fall of the Phibun Government, 1944', *Journal of the Siam Society*, July 1974.

______ (comp. and ed.), *Siam's Political Future: Documents from the End of the Absolute Monarchy*, Data Paper No. 96, Southeast Asian Program, Ithaca: Cornell University, July 1974.

Benedict, Ruth, 'Thai Culture and Behavior: An Unpublished War Time Study Dated September, 1943', Data Paper No. 4, Ithaca: Southeast Asia Program, Cornell University, 1952.

Blanchard, Wendell, *Thailand: Its People, Its Society, Its Culture*, New Haven: HRAF Press, 1958.

Botan, *Letters from Thailand*, trans. by Susan Fulop Morell, Bangkok: D. K. Book House, 1977.

Brailey, Nigel (ed.), *Two Views of Siam on the Eve of the Chakri Reformation*, Whiting Bay (Scotland): Kiscadale Publications, 1989.

Brown, Ian, *The Élite and the Economy in Siam c.1890–1920*, Singapore: Oxford University Press, 1988.

Buddhist Education in Thailand, Bangkok: Mahamakut Educational Council, Buddhist University of Thailand, 1961.

Bunnag, Jane, 'Loose Structure: Fact or Fancy?: Thai Society Re-examined', in Clark D. Neher (ed.), *Modern Thai Politics: From Village to Nation*, Cambridge: Shenkman Publishing Co., 1976.

Bunyaraks Ninsananda, 'The Structural Adjustment for Sustainable Growth: Thailand', Paper presented at the Asian Development Symposium, Tokyo, 1988.

Chatthip Nartsupha and Suthy Prasartset (eds.), *The Political Economy of Siam, 1851–1910*, Bangkok: Social Science Association of Thailand, n.d.

Chatthip Nartsupha et al. (eds.), *The Political Economy of Siam, 1910–1932*, Bangkok: Social Science Association of Thailand, n.d. [1978].

Che Man, W. K., *Muslim Separatism: The Moros of Southern Philippines and the Malays of Southern Thailand*, Singapore: Oxford University Press, and Quezon City: Ateneo de Manila University Press, 1990.

Chirayu Isarangkun na Ayuthaya, 'Conditions in the Industrial Sector and Aims of Industrialization Policy', in Vichitvong na Pombhejara (ed.), *Readings in Thailand's Political Economy*, Bangkok: Bangkok Printing Enterprise, 1978.

Coughlin, Richard J., *Double Identity: The Chinese in Modern Thailand*, Hong Kong: University of Hong Kong Press, 1960.

Chula Chakrabongse, *Lords of Life: A History of the Kings of Thailand*, 3rd edn., Bangkok: DD Books, 1982.

Cushman, Jennifer W., 'The Chinese in Thailand', in Leo Suryadinata (ed.), *The Ethnic Chinese in the ASEAN States: Bibliographical Essays*, Singapore: Institute of Southeast Asian Studies, 1989.

Darling, Frank, 'Marshal Sarit and Absolutist Rule in Thailand', *Pacific Affairs*, December 1960.

______, *Thailand and the United States*, Washington, DC: Public Affairs Press, 1965.

Donner, Wolf, *The Five Faces of Thailand: An Economic Geography*, St. Lucia: University of Queensland Press, 1978.

Embree, John, 'Thailand—A Loosely Structured Social System', *American Anthropologist*, April–June 1950.

Feder, Gershon et al., *Land Policies and Farm Productivity in Thailand*, Baltimore: Johns Hopkins University Press, 1988.

Feeny, David, *The Political Economy of Productivity: Thai Agricultural Development, 1880–1975*, Vancouver: University of British Columbia Press, 1982.

Fujinaga Takahiro, *Thai wa Ima: Kyu Seicho o Togeru Ajia Power* [Thailand Today: A Rapidly Growing New Asian Power], Tokyo: Diamond-sha, 1989.

Girling, John, *The Bureaucratic Polity in Modernizing Societies: Similarities, Differences, and Prospects in the ASEAN Region*, Singapore: Institute of Southeast Asian Studies, 1981.

______, 'Is Small-holder Cultivation Viable?: A Question of Political Economy with Reference to Thailand', *Pacific Affairs*, Summer 1986.

______, *Thailand: Society and Politics*, Ithaca: Cornell University Press, 1981.

Gould, J. S., 'Preliminary Estimates of the Gross Geographical Product and Domestic National Income of Thailand 1938/39, 1946–1950', Mimeographed paper presented to National Economic Council, Bangkok, 1952.

Griswold, A. B., 'King Mongkut in Perspective', *Journal of the Siam Society*, April 1957.

______, *King Mongkut of Siam*, New York: Asia Society, 1961.

Grit Permtanjit, *Political Economy of Dependent Capitalist Development: Study on the Limits of the Capacity of the State to Rationalize in Thailand*, Bangkok: Social Research Institute, Chulalongkorn University, 1982.

Hanks, L. M., 'Merit and Power in the Thai Social Order', *American Anthropologist*, 1962.

Harada, Yutaka, *Tai Keizai Nyumon* [Introduction to the Thai Economy], Tokyo: Nihon Hyoron-sha, 1988.

Hashimoto Takashi, 'Thai no Chiho Gyosei to Noson Kaihatsu' [Local Administration and Rural Development in Thailand], *Ajia Keizai*, October 1984.

______, 'Thai Nanbu Kokkyo Ken Mondai to Malay Muslim Togo Seisaku' [Problems in Southern Border Provinces and Malay-Muslim Integration Policy], *Tonan Ajia Kenkyu*, September 1987.

Hewison, Kevin, *Power and Politics in Thailand*, Manila: Journal of Contemporary Asia Publishers, 1989.

Hindley, Donald, 'Thailand: The Politics of Passivity', in Clark D. Neher (ed.), *Modern Thai Politics: From Village to Nation*, Cambridge: Shenkman Publishing Co., 1976.

Industrial Development in Thailand, Bangkok: Industrial Finance Corporation of Thailand, n.d. [1991].

Ingram, James, *Economic Change in Thailand, 1850–1970*, Stanford: Stanford University Press, 1971.

______, 'Thailand's Rice Trade and the Allocation of Resources', in C. D. Cowan (ed.), *The Economic Development of South-East Asia: Studies in Economic History and Political Econony*, London: Allen & Unwin, 1964.

Iwaki, Yujiro, *Nittai Hikaku Bunka-ko* [A Comparison of Thai and Japanese Cultures], Tokyo: Keiso Shobo, 1985.

Jackson, Peter A., *Buddhism, Legitimation, and Conflict: The Political Functions of*

Urban Thai Buddhism, Singapore: Institute of Southeast Asian Studies, 1989.

Jacobs, Norman, *Modernization without Development: Thailand as an Asian Case Study*, New York: Praeger, 1991.

Jansen, Karel, *Finance, Growth and Stability: Financing Economic Development in Thailand, 1960–86*, Aldershot: Gower Publishing Co., 1990.

Johnston, David Bruce, 'Rural Society and the Rice Economy in Thailand, 1880–1930', Ph.D. thesis, Yale University, 1975.

Juanjai Ajanant et al., *Trade and Industrialization of Thailand*, Bangkok: Social Science Association of Thailand, n.d. [1986].

Kanok Wongtrangan, 'The Revolutionary Strategy of the Communist Party of Thailand: Change and Persistence', in Lim Joo-Jock (ed.), *Armed Communist Movements in Southeast Asia*, Aldershot: Gower Publishing Co., 1984.

Kasem Udyanin and Smith, R. D., *The Public Service in Thailand*, Brussels: International Institute of Administrative Sciences, 1954.

Kawabe, Toshio, *Taikoku Rikai no Key Words* [Key Words for Understanding Thailand], Tokyo: Keiso Shobo, 1989.

Keyes, Charles F., 'Buddhism and National Integration in Thailand', *Journal of Asian Studies*, 1971.

_____, *Thailand: Buddhist Kingdom as Modern Nation-State*, Bangkok: Editions Duang Kamol, 1989.

Khoontong Intarathai, 'The Impact of Direct Private Foreign Investment on the Industrialization of Thailand', Ph.D. thesis, University of Illinois, 1974.

Knodel, John et al., *Thailand's Reproductive Revolution: Rapid Fertility Decline in a Third-World Setting*, Madison: University of Wisconsin Press, 1987.

Kraisak Choonhavan, 'The Growth of Domestic Capital and Thai Industrialization', *Journal of Contemporary Asia*, 1984.

Kulick, Elliott and Wilson, Dick, *Thailand's Turn: Profile of a New Dragon*, London: Macmillan, 1992.

Kumut Chandruang, *My Boyhood in Siam*, New York: John Day, 1938.

Likhit Dhiravegin, 'Demi-Democracy: Thai Politics in Transition', Unpublished manuscript, 1987.

_____, 'The One-and-a-Half Party System and the Halfway Democracy: A Comparative Perspective', in Kunio Yoshihara (ed.), *Thai Perceptions of Japanese Modernization*, Kuala Lumpur: Falcon Press, 1989.

_____, *Thai Politics: Selected Aspects of Development and Change*, Bangkok: Tri-Sciences Publishing House, 1985.

Maekawa, Ken'ichi, *Bangkok no Koki-shin* [Curiosity about Bangkok], Tokyo, Mekon, 1990.

The March of Thailand: A Survey of Various Aspects of Post-war Thailand, Bangkok: Department of Publicity, 1950.

Mattani Mojdara Rutnin, *Modern Thai Literature*, Bangkok: Thammasat University, 1988.

A Memoir of His Majesty King Bhumibol Adulyadej of Thailand, Bangkok [printed by Bangkok Printing (1984) and Mr Mok Rungkamol Printer], 1987.

Mingsarn Santikarn Kaosa-ard, 'Japanese Investment in Thailand: Looking Back and Into the Future', in Seiji Naya and Akira Takayama (eds.), *Economic Development in East and Southeast Asia: Essays in Honor of Professor Ichimura*, Honolulu: East–West Center, and Singapore: Institute of Southeast Asian Studies, 1990.

Moffat, Abbot, *Mongkut: The King of Siam*, Ithaca: Cornell University Press, 1961.

Moore, Frank, *Thailand: Its People, Its Society, Its Culture*, New Haven: HRAF Press, 1974.

Morell, David and Chai-Anan Samudavanija, *Thailand: Reaction and Revolution*, Cambridge: Oelgeschlager, Gunn & Hain, 1981.

Mosel, James N., 'Thai Administrative Behavior', in William Siffin (ed.), *Toward the Comparative Study of Public Administration*, Westport, Connecticut: Greenwood Press, 1957.

Motooka, Takeshi, 'Rice Exports and the Expansion of Cultivation', in Ishii Yoneo (ed.), *Thailand: A Rice-growing Society*, Honolulu: University Press of Hawaii, 1978.

Mulder, Niels, *Inside Thai Society: An Interpretation of Everyday Life*, Bangkok: Editions Duang Kamol, 1990.

_____, *Monks, Merit and Motivation: Buddhism and National Development in Thailand*, DeKalb: Center for Southeast Asian Studies, Northern Illinois University, 1973.

Murashima, Eiji, 'Gendai Thai ni okeru Koteki Kokka Ideology no Keisei' [The Formation of an Official Ideology Regarding the State in Modern Thailand], *Kokusai Seiji*, February 1987.

_____, 'Local Elections and Leadership in Thailand: A Case Study of Nakhon Sawan Province', *Developing Economies*, December 1987.

_____, 'The Origin of Modern Official State Ideology in Thailand', *Journal of Southeast Asian Studies*, March 1988.

Muscat, Robert, *Thailand and the United States*, New York: Columbia University Press, 1990.

Nagai, Hiroshi, *Sareru Gawa kara Mita Enjo: Thai kara no Hokoku* [Japanese Economic Aid, Viewed from a Recipient Country: A Report from Thailand], Tokyo: Keiso Shobo, 1983.

Narongchai Akrasanee and Somsak Tambunlertchai, 'Transition from Import Substitution to Export Expansion: The Thai Experience', in Seiji Naya and Akira Takayama (eds.), *Economic Development in East and Southeast Asia: Essays in Honor of Professor Ichimura*, Honolulu: East–West Center, and Singapore: Institute of Southeast Asian Studies, 1990.

Narongchai Akrasanee et al., *Thailand's Export-led Growth: Retrospect and Prospects*, Policy Study No. 3, Bangkok: Thailand Development Research Institute, 1991.

Neher, Clark D., 'Constitutionalism and Elections in Thailand', in Clark D. Neher (ed.), *Modern Thai Politics: From Village to Nation*, Cambridge: Shenkman Publishing Co., 1976.

_____, 'Political Corruption in a Thai Province', *Journal of Developing Areas*, July 1977.

Nikom Chandravithun, *Thai Labour: A Long Journey*, Bangkok: Thai Watana Panich, 1982.

Pasuk Phongpaichit, *The New Wave of Japanese Investment in ASEAN*, Singapore: Institute of Southeast Asian Studies, 1990.

_____, 'The Politics of Economic Policy Reform in Thailand', Updated version of the paper presented at the Seminar on Politics of Economic Policy Reform, Institute of Management, Manila, 14–15 October 1991.

Phillips, Herbert, 'Relationships between Personality and Social Structure in a Siamese Peasant Community', in Clark D. Neher (ed.), *Modern Thai Politics: From Village to Nation*, Cambridge: Shenkman Publishing Co., 1976.

_____, 'The Scope and Limits of the "Loose Structure" Concept', in Hans-Dieter Evers (ed.), *Loosely Structured Social Systems: Thailand in Comparative Perspective*, New Haven: Southeast Asia Studies, Yale University, 1969.

_____, *Thai Peasant Personality: The Patterning of Interpersonal Behavior in the Village of Bang Chan*, Berkeley: University of California Press, 1965.

Piker, Steven, 'The Relationship of Belief Systems to Behavior in Rural Thai Society', in Clark D. Neher (ed.), *Modern Thai Politics: From Village to Nation*, Cambridge: Shenkman Publishing Co., 1976.

Pisit Leeahtam, *Thailand's Economic Adjustment in the 1980s: From Crisis to Double Digit Growth*, Bangkok: Dokya Publishing House (1988) Co., 1991.

Piti Sithi-Amnuai, *Finance and Banking in Thailand*, Bangkok, privately published, 1964.

Potter, Jack M., *Thai Peasant Social Structure*, Chicago: University of Chicago Press, 1976.

Prasert Yamklinfung, 'Contrasting Sociological Factors in Rural Development of Japan and Thailand', Paper presented at the Conference on a Comparative Study of the History of Rural Development in Japan and Thailand, Pattaya, 31 July–2 August 1981.

______, 'The Problem of Modernization of Thai Society', *Area Studies Tsukuba*, March 1991.

______, 'Thailand: Reflections on Changing Social Structure', in Ann Buller (comp.), *Proceedings of the International Conference on Thai Studies*, Australian National University, 3–6 July 1987, Vol. 3, Part One.

Prizzia, Ross, *Thailand in Transition: The Role of Oppositional Forces*, Honolulu: University of Hawaii Press, 1985.

A Public Development Program for Thailand, Baltimore: Johns Hopkins Press, 1959.

Puey Ungphakorn, *Best Wishes for Asia*, Bangkok: Klett Thai Publications, 1975.

______, 'Thailand's Economic Prospects', Paper presented at the Siam Society, Bangkok, 5 February 1970.

______, 'Violence and the Military Coup in Thailand', *Bulletin of Concerned Asian Scholars*, 1977.

Ramsay, Ansil, 'The Political Economy of Sugar in Thailand', *Pacific Affairs*, Summer 1987.

Reeve, W. D., *Public Administration in Siam*, London: Royal Institute of International Affairs, 1951.

Reflections on Thai Culture: Collected Writings of William J. Klausner, Bangkok: Siam Society, 1987.

Reynolds, Craig, 'The Case of K. S. R. Kulap: A Challenge to Royal Historical Writing in Late Nineteenth Century Thailand', *Journal of the Siam Society*, July 1973.

______, *Thai Discourse: The Real Face of Thai Feudalism Today*, Ithaca: Southeast Asian Program, Cornell University, 1987.

Riggs, Fred W., 'Interest and Clientele Group', in Joseph Sutton (ed.), *Problems of Politics and Administration in Thailand*, Bloomington: Department of Government, Indiana University, 1962.

______, *Thailand: The Modernization of a Bureaucratic Polity*, Honolulu: East–West Center Press, 1966.

Saito Chikanori, *Bangkok Taizai Monogatari* [A Story of My Stay in Bangkok], Tokyo: Gakusei-sha, 1990.

Samart Chiasakul and Koji Taniguchi, *The Role of Foreign Capital in the Manufacturers Market Development in Thailand*, Joint Research Programme Series No. 89, Tokyo: Institute of Developing Economies, 1991.

Sataporn Jinachitra, 'Monetary Policy: Achievement and a Look to the Future', in Vichitvong na Pombhejara (ed.), *Readings in Thailand's Political Economy*, Bangkok: Bangkok Printing Enterprise, 1978.

Scott, James C., 'Corruption in Thailand', in Clark D. Neher (ed.), *Modern Thai Politics: From Village to Nation*, Cambridge: Shenkman Publishing Co., 1976.

Seni Pramoj and Kukrit Pramoj, *A King of Siam Speaks*, Bangkok: Siam Society, 1987.

Sharp, Lauriston, 'Cultural Differences and Southeast Asian Research', in Clark D. Neher, *Modern Thai Politics: From Village to Nation*, Cambridge: Shenkman Publishing Co., 1976.

Shishido, Toshio (ed.), *Tai Keizai Hatten no Sho-joken* [The Conditions for Thai Economic Development], Tokyo: Institute of Developing Economies, 1973.

Shor, Edgar, 'The Public Service', in Joseph Sutton (ed.), *Problems of Politics and Administration in Thailand*, Bloomington: Department of Government, Indiana University, 1962.

A Siamese for All Seasons: Collected Articles by and about Puey Ungphakorn, Bangkok: Kamol Keemthong Foundation, 1981.

Siffin, William, 'Economic Development', in Joseph Sutton (ed.), *Problems of Politics and Administration in Thailand*, Bloomington: Department of Government, Indiana University, 1962.

_____, *The Thai Bureaucracy: Institutional Change and Development*, Honolulu: East–West Center Press, 1966.

Silcock, T. H., 'Thai Money: Review Article', *Malayan Economic Review*, April 1966.

_____ (ed.), *Thailand: Social and Economic Studies in Development*, Canberra: Australian National University Press, 1967.

Skinner, G. William, *Chinese Society in Thailand: An Analytical History*, Ithaca: Cornell University Press, 1957.

Somboon Suksamran, *Buddhism and Politics in Thailand: A Study of Socio-Political Change and Political Activism of the Thai Sangha*, Singapore: Institute of Southeast Asian Studies, 1982.

_____, *Political Buddhism in Southeast Asia: The Modernization of Thailand*, London: C. Hurst & Co., 1977.

Somjai Phagaphasvivat, *Thai Capital Market*, Bangkok: S. S. Consultant & Research, 1988.

Sompop Manarungsan, *Economic Development of Thailand, 1850–1950*, Bangkok: Institute of Asian Studies, Chulalongkorn University, 1989.

Somsak Tambunlertchai, *Japanese and American Investments in Thailand's Manufacturing Industries*, Tokyo: Institute of Developing Economies, 1977.

Somsakdi Xuto (ed.), *Government and Politics of Thailand*, Singapore: Oxford University Press, 1987.

Stanton, Edwin, *Brief Authority: Excursions of a Common Man in an Uncommon World*, London: R. Hale, 1957.

Statistical Yearbook, Thailand, Bangkok: National Statistical Office, Office of Prime Minister, 1990.

Stowe, Judith A., *Siam Becomes Thailand*, London: Hurst & Co., 1991.

Suchart Prasith-rathsint, 'Fertility Control Policies in Thailand', Bangkok: National Institute of Development Administration, October 1986.

_____, *Thailand's National Development: Policy Issues and Challenges*, [Bangkok], Thai University Research Association and Canadian International Development Agency, 1987.

Suchit Boonbongkarn, 'Political Power of Thai Military Leaders: A Comparative Study of Field-Marshal P. Pibulsongkram and Field-Marshal Sarit Thanarat', *Social Science Review*, 1977.

Suehiro, Akira and Yasuda, Osamu (eds.), *Tai no Kogyo-ka: NAIC eno Chosen* [Thai Industrialization: A Challenge to the NAIC], Tokyo: Institute of Developing Economies, 1987.

Suntaree Komin, *Psychology of the Thai People*, Bangkok: National Institute of Development Administration, 1990.

Sunthonraphot, Bothbaht, la Lhamkhwahn doi Dr Puey Ungphakorn [Speeches, Articles, and Congratulatory Messages by Dr Puey Ungphakorn], Bangkok: Bank of Thailand, 1964.

Supachai Panitchpakdi, *Financial Development in Thailand and Other Developing Countries*, Bangkok, privately published, 1985.

_____, *Issues in Banking and Finance in Thailand*, 1975–1980, Bangkok, privately published, 1981.

Suphaap Phatsaong and Krithanah Chingchit, 'Phai Luang: Kaan Long Tun Khong Ipun Nai Prathet Thai' [Yellow Peril: Japanese Investment in Thailand], *Social Science Review*, 1972.

Supote Chunanuntathum et al., 'Trade and Financing Strategies for Thailand in the 1980s', Paper presented at the Seminar on New International Economic Order, Faculty of Economics, Thammasat University, 1986.

Surachart Bamrungsuk, *United States Foreign Policy and Thai Military Rule, 1947–1977*, Bangkok: Editions Duang Kamol, 1985.

Surin Pitsuwan, *Islam and Malay Nationalism: A Case of the Malay-Muslims of Southern Thailand*, Bangkok: Thai Khadi Research Institute, Thammasat University, 1985.

Suthy Prasartset, 'An Emerging Trade Pattern since the New Wave of Japanese Direct Investment in Thailand', in Kunio Yoshihara (ed.), *Japan in Thailand*, Kuala Lumpur: Falcon Press, 1990.

Sutton, Joseph, 'Political and Administrative Leadership', in Joseph Sutton (ed.), *Problems of Politics and Administration in Thailand*, Bloomington: Department of Government, Indiana University, 1962.

Tambia, S. J., *World Conqueror and World Renouncer: A Study of Buddhism and Polity in Thailand against a Historical Background*, Cambridge: Cambridge University Press, 1976.

Tanaka, Tadaharu, *Tai-Nyumon*, Tokyo: K.M.S, 1989.

Thai-Vietnam to Nihon, Tomita Takejiro Kyoju Taikan Kinen Ronbunshu [Thailand, Vietnam, and Japan: A Collection of Essays in Commemoration of the Retirement of Professor Tomita Takejiro], Osaka: Division of Thai and Vietnamese Languages, Osaka Foreign Language University, 1984.

'Thai Airways International: 32nd Anniversary', *Sawadee* [inflight magazine], May 1992.

Thailand: Private Enterprise Investment Opportunities, Bangkok: Board of Investment, July 1968.

Thak Chaloemtiarana, *Thailand: The Politics of Despotic Paternalism*, Bangkok: Thai Khadi Institute, Thammasat University, 1979.

_____ (ed.), *Thai Politics: Extracts and Documents, 1932–1957*, Bangkok: Social Science Association of Thailand, 1978.

Thamsook Numnonda, 'Pibulsongkram's Thai Nation-building Programme during the Japanese Military Presence, 1941–1945', *Journal of Southeast Asian Studies*, September 1978.

Thompson, W. Scott, *Unequal Partners: Philippine–Thai Relations with the U.S., 1965–75*, Lexington: Lexington Books, 1975.

Tong Chee Kiong, *Perceptions and Boundaries: Problematics in the Assimilation of the Chinese in Thailand*, Working Paper No. 92, Singapore: Department of Sociology, National University of Singapore, 1988.

Tourret, Richard (ed.), *Thailand*, London: Euromoney Publications, 1989.

Turton, Andrew, 'Local Powers and Rural Differentiation', in Gillian Hart et al. (eds.), *Agrarian Transformation: Local Processes and the State in Southeast Asia*, Berkeley: University of California Press, 1989.

——, 'Thailand: Agrarian Bases of State Power', in Gillian Hart et al. (eds.), *Agrarian Transformation: Local Processes and the State in Southeast Asia*, Berkeley: University of California Press, 1989.

—— et al. (eds.), *Thailand: Roots of Conflict*, Nottingham: Spokesman, 1987.

Van der Meer, Cornelis L. J., 'Pattern and Consequences of Agriculture Growth in Thailand', in *Rural Thai Society: Development of Thai Economy*, Vol. I, Proceedings of the International Conference on Thai Studies, Bangkok, 22–24 August 1984.

Varaporn Bovornsiri, 'An Analysis of Access to Higher Education in Thailand', Occasional Paper No. 23, Singapore: Regional Institute of Higher Education and Development, 1985.

Vella, Walter, *Chaiyo! King Vajiravudh and the Development of Thai Nationalism*, Honolulu: University of Hawaii Press, 1978.

——, *The Impact of the West on Government in Thailand*, Berkeley: University of California Press, 1955.

Vickery, Michael, 'Thai Regional Elites and the Reforms of King Chulalongkorn', *Journal of Asian Studies*, August 1970.

Vilas Manivat (comp.), *M. R. Kukrit Pramoj: His Wit and Wisdom, Writings, Speeches and Interviews*, Bangkok: Editions Duang Kamol, 1983.

Virabongsa Ramangkura and Pakorn Vichyanond, 'Manifold Dilemmas behind External Debt Management', in Seiji Naya and Akira Takayama (eds.), *Economic Development in East and Southeast Asia: Essays in Honor of Professor Ichimura*, Honolulu: East–West Center, and Singapore: Institute of Southeast Asian Studies, 1990.

Wales, H. G., *Ancient Siamese Government and Administration*, New York: Paragon Book Reprint Corp., 1965.

Warr, Peter and Bandid Nijathaworn, 'Thai Economic Performance: Some Thai Perspectives', *Asian-Pacific Economic Literature*, May 1987.

Watson, Keith, *Educational Development in Thailand*, Hong Kong: Heinemann Asia, 1980.

Wibha Senanan, *The Genesis of the Novel in Thailand*, Bangkok: Thai Watana Panich, 1975.

Wilson, David, 'Political Tradition and Political Change in Thailand', in Clark D. Neher (ed.), *Modern Thai Politics: From Village to Nation*, Cambridge: Shenkman Publishing Co., 1976.

——, *Politics in Thailand*, Ithaca: Cornell University Press, 1962.

Wira Wimoniti, 'Historical Patterns of Tax Administration in Thailand', Master of Public Administration thesis, Thammasat University, 1961.

Wright, Joseph, *The Balancing Act: A History of Modern Thailand*, Oakland: Pacific Rim Press, 1991.

Wyatt, David, *Thailand: A Short History*, New Haven: Yale University Press, 1984.

Yamazawa, Ippei and Somsak Tambunlertchai, *Manufactured Exports from Developing Countries: Mechanisms and Policies—A Study Based on Interview Survey of Textile Firms in Thailand*, Working Paper No. 18, Tokyo: International Development Center of Japan, 1981.

Yasuda, Osamu, *Tai* [Thailand], Chuo Shinsho 889, Tokyo: Chuo Koron-sha, 1988.

Index

THE PHILIPPINES

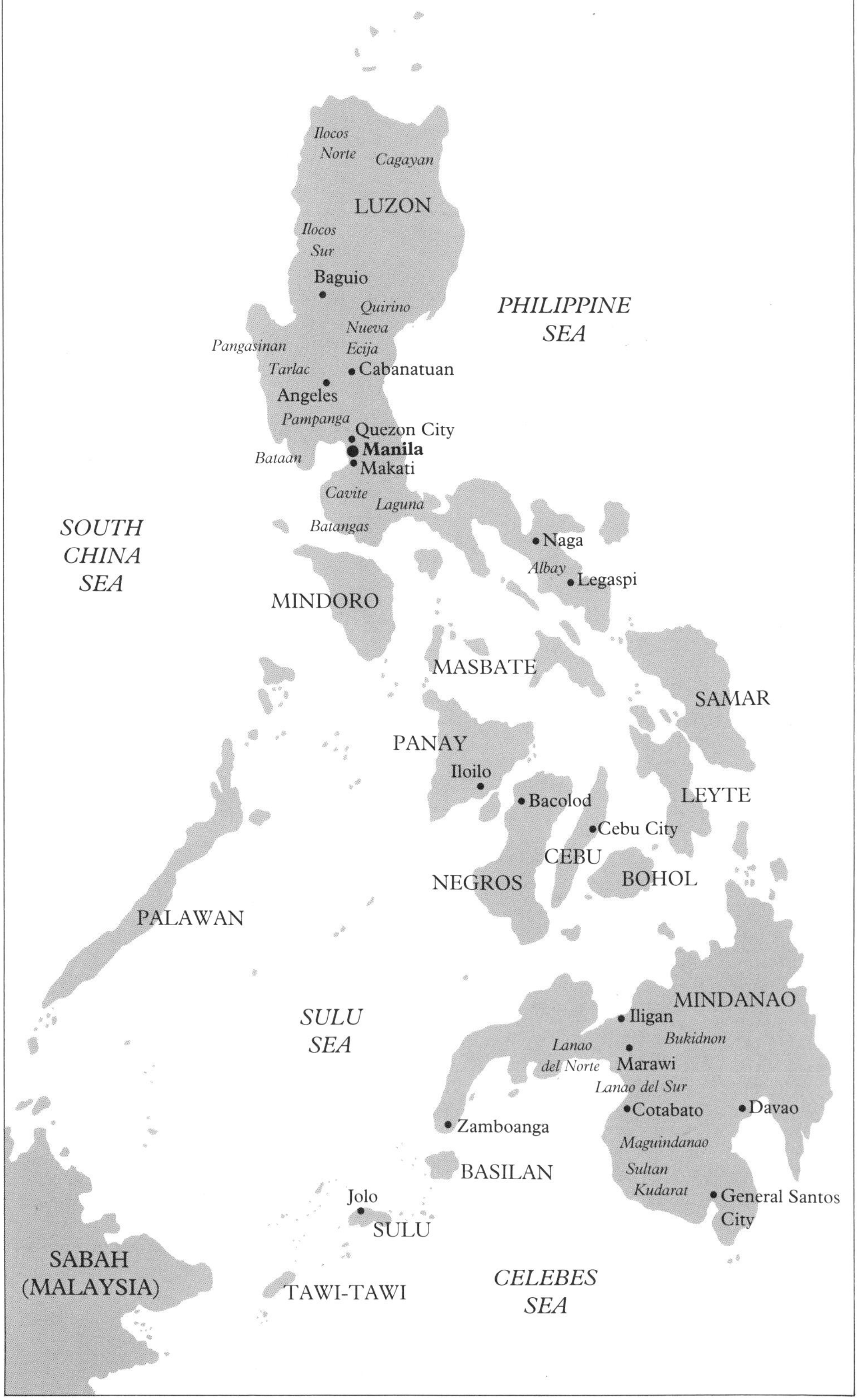